SOCIAL PHILOSOPHY AND ECOLOGICAL SCARCITY

SOCIAL PHILOSOPHY AND ECOLOGICAL SCARCITY

Keekok Lee

ROUTLEDGE
London and New York

First published 1989 by Routledge
11 New Fetter Lane, London EC4P 4EE
29 West 35th Street, New York NY 10001

© 1989 Keekok Lee
Printed in Great Britain by T. J. Press (Padstow) Ltd
Padstow, Cornwall

British Library Cataloguing in Publication Data
Lee, Keekok, 1938 –
Social philosophy and ecological scarcity.
1. Politics. Environmental aspects
I. Title
320

Library of Congress Cataloging in Publication Data
Lee, Keekok, 1938 –
Social philosophy and ecological scarcity / Keekok Lee.
p.   cm.
Bibliography: p.
Includes index.
1. Economic development – Environmental aspects.
2. Economic development – Social aspects.
3. Human ecology.
4. Cooperation.
I. Title.
HD75.6.L44   1989
333.7 – dc 19   88-26813
ISBN 0-415-03220-2

For my children, Jonathan and Rebecca,
and all other children, their children
and their children's children

CONTENTS

ACKNOWLEDGEMENTS

I wish to thank Harry Lesser for his generosity with his time and energy in reading and commenting on the whole book, as well as discussing numerous points and issues, whenever I needed clarification of them. I am equally indebted to the unknown referee who also read it with great care and made many constructive criticisms. However, I have, also, stubbornly resisted some of their ideas. Perhaps, I have been foolish in doing so. But what I can be sure about is that the book is a much better product as a result of their many suggestions for improvement.

I also wish to thank all those colleagues, in particular, Liz Brock, Gordon Neal and Toni Smith who happened to live along my corridor and bore the brunt of my ignorance about machines; without their kind willingness to help in coaxing word-processors and other such gadgets to behave properly, this book could not have been produced.

I wish to apologise to the reader for any typographical errors, stylistic lapses and other such faults that, no doubt, still remain, in spite of strenuous efforts to eliminate them. One pair of tired eyes has severe limitations — that is my excuse.

PREFACE

Our industrial civilisation can be said to date from the seventeenth century onwards, at least as far as its theoretical foundations are concerned. It is one based on using science and technology (but a technology which can be described as ecologically insensitive) to dominate Nature, and to make her serve our human ends. Concepts of science and technology are part of the seventeenth century notion of progress and modernity and the eighteenth century notion of the Enlightenment. The theoretical foundations of such a civilisation are based, amongst other things, on (classical) physics as the paradigmatic science and on its mechanistic linear paradigm of cause and effect.

Our major contemporary social philosophies — the first world of liberal representative democracy *cum* (bourgeois) capitalism and the second world of the people's democracy *cum* (state) capitalism — are constructed upon the industrial civilisation as characterised above. Locke, the theorist *par excellence* of liberalism, and Marx, the theorist *par excellence* of socialism/communism, have much in common in spite of their differences.

Unfortunately, in spite of its many undoubted successes, that civilisation is also running into difficulties and crises which cannot, however, be solved within its own scientific, technological, economic or ethical framework. The fatal flaws stem from its adherence to the mechanistic paradigm of causation, from its elevation of classical physics to be

ix

the paradigmatic science and, hence, its ignoring, in the main, of the laws of at least one other fundamental science, that of thermodynamics, and the basic principles of the science of ecology, as well as its non-linear model of cause and effect.

A civilisation erected on such crucially flawed assumptions cannot be expected to last. A social philosophy constructed upon them cannot be said to be either adequate or relevant; indeed, it may be said to be fantastic. Such a civilisation promises falsely to guarantee an infinite, inexhaustible supply of material goods. The dominant social philosophies of our times reflect and celebrate such a cornucopia, mirage though it may be. They, therefore, urge as their criteria of the 'good society' and the 'good life' ever expanding economic growth, ever increasing possession and consumption of external material things.

These criteria would not do, as the goal of growth and consumption, for ever more, is both a physical impossibility as well as a conceptually incoherent ideal. We need to construct a new social philosophy, one which is in keeping with the laws of thermo-dynamics and the principles of ecology. Through our understanding of how living processes interact with non-living (physical/chemical) processes in the biosphere, we can begin to work out new conceptions of what the good society and the good life amount to. In other words, we will be able to answer afresh, hopefully, more rationally and adequately, the peren-nial central questions of social philosophy, those pertaining to the endurance of human society and to human flourishing within it. But this time, we should realise that these quintessentially human preoccupations cannot be divorced from the endurance of the natural world of which we human agents are a part, and from the flourishing of non-human life forms and non-living processes, upon which we are dependent, and all of which are interdependent. We must, in other words, turn our backs upon the seventeenth and eighteenth century notion of progress which the late twentieth century has outlived, and which could only lead the world to perdition, even if one were to grant that it enables some human beings (primarily in the European world) to achieve spectacular improvements in their standard of living over the last hundred years or so. But such improvements cannot be sustained indefinitely, either for the already privileged, never mind all human agents, both living now and in the future.

The new social philosophy, whose outline is developed in this book, will urge, instead, as criteria for the good society and the good life, (a) an attempt to meet human needs by means, which make less, rather than more, demands on the absolutely scarce supply of low entropic energy/matter; (b) a focus on the achievement of internal goods rather than the possession and consumption of external goods, as the source of abiding human satisfaction; (c) and in so doing, to make possible co-operation rather than competition, a non zero-sum rather than a zero-sum game in life, an ethical lifestyle which cuts across the crude dichotomy of egoism and altruism, and undermines to a greater extent the instrumental conception of work as a curse.

This book has two readerships in mind:

i. to convince students of social philosophy that the sciences of thermodynamics and ecology have profound significance for their own discipline. But such students usually know little or nothing about these two bodies of knowledge, and so have first to be introduced to them, before their implications, for the traditional issues in social philosophy, can be spelt out;

ii. for those who are already familiar with the findings of thermodynmics and ecology, those chapters and sections dealing with them contain nothing new that they do not already know. However, they may, nevertheless, wish to see how the outline of a systematic coherent social philosophy may be constructed based on their implications.

This exploration is offered as part of a rethinking and reconceptualisation which theorists, convinced of the relevance of these sciences, are already undertaking. So far, these theorists, in the main, come from fields as diverse as economics, demography, ecology itself, theology and even futurology. But surely social philosophy ought to be crucially concerned and involved? It is in this spirit that the outline has been delineated.

The book is structured in such a way that Chapter One lays down the broad philosophical framework within which the arguments for the central thesis, namely, the outline of a social philosophy based on ecologically sensitive values (ESVs for short) and not ecologically insensitive values (ESVs), will be advanced and marshalled. That framework, epistemologically speaking, is both a naturalistic and a fallibilistic one. Moreover, it also recognises that value discourse is a type of rational discourse, in which arguments could meaningfully be put forward and assessed by the usual critical canons, which obtain elsewhere in discourses which do not apparently involve or refer to values, and are considered to be unproblematically critical and, therefore, rational. It advocates as one of the important tests of the adequacy or otherwise of social theories that such theories should be in accordance with our scientific understanding of the world — in this case, in particular, the fundamental science of thermodynamics and the principles of ecology.

There is a further section to this chapter designed to meet the argument put forward by so-called 'hard-headed' egoists, that ecological viability and sustainability is of no concern to them, as long as they themselves are not directly affected by ecological degradation and bankruptcy. It will be shown that their thesis, far from being 'hard-headed' (which usually implies being critically impregnable), is not a coherent one and is deeply flawed. In this way, I hope to have cleared the way for the central positive task of constructing the outline of a social philosophy, which is in accordance with a proper understanding of the biophysical foundation of life, and of how the natural world works in terms of the laws of thermodynamics and the principles of ecology.

Chapters Two and Three, therefore, go on to give an account of these two sciences, and to emphasise the significance of the existence of ecological (absolute) scarcity which inevitably follows, if what these sciences maintain, is correct and true.

Before exploring further the implications of ecological scarcity for human life, one needs first to clarify what it is to be a human being or agent. This, Chapter Four does, teasing out the implications of human agency and its entailed notion of human action for human agents themselves, as well as for other non-human agents in the world, through the impact of human actions upon the environment. These show that the normal dichotomy in moral theorising between egoism and altruism is not germane to the human predicament — rather, in a world governed by the laws of thermodynamics and ecology, morality displays both egoistic and altruistic aspects at once.

The significance of ecological scarcity for human agency and action may be assessed primarily in terms of three of its activities — the rate of reproduction of human agents, the rate of consumption by such agents, the mode of production employed by such agents in satisfying their appetites for consumption. Chapter Five deals with the first two types of human activities, and Chapter Six with the third, where it is argued that orthodox economics (both bourgeois and non-bourgeois), based on exponential growth and ecologically insensitive technology (EST), are not compatible with the laws of thermodynamics and the principles of ecology which govern the functioning of the complex ecosystems in the world.

Chapters Four, Five and Six try then to to deal with a central question in social philosophy, namely, the problem of the endurance of human society. Chapter Seven goes on to deal with a second central issue in social philosophy, how not simply to survive and endure as a society, but also how to flourish as a society, as well as how to flourish as individuals within it — the traditional questions addressed to this set of problems being, 'what is the good society?', 'what is the good life?', 'what is the good person?' 'what sort of person ought I to be?' The answers then constitute the core thesis of the book — the adoption of ESVs and the rejection of ESVs.

The crucial differences between ESVs and E$\underline{S}$Vs are illustrated by their respective attitudes to the theme of work or labour. In this context, a plea for the adoption of a frugal model of socialism is made, and the corresponding rejection of a cornucopic model of socialism. And it is in this context, too, that Fourier and Morris would be assessed as instances of the former and Marx as a paradigm of the latter. Chapter Eight looks at this set of issues.

The adoption of ESVs and of the frugal model of socialism presupposes a particular type of distributive value, namely, equality. Chapter Nine is designed to explicate and defend this value.

And finally the adoption of ESVs and the frugal model of socialism also presupposes the concepts of sufficiency, capacities and needs. Chapter Ten attempts to clarify these concepts.

Autumn, 1988
Manchester

CHAPTER ONE

A RATIONAL BASIS FOR A NATURALISTIC ETHIC AND SOCIAL PHILOSOPHY

1. Traditionally, moral and social philosophers, when pushed to give a ground or foundation for their systems of values or norms, have relied on the following methodologies:

(a) that God is the final source and authority, whether divinely revealed or through the use of human reason;

(b) that they rest ultimately on intuitions which one simply and self-evidently perceives to be true;

(c) that they are to be justified by reference to facts about the world and ourselves;

(d) that the will is the final arbiter, that is, the individual human will chooses certain values while rejecting others, not in a rational but irrational or non-rational, though sincere manner.

Method (a) — the transcendent route — is no longer available in a secular age, quite apart from its inherent logical and conceptual difficulties. Method (b) cannot overcome the fundamental criticism that different people appear to subscribe to very different self-evident truths, without conceding either a form of mysticism or a form of subjectivism about values, thus collapsing into method (d) above. Method (d) itself openly admits that systems of values are, at their very basis, no more than arbitrary subjective choices or commitments, albeit sincere ones made by the will — it is held that while matters pertaining to the cognitive faculty may be said to be true or false, it is inappropriate to maintain that matters pertaining to

1

the will may be said to be true or false; however, they may be said to be sincerely or insincerely committed to. Method (c) is therefore the only hope remaining to those who wish to construct a rational naturalistic system of values.

However, method (c) is considered by many philosophers (especially since the beginning of this century) to be irredeemably logically flawed, for it commits the so-called Naturalistic Fallacy, that is to say, it attempts logically to derive 'ought' from 'is'. If this charge were valid, then I think one must concede defeat. But I do not accept the indictment. Whilst it is true that logical derivation of an 'ought' or normative proposition from an 'is' or factual proposition constitutes a fallacy, it is not true that moral and social philosophers using method (c) try to do what is logically misconceived. Their aim is not to achieve logical derivation, but something else, to show that another logical relationship, which I have called epistemic implication, obtains between 'ought' and 'is' propositions, that will provide a warrant for a rational passage from factual evidence to prescriptive or normative conclusion. [1]

If my defence above survives critical scrutiny, then method (c) is back in business. I also maintain that a moral/social theory, like theories put forward in other fields of inquiry, may be subjected to criticism. I suggest four tests of adequacy which could be used to decide between competing moral/social theories. These are: (1) the check of logic, (2) the check of facts, (3) the check of empirical/scientific assumptions and claims, (4) the check of the problem. [2]

My task in this book is a slightly different one. This time, I hope to construct the outline of a social philosophy in accordance with these tests of adequacy, and in that way to justify rationally the system of values in question. I will in particular pay attention to checks (2) and (3), and to argue that social theories which do not pass such tests are fantastic theories with no application to the real world you and I, as human agents, occupy. Such theories *ipso facto* also fail check (4), the check of the problem. Social problems arise because of certain features about human agency and the environment within which it acts and interacts. Such problems cannot be solved by theories which conjure away those very features about ourselves and the world, which in the first instance, give rise to them.

But as my meta-ethical approach leads to the claim that it is possible to justify values critically and, therefore, rationally, I feel obliged to say something more about the state of meta-ethics in general. Contemporary Western moral philosophy (using Weber and G. E. Moore as convenient starting points), by and large, subscribes to the contrary thesis of value irrationalism, namely, that all values (including social/moral values) are incapable of being critically and, therefore, rationally justified. This is inferred from the invalidity of method (c) raised above. Three sub-theses follow from it: (1) that it makes sense to talk about a disagreement in values or attitudes towards a state of affairs between two people, even in the absence of any disagreement about the facts of the case; (2) that it makes sense to conceive of values remaining unchanged, even in a world very different from the one currently occupied by human agents; (3) the individual ego (or the communal consciousness) is the moral sovereign, and each ego creates its own moral universe. I wish here to look more closely at these three entailed sub-theses, rather then the main one of value irrationalism itself.

The apparent intelligibility of (1) partially rests on the habit of many moral philosophers of constructing artificial and, therefore, highly simplified and schematic examples of moral disagreement between people. Quite often, it even simply consists of asking the reader or hearer to imagine disputant A being still able to disagree with disputant B about the morality of the case, even if A were to agree with B that the facts he, A, relied on, were wholly false, and that those, which B relied on, were acceptable. Suppose the case to be the morality of euthanasia. A maintains that to permit euthanasia is morally wrong on the grounds that foolproof safeguards could never be devised to prevent abuse. Next imagine that B could assure A that such safeguards are after all available. It is then claimed that it would still be meaningful for A to hold against B, that to permit euthanasia is wrong, in spite of the (hypothetical) agreement on the part of both that adequate safeguards are available to prevent abuse.

But apart from the constant iteration that such disagreement of values can occur, it is not obvious that it does make sense. If A really were to agree that the facts he relied on turned out on more careful consideration to be false, and if A had agreed in advance that these were the basis for his original claim that permitting euthanasia was wrong, then A could not stubbornly carry on maintaining the original claim, after having conceded that his reasons turned out to be false or untenable. If he were to do so, this would show that those reasons either (a) were not the real reasons he claimed that they were, or (b) that they were not the only reasons as he had admitted in the first instance, (c) but that he had some other reasons (more adequate perhaps) for believing that euthanasia was wrong.

If one could at the start of the discussion get A to agree that (i) the reason he cited (in this case, the lack of safeguards to prevent abuse) is his real reason for maintaining that euthanasia is wrong, and (ii) it is also his only reason for holding such a moral belief, then, should he in the course of the discussion, come to agree with B that, after all, adequate safeguards could be erected, then he would be perverse from the standpoint of a critical and rational methodology to go on holding that permitting euthanasia remained morally wrong.

At every stage of the (real) moral argument between A and B, the same methodological procedure as outlined above could be adopted and the same implication would obtain, that a disputant who violates these rules is guilty of perversity from the critical, rational standpoint.

In real life moral disputes, such as the morality or otherwise of nuclear armaments, of racism, of sexism, of orgiastic consumption, etc. disputants do differ about matters of fact. For example, as we shall see (in Chapter Three), those who hold that a lifestyle of orgiastic consumption is morally acceptable believe as a matter of fact (i) that there is no absolute scarcity, (ii) that, instead, there is relative scarcity, but it can be successfully overcome by more and more sophisticated technology. In real life moral arguments which involve very complicated facts, it may not be a simple matter to convince such people that they are factually (and scientifically) mistaken. In a good many cases, it involves projection about future consequences which could flow from a proposed course of action. But the projection is only valid if the various parameters presupposed by the course of action would obtain and continue to obtain. As a result, this can give rise to (factual) disputes about the facts. And because of this, disputants can hang on to their respective moral views without actually violating the methodological procedure outlined above.

But this, however, should not be interpreted to mean that in any one instance when all the reasons cited by disputant A, say, in support of his case turn out to be factually mistaken or unsound in other ways (such as, by failing the check of logic), that it is intelligible to maintain that A could continue maintaining that he is right, and that B, his opponent is wrong, even though he now agrees that B's reasons in support of his claim are sound and that his own are faulty.

However, to talk in a blanket way of the disagreement of facts between people is already to oversimplify matters grossly. For there are at least two types of factual disagreement. (I have already referred to one variety, that based on projection about future consequences of action.) The first is the more familiar straightforward kind — A believes that p is the case, whereas B believes that -p is the case. A maintains that X is morally right because he believes that p obtains, whereas B maintains that X is morally wrong because he believes that -p obtains. This presupposes that A and B are agreed that whether p obtains is crucial to the outcome. So if it can be shown that -p obtains, say, then A must concede that he can no longer hold X to be morally right; otherwise, he could be accused of methodological perversity.

The other kind exists where A does not seem to be aware that certain facts obtain whereas B does. As A is unaware of them, he naturally does not mention them. Call these q. But as B knows that q obtains, B cites q, not only p which A also cites, as the sole reason for holding that X is morally right. Suppose the dispute between A and B to be whether capitalism in Britain since its inception 400 years ago, could, on the whole, be said to be a morally acceptable system. A holds that it is. In evidence, he agrees with B that while it was true that in some period like the nineteenth century, the proletariat suffered greatly (that is p_1), but even the proletariat benefited(s) as economic growth occurred and continues to occur (that is p_2). B accepts p_1 and p_2. If p (that is, p_1 and p_2) is all that is under discussion, it is conceivable that B would concede that, on the whole, capitalism in Britain is a morally acceptable system. But B cites further evidence q.

q takes the following form: (i) that the suffering of the majority of people in Britain was not simply confined to the nineteenth century, although this is the most publicised aspect of it, but that it started to occur much earlier when the Enclosure Laws (even beginning in Tudor times) forced people off the land to provide labour for the growing industries, like the woollen industry (operating initially as homework), and later to drift into the developing industrial urban centres to nourish the factory manufacturing sector of the economy; (ii) that the economic growth enjoyed by Britain was made possible (a) by the enslavement of African peoples, whose labour was required to develop the newly conquered north American continent, whose indigenous population had been either killed off deliberately or unwittingly (Britain is not the only culprit but for the sake of simplicity, I only mention her and not others); Britain benefited directly and indirectly by colonial development in general, and

directly by engaging in the slave trade itself; (b) by
the countries of her empire which supplied cheap raw
materials to feed the metropolitan economy, and, in
turn, to function as captured markets for the goods
produced by her factories; (iii) today Britain, it is
true, has no empire, but the terms of trade between
her and other developing economies (which include
former colonies) and the penetration of multi-national
capital are such that though formal colonialism has
ended, it is not obvious that economic domination
ended with it.

It is difficult to conceive A still holding on to his
original view given the new information now made
available to him, and assuming, of course, he finds it
hard to dispute it. (But if he does dispute it, the
dispute remains a factual one and does not jeopardise
the methodological requirement that if all facts are
agreed upon, it is perverse for A to continue to
disagree with B. Indeed, his attempt to dispute the
facts indicates that he actually abides by the
methodological procedure, as he is implying, that it is
only intelligible for him to continuing disagreeing with
B morally, provided that he and B are in disagreement about the facts of the case, which constitute the
reasons to justify his moral assessment.) It would only
make sense for him to do so, if in addition to p and
q, he now goes on to maintain something else, such
as that while the fate of white British people matters
(whether they prosper or not under capitalism), the
fate of many more non-white peoples does not.
However, this shifts the dispute about the morality or
otherwise of capitalism in Britain to another issue, the
morality or otherwise of racism. But whether racism
itself is morally justified involves a critical assessment
of the reasons used by A (and others) to justify the
claim, including the factual reasons he may cite. The
same critical methodological procedure applies here as
it applies in the original debate.

Sometimes in a real life argument disagreement is
not even about what may be called 'naturalistic facts',
that is, matters pertaining to the world we agents,
here and now, occupy or did occupy. (In the case

7

just examined, for instance, whether African peoples were captured, bought and sold as slaves to fuel Western economies in the modern era is such a matter.) Sometimes, it shifts to other things, such as whether there is a God, what kind of God He is, what His will is, the relation between God and His creatures, etc. In a debate on abortion, suicide (and even euthanasia), quite often, and quite soon in the discussion, theology enters the picture which brings with it its own complexities. Since I myself am not interested in grounding morality on theology (nor do I believe it is possible to do so), I leave this possibility alone, and confine myself to disagreement of 'naturalistic facts'.

When the 'naturalistic facts' involved are relatively simple, it is not difficult to show that A suffers from 'prejudice', if A continues to hold the original moral assessment, even though the evidence he cites, in support of it, turns out to be false and without basis. A sexist might maintain that women ought to be treated in a manner inferior to men because females have lower I.Q.s than males. It can be shown that this is incorrect. If A continues to discriminate against women unfavourably (without citing further conceivably relevant and true evidence) then he could be convicted of sexual prejudice. 'Prejudice' is precisely defined as 'preconceived opinion', 'unjustified attitude' — preconceived because it is not formulated in the light of correct evidence but independent of it and unjustified, because the evidence cited in support of the attitude is not well-founded.

I do not, however, wish to create the impression that moral disagreements turn round only on factual disputes, and that they are capable of being easily settled at that, although factual matters must constitute a very important element. Another very significant element determining who has the better argument is, of course, bringing to bear on the discussion the usual panoply of principles of critical and rational thinking, such as the principle of consistency, of avoiding fallacies of reasoning, etc. These are just as relevant to moral discourse as to other forms of discourse which claim to be critical.

Sub-thesis (2), reinforced by (1) gives rise to the illusion that social/moral values float in a vacuum, entirely divorced from the world and what it is like as occupied by human and other agents. Such an illusion enables philosophers to argue, for instance, that the moral norm against maiming, assault, etc. would still remain in place and occupy the central place it does in morality, should it turn out to be false, that if X (a human agent) chops off Y's (another human agent) arm, Y feels great pain, Y will not grow another arm instantly to replace the chopped off one, and Y will not be able to carry on life as it used to be before the episode. If it turns out that we are simply mistaken about certain matters, that sharp devices could penetrate human flesh and sometimes even bones, causing injury and pain, that we, human organisms, contrary to what we have always believed, have the capacity for instant organ renewal and not merely tissue renewal, then surely, it would not be sensible to attach urgency to the moral norm against injuring, maiming others. Perhaps, instead, we might even encourage competitions to see who could chop off the most number of arms and legs within a minute, and consider it great fun to do so.

Conversely, it also encourages what I have called 'fantastic' social/moral theories which presuppose a world radically different from the one we occupy, thereby rendering them irrelevant as solutions to the problems which face us in the real, non fantasy world. These problems arise crucially because the world possesses certain characteristics and we, human agents, as part of that world, also possess certain features, and because of the necessity of exchange in our actions between ourselves and the world of nature. An adequate social/moral theory must, therefore, address itself to these characteristics and the character of the exchange. If it does not, whatever solution it has to offer is of no relevance or significance to our preoccupations and problems.

If no facts about the world are ever pertinent to the (critical) assessment of social/moral theories, then it is indeed possible for the individual ego to establish itself as the moral sovereign, each creating her/his moral universe (sub-thesis 3), regardless of what the world is really like. The ego and its will could then be entirely unfettered, entirely 'free' to choose whatever norm it pleases its fancy or whim to adopt. But if facts about the world are pertinent to the issue of norm-creation, then it cannot be up to the individual ego and its will arbitrarily to decide what ought to be done.

The will will have to take into account certain sorts of facts, to follow the requirements of the critical assessment of facts and the formal principles of rationality. If so, there cannot be as many moral universes as there are individual egos, each of them held to be as correct, valid, adequate, relevant as the other. There may be only one moral universe which it makes sense for all of us to create and to share. This moral universe, this book argues, is the one which recognises absolute or ecological scarcity, the details of which will be presented and argued for in the rest of the book.

This approach invites the following retort — those who adhere to value irrationalism will argue that it is a waste of my time to try to establish that there is ecological scarcity, for on their view, my ability to shift the position of my opponent from one of endorsement of the morality of our contemporary civilisation to one of condemnation presupposes that such a person already is predisposed favourably to an ecologically sustainable lifestyle. If such a favourable attitude did not already exist, then no amount of facts would, and could, shift his position.

However, this retort would not do, for it turns out to be a mere dogmatic reassertion of sub-thesis (1), rather than an argument in its defence. It simply assumes that it makes sense to say that even if both parties agree about all the facts of the case, in this instance, about ecological scarcity, they could adopt opposing attitudes to the same set of evidence. The agreement, I am hoping to achieve is, hence, no more than a matter of happy coincidence that those I am arguing with, may turn out in the end, after all, to have a pre-ordained, though up to now hidden, favourable attitude towards an ecologically sustainable lifestyle. What I cannot hope to show is that they can come to agree (on critical, rational grounds), based on the evidence to be cited, that an ecologically sustainable lifestyle is morally the correct one to adopt.

To say that the attitude must already be there, and hence pre-ordained, is to create more mystery than is necessary. It is in danger of turning the thesis into the doctrine of innate moral ideas. Such a doctrine is implausible as it is obviously irreconcilable with the rich diversities of moral beliefs in human cultures throughout history. It is odd to think that human agents have pre-ordained beliefs (which often contradict one another) about the morality or immorality of wearing skirts of a certain length, of pre-marital sexual intercourse, of euthanasia, etc. (What I deny is innateness of specific moral ideas like those mentioned; I am not denying that human agents are born with certain capacities, such as for cruelty, for kindness, for fear, for love and so on, without which no morality is possible.)

The mystery deepens because it also holds that the innate, pre-ordained favourable attitude towards an ecologically sustainable lifestyle will remain hidden, until elicited by the set of evidence I intend to use. The question then arises — will it be elicited by this type of evidence only or any old evidence? Clearly not the latter; otherwise, I might as well recite the story about Father Christmas instead of writing a book of social/moral philosophy on the subject. If the former, then it must be because the evidence is pertinent. Hence, a far simpler way of looking at the matter is to say that in the light of the evidence cited, one could be persuaded (rationally and critically) to drop extant moral beliefs and attitudes and adopt new ones. This way renders the adoption, the modification of moral beliefs and attitudes unmysterious and economical. It is also to be recommended then in terms of Ockham's razor.

After this detour into contemporary meta-ethics, let me return to completing the outline of the task I have set myself in this book. I take it that all social philosophers, who have ever addressed themselves to the question of constructing such systems of philosophy, have assumed the continuance of the human species (if not other species) and, therefore, the endurance of human society in some form. As they see it, their job is not to query whether human beings as a species should continue to survive or whether society should be destroyed with the extinction of *homo sapiens*. Rather, their job is to build what, in their view, is the best framework within which human beings could live and flourish, to construct a good society that can and would endure.

But of late, a new element seems to have appeared to challenge this very assumption. Up to recent times, although human beings knew how to get rid of other human beings, deliberately through war or not so deliberately through action eventually causing disease or famine, we did not have the means which we could knowingly use to kill the entire human species (and other species), or to render the habitat no longer a viable one for human existence in general. But now we have the technology alas. Nuclear weapons are just such a technology. Less dramatically, technologies in the sphere of production (the non-armament sector of the economy) also seem to have effects which, unchecked in the longer term, could render the earth no longer able to support *homo sapiens* and therefore eventually lead to its extinction.

Some philosophers, as a result of these possibilities, have seen fit to raise the issues whether it might not be acceptable after all to permit the extinction of human and/or other species through its war and productive technologies. [3] I am, however, not concerned in the main with this set of problems. I am assuming, like the classical philosophers, that the continuance of the human species is a good thing (subject to its leading a lifestyle which does not needlesssly destroy other species and forms of matter), and that one's task as a social philosopher is to

12

construct an enduring framework within which human beings could live and flourish, an existence which flows from the recognition that life has biophysical foundations, that cannot, and should not, be ignored. So I will not be spending too much energy on combating those who argue 'eat, drink and be merry for tomorrow we (the human species) die', although I will be devoting some time to arguing against such a view. (See section 3 below.)

From the point of view of Nature and evolutionary changes *per se* it is, of course, neither here nor there that human beings go out of existence. If we do, some other species, either existing or new, would probably evolve to take our place of ascendancy in the evolutionary chain. In other words, the continuance, the flourishing or otherwise of the human species, is entirely a human concern and preoccupation. We are organisms which are not only conscious, but also self-conscious; moreover, we are also capable of consciously and deliberately monitoring our own activities. It is in virtue of our possessing such capacities that it is meaningful to address ourselves to the issue about the impact of our actions upon the environment, and the problem of ecological responsibility in our exchange with Nature.

In the description of this task, the operative words are 'endurance', 'live' and 'flourish'. The problems, therefore, are set by these terms. But baldly as they stand, they are not helpful, for they immediately bring to mind contentious issues like 'endure, but for how long?', 'what counts as living and flourishing?' To many contemporary philosophers, especially for those who adopt method (c), these issues raise the charge that they are essentially contestible, and, therefore, incapable of a rational solution even in the very long run. But I hope to rely on checks (2) and (3), in particular, to fill out accounts of endurance and human flourishing which would surmount the charge of essential contestedness.

In other words, a social philosophy which in its argument and its recommended arrangements ignores or goes against checks (2) and (3) is irrelevant, and if acted upon, would yield a non-viable society in the long run. (A society based on such a system may endure for a relatively short span — for instance, civilisation as we know it, since the seventeenth century in Europe, may be such a short term one.) Most modern (that is, from the seventeenth century onwards) social philosophies in their constructions have, as a matter of fact, ignored much of how science understands the world to work. To put it in another way, they have made a very narrow selective view of what science has on offer, and opted for a partial understanding provided by a few of the sciences, the most prestigious of which being classical physics. But such partial understanding is not enough. One needs to go beyond the mechanistic paradigm [4] and the linear model of causation embedded in classical physics to comprehend as well those sciences which involve the study of living organisms, and their processes of interaction with non-living things.

The reason for reaching out beyond inert matter (the subject matter studied by physics) is the obvious one that, to begin with, we human beings are living organisms, and that our existence, amongst other things, depends vitally upon the existence of other living organisms and certain chemical processes at work. So before one pontificates how human beings ought to behave towards other human beings, or how they ought to flourish, one should at least have some understanding how the world of Nature works and the roles human agency plays, both as constituent of that world and as a potential bringer of change to it, through our intervention in the way it works.

At the very least, we need then to have some fairly clear ideas (in so far as science itself as a corporate fallible body of knowledge allows such clear ideas to emerge) as to how (a) Nature at large works — this means, as I said before, not only a study of physics and chemistry, but also the live sciences, as well as the very fundamental science of thermo-dynamics together with the science of ecology; (b) how we, as a species, are a part of (a); (c) how we as individuals of the species reproduce, grow, mature, develop and die against the background of (a); (d) how we in the way we produce things like food, shelter etc. in order to 'live and flourish' and to reproduce can affect (a); (e) in turn how such affected and changed Nature can have consequences on our mode of production, reproduction and our attempts to 'live and flourish'.

So very fundamental is the science of thermo-dynamics that I was even tempted to incorporate it into the very title of this book. This is because if a very brief answer is to be given to the basic problems of any social philosophy, namely, 'what counts as endurance?' and 'what constitutes living and flourishing?', I would say that the limit of endurance is, as a matter of fact, set by our understanding of the world given to us by the principles of thermodynamics, and that the conception of human existence and flourishing must also be in keeping with that understanding.

The next chapter must, therefore, say something about this science. But one basic relevant point to emphasise here and now is that our solar system, of which our planet earth is a part, will eventually run down. The sun is our ultimate source of energy and also, therefore, the source of life as we know it. When that energy source winds down, we can take it that human existence will no longer be supported. So human existence and society would not last forever. Our endurance is, hence, predicated upon the endurance of the sun in so far as it is the provider not only of energy *per se* but also of a certain strength and quality by the time it reaches the earth. But although the ultimate extinction of life on earth is an unavoidable outcome, this does not mean that human activity cannot and does not play a part in determining the rate at which life might become extinguished or impoverished. Social philosophy cannot concern itself with things which are beyond human control. But it must crucially concern itself with things which are within human control.

Some forms of human existence and flourishing may indeed contribute to altering the strength and quality of that solar energy as it reaches us. For instance, there is grave concern about the possible destruction of the ozone layer of our atmosphere by the release of chlorofluorocarbon gases through the use of spray cans, fast food cartons and in refrigeration, amongst other activities. The thinning of the ozone could mean that harmful ultra-violet rays from the sun would filter through to cause skin cancer and other ills. The gases also prevent radiated heat from escaping, thus helping to produce the 'greenhouse effect'. A style of living and flourishing which relies on the convenience of spray cans and fast food cartons may be said not to be in keeping with our understanding of (a) how Nature works, (b) how our mode of production and consumption in persuance of a certain style of existence could affect Nature, that is, in this case, to deplete the ozone, and (c) how in turn this destruction of this part of Nature could affect human existence.

So the realisation that the sun would finally disappear as a source of energy, and with it life as we know it to be, is itself of no great relevance to social philosophy. However, while the sun still shines, there are lots of things which, were we to do them, would pretty quickly deplete the stocks of low entropic energy and matter (which are all absolutely scarce — see Chapter Three), and at the rate with which the depletion takes place, would overload the ecosystems so that they would no longer be able to cope with the end products of such use and consumption. It is this issue which is of fundamental significance to social philosophy. The issue is about matters which are perfectly within our control — how much we deplete and how fast, and the undesirable consequences of overloading are avoidable, provided we are prepared to inform our conduct by ideals and values, which are ecologically sensitive, to replace the extant ecologically insensitive ones.

Up to now, we have failed to take seriously into account the workings of the laws of thermodynamics and the principles of ecology in our daily activities of production and consumption. As a result, such activities are producing unwanted side effects which increasingly pose a threat to the continuing well-being of the human as well as other species. Yet these cumulative consequences are readily explained (and in broad outline readily predictable) by reference to the laws of thermodynamics and ecology. The lesson to be learnt must surely be to pay more careful attention to what these sciences have to tell us and, if needs be, to reduce, or even revise our activities of production and consumption (and in turn our other values), so that they will be in accordance with this more complete scientific understanding of the world we live in.

2. Next, let me say something about a methodological matter which I raised earlier in the last section. If a social philosophy is to be in accordance with the deliverances of science and in that sense to be justified by science, does this not presuppose that scientific knowledge itself must be certain, unchanging, in order to provide the requisite foundation for social philosophy?

This is the old philosophical search for certainty. But scientific knowledge, alas, is not absolutely certain. Indeed sceptics point out delightedly that theories held to be correct even for centuries have in the end been overthrown. So is it not fruitless to try to construct a social philosophy based on shifting sands?

To meet this objection, I will confine myself to saying only two things: (1) my epistemological framework is a fallibilistic one. Theories, whether in the domain of the natural sciences or in the sphere of social philosophy, are all fallible. Fallibilism, it is true, cannot yield truths which are guaranteed to be certain and absolute; but it does not mean that one can never decide between theories in a rational manner (provided that 'rational' is not equated with 'logical proof' or 'logical derivability'). It does, however, mean that in the future, should further new evidence become available to challenge the existing best theory, there is no privileged status of 'keep off, don't challenge' attached to it. As a result of a serious challenge, it may no longer be the best theory available;

(2) it follows from my epistemological stance that should there be a major change in scientific understanding, and the laws of thermodynamics were to be replaced by a quite different set of laws, then the social philosophy constructed on the extant laws would be rendered irrelevant, and a new attempt would have to be made. There is nothing inherently alarming about such a prospect. Indeed, it is in this spirit that I am now engaged in the task of constructing the outline of a social philosophy in accordance with a fundamental science, namely, the science of thermodynamics whose principles were not clearly grasped and articulated till the nineteenth century, to supersede the social philosophies such as Locke's and Marx's which did not take that science into account — in the case of Locke, clearly he lived well before that and so Locke himself could not be blamed, and in the case of Marx, he too could probably not be wholly blamed even though he lived in the nineteenth century, as the implications of ideas from another field take time to be recognised and absorbed. [5] So strictly speaking, one is not so much criticising Locke and Marx as those who, today, still pursue the neo-Lockean and neo-Marxist social philosophies without any awareness that their views, though regarded as competitors and rivals, are in actual fact united in their basic assumptions about a world, which do not specifically recognise the relevance of the laws of thermodynamics and the principles of ecology, and the limitations to human actions as well as the consequences which flow from them. (See Chapter Six.)

In principle, fallibilism accepts the possibility that the laws of thermodynamics may one day be challenged and overthrown. In practice, one can (as a lay person) only look for guidance to the community of scientists and their considered opinion. In the judgment of at least one very eminent member of that community, namely, Einstein, those principles are unlikely to be seriously challenged. He writes:

> A theory is more impressive the greater is the simplicity of its premises, the more different are the kinds of things it relates and the more extended its range of applicability. Therefore, the deep impression which classical thermodynamics made on me. It is the only physical theory of universal content which I am convinced, that within the framework of applicability of its basic concepts will never be overthrown. [6]

Another prominent scientist, Arthur Eddington has also observed:

> The law that entropy increases — the Second Law of Thermodynamics — holds, I think, the supreme position among laws of nature. If someone points out to you that your pet theory of the universe is in disagreement with Maxwell's equations — then so much the worse for Maxwell's equations. If it is found to be contradicted by observation — well, these experimentalists do bungle things sometimes. But if your theory is found to be against the Second Law of Thermodynamics, I can give you no hope; there is nothing for it but to collapse in deepest humiliation. [7]

3. The primary purpose of this book is to explore the elements and themes that make up a social philosophy, which is ecologically sensitive. However, it could be said that this vision of an ecologically sensitive society, based on the self-denial of consumerism, on self-development or the acquisition of internal goods rather than of external material goods as the main source of fulfilment and happiness, on co-operation rather than competition (see especially Chapters Four, Five and Seven), could be easily undermined by those who argue against it from the perspective of the self-interest of the individual. So I

need to look at this challenge to see if it could be deflected.

However, it is not the aim of this book to write a comprehensive critique of the notion of self-interest, as to do so would alter the fundamental purpose and character of the book. Moreover, its menacing challenge is relevant not only to someone like myself, who wishes to argue for ESVs as the core of civilisation. It poses a threat to all social/moral theorists who argue for the possibility and desirability of some form or other of altruism, or at least to those who argue against egoism. My own account is based not so much on altruism, as on a rejection of the sharp dichotomy between egoism and altruism and for a mode of looking at human conduct which, at once, recognises so-called egoistic and altruistic aspects as being inextricably intertwined. (See Chapter Four.)

The literature in favour of the concept of self-interest in moral/social philosophy is, to say the least, extensive; so is the literature in criticism of it. It is therefore neither possible nor desirable for me here to examine every argument which has been advanced on its behalf, and to try to meet them all. Instead what I propose to do is to consider one particular line of argument from self-interest which has a direct bearing on the position I am trying to advance, namely, that my arguments in defence of ESVs would cut no ice with the hard-headed proponents of self-interest, the most extreme of which maintain that generations, other than their own, have no claim upon themselves, the present generation, so that the latter, if it so wishes, could use up all of Nature's 'capital' and 'income' on itself, at one go, so to speak.

To meet this type of argument, one needs to distinguish, first of all, between those commonly called psychological egoists and those who are ethical egoists. [8] The former holds that human beings are so constructed that they cannot, as a matter of psychology, desire anything but to advance their own individual interests. The latter are those who maintain that irrespective of whether as a matter of fact they act only to advance the interests of the self, they ought to. This is a normative claim, and can be understood as either a moral normative or a prudential normative claim.

Psychological egoism, upon examination, turns out to face immense difficulties and in the end to transform itself from being a purely factual truth to become a non-factual one, that is, as a tautological truth whose necessity and certainty are guaranteed by linguistic fiat. The transformation would occur as follows: suppose an opponent challenges the (empirical) truth of the claim that all human beings act out of self-interest, by citing obvious counter examples like self-sacrificing mothers, who would rather themselves starve to death in order that their offspring could survive on whatever little food there might be available, or patriots and supporters of causes, who are prepared to try to assassinate their opponents by using themselves as 'walking hand grenades'. Are these not clear cases of people acting, not so much to promote their own interests, but the interests of others?

Surely, whatever else self-interest might mean, it must at least mean survival and preservation of the self? Such people, indeed, are what we typically call heroines and martyrs, that is, people who give up their own lives in order to ensure the survival and protection of others. (Moral philosophers call such actions supererogatory duties).

If the psychological egoists accept these as genuine counter examples, then they would have to modify their thesis considerably — from the claim that it is never the case that people act against their self-interest to the more reduced claim that they act, most of the time, perhaps, to advance their self-interests, but that they can, at times, also act against their self-interests.

From the point of view of my thesis that we, the present generation, should curb our acquisitive appetites for material goods for the good of future generations, such a reduced psychological egoistic claim is no longer threatening, for it concedes that human agents can act to promote the interests of

21

others, at times, even at the expense of their own. After all, to give up orgiastic consumption is a smaller sacrifice than to give up one's life to preserve that of others. To concede that the latter is possible implies that a concession to the former is also possible. Moreover, moral philosophers, surely, would not regard abstinence from overconsumption as a supererogatory matter. Or would they?

However, some psychological egoists might be unwilling to accept that these cases are genuine counter examples. They would argue that behind such cases of apparent self-sacrifice lurks self-interest, because individuals would not act unless they are motivated by self-interest. As these individuals did act, then there must be a hidden self-interest motive behind the action. But what could be the hidden motive?

In the case where an agent, say, leapt in to save someone at real risk to her own life, they could argue that it is because the agent was motivated by the adulation and praise she would receive from society for such an act of bravery, should she survive the rescue operation. But what if such an agent were to be interviewed and queried closely as to her motivation. Suppose she denied that such thoughts had ever crossed her mind at the time of the rescue. Would this not constitute evidence to falsify the claim asserted by the adamant psychological egoists? If they were to reject refutation, they could go on to maintain that, although the agent had no such conscious motivation, there must have been such motivation at the unconscious level.

As we know, there are well-known objections to this kind of 'Freudian' claim about universal unconscious motivation. It suffices to mention only one such, namely, that the search for unconscious motivation is only imperative and relevant if the ostensible and avowed reason for action is inadequate to explain the behaviour in question. Take as an example someone who washes his hands every five seconds of his waking life, and gives as his reason for this cleansing act that his hands are dirty, when it is quite obvious to a bystander that they are quite clean. In such an instance, it would be appropriate to invoke a possible unconscious motive for the act, that perhaps, the agent has committed a murder, and that his unavowed guilt manifests itself through obsessive washing of the hands to get rid of the blood.

But the example of the rescuer is not comparable to the obsessive hand washer. The former's avowed reason that she wanted to save the drowning person is sufficient and adequate to explain the behaviour in question. The claim then that no behaviour is adequately explained, unless one goes beyond conscious motivation to an unconscious one, is an unjustified metaphysical dogma. (Not all forms of metaphysics are unjustified, but this one is.)

Another strategy employed by determined psychological egoists is not so much to resort to unconscious motivation, but to argue that the self-interest works in the form of a 'glow of satisfaction' at the thought of doing good to others. Suppose the martyr in question (a) does not believe in an after life for which s/he would be rewarded for the good deed by the Almighty (some, of course, do), (b) does not believe either that s/he would survive the operation to receive public acclaim, on the rational grounds that short of a miracle such a type of dangerous operation involves the practical certainty (logically, of course, miracles are possible) of one's death. Where then does the 'glow of satisfaction' come from? It comes from the contemplation on the part of the agent of the posthumous adulation s/he would receive.

One does not wish to write off such a 'glow' totally. For all I know, some heroines and martyrs could well feel such a 'glow'. But the conceptual point remains, that the 'glow' could not account for the agent's action unless the agent already has a conception of advancing the interests of others, even at the expense of one's own; otherwise, conceptually speaking, the 'glow' cannot exist. The 'glow' is conceptually posterior to the conception of self-sacrifice itself. If the glow does not exist, it cannot explain the behaviour; if it does exist, it can only be a secondary, not the primary cause, from the conceptual point of view.

What if the psychological egoists refuse to concede defeat, and go on to maintain that the 'glow' must exist on the grounds that no action could emanate from an agent, unless the agent is motivated by self-interest? This claim is like the Freudian resort to unconscious motivation, which, I have argued, is an unjustifiable metaphysical dogma. There is no independent existence of such a 'glow'. It is imported solely to fight off refutation.

The thesis that the agent could not have acted unless out of self-interest has ceased to be an empirical claim, which could be refuted by counter examples. No counter example is considered to be genuine by the technique of redefining the meaning of the term 'selfish'. In normal usage, A is selfish if A tramples on the interests of others to advance her own. A is unselfish if A allows her own interests to be side-stepped in favour of the interests of others. But the determined psychological egoists have redefined the term 'selfish' to mean no more than this — any action that proceeds from the self is selfish.

On the revised definition, it is necessarily true that every agent acts 'selfishly', for all actions emanate from the self or agent. Under this revision, we can no longer distinguish between selfish and unselfish behaviour in the normal understanding of such characteristics. If the psychological egoists were to try to preserve such a distinction in their new terminology, then this would bring back the problems they thought they had expelled. They appear finally to end up with a claim which is necessarily true (as a tautology). But such a claim is a trivial, non-informative truth which we can safely ignore.

Let us next look at the ethical egoists. They in turn can be divided into (a) those who believe that self-interest can be construed more broadly to include enlightened self-interest and (b) those who do not. The former group could cover those who hold that the advancement of one's self-interest may often include advancing the interests of others, like those of other generations. Although the moral motive is not one of altruism but simply that of enlightened self-interest, as such, these theorists are not necessarily a threat to my case. (There is further elaboration of this point later on.)

However, there may be another group of ethical egoists who maintain that although they have a notion of enlightened self-interest, in their calculation, its scope of application does not include the welfare and interests of generations other than their own. If so, as far as the issue of the provisions for future generations is concerned, they collapse as a matter of fact into category (b) above, that is, those who simply hold the ideal of crude self-interest *simpliciter*.

An example to illustrate this type. Some years ago the newspapers reported that a group of old age pensioners living in San Diego, USA, refused to pay, through local income tax (comparable to rates in this country), for the education of the young in the community. They argued that they themselves had neither children nor grandchildren living in the area, who could conceivably benefit from the education provided out of direct taxation.

Suppose one were to point out to them that they were somewhat short-sighted — even though their own posterity would not benefit, they themselves would derive benefit from educating the young, as surely they would like to be served efficiently by literate milkmen and skilled electricians and plumbers, etc. when the young finally entered the labour market.

They responded (or could respond), however, by saying that they were not likely to live that long to enjoy the benefits of their 'investment'. Moreover, should they survive long enough to see the present generation of the young reach the age of employment, it might, nevertheless, be still cheaper for them to pay for imported literate and skilled labour (from other states or countries) than to pay the taxes required to educate the young. In crude self-interest terms, they justified their refusal to pay taxes to support the education of the young.

Their logic looks insuperable and impregnable. But is it really as tight as it appears? Perhaps not. Their crude self-interest only works (that is, that they would still be able to enjoy the fruits of education without paying so much for them, or not paying for them at all) by shifting the cost of education on to other communities and societies. In other words, these communities and societies in turn could not be crude ethical egoists and refuse to educate their young.

If every community were to be a community of 'hard-headed' and 'hard-hearted' ethical egoists like themselves, no-one would feel obliged or want to educate their young. As a result, the next generation would be totally illiterate and unskilled. This would surely not be in the self-interest of the tight-fisted selfish OAPs. In other words, as a universal precept, ethical egoism — one (meaning everyone) ought to be a hard-headed crude egoist — leads to consequences which are injurious to hard-headed egoists themselves.

The advantages to not investing in the education of the young could only exist if the majority of agents in other communities are not egoists in the way envisaged. Yet as ethical egoism is meant to be a universal doctrine which all people ought to practise, at the theoretical level, it is not possible for the benefits to occur if everyone were to act on it. At the factual practical level, of course, the story may be somewhat different, because not everyone believes that ethical egoism is either an attractive or convincing moral doctrine anyway and, hence, would not act on it. Or it could be that a sufficient number of convinced ethical egoists are silly enough to have got their sums wrong and agreed to pay for the education of the young.

The above criticisms also apply against the earlier stage of the ethical egoistic argument, namely, those OAPs who said that they would die before the children could become employable. For these too had shifted the cost to other people, namely, those before them who had paid for the cost of educating the workers now serving them as literate milkmen and efficient electricians and plumbers. If everyone (including the past generations) had acted on crude ethical egoistic grounds because they believed it would be right to do so, then they, the present generation of OAPs, would not now be reaping the benefits of other people having borne the costs.

Again at the theoretical level, such a possibility of shifting costs elsewhere could not occur. But again at the practical level, of course, they could take advantage of the fact that not everyone in the generation before their own had behaved and acted on the doctrine, or that even as ethical egoists they had acted foolishly and made mistakes in their calculation.

In other words, to be theoretically coherent, at least as far as the consequences of acting upon egoistic grounds are concerned, the doctrine cannot be formulated as a universal claim and must be modified to 'some people ought to act on crude egoistic grounds, but not all'. This raises a difficulty, however. To be rational seems to require that a reason must be given to differentiate between two groups otherwise similar. In this case, it would have to justify differentiating between those who ought to act on egoistic grounds and those who ought not to.

Ethical egoism has no resources within itself to do so. Other moral social doctrines could invoke God or natural law, etc., but ethical egoism prides itself on being 'hard-headed' and 'no-nonsense' in its approach and so cannot fall back on obscure and problematical constructs, like God or natural law. It also prides itself on being a rational doctrine — as such, it cannot simply fall back on the fashionable meta-ethics of saying that one has arbitrarily and irrationally decided that some ought to be rational ethical egoists and others ought not to be. And in its modified reduced form in any case, it is incompatible with its original claim of being a universal rational moral doctrine.

And in its original form, no attempt, as far as I know, has been made to justify itself as a rational doctrine. While it is plausible to maintain that it is rational to take into account one's interests, crudely and narrowly defined, as an important consideration in determining how one ought to act, it is not obviously plausible to maintain that it is rational, always and only, to advance one's interests crudely and narrowly defined. It is simply dogmatically asserted to be a rational moral (or prudential) truth. It arrives at this 'logically impregnable' status by the usual tactic of linguistic fiat, of defining the term 'rational' in such a way that any one, who does not act on crude egoistic grounds, is said to be 'not rational' or 'irrational'. This 'triumphant' feat, like that of psychological egoism, is built on philosophical sands. It could, of course, be maintained as a self-evident truth. But what is self-evident to one is not self-evident to another. So it is equally unsatisfactory to hold it as a mere self-evident truth.

To summarise the arguments against egoism so far. Psychological egoism is (empirically) false or vacuous. Ethical egoism, in so far as it covers enlightened self-interest, is not an enemy but an ally, as far as my central thesis of concern for posterity goes. (See below for further discussion on this point.) In so far as it is narrowly interpreted to refer to crude self-interests only, it faces many insuperable conceptual hurdles. As a universal precept, on the theoretical level, it is riddled with inconsistencies, if not out-right contradictions. And as for the claim in general that ethical egoism in all its different forms is a rational moral (or prudential) doctrine, its epistemological foundation is just as insecure as that of its counterpart, psychological egoism. For its claim to be a rational doctrine is equally vacuous.

I have now commented in general on psychological and ethical egoism and have shown that both forms run into difficulties. Let me now turn my attention to the more specific claims that self-interested individuals could not and need not be concerned with (a) the non-sustainability of our current ecologically insensitive civilisation, (b) the welfare of generations other than our own, including those already existing or just about to exist, (c) the welfare of remote future generations. (For the purpose of this discussion at the moment, let us interpret 'remote' to mean any generation after that of grandchildren.)

Take claim (a). Its plausibility may have been greater even ten years ago, but today evidence is growing daily that no one, not even so-called hard-headed egoists, could afford to be quite so complacent about the matter. I take it that the hard-headed egoists in question are not so much the hard-headed egoists who are octogenerians about to 'shuffle off this mortal coil', but younger generations who have forty to sixty years or more ahead of them. While it might be plausible for the former to be cavalier about the issue, it is much less so for the latter categories.

To take only three examples of grave concern today which even governments in the so-called first (affluent industrialised) world, with the exception of Great Britain, are prepared to act upon, but which they could, up to a few years ago, turn a blind eye to — (i) the depletion of ozone in the atmosphere caused by the emission of CFC gases, the alarming nature of which is now being reinforced by the very recent discovery of 'a hole' in the ozone layer above the Antarctic, (ii) the death and debilitation of trees, the precise cause or causes of which are still not completely understood, but of which it would be safe to say that they have something to do, either directly or indirectly, with increase in atmospheric pollution, even if it were true that acid rain is not the sole component, (iii) the pollution of water supplies and damage to many forms of life, through the excessive use of artificial fertilisers, herbicides and pesticides in modern agriculture.

It is difficult to see how the hard-headed egoists could shrug off these and other already extant or imminent threats to their well-being, unless they try to get out of this kind of tight corner by redefining 'self-interest' to mean something, which no longer has anything to do with well-being, but to mean, whatever the individual may care to define as 'self-interest'.

'Well-being' is minimally understood to mean 'not being poisoned', 'not fearing the possibility of suffering from, say, skin cancer' and so on. And the notion of self-interest in turn must minimally include these desirable states. The hard-headed egoist may now be seen to maintain that, for them, the advancement of their self-interest is compatible with their being poisoned or suffering from skin cancer, etc. Under this revision, the original universal precept of ethical egoism — one ought to advance one's self-interest — becomes an empty injunction. It has become simply the injunction — one ought to advance whatever each one believes to constitute her/his own self-interest.

Being substantively empty, it is no longer a threat to someone like myself who wishes to argue for an ecologically sensitive lifestyle, as it is logically compatible with all possible lifestyles. It is just the case that my understanding and definition of the notion of self-interest happens to include my own well-being and the well-being of others, including other already existing generations and generations to be born, which is not shared by the hard-headed egoists, whose conception of self-interest includes ignoring the well-being of other generations as well as the strong likelihood of their being poisoned, of their suffering from certain diseases and even painful death.

As we have already seen, such a meta-ethics based on subjective choices of values, involving definitions of terms by individuals, is clearly not compatible with the claim of ethical egoism as a rational universal doctrine. In its revised form as a crudely subjective morality, the ethical egoists could not claim in any meaningful sense that I and others like-minded are wrong in choosing ecologically sensitive lifestyles and values, or that they themselves are right in rejecting them. Within such a meta-ethics, we are each 'right'. But if we are each 'right', it follows that the ethical egoists cannot criticise my conception of self-interest, or indeed my conception of any other moral ideal. If that is so, I and similar spirits should be left well alone, at least at the theoretical level, to pursue our own conception of the good without any fear of further harassment from such ethical egoists.

The arguments that I have just rehearsed would apply equally to those ethical egoists who might argue that their conception of self-interest includes running risks of incurring disease and even death provided that, in their calculations, there are other compensations to balance such risks, like eating junk food sealed in plastic cartons, using aerosols or spray cans etc., all of which in many countries still involve processes that release CFC gases into the atmosphere. To such people, the convenience or pleasure they get out of the presentation of 'fast food' is of greater value than the 'inconvenience' or 'displeasure' attendant upon getting skin cancer, through eventual over exposure to the sun's ultra-violet rays.

This is the obverse to the coin about the so-called gambler's choice. The gambler is prepared to run the very great risk of losing five pounds on the very small chance of winning a million pounds. The ethical egoist rates more highly the convenience or pleasure of using spray cans to the risk that s/he personally runs of acquiring skin cancer or being poisoned. However, 'chacun á son gout' presents no real problem to someone who does not wish to make such a choice. We have already seen the drawbacks of such a meta-ethics.

Next claim (b). To assess this properly, one needs first of all to distinguish between the notion of self-love and that of selfishness. We have already seen that 'selfishness' means 'trampling upon the interests of others in order to advance one's own'. 'Self-love', however, means something quite different. According to Kant, as rational agents, we each have to work out a conception of self-love, that is, of what constitutes happiness for ourselves. (For Kant, of course, self-love is only at the level of prudential reason and not moral reason. To be a rational moral agent, one needs to go beyond the maxim of self-love to the Categorical Imperative itself.) Happiness, for Kant, is not the Benthamite utilitarian one of greater pleasure over pain in terms of sensations of pleasure and pain, but the harmonising and prioritising of our objectives and goals in life, so that they form an ordered whole.

Suppose individual A's conception of self-love or happiness does not include the procreation of children, but individual B's conception does. Suppose further that A's motive for being childless has nothing to do with concern about the problem of overpopulation, or any larger issue of ecological and social significance. A simply wants no demands made upon her/his time and energy, which would inevitably be made, if s/he were to have a child or children. Being childless would enable such individuals to concentrate all on developing their own potential, be it in running a business, writing a novel, playing football.

Such individuals are not necessarily being selfish; nor could they be said to be altruistic or self-sacrificing either. They have simply chosen to lead a childless existence as part of their conception of happiness or self-love. Such individuals (a) are not advocating that everyone of an age capable of reproduction ought, like themselves, to be childless; (b) may well be intelligent enough to realise that childlessness, as a universal prescription, leads to unacceptable consequences such as the exinction of the human race; indeed as rational egoists they would realise that their own welfare in their old age depends on the continuing contribution of younger generations to upkeep the fabric of human existence; (c) are, therefore, duly mindful that generations other than their own, have claims to welfare and well-being.

Although their own conception of self-love does not include themselves personally producing children, the procreation of children by other people (so long as it is not overdone) is a good and a necessary good, and hence they would not grudge even paying taxes to nurture the young. They could, and would recognise that people have a right to procreate as well as a right not to procreate, should they so choose. Such a type of rational egoists is not a threat to my defence of the thesis that we should care about the quality of the environment and of life that our children and grandchildren might have to face. They could well be on my side.

It goes without saying that I do not disagree with, or need to fear those egoists who maintain that their conception of self-love involves wanting children and providing an optimal environment for their well-being. On this issue, we are of one mind.

This brings me to claim (c). This kind of egoists may in turn also be divided into those who might themselves want children and grandchildren whose claim to concern they recognise and those who, while not wanting them themselves, might still recognise that other people's children and grandchildren have a legitimate claim to concern. But both types would deny that their own concern needs legitimately extend beyond the welfare of the next two generations.

With this kind of egoist, I think, appearance to the contrary not withstanding, there is, nevertheless, quite a lot of common ground between their position and mine. Such egoists (and non-egoists for that matter) might naturally wish to do the best they can for their own children and grandchildren. The more conventional way of trying to do the best for them consists of setting up investment trusts which would avoid paying inheritance taxes, taking out covenants for their privately purchased education, etc. The more thinking of them could well come to realise that these might not be enough, and that doing one's best for one's offspring might well include that of ensuring, that they do not live in an ecologically degraded and hazardous environment, running the risk of being poisoned, even suffering painful diseases and deaths, etc.

In ecological terms then, doing one's best for one's offspring involves leading a lifestyle which is ecologically sensitive, minimally, to the extent of leaving an environment which is no worse than the one they have found it themselves at the start of their lives, and maximally, even to the extent of reversing the damages already caused by previous generations, and the present generation of mature agents.

This latter possibility is not too fanciful, for egoists of such ilk frequently say that they are prepared to work hard, so that their children and grandchildren could have a better life than the one they have themselves. They could, therefore, be prepared to make considerable self-sacrifice even in terms of their own lifestyle.

If every generation were to be informed even by this type of egoistic spirit, then the environment might not get significantly worse than it is, and might even get better. If so, such egoists and I are allies. In other words, whether, as a matter of fact, they acknowledge the legitimate claim of more remote future generations becomes, on this understanding, an irrelevant academic matter. The maxim 'leave the environment at least no worse off, if not better off, for your children and grandchildren', if acted upon conscientiously by each generation, would secure continuous desirable ecological outcomes.

However, it could still be argued that I have not dealt with yet another kind of ecological context which the determined egoists could take advantage of. They might maintain that some, though not all of the bad ecological consequences of their actions may take, say, 200 years or 300 years to manifest themselves. Since such a long span of time is well beyond that occupied by themselves, their immediate posterity and that, these consequences would only affect very remote generations, they need not regard such consequences as any concern of theirs.

To meet such a type of rational egoistic outlook, let us recall two earlier arguments. The first is the claim that the thesis of rational egoism itself — one ought always to advance one's own self-interests — turns out on examination to be an empty injunction. It becomes re-written as 'one ought always to advance whatever one believes to constitute one's own interest'. Moreover, this reading is in keeping with the presupposition of the theory that the individual ego is the final (and indeed the only) arbiter of what constitutes one's own self-interests. If so, it is conceivable that there are as many conceptions of self-interest as there are individuals.

The second is the distinction between self-love and selfishness. The former may legitimately form part of one's self-interest. One's conception of self-love may, indeed, extend to a concern about the well-being of even remote generations. It is neither absurd nor un-intelligible for self-interested agents to hold that they would be very unhappy at the thought of remote future generations suffering the bad ecological conse-quences of their present actions.

The cut-off point for concern at the generation of grandchildren is only a pragmatic consideration, and has no logical import, as far as one's concern for the welfare of posterity is concerned. In life, it is true that for most people, they are likely to live to an age to see no more than their grandchildren. But some may never do so, of course. Yet others may live to see even their great great grandchildren. Those who achieve the distinction of being 'glamorous grannies' at the age of 34 stand a good chance of still being around when their great great grandchildren will be born (if the family keeps up its tradition of early child-bearing). There is no reason why such egoists might not include the well-being of such descendants in their conception of self-love. In other words, it does not matter whether the agent is alive to confront these descendants. Conceptually speaking, if it is possible for one to be concerned with the well-being of one's immediate posterity, it is also possible for one to be concerned with the well-being of future remote posterity.

Morever, a psychological mechanism exists to trigger off this concern. If any one generation of ethical egoists were to include the well-being of its children and grandchildren in its conception of self-love, and if each succeeding generation were to do likewise, then each generation could incorporate in its own conception of self-love concern for the well-being which its immediate posterity would have for the well-being, in turn, of its own immediate posterity. In other words, if A were to love X dearly, A would want X to be happy. X in turn loves Y dearly and would want Y to be happy. The unhappiness or hap-piness of Y becomes the unhappiness or happiness of X which, in turn, becomes the unhappiness or hap-piness of A. The happiness or unhappiness of agents further down the series, in a relationship of love and concern, is transitive in the way outlined.

A combination of these arguments above would then ensure that it makes sense to say that even self-interested agents could have an interest in the well-being of posterity, and that it would be right for them to act in a way which would not injure the well-being of remote future generations.

The preceding discussion, I hope, satisfactorily takes care of the claims which rational egoists could possibly make. However, there is one more claim I wish to consider. This concerns those egoists who I shall call the 'doomsday egoists', that is, those who hold 'après mois, le deluge' — that they themselves, their own generation, have the sole right to do what they please with Nature and the environment, including using up, all at once, the low entropic energy and matter available, and in the process, foul up the environment to such an extent that Nature's ecosystems cannot cope with the waste. [9]

This type is often put forward as the most hard-headed of hard-headed egoists. However, their position appears to be unassailable only if we do not examine critically the presuppositions behind it. One presupposition is that there is nothing problematic about identifying the generation, after which, is the deluge. But which is that generation which assigns to itself the exclusive right and privilege to dispose of Nature as it pleases? Is it the advanced octogenerian and septuagenerian class about to shuffle off its mortal coil (call it A)? Is it the class of the 50 and 60 years old (call it B)? Is it the 30 and 40 years old (call it C)? The 20 and 30 years old (call it D)? Or the 20 and below years old (call it D)?

In any case, classes of certain age ranges are not what is necessarily meant by 'generations'. A generation, on one definition, designates the reproductive distance between people — X is one generation older than Y, if X is of an age such that X could have reproduced Y, that is, if X could have been the parent of Y. X is two generations older than Y if X could have been Y's grandparent. So the classes of children, parents, grandparents constitute three generations.

But any one individual may stand with regard to Y as parent, but as child with regard to Z, and so on. The exact ages of two individuals are not actually relevant to determining the generational relationship between them apart from meeting the minimal one mentioned above, namely, the age difference must be such that X could have reproduced Y in terms of biological development. In other words if X is the parent of Y, then X could not be less than than 13 years older than Y (that is, of one were to take 13 as a rough guide and indicator of the male or female reaching sexual reproductive maturity). Similarly, X could not be so much older than Y that X would have reached her menopause (in the case of a woman) by the time Y was born. In the case of men, it might be more difficult to lay down an exact limit, as men's spermal activity could carry on to a much older age, with no great dramatic and obvious changes to their sexual lifecycle. (If modern technology for egg/sperm storage and 'rent a womb' were to become the norm, then this would complicate the picture even more.)

So the criterion by actual ages of individuals, although a rough and ready guide, does not yield the same set of individuals when the criterion of actual biological relationships is used. Using the first criterion, one would expect that a 60 year old man is likely to have a 30 year old child, and a grandchild who is a baby or toddler. (One popular definition of 'generation' is that one generation is separated from another by a 30 year gap.) But a 60 year old man could be the father of a baby or a mere toddler.

Does this kind of 'doomsday egoist' pick on class A as that privileged class of final destroyer of the earth's fabric, so that, by and large, it is the grandparent generation which bears this awesome privilege or burden? Or is it class B, that is, the class of the parent generation? Or is it even to be the class of teenagers, toddlers and babies, that is, the child generation that decides?

As any society normally has three generations coexisting at any one time, the picture of 'après mois, le deluge' becomes much too blurred and fuzzy to be of use to clear thinking, and as guide to action.

Suppose the egoists pick on the grandparent generation as the privileged generation. This generation would then either ignore the interests of the generations of their children and grandchildren, as well as the interests of yet unborn great grandchildren, and so on, or ignore only the interests of the yet unborn great grandchildren, but include those of their children and grandchildren, who are already in existence. In the extreme former case, it is then simply assumed that the interests of generations, even already in existence, have no legitimate say about how the world is to be disposed of ecologically.

There is no argument put forward why it alone has this right and nobody else should have a look in. As no arguments have, to my knowledge, been provided, I shall not bother to try to provide some on their behalf, as I do not think that any sound argument could be advanced in its support. Why, after all, should the other already existing generations, who are presumably also rational egoists, agree that it would be to their interest to allow the grandparent generation to initiate the 'big bang'?

In the less extreme case, it is also assumed that the grandparent generation has the right to ignore the concern of the parent generation for the well-being of their own grandchildren, and of the present child generation for the well-being of its own yet unborn children and grandchildren. Their conception of self-interest can, as we have seen, include those of these generations and, hence, their concern about the ecological inheritance left to them. As rational egoists of such a kind, their self-interest would not be advanced by the destruction of the earth's fabric.

Similar problems arise if the generation of parents is chosen as the privileged one. But what if the generation of grandchildren is chosen as the privileged one. Here, one faces the difficulty that babies, toddlers, immature teenagers who either have no knowledge nor conception of what the world is like, or at best only a limited understanding, be vested with this right of initiating doomsday. As it is so bizarre a possibility even to contemplate, I will not waste my time pursuing the matter further.

To sum up, there are two major difficulties facing 'doomsday egoists' — (1) that of identifying the generation in which this awesome right, burden or privilege of bringing about ecological destruction is vested; (2) that of justifying why that generation, even if there exist clear-cut, non-problematic critieria for identifying it, should have that right or privilege. As no justification is forthcoming, except the reaffirmation that as rational egoists one has such a right, the claim is reduced to a mere tautological one. In any case, why should other rational egoists allow them to get away with it?

The difficulty, raised under (1) above, shows the immense complexities behind life as it is actually led, presented by the fact of the overlapping of generations. While some are ageing and dying, others are being born and yet others are slowly reaching maturity. If these complexities were conjured away somehow, and one were talking of a science fiction world, where one generation exists, which is clearly identifiable, with no parents alive and no children yet born, then it might be more plausible (but only in this kind of fantasy world) to raise the issue, whether such a generation could not blow up everything in one big bang, and exit in a cloud of pollution. But as I have good reasons in general for rejecting fantastic theories in social philosophy, I will not waste more time here pursuing this issue either.

But there remain two other aspects related to the 'doomsday egoist' argument that I wish to comment on. The first concerns the rhetorical question often posed by the proponents of this view, 'What has posterity done for me?' The posing of this very question is expected to present an insuperable stumbling block to those who wish to argue against the 'doomsday egoist'. Clearly, egoists would at best take into account the interests of other agents only on a *quid pro quo* basis. *Ex hypothesi*, future agents are not there to enter into such a type of contract. Hence, 'doomsday egoists' could dismiss the interests of such future agents.

However, the posing of this rhetorical question is conceptually misconceived. Necessarily it is the case that future agents cannot be a party to the kind of contract envisaged by the egoists. It is also the case that while the actions of present agents may and can affect future agents, while present agents may and can be affected by the actions of past agents, the actions of future agents cannot affect present and past agents. The behaviour of future agents (as opposed to what present agents believe the behaviour of future agents to be), logically and causally speaking, cannot enter into the calculation of present agents. The question posed is precisely rhetorical because of such considerations. The correct conclusion to draw then is not that the egoists have a watertight case, but that it makes no sense for them to raise such a question in the first instance.

A *quid pro quo* relationship does exist between human agents but it is not one which occurs, like in the standard case, between two existing agents capable of confronting each other. It is a much more complicated type of *quid pro quo* relationship. The parties involved may be trans-generational, and therefore, would not be able to confront one another. If generation A does generation B a good turn, generation A might well be dead and gone by the time generation B comes to enjoy the benefit. B cannot reciprocate A, A being dead. B could, however, discharge this duty of reciprocation indirectly by doing generation C a similar favour. If my grandfather planted an apple tree in his garden shortly before he died, I now benefit from that act of his, harvesting the apples produced. I, causally and logically speaking, cannot return this act of kindness directly as far as my grandfather is concerned, unless ancestor worship is regarded as a suitable substitute. But I could plant a pear tree, perhaps, so that my grandchildren and so on can eat the fruit of that tree. In other words, the notion of reciprocity, admittedly a genuine moral notion, nevertheless does not apply in this kind of context in the same straightforward way as when two extant agents are involved, which is what is presupposed by the 'doomsday egoists'. The only way in which one can discharge the duty of reciprocity towards past agents is by acting in such a way as to benefit future agents. The 'doomsday egoists' simply ignore these complexities of human existence, and in so doing raise a question which is actually not merely rhetorical but also unintelligible.

The second issue is that remote future generations (generations after that of grandchildren) are somehow shadowy because they do not yet exist, and are not worthy of consideration. Although the individuals belonging to the class of remote future generations by definition and *ex hypothesi* are not identifiable by names and life histories, the class itself is not thereby rendered a null class. It would only be rendered a null class if the privileged generation of 'doomsday egoists' could provide good reasons to convince the already existing generations that all of them, on egoistic ground, should cease reproducing. As no good reasons are likely to be offered, which are also overwhelmingly convincing and overriding in their implications, not all such egoists could be persuaded. Those who are not might want posterity as part of their conception of self-interest.

This in turn raises the problems already rehearsed which arise under the fragmentation of the notion of self-interest into at least two competing and contrasting sub-conceptions — that which includes desire for, and concern about posterity, and that which does not — which fail to be resolved rationally in favour of the anti-procreation lobby. Indeed, as we have seen, there may be good reasons in favour of the procreation lobby.

These could be further developed along the following lines: in the real world where not everyone dies simultaneously (unless the anti-procreation lobby were to advocate simultaneous communal suicide, in which case, it is even less likely to be convincing on egoistic grounds than ever before), it would not be in the self-interest of those who die later to have no one to look after them, as they get older and weaker. Hence, even on crude grounds of self-interest, it would pay to have children and grandchildren, etc. One could imagine that some of these procreation egoists are moved by such a consideration alone. But again not necessarily all of them would be thus moved. Many perhaps, while appreciative of this line of thought, might well have a conception of self-interest, happiness or self-love which includes the well-being of their descendants.

It could, however, be retorted that I have engineered an easy victory by the simple device of arguing that self-interest could include a conception of self-love, based on the desire for posterity in general, as well as a desire for their well-being, thus winning many egoists over to my side, without so much as firing a shot. But I do not think that I am getting the results by a mere sleight of hand.

It is no part of the doctrine of egoism (at least of the ethical variety) to maintain that individuals cannot, and should not, desire anything other than what touches their own direct immediate persons. Ethical egoism, of course, advocates that an invididual ought to grab whatever food is available before B gets it, if that food is necessary for one's own survival. But ethical egoism does not necessarily rule out of court a conception of self-interest which includes the interest of selves other than one's own, related to it in some special way. To say dogmatically that this is not permitted is to confuse ethical egoism with psychological egoism, a doctrine whose coherence I have already shown earlier to be wanting.

One has seen that the notion of self-interest is not unambiguous. It could mean something very narrowly defined, such that an individual, imbued by its spirit, would literally disregard the interests of any and everybody including parents, children, friends. But such a narrow conception of self-interest is difficult to justify in rational terms for all contexts of behaviour, however one defines the term 'rational', save in the tautologous sense. If 'rational' is understood in utilitarian terms, it would not be easy systematically to justify such a narrow egoistic morality. More often than not, acting in such a way could lead to very bad consequences for the individual. And as a universal precept, which it is presumably meant to be, consequences overall for everyone would also be very bad indeed. Moreover, as we have seen earlier, if everyone were to act upon it, the advantages which the individual egoist expects to obtain for her/himself — that is, of reaping benefits based upon the burden of costs being borne by others — would fail to materialise. This contradictory character of egoism as manifested in free-riding behaviour, as a universal precept, will be looked at in greater detail in Chapter Four.

Of course, it would be rational for an individual egoist to take advantage of others if an appropriate situation occurs. But such an egoist would not be able to communicate the principle of her/his action to others, or to advocate that others act upon it. For its very communication and public declaration leading to its adoption as a principle of action by all other egoists, or even a substantial number of them, would be sufficient to nullify the advantageous position, which such (necessarily a minority, and in extreme cases even a minority of one) egoists hope to enjoy. It is, therefore, a theory of rationality which sets severe limits to its own rationality. Its success depends on preserving it as an 'official secrets act', never to be publicly acknowledged, avowed or taught to others. In other words, it cannot be held as a universal precept (either as a moral or a prudential one), such as its usual 'surface' formulation — one ought always to advance one's own interest — might lead one to believe.

A more viable form of self-interest is that of enlightened self-interest, or of a conception of self-interest which includes the notion of self-love, which could:
(a) include recognising the interests of others and making room for them, even if the recognition is no more than that of seeing it, as a means to the end,

of promoting one's own self-interest. After all, a successful business man might not care intrinsically about the well-being of his customers, but he would care about it to the extent that if they were to become ill or unemployed, he could be losing their custom;

(b) allow for the well-being of, at least, some other individuals, namely those related closely to the self as parent, children, other relatives, etc., to enter into one's own conception of self-interest. Here the relationship between the interest of the self and the well-being of these special others transcends the merely means/end relationship. Such an ethical egoist would be genuinely upset, unhappy and disturbed when s/he sees or contemplates these other selves suffering, or are in a bad way. However, such egoists cannot, without losing their identity as egoists, extend their genuine concern and consideration to cover everyone else, in conditions similar to those, suffered by people who are their descendants. (Self-love can, indeed, even accommodate the well-being of remote descendants, as we have seen.) To do so would mean that they have ceased to be ethical egoists and to have become moral theorists, who believe that all agents have needs and legitimate claims, which have to be met against their own claims to furthering self-interest, based on the possession by all agents of certain characteristics that entitle them to have their needs met. (See Chapter Ten for further discussion of this point.)

Such a more hospitable conception of self-interest may be more readily defensible in utilitarian terms. But its weakness lies in its drawing the line between kith and kin, on the one hand, and non kith and kin, on the other. Such a distinction may not be so readily defensible. But as this book is not meant to be a detailed critique of egoism in all its forms, I will leave the matter, having just raised it. However, as I have shown, as far as the more specific issue of ecologically insensitive versus ecologically sensitive values is concerned, it is sufficient to note that this variant does not lead to the choice of the former. And I am happy to welcome it as an ally on this front, provided such egoists do not in turn embrace eco-fascism — see Chapter Nine on this point, where I deploy further arguments against eco-fascism itself.

In final conclusion, let me put matters in this way. Under close critical scrutiny, it turns out that ethical rational egoism, as far as the issue of ecologically sensitive versus insensitive lifestyles is concerned, is not a single claim, but a disparate set of very different claims, some of which are not necessarily hostile to those like myself who defend ecologically sensitive values. Indeed they appear to be on my side and we could be working allies, though not moral twins. Of the versions which are really hostile, it is not obvious that their claims are either easy to state clearly and coherently, or are claims relevant to human existence as it is led, as opposed to how it might be led, in a fantasy or science fiction world. As for psychological egoism, I have said enough earlier on to show that it is either a false empirical claim or a true, but vacuous one. The charge of being a vacuous claim, as it turns out, is also applicable to ethical rational egoism, once it is conceded (i) that it is not irrational or against one's self-interest to want to be harmed by such things, as polluted air, poisoned water and food, etc. because (ii) the individual ego is the only arbiter of what constitutes one's self-interest. The injunction — it is rational and, therefore, one ought always to advance one's self-interest — clearly becomes an empty tautology.

CHAPTER TWO

THE PRINCIPLES OF ECOLOGY AND THE LAWS OF THERMODYNAMICS

1. The first account of what ecology is was given by E. Haekel in 1870:

> By ecology we mean the body of knowledge concerning the economy of nature — the investigation of the total relations of the animal both to its inorganic and to its organic environment; including above all, its friendly and inimical relation with those animals and plants with which it comes directly or indirectly into contact — in a word, ecology is the study of all the complex interrelations referred to by Darwin as the conditions for the struggle for existence. [1]

A more recent characterisation is as follows:

> Ecology concerns itself with the interrelationships of living organisms, plant or animal, and their environments; these are studied with a view to discovering the principles which govern the relationships. That such principles exist is a basic assumption — and an act of faith — of the ecologist. His field of study is no less wide than the totality of the living conditions of the plants and animals under observation, their systematic position, their reactions to the environment and to each other, and the physical and chemical nature of their inanimate surroundings. . . . [2]

The living organisms, plants, animals and microbes form the biotic components which interact with the abiotic (non-living) physico-chemical environment, through the movement of energy as well as nutrient elements, such as carbon dioxide, water, nitrogen, phosphorus, sulphur, magnesium and others. The two components, a specific biotic assemblage of plants, animals and microbes, in a particular abiotic physico-chemical environment, constitute an ecosystem. An ecosystem has a structure and function which it is the business of ecology to study. But ecosystems are not static systems. The two major (though not the only) ecological processes of the movement of energy and nutrients, involving interaction between the biotic assemblage and the abiotic environment, account for the dynamics of the system, which includes growth, development, homeostasis, adaptation, change and evolution.

While the movement of energy is unidirectional and noncyclical, that of the movement of minerals is cyclical. (In the next chapter, we will see how the latter cyclical processes may be integrated with the non-cyclical nature of the former.) Let us look at the flow of energy first. Plants with chlorophyll absorb the radiant energy from the sun, synthesising carbon dioxide into carbon compounds. Solar energy in this process is transformed into chemical energy. These plants not only sustain themselves in this way, but also provide food (and therefore energy) for the herbivores, who in turn provide food for the carnivores. Except for a few odd plants which are carnivorous (like venus fly trap), by and large plants do not eat animals while animals eat plants. The flow of energy is, therefore, unidirectional. It is noncyclical because at every stage of the food chain, some energy is lost; nor is all that is retained, in every link of the chain, used up with one hundred percent efficiency. (There will be a further discussion of this point in section 4.)

Plants, which die naturally, return minerals they have absorbed to the soil, while the minerals in plants, eaten by animals, are also returned eventually to the soil. Bacteria and fungi (called decomposers) produce enzymes, which break down the dead organic matter of plants and animals, releasing the minerals back to the soil, to be reused by the plants. The nutrient cycle is thereby completed.

Ecosystems are self-organising systems. Other examples of self-organising systems are cells, organisms, social systems. But in the account that follows, I will be using only biological instances. As such, they display the following essential characteristics:
1. they are capable of self-maintenance and self-renewal. For instance:

> an organism is primarily engaged in renewing itself; cells are breaking down and building up structures, tissues and organs are replacing their cells in continual cycles. Thus the pancreas replaces most of its cells every twenty-four hours, the stomach lining every three days; our white blood cells are renewed in ten days and 98 percent of the protein in the brain is turned over in less than one month. All these processes are regulated in such a way that the overall pattern of the organism is preserved, and this remarkable ability of self-maintenance persists under a variety of circumstances, including changing environmental conditions and many kinds of interferences. [3]

2. from the above, one can see that there is stability but the stability may, nevertheless, be said to be dynamic. The process of self-renewal, embodying such dynamic stability, is rendered possible because such systems are open systems (see section 4 below), that is, they have to exchange energy and matter continuously with their environment to stay in existence. What they take in is nutrients as food, to do 'work' to keep alive. As such they are in a state of non-equilibrium, as total equilibrium is achieved only in death, non-existence;
3. they are in a state of continual fluctuation as they are constituted of a host of interdependent variables, each of which can vary between an upper and a

lower limit. The state of continual oscillation between these limits may be called homeostasis. For instance, our heartbeat fluctuates, say, during a twenty-four hour period, but for each of us, there is an upper and a lower limit beyond which it does not stray;
4. however, when there are external disturbances from the environment, such systems rely on negative feedback mechanisms to correct the imbalance caused and to reduce the deviation from the homeostatic state.

To maintain the homeostatic state, the feedback must be of the negative sort, regulating a process or set of events by turning it off or slowing it down. Such negative feedback is the basic principle of the home thermostat which 'turns off' the heating unit when the temperature exceeds a present level but allows it to operate when the temperature is below the set level. Similar feedback occurs at sublevels in the ecosystems; when nutrient release exceeds a certain level, feedback largely through chemical equilibria inhibits further release; when a given population exceeds a certain size various events are triggered which curtail further reproduction. [4]

5. but negative feedback is not the only mechanism available for systems capable of self-organisation through fluctuations. There is also positive feedback 'which consists of amplifying certain deviations rather than damping them. . . .This phenomenon plays a crucial role in the processes of development, learning and evolution'. [5] This may be called the principle of 'self-transcendence'. [6] This capacity enables new levels of structure to emerge and indeed new systems eventually to evolve.

It is of the utmost importance to stress that ecosystems are capable of using, not only negative feedbacks, but also positive feedbacks. While the former enables the systems to attain stability through near equilibrium, the latter enables small initial deviations, sometimes, to break through existing systemic boundaries to create a new set altogether. The early days of cybernetics emphasised the first type of mechanism, through its study of completely self-regulating and equilibrating systems like thermostats, automatic steering devices, and even physiological systems, like the regulation of body temperature (an example cited above).

However, later investigation of other systems shows that positive feedbacks are just as important. When deviations occur, it is not always the case that the system succeeds in relying on negative feedbacks to restore it to near equilibrium. To illustrate the latter point, take an example from C. S. Holling's writings. This concerns the responses of fish populations to fishing pressure.

The fisheries of the Great Lakes have always selectively concentrated on abundant species that are in high demand. Prior to 1930, before eutrophication complicated the story, the lake sturgeon in all the Great Lakes, the lake herring in Lake Erie, and the lake whitefish in Lake Huron were intensively fished . . . In each case, the pattern was similar: a period of intense exploitation during which there was a prolonged high-level harvest, followed by a sudden and precipitous drop in populations. Most significantly, even though fishing pressure was then relaxed, none of these populations showed any sign of returning to their previous levels of abundance. This is not unexpected for sturgeon because of their slow growth and late maturity, but it is unexpected for herring and whitefish. The maintenance of these low populations in recent times might be attributed to the increasingly unfavourable chemical or biological environment, but in the case of the herring, at least, the declines took place in the early 1920s before the major deterioration in environment occurred. [7]

And now an example to illustrate the positive feedback mechanism at work. Take the weathering of rock.

A small crack in a rock collects some water. The

water freezes and makes the crack larger. A larger crack collects more water, which makes the crack still larger. A sufficient amount of water then makes it possible for some small organisms to live in it. Accumulation of organic matter then makes it possible for a tree to start growing in the crack. The roots of the tree will then make the crack still larger. [8]

A system which starts off by being predominantly rock may end up being a system consisting of rocks, soil, a rich variety of fauna and flora. This, then, is what is meant by the principle of self-transcendence.

From the above account of ecosystems, one can argue that two principles distinguish the study of the subject of ecology from the causal mechanistic paradigm of classical physics. In the latter, it is usually said the whole is no more than the sum of the parts. The favourite example cited is that of a watch. As each component is no more than a part of the aggregate, the removal or loss of one component has no particular effect on the remaining bits. If the winding up knob of a watch went missing, the watch, it is true, might stop after a bit, but nothing else in the system would have changed. If a new winder were screwed on and the watch wound up again, the *status quo* would be restored.

However, in ecological studies, it is held that the properties of the ecosystems themselves cannot be predicted from the properties of each of the entities of the biotic and abiotic components, any more than the properties of a cake are predictable from the properties of the separate ingredients which make up the cake. (This poses for philosophy the so-called problem about emergent properties or supervenience.) The entire biosphere or ecosphere, which includes the ecosystems and their interactions, is a unity governed by its own sets of laws, which it is the business of ecology to uncover.

From this principle, sometimes called the principle of holism (or wholism), flows another, that of interdependence.

Everything within any ecosystem one chooses to examine can be shown to be related to everything else. Moreover, there are no linear relationships; every effect is also a cause in the web of natural interdependency. Of course, not all relationships are equally important or equally sensitive, and most of them are indirect. In general, however, interdependence is total. Certain kinds of important interrelationship are intuitively obvious even to the casual observer. We all know that there are predators and prey, that microbes can cause disease, and that worms will inherit our bodies when we are buried. However, the casual observer is unaware of the numerous other interrelationships in nature, many of critical importance. [9]

It follows, then, that the removal of an organism(s) or an element from an ecosystem, or the addition of one, could have effects throughout the system. As an example of the former, the cutting down of forests in the tropics could lead to rapid soil erosion, to changes in the local climate, which in turn lead to further erosion. As an instance of the latter, take the case of caesium-137 (a radioactive isotope) which was carried by winds from the nuclear disaster in Chernobyl to Lapland. The caesium-137 is absorbed by the lichen (called reindeer moss) which is the food of the Lapland deer, which in turn is the food of the Laplander. The caesium-137 in the deer has recently been reported to be well above the limit which is considered safe for human consumption. As a result, the Laplanders' livelihood and way of life are ruined. Caesium-137 has a half-life of 30 years; this would ensure that the traditional Laplander's existence is as good as extinct. The retreat of human agents from the area can in turn over time cause certain changes to the ecosystem itself. (See below for further discussion of this point.)

The science of ecology provides, not only understanding of how processes in one part of Nature are linked to those of another part, but also the very model of non-linear causation, which is so very different from the mechanistic linear model of cause and effect used by classical physics. [10] In classical physics proper, particle C (billiard ball) moves because particle B (another billiard ball) knocks against it, and particle B moves because particle A (yet another billiard ball) hits it, and so on. → A → B → C. (→ is the causal arrow). C does not in turn cause A to move. Moreover, when A imparts motion to B, classical physics assumes that A and B themselves are not altered in any other way apart from moving across a certain portion of space.

But in the example about the depletion of the ozone layer, B, the human agents who release the CFC gases into the air, cause a change in the ozone layer (designate this state by A_1), and A_1 (the depleted ozone layer) in turn, causes a change in the human agents (designate this state by B_1 — the state of having skin cancer).

Or take another example. In an area where there is shortage of water, some human agents may dig deeper wells by using a new, more advanced type of technology. As a result, herdsmen feel able to increase their herds as more water becomes available. The increase in supply also encourages herdsmen from other drier regions to gravitate to the new water holes. The end result could well be a worsening of the situation in the long run — as the water in the newly dug wells dries up, the increase in population, both human and animal, intensifies and magnifies the original problems of water shortage and insufficient vegetation for grazing.

In these examples, the direction is not so much linear as loopish. The causal agents bring about changes (not simply a change of position as in the laws of motion) in the objects they work upon. To rely wholly on the linear model of causation implicit in classical physics would be misleading, as the natural processes do not appear to conform to it.

This, however, is not to deny that outside of biological, ecological phenomena, the model of loopish non-linear causation is not relevant or does not exist.

Indeed, the concept of 'negative feedback', embedded in this model of causation (although, as we have seen, ecosystems do not only employ this mechanism in coping with disturbances in the environment), is applied, in diverse forms of technology, ranging from that of the Watt steam engine, in the earlier history of modern technology, to that of the most sophisticated computer today. The latter, together with information theory, generally referred to as IT (information technology) has put the notion of negative feedback in the centre of the stage so to speak. (But see below for crucial qualifications about the importance of negative feedback for an understanding of how ecosystems behave.) Although the steam engine in its time also transformed the technological, economic and social scene, its presupposed model of causation did not seriously challenge that of classical physics, both inside the domain of the physical sciences and outside it. The prestige of classical physics has so dominated modern thinking up to now, especially outside the domain of the natural sciences, that, by and large, social, moral and political theorising still rests unthinkingly on the mechanistic linear causal paradigm.

Two sets of issues in social theories spring immediately to mind as illustrations of this deep-seated trend, the discussion of which in the standard literature presupposes a purely mechanistic linear model of causation — (a) the relationship between the economic base and the superstructure and (b) the relationship between the individual and society.

In the first example, Marx, in spite of lapses into dialectical talk, appears to adhere to the linear model as much as his critics. They both seem to assume that if A causes B, then B in turn can have no effect on A. If the economic base is the cause of the ideological superstructure, then the latter cannot in turn have any effect on the former, just as, if the motion in billiard ball A is the cause of the motion in billiard ball B, then the latter's motion cannot in turn have any effect on the first ball. However, on the model of loopish non-linear causation, it is not inconceivable that while changes in the economic base cause changes in the superstructure, in turn the changes in the latter can have an effect on the base, either reinforcing it in some cases, or modifying it in others. As the process of causation is a dynamic ongoing one, the reinforced or modified base, in turn, can have further effects on the superstructure, and so on.

The critics of Marx assume that they have 'falsified' or 'refuted' his thesis, when they can show that it is not always and only the case that the economic base causes changes in the superstructure, but that sometimes changes in the latter can bring about changes in the former. Some supporters of Marx refuse to accept such a refutation, by arguing that the superstructure cannot affect the base, as the base is the cause and the superstructure is its effect, and that, whatever is cause, cannot also be effect and *vice versa* However, both sides share the assumption that A cannot be said to be the cause of B (its effects), if B, in turn, can cause A to change or produce effects in A.

This implied assumption works as a kind of methodological rule, if not as a piece of scientific metaphysics. It may be analogous to the methodological rule, same cause same effect. In the case of the latter, one argues that if the effect is different, then the causal conditions cannot be identical and that we, the investigators, have overlooked the difference, which is responsible for the outcome being dissimilar. This prompts us to look hard, and often we find and identify the factor, which makes the difference. So, adhering to that rule of procedure is fruitful and leads to good results. However, adhering to the former does not seem to be fruitful. Instead, it seems to lead to bad results, as it makes us overlook causal links, which may be vital for a proper understanding of how the world works.

There is one move which those who hold the implied assumption — if A is the cause of B, B cannot be the cause of A — can resort to. That is, to preserve its formal validity, by refining the descriptions of A and B, such that what happens may be more accurately portrayed as follows: A_1 (say the shortage of water) causes B_1 (lack of vegetation); B_1 causes C_1 (human agents) to dig deeper wells; C_1 and C_2 (other human agents) by increasing their respective flocks cause A_2 (the water in the new wells to disappear as well); A_2 plus C_1, C_2 and D (increase in animals) in turn lead to B_2 (greater loss of vegetation).

In this way, honour may be formally satisfied. But it would be misleading to describe the more elaborrately refined causal nexus as satisfying the purely linear model of causation. The model appropriate to its understanding is that of the open-ended loop, which involves both negative and positive feedback mechanisms.

The second example illustrates problems similar to those just discussed. So-called methodological individualists [11] hold that the behaviour of individuals causes society to display certain features or characteristics (and thereby fully explains these characteristics or effects) — hence, how society works, and what it is, can be explained and accounted for, in terms of the behaviour of the individuals, which make up society and constitute its cause. So-called collectivist theorists reverse the causal order, and hold that it is society which causes individuals to behave in certain ways. Hence, society is the cause and individual behaviour the effect. The truth of the matter may be more complex than either side assumes — as the processes of interaction between individuals and society are open-ended and loopish, the one (the individuals) has effects upon the other (society), just as surely as the latter has effects on the former.

My two examples come from the domain of social theorising. This fact is itself significant, as I will try to show. Today, in the physical or natural sciences, Newtonian physics has to share pride of place with Einsteinian physics, even if it is correct to say that it has not been entirely superseded or displaced by the latter. The prestige of the former has suffered something of a knock and a dent. It is often the case, however, that theories, outside of the physical sciences, continue to be influenced by notions and concepts used by the prestigious 'hard' sciences, long after the 'hard' sciences themselves have lost enthusiasm for them. The lag may be a considerable one. But it is time for theories in the social and moral domain to sidestep the model of mechanistic linear causation, long outgrown by parts of physics itself, by-passed by biology and ecology, as well as technologies as diverse as those based on the Watt governor and electronic equipment.

The sciences which have the most direct and relevant significance for social theories are sciences like biology and ecology, not classical physics. (But, to say this is not to say that the laws of biology and ecology themselves are not in accordance with the laws of physics. The latter, however, can only constitute necessary, but not both necessary and sufficient conditions, for explaining biological and ecological phenomena. These exist at a higher level of organisational complexity than purely physical phenomena, displaying emergent properties, which cannot be completely accounted for, solely in terms of physical behaviour at a lower level of organisational complexity.)

It is to them and their implied model of non-linear causation that one must turn, in the construction of social, moral theories. This is because (a) we are ourselves biological organisms, (b) the level at which we interact with Nature most directly is the ecological level, and not at the purely physical level. Hence, the results of these interactions cannot be properly understood except at the ecological level, presupposing the loopish non-linear model of causation. At the level of (macroscopic) physics, there can only at best be partial understanding of how Nature behaves, as that science presupposes the mechanistic linear model, and has nothing to say about levels of organisation beyond its domain. This partial understanding can, and does, mislead us, in the way we, human agents, treat Nature.

But what more precisely does non-linear causation involve? My remarks so far have hinted that, unlike the linear model implied in classical physics, it is not mechanistic, and that it is loopish. The former, as I have used the term, is understood in the following way: what is said to be the cause, when it occurs, would bring about the effect, and if removed, would eliminate the effect, without affecting anything else, like the parts of a machine which may be removed and then replaced after an interval, without affecting the character and functioning of the machine itself. A loopish model (note that this sense of loopish does not involve either circular time nor backward time travel) implies (i) the denial of mechanism as just delineated, and (ii) a complex causal nexus in which it is not only the case that what is said to be the cause can have an effect, but that the effect in turn can act upon the original cause, to produce other effects.

This more complicated type of causal nexus can perhaps be further explored by first looking more closely at the presuppositions of linear causation themselves. These seem to be:
1. cause and effect are events;
2. events are phenomena considered in isolation from, and are understood without reference to, any systemic boundaries;
3. causes and effects are, therefore, simply additive or subtractive;
4. causes, therefore, do not include background or standing conditions, for these are not events but are part of what constitute the systemic boundaries.

A model with such presuppositions cannot, as a. result, do justice to at least three types of phenomena which are of crucial significance to ecological understanding, namely, (a) threshold effects, (b) synergisms, (c) exponential growth.

As the four presuppositions are interrelated, I shall deal with them together. Without embarking upon a thorough exploration of the concept of events, [12] one could, perhaps, uncontroversially say that events are happenings — the slate fell off the roof or the kettle of water has just boiled — which involve change and, therefore, extend over intervals of time. At time t1, the slate was on the roof but at time t2, it was lying on the ground; at time t1, the water in the kettle was well below boiling point, but at time t2, it was at such a point. The first example may involve either change of place only or change of place and other changes, that is, it could also have been broken or chipped. The second involves a qualitative change (although to be exact, there was also a quantitative change involved, as some of the water had evaporated).

Events are contrasted with background or standing conditions, which are not considered themselves to be events but are, more or less, enduring states. For example, if we say that the event, the lightning hitting the haystack, is the cause of the fire, this event is contrasted with standing conditions such as the dryness of the hay, the strength and direction of the prevailing winds at the time, the presence of oxygen in the air. (These standing conditions exist and endure through intervals of time, but they do not involve change.) Similarly, if we say that the event, the leatherbound volume of *War and Peace* falling on X's head, is the cause of X's death, this event is contrasted with standing conditions, such as, the egg-shell nature of X's skull, the distance and position of such a skull relative to the book on the shelf, etc.

A commonsensical way of arriving at this distinction is to consider the issues in the following manner — the hay had been dry for quite some time, the prevailing winds had been prevailing for some time and oxygen had been present in the air all the time, and yet no fire had occurred. What made the difference? The event of the lightning introduced into the cluster of standing conditions. The same goes for the death. X had an egg-shell skull all his life, he had been sitting by the bookshelf for quite some time and yet there was no death. What made the difference was the book falling off the shelf hitting him on the head.

Sometimes, this commonsensical way of singling out the event in question as the cause is justified in terms of the distinction between the so-called scientific and the ordinary everyday concepts of cause. Hart and Honoré, [13] who make this distinction, are themselves manifestly interested only in the latter, and their account of it may be said to be close to, if not identical to, what I have described above. [14] They claim they are concerned with it because they are dealing with causal matters in an attributive context, namely, with the question, what or who is to be blamed or to be held liable in the law and in everyday life, when damage to something or somebody occurs?

They contrast this with the scientific concept of cause which occurs in an explanatory context. In such a context, the whole set of necessary conditions, which is jointly sufficient for the occurrence of the effect, is said to be the cause. The death is explained in terms, then, of both the event (the falling of *War and Peace* upon X's head) as well as the standing conditions, such as the distance and position of X's head, and the fragility of the head itself. Similarly, in the case of the fire, the necessary conditions, jointly sufficient for its occurrence, include not merely the event of the lightning hitting the haystack, but such standing conditions as the dryness of the hay, the state of the prevailing winds, the presence of oxygen in the air.

Whether Hart and Honoré are right about their analysis of the ordinary commonsense notion of cause in an attributive context in daily and legal life is not germane to the discussion here. What is of interest is their remark about the scientific concept in an explanatory context. On this point, I think, they are correct. Such a concept of cause involves both events and standing conditions, individually necessary but jointly sufficient for the occurrence of the effect. But what has gone wrong is that many other philosophers, and some scientists as well, might have unthinkingly borrowed the distinction between event and standing condition, crucial to an analysis of the commonsense notion of cause, and applied it to the scientific explanatory context.

In singling out the occurrence of the event which makes the difference to the outcome as the cause, while excluding the standing conditions which, nevertheless, must obtain, such an analysis then tends to regard events (either as cause or effects) as happenings which could take place in isolation, and in abstraction, from the systemic boundaries presupposed by the explanation in question. [15] (The standing conditions are part of the systemic boundaries.) This abstraction can lead scientists and philosophers astray in the following way: (a) to begin with, they accept that whatever event is said to be the cause could only be so designated if, whenever the cause occurs, the effect occurs; but if (b) it is obvious that, on some occasions, the event designated as cause occurs without the effect occurring, then (c) this leads them to conclude that the event designated as cause cannot be the cause (or part of the cause) of the effect.

Take the controversy whether exposure to a certain level of radiation causes cancer of the blood, like leukemia. In some cases, such exposure is sufficient to bring about the cancer. Yet in others, it appears not to be so. As a result, it is concluded that radiation cannot be the cause (or part of the cause) of leukemia. However, the truth of the matter may be more complex — exposure to radiation is an event which together with other standing conditions, such as the immune system of the body being in a certain state, the emotions of the person being in a certain condition, the genetic constitution being of a certain sort, etc., are jointly sufficient to explain the existence of the leukemia. However, if one or more of the standing conditions do not obtain, then the leukemia may fail to occur, in spite of the exposure to radiation. By restoring standing conditions to the notion of cause, the scientific account may be seen to be faithful to the goals in science of establishing (non-accidental) generalisations and of getting hold of a theory or theories which can satisfactorily explain why these generalisations obtain. [16]

Scientists and philosophers may also have been led into holding the mistaken view, that what counts as the cause of an effect must be present in all instances in which the effect occurs and absent when the effect does not occur, by a less than careful reading of

Mill's methods of agreement and difference. Mill's canons of induction (of which these two methods are a crucial part) are acknowledged to provide the philosophical and methodological basis for the notion of the controlled experiment, a notion indispensable to scientific procedure itself. The methods may be schematised as follows:

	Antecedent	Consequent
Agreement:		
instance 1	ABC	XYZ
instance 2	ADE	XVW
	A is the cause of X	
Difference:		
instance 1	ABC	XYZ
instance 2	-BC	-YZ
	A is the cause of X	

Mill is understood to say that under the method of agreement A cannot be said to be the cause of X if A occurs (as in instance 2) but X does not obtain. He is also understood to say that under the method of difference the absence of A (as in instance 2) is the cause of the absence of X. Under the joint methods of agreement and difference, it follows that from the presence of A and the corresponding presence of X, and from the absence of A and the corresponding absence of X, one can safely infer that A is the cause of X.

But Mill is actually much more careful in his formulation of the two methods than he is normally taken to be. Under the two methods, he says, when the conditions obtain as schematised above, A may be said to be either the cause or part of the cause of X. This latter qualification saves Mill from the mistaken charge referred to above. Under the method of agreement, as A may be said to be part of the cause of X, this leaves room for the possibility that X would not occur unless A occurs in conjunction with other conditions, namely B and C. Under the method of difference, this leaves room for the possibility that

62

the absence of X may be accounted for not merely by the absence of A, but also perhaps the absence of, say, B or C or both; the absence of A may thus be said to be part of the cause of the absence of the effect X.

This more careful reading of Mill then makes it possible for one to say that A is a necessary condition for the occurrence of X which together with other necessary conditions, like B and C, are jointly sufficient for the occurrence of X. Often it may be difficult to track down what the set of necessary conditions may be by using Mill's methods; but at least in principle he, unlike others who have unthinkingly absorbed his thoughts but got them (partially) wrong, could allow for what is said to be the cause of a phenomenon to be such a complex set of necessary conditions sufficient for its occurrence.

Adhering to the thesis that causes are merely events, considered in isolation from, and without reference to, any systemic boundaries also gives rise to the views that (i) causation is not loopish, and (ii) that causes and effects are simply additive or subtractive. Consider the latter first *via* the example of a spring balance. If you hang a weight on it, the spring depresses, say, by 1 inch (which is registered on a calibrated scale as 1 lb). If you hang another similar weight B on it, the spring depresses by another 1 inch, and so on. The total length of the spring is 1 inch X N weights.

For every weight removed, from N to A, the spring retracts by an inch. Therefore, the cause of the spring being depressed by an inch is the addition of weight A or B or . . .; similarly, the cause of the spring retracting by an inch is the subtraction of weight A or B or . . . . The addition or subtraction of the cause and its corresponding effect apart, everything else is unaffected and remains intact.

However, this is more apparent than real. Everything else remains intact only provided the spring is not overloaded. If the spring could not tolerate more than 20 lbs, and more than 20 (1 lb) weights were added on to it, the spring would break. In other words, the conception, that causes and effects are simply additive or subtractive, is an abstraction, which makes no reference to systemic boundaries. The boundaries or parameters in this case are laid down by the strength and make-up of the spring balance, and its tolerance for maximum weight. But once systemic boundaries are taken into account, causes are no longer simply additive or subtractive, but may be said to be cumulative. With the addition of each further weight, the strain upon the spring increases, until the addition of one more weight causes it to break altogether. The proverbial wisdom about the last straw breaking the camel's back should be taken very seriously in causal matters. (See below for further discussion of threshold effects.)

Let us look at another example, the billiard balls already mentioned. Again the standard account of the movements of these balls leaves out any reference to systemic boundaries. In reality, billiard balls, as we know, operate within the confines of a billiard table. Ball B, while being hit by A, may itself through this impact hit the edge of the table, and in turn hit back at A. This, then, shows that even in such a paradigmatic case of mechanistic linear causation, the model is inadequate. The cause, that is, A, can have an effect on B which, in turn, can have an effect on A *via* its impact upon the edge of the table. It is, therefore, a case of loopish non-linear causation. Events, as causes and effects, cannot be properly considered in isolation from one another and the system of which they are parts. [17]

If the conception of mechanistic linear causation is barely adequate for characterising the behaviour of weights and spring balance, or billiard balls and table, it is highly unlikely to be adequate for characterising the causal links between ecological phenomena. So let us turn our attention next to see where precisely its inadequacies lie.

I mentioned earlier what is sometimes called the phenomenon of the threshold effects. In Chapter Four, I will be using Hardin's tragedy of the common to illustrate yet another related problem, namely, about the accumulation of the unintended consequences of individual actions. But it certainly illustrates extremely well the issue of threshold effects, and thereby shows up clearly the inadequacy of the linear model of causation.

Very briefly, the tragedy of the common involves the addition of one animal by each shepherd to graze the common, such that the common becomes ecologically degraded, and no longer capable of sustaining even the original number of animals. But if causation in this kind of context were truly linear, the degradation would not, and could not, appear.

Consider the following data: 1 cow eats on average 150 lbs of grass a day; it eats 54,750 lbs a year. This pasture can produce 5,475,000 lbs a year. Conclusion: it can support 100 cows a year (indefinitely). Now mathematically speaking and in terms of causes and effects being merely additive or subtractive, this is quite correct. But the ecological degradation of the pasture is not equivalent to the sum of the acts of depleting 150 lbs of grass per cow per day by 100 cows for 365 days. The consequences of each cow chewing up so much grass daily are not identical from the causal point of view. The causal consequences of cow 1 devouring 150 lbs per day for a year, when no other cows are in the pasture (call this condition A), are not the same as those when cow 100 is so doing and 99 others are also grazing the common (call this condition B). Cow 1, under condition A, does not cause the pasture to become barren or degraded. But cow 100, under condition B, might produce precisely that effect.

To understand the asymmetry between the two events of grass chewing from the causal point of view, one must refer to the standing conditions and to the systemic boundaries, which include the type of grass grown, whether other plants (such as clover) grow on it as well, the condition of the soil, the climate, how often it is cropped, how many feet trample upon it, how long is each trampling and how often are the tramplings, whether it ever lies fallow, etc. The tolerance of the pasture for sustainable grazing is dependent on a combination of all these causal factors. When the maximum tolerance is exceeded, the degradation sets in. But before the degradation becomes manifest, each additional animal to the respective herds of the shepherds contributes to the threshold effect. Once the threshold has been reached, the bad effects may quite suddenly and dramatically appear. The mere addition of one more cow could trigger them off. Yet, from the standpoint of cause and effect being merely additive, such effects become mysterious and inexplicable, as according to it, any one cow indifferently consumes 150 lbs of grass a day, and this act of daily depletion is considered in isolation from any other such acts, and with no reference to the systemic boundaries.

Let me quote at some length other examples cited by ecologists:

Mankind's environmental predicament is also greatly aggravated by situations where relatively small changes in inputs may cause dramatic changes in the environment's response.

Threshold effects are one such type of situation. For example, below a certain level of pollution, trees will survive in smog. But when a small increment in the local human population produces a small increment in smog, living trees become dead trees. Perhaps 500 people can live around a certain lake and dump their raw sewage into it, and its natural systems will be able to break down the sewage and keep the lake from undergoing rapid ecological change. But 505 people may overload the system and result in a polluted or eutrophic lake.

Such thresholds characterize the responses of many organisms or groups of organisms to many different kinds of evvironmental changes: fish die when water temperature exceeds a certain threshold or when dissolved oxygen content falls below a certain threshold; different crops have different thresholds for tolerance of dissolved salts in irrigation water; carbon dioxide is fatal to humans at high concentrations, but, as far as we know, causes only reversible effects at low concentrations. Scientists describe such situations as displaying a nonlinear dose-response relation. Nonlinear in this context means that a graph plotting response (say, percentage of deaths in a population of fish) versus dose (say, temperature in the habitat) will not be a straight line. [18]

Synergisms are equally mysterious and inexplicable under the model of linear causation. In synergism:

one is concerned with the simultaneous interacting effects of two or more kinds of input, where each kind of input acts to intensify the effects of others. For example, sulfur dioxide and various cancer-causing kinds of particulate matter are found at the same time in city air and for hundreds of miles downwind. One of the effects of sulfur dioxide is to impair the cleaning mechanisms of the lungs, thus increasing the time that the carcinogenic particles spend in the lungs before being discharged. Thus the joint effect is synergistic; it exceeds the sum of the individual effects expected if sulfur dioxide and cancer-causing particles had been present separately. [19]

Another disturbing example of synergism from the environmental point of view is:

the combined effect of DDT and oil spills in coastal waters. DDT is not very soluble in sea water, so the concentrations to which marine organisms are ordinarily exposed are small. However, DDT is very soluble in oil. Oil spills therefore have the effect of concentrating DDT in the surface layer of the ocean, where much of the oil remains, and where many marine organisms spend part of their time. These organisms are thus exposed to far higher concentrations of DDT than would otherwise be possible. As a result, the combined effects of oil and DDT probably far exceed the individual effects. [20]

Ecologists acknowledge that investigating synergistic and threshold effects is one of the most difficult, though highly crucial areas of environmental analysis. For instance, in determining the hazards of pollutants, the following difficulties (amongst others) present themselves:

3. Which pollutant among many candidates is actually responsible for the suspected damage is often unknown. In many if not most cases, the agent doing the damage is a 'secondary' substance produced by the chemical or radioactive transformation of the 'primary' pollutant produced by human activity.
4. The preceding difficulty is multiplied many times over by the importance of *synergisms*, wherein the effect of two agents acting in concert exceeds the sum of the effects to be expected if the two acted individually. One or both agents in a synergism might be secondary substances produced from pollutants, one might be a naturally occurring agent, or there might be more than two actors involved. . . .
8. Very large sample populations (of animals or people) are needed to investigate effects at low doses of pollutants, where only a small percentage of those exposed will manifest the suspected effect even if the cause-effect relationship is genuine. It cannot be assumed that the dose-response relation is linear with dose, that is, that effects occur in the same direct proportion to dose from low doses to high ones. For some agents, low doses may produce more damage per unit of exposure than high doses; for others, there may be a threshold in dose below which no ill effect occurs. It has been customary in regulation of pollution to assume that evidence obtained at high doses can be extrapolated linearly to low ones, this will be overcautious in some cases and not cautious enough in others. [21]

Difficult though this kind of causal nexus may be to unravel in practice, at least ecologists are well aware that the model of linear causation is an inept and inadequate conceptual tool to use in trying to work out the complex causal links between phenomena.

In Chapters Three and Five, I will be concerned with the problem of exponential growth and its potential impact on ecoystems, and in Chapter Six, with the problems of economic growth as exponential growth and its attendant impact on ecosystems. Exponential growth is a key consideration in trying to understand the ecological crisis that is facing us today. But linear causation is no more relevant or adequate to an understanding of its operation than to that of synergistic effects. It is clear that exponential growth is not merely additive. The effects are much greater than if they were. The example of the lily which doubles its size every day (cited in Chapter Three) shows that on the 28th day of growth, the lily would cover only a quarter of the fish pond; on the 29th day, half of the pond. But by the 30th day, the entire pond.

Moreover, exponential growth, considered not merely as a mathematical possibility, will soooner or later run up against systemic boundaries. The fish pond is of limited size. Physical systems are finite; only mathematical progressions are infinite. This shows that the causal relations involved in exponential growth, occurring in actual physical systems, must refer not only to events (considered in isolation), but also to standing conditions, which can act and react on one another, together forming a set of conditions sufficient for explaining the phenomenon in question.

There is yet another kind of ecological phenomenon which would be rendered inexplicable and unpredictable if the additive view of cause is adhered to. Suppose the original situation to be Y. Then Y was observed to have become not-Y. Suppose X were the postulated cause that brought about the change from Y to not-Y. According to the additive view, upon the removal of the cause X, the *status quo* is expected to return. But it might not always be so. The example given by C. S. Holling, [22] which was cited earlier to emphasise the point that negative feedbacks do not always work with ecosystems, may also be used to illustrate the limitation of this view. The case study shows clearly that the causation at work cannot be said to approximate to the mechanistic linear model; the removal of the cause, the overfishing in the Great Lakes, simply did not restore the *status quo*.

In the light of the above exploratory discussion, one could say that non-linear causation may involve the following features and assumptions:

(1) cause may include both events and standing conditions;

(2) standing conditions are part of the systemic boundaries;

(3) a cause produces an effect, but the effect may in turn be a cause which has an effect on the original cause, and so on, such that the causal nexus approximates to the following schema — $A_1 \rightarrow B_1 \rightarrow A_2 \rightarrow$ . . . ($\rightarrow$ is the causal arrow);

(4) (1), (2) and (3) above imply that causes and effects are not simply events, which can be considered and understood as happenings isolated from one another, and independent of systemic boundaries. As a result, causation may be said to be loopish;

(5) (4) in turn implies that causes and effects are not merely additive or subtractive. The additive view cannot account for (i) threshold or cumulative effects, (ii) synergistic effects, (iii) exponential effects, (iv) changes to systemic boundaries such that a new set may be said to have emerged. To explain this, one needs to resort to a model of causation which involves not merely negative but also positive feedback loops.

2. Let us next look at the science of thermodynamics. There are actually four laws in the modern science of thermodynamics, which is concerned with the study of the transformation of energy in all its forms. [23] But for our purpose, we need only to look at the First and Second Laws. The First Law is sometimes stated as 'Energy is conserved' and sometimes as 'Total energy content of the universe is constant'. The Second Law is sometimes formulated as

'The entropy of the universe is always increasing'.

The science began originally as the study of heat, and was initiated by a French army officer and engineer, Sadi Carnot, who wanted to understand how the steam engine works and how to improve its efficiency. He thought the English to be superior both in war and in industry because they possessed the steam engine. He found that there is an intrinsic inefficiency in the conversion of heat into work. The steam engine works because parts of it are very hot, and parts very cold. Heat moves from the hot to the cold part and in so doing, work is performed. But when the two parts reach the same temperature (that is, a state of equilibrium), no more work can be performed. For work to occur there must be a difference in energy concentration, or in other words, a difference in temperature between parts of the system. Moreover, as energy moves from a higher to a lower level, less energy is available for work on the next round. For instance, in a waterfall, the water, as it falls, can be used to drive a wheel, but once it reaches the pool at the bottom, it is no longer available to perform any further work.

From such practical beginnings grew the abstract fundamental science of thermodynamics, to which famous scientists like Joule, Kelvin, Clausius and Boltzmann contributed. The latter's contribution consists of linking the behaviour of matter at the macro level to the behavioiur of matter at the micro atomic level, and in this way to provide a unifying theory of vast scope to explain the nature of change in the world. Atkin writes:

The aims adopted and the attitudes struck by Carnot and by Boltzmann epitomize thermodynamics. Carnot traveled toward thermodynamics from the direction of the engine, then the symbol of industrialized society: his aim was to improve its efficiency. Boltzmann traveled to thermodynamics from the atom, the symbol of emerging scientific fundamentalism: his aim was to increase our comprehension of the world at the deepest levels then conceived. Thermodynamics still has both aspects, and reflects complementary aims, attitudes, and applications. It grew out of the coarse machinery: yet it has been refined to an instrument of great delicacy. It spans the whole range of human enterprise, covering the organization and deployment of both resources and ideas, particularly ideas about the nature of change in the world around us. Few contributions to human understanding are richer than this child of the steam engine and the atom. [24]

The First Law is not difficult to grasp. Energy can neither be created nor destroyed. It can only be transformed from one state to another. When a tree grows or when a shed is put up, the energy used is imported from elsewhere. When the tree dies or the shed decays, the energy as such does not vanish; it is merely transformed so that the tree eventually becomes soil, dust and so on.

The Second Law can also be grasped quite readily *via* the principle that heat flows from hot to cold, and common knowledge, that once we have burnt a piece of coal or wood, we cannot reburn the ashes to produce heat, to do work. The example of the coal conveys to us vividly, as a matter of fact, the message of both the First and the Second Laws. The energy in the coal is transformed to become heat, ashes, sulphur dioxide and other gases. Thus the total amount of energy remains the same, but it now occurs in forms, which are no longer available as such for further useful work.

Entropy is the technical term introduced by Classius in 1868 as a measure of the amount of energy no longer capable of converting into work. The piece of coal, before we burn it, is capable of converting into work (or is available for work); but after it has been burnt, it is no longer thus capable (or has become unavailable for work), for, in the process of burning, entropy has increased. Entropy increase is sometimes referred to as positive entropy. Before burning, the energy in the coal is highly concentrated; after burning, it exists in low concentration. The movement of energy from high to low concentration is another way of referring to an increase of entropy.

Yet another way of characterising the same phenomenon is to say that energy moves from an ordered state (non-random) to a disordered (randomised or dissipated) state. Energy at high concentration, available for work, is also at its most ordered. Conversely, energy at low concentration, when it is least available for useful work, is also at its most disordered. Again, commonsensically, we can grasp this point through the general recognition that things left to themselves sooner or later become disordered. And to restore order requires an expenditure of energy in the tidying, cleaning, repairing and rearranging processes.

In the literature, one finds therefore the following terms to characterise energy:

high concentration	low concentration
available; free	unavailable; bound
ordered (non-random)	disordered, randomised, dissipated
low, negative entropy	high, positive entropy (entropy increase), heat death, waste, pollution

The Second Law holds true for all transformations of energy, both by human and non-human agents. All natural processes use up available energy and produce entropy increase. So the Second Law may also be formulated as 'Natural processes are accompanied by an increase in the entropy of the universe.' (See also section 5.)

On this understanding, all processes that take place in the world produce entropy, what is sometimes commonly called 'waste'. But the 'waste' produced by non-human transformation of energy is, on the whole, recycled, and then re-absorbed within the ecosystem. When an animal breathes, carbon dioxide is produced; when it shits, dung is produced. The carbon dioxide is re-absorbed by the plants in the ecosystem, of which the animal is a part; the cow-pat is worked upon by organisms, such as beetles and bacteria, to break it down into elements, which become part of the soil, which then sustains the plants, which the animal in turn eats.

Before the discovery and the intense application of EST in the history of mankind, human transformations of energy in their productive activities have, on the whole (there have been some exceptions), been on a relatively smaller scale, and also qualitatively of a kind such that the 'waste' produced by them could be recycled and re-absorbed within the ecosystems. Traditional farming methods (which do not overtax the soil to produce soil erosion) enable the 'waste' from animals, plants and, indeed, even human beings to be returned to the soil to sustain further plant growth and agricultural activities. [25]

But the arrival of EST has changed the situation. Human productive activities, particularly in the advanced industrialised societies, are not only on a much larger scale, but also such that the transformations of energy involved are qualitatively different from traditional transformations of energy. Substances, created by human agents, are introduced into the ecosystems, which the natural processes involving chemical, physical and biological agents, cannot break down. The waste (no quotes need be put around this word in this context) produced is also on such a scale, that even though it can in principle be broken down, recycled and re-absorbed within the ecosystems, in practice, ecosystems just cannot cope. It is in this context that one can refer to the increase of entropy as pollution.

The main message, then, of the Second Law (also called the Entropy Law), for the purpose of constructing a social philosophy, may be summed up by saying that work may be performed but only at a price, the price being that the amount of available energy for further work in the future has diminished. An increase in entropy is then simply a corresponding decrease in the amount of energy available for future work. This, together with the First Law which says that energy can neither be created nor destroyed but only transformed, with each transformation producing an increase of entropy, means that the faster the rate of transformation by human agents in their productive activities, the greater the entropy, or the greater the rate at which available energy for work decreases.

This means that (a) with regard to non-renewable stocks of energy (and matter), the faster the rate of depletion, the sooner will the stocks run out, and the greater the quantity of waste produced; (b) with regard to renewable forms of energy and matter, the faster the rate of consumption, the greater the quantity involved, the less able will the ecosystems be to recycle the waste — hence the greater is the pollution, and the less able will the ecosystems be to refurbish themselves; (c) with regard to the introduction of substances which ecosystems cannot break down and absorb, the greater the threat such pollution poses to the continuity of the ecosystems and the agents, both human and non-human, within them.

In other words, a proper understanding of the laws of thermodynamics and the principles of ecology would enable one to appreciate that scarcity is absolute, not relative, for we are here not simply referring to the scarcity of particular items like oil, helium or whatever, but the finitude of low entropic energy (and matter) itself, and the limitation of the biosphere (the ecosystems and their environments) itself, to cope with the problems raised under (a), (b) and (c) above. (But this is to anticipate the discussion in Chapter Three.) And this realisation in turn has implication and great significance for social philosophy.

3. It is sometimes said that science is really concerned to demonstrate that certain things are impossible, to produce so-called impossibility theorems. In the science of mathematics, one impossibility theorem is — you cannot square the circle. Those who tried, like Hobbes, are considered to be quite crazy. A popularly formulated impossibility theorem in the science of thermodynamics is — you cannot build a perpetual

motion machine.

While mathematicians are not tempted to try to square the circle, even reputable scientists have attempted to challenge the impossibility theorem of thermodynamics. The most serious and eminent of these is J. C. Maxwell:

> Maxwell suggested that an intelligent being tiny enough to handle individual molecules might be capable of violating the second law. . . . Maxwell posed the following hypothesis. Take an enclosure, he said, that is divided into two compartments, separated by a small door. The enclosure, which is totally isolated, contains a gas at a 'uniform temperature'. Now at uniform temperature the Entropy Law says that no work can be performed. Maxwell proposed to get around that problem by putting a little demon at the tiny door separating the two compartments. The demon, being sharp of eye, would then open and close the door, permitting molecules with greater than average velocities to pass from left to right and molecules with less than average velocities to pass from right to left. 'Since high speed molecules correspond to a high temperature and low speed molecules to a low temperature, the gas in the right-hand compartment would become hotter and the gas in the left-hand compartment colder.' . . .'Once the difference in temperature was established, it could be used to drive a heat engine that would deliver useful work.' [26]

The demon as a matter of fact does not exist in the real world. But even as a theoretical possibility, can it exist? For if it does, then Maxwell would have envisaged a theoretical situation where the Second Law is violated. However, such a situation does not obtain:

> [Maxwell] supposed that his demon would be able to sense the velocity (speed and direction) of individual molecules and then act accordingly. . . .

As the demon peers into either side of the isolated enclosure at uniform temperature, the uniformity of radiation throughout does not permit him to see anything. The sameness in the enclosure would allow him to perceive the thermal radiation and its fluctuations, but he would never see the molecules. . . .We conclude that the demon needs his own supply of light to disturb the radiation equilibrium within the enclosure, so we equip him with a light to enable him to see the molecules. The high quality energy that the light pours into the system provides the demon with the information he needs to operate the door to separate the high speed molecules from the low speed ones. Although the demon is able to increase the net order of the gas (and hence decrease its own entropy), a greater increase in disorder and entropy must occur in the light source. That is, for the entire system, light source, demon and gas, there will be a net increase in entropy as required by the second law, thus rendering the perpetual motion machine impossible. [27]

The impossibility of squaring a circle is of course a logical impossibility. The impossibility of building a perpetual motion machine, or of work being performed indefinitely at a constant rate (in a closed system) is not a logical impossibility, but a (natural) physical impossibility. While philosophers have no difficulty with the notion of logical impossibility, many of them have been loth to accept the notion of natural or physical impossibility. The implicit contrast they make is between logical impossibility as opposed to natural contingency. Either something cannot happen because that something is logically impossible or absurd and, therefore, logically inconceivable, or that something is logically conceivable and may exist, being, therefore, contingent.

But what is contingent may be divided into those which are likely to happen (the probability of their occurrence is high) and those which are unlikely to happen (the probability of their occurrence is low). Nevertheless, it remains true to say that the highly

77

improbable is logically possible.

In this way, such philosophers retain logical impossibility as the only type of impossibility. On this view the physically impossible is simply a kind of highly improbable contingency. But to say that something is physically impossible is to say that it cannot happen, given our understanding of how Nature works. To say that something is highly improbable is not to rule out in principle that it cannot happen, but that it could happen, though highly unlikely to do so.

Scientists who have implicitly taken over this philosophical view under which physical impossibility is redescribed as improbability, have then tried to present the Second Law of thermodynamics, not as laying down the boundaries of physical possibility or impossibility, but as laying down guidelines about phenomena which are likely to happen and those highly unlikely to happen. We find Boltzmann, one of the major contributors to the science, doing precisely this, in what he calls statistical thermodynamics. Here he maintains that it is not so much (physically) impossible for energy to move from a cold part of the system to a hot part, it is highly unlikely to do so. On this interpretation, ashes of a spent fire are simply very unlikely to be used to heat a kettle again, and corpses are highly unlikely to come to life again.

This way of denying physical impossibility may then be seen as an attempt to attenuate the insights of the science or to soften the message of those laws. For the eternal optimist could argue that one day perhaps, through further manipulations of Nature, what is now highly improbable may become probable. There is then always this hope that the Entropy Law may be sidestepped and all would be well. But it may be a hope based on science fiction rather than science. In this spirit, some have maintained that the sun over a very, very long time span, may be able to transform all the random metal molecules into concentrated forms again. But this statistical possibility, however, can give us no real comfort, since no one knows how long, although one can safely say billions of years. But, perhaps long before that, the human species itself might well have become extinct. (See section 6.) Or indeed, it might take so long that even the sun itself might have been extinguished.

4. There is another kind of issue which claims exemption from the operation of the Second Law. It is held that biological processes are immune, so that it is not true that all processes in Nature increase entropy.

At first sight, this seems to be a plausible claim, for plants, for instance, are highly ordered and structured and are capable of creating order (non-random arrangements) out of the free energy in their environment. So evolution seems to occur in defiance of the Entropy Law.

But this is an illusion. Plants and animals alike ultimately depend on solar energy — plants absorb it directly and, through photosynthesis, create structure and order. Animals cannot perform photosynthesis, so they eat the plants which can. Yet other animals, like ourselves, cannot ingest grass (although we can ingest other limited sorts of plant life), and so we eat the animals that can.

However, plants in the process of photosynthesis produce entropy. The Second Law is not violated as long as it is realised that 'the small local decrease in entropy represented in the building of the organism is coupled with a much larger increase in the entropy of the universe.' [28]

The puzzle presented by living processes is removed by clarifying the distinction between 'closed systems' and 'open systems'. A closed system is one which exchanges energy but not matter with its environment. The earth is such a system relative to the rest of the universe. It gets energy from the sun, but apart from the odd bit of meteorite which comes through our atmosphere, our planet receives no influx of matter from outside itself. The Second Law is about such a closed system — it is equilibrium thermodynamics. In such a system entropy tends toward a maximum, that is, the difference in energy levels evens out. The boiling water in the kettle soon becomes cool (when the source of heat is turned off), having lost its heat to the surrounding air, until eventually its temperature is the same as that of the air around it. It has reached the state of equilibrium when there is no more difference in the energy levels. As a result, no more work can be performed. The water can only become hot again if a new source of free or available energy is applied to it.

An open system is one which exchanges both matter and energy with its surrounds. Living things have to absorb and transform both available energy and matter from the outside. Such a state comes under non-equilibrium thermodynamics. But in trying to maintain a near steady state, that is, to decrease entropy within their own systems, living things, nevertheless, produce a far greater amount of entropy in the environment at large.

To illustrate this vast imbalance of great increase of entropy at large over the small decrease of entropy within the living system, take a look at the food chain. Suppose the chain to consist of grass, grasshoppers, frogs, trout and humans. [29] Suppose in a year a man needs to eat 300 trout to keep alive. The trout must eat 90,000 frogs. The frogs must eat 27 million grasshoppers and the grasshoppers in turn must eat 1,000 tons of grass. Miller, who gives this example, comments: '. . .about 80-90% of the energy is simply wasted and lost to the environment' [30], whenever the predator eats the prey. This means that only 10 to 20% has been absorbed by the predator to remain in its cells to pass on to the next predator further up the food chain.

On this view, while it remains true to say that every stage higher up the evolutionary scale displays greater complexity, there is a price to be paid. The price is that a greater amount of energy has to be fed into it to maintain it, and as a result a greater amount of disorder or entropy is created in the environment at large. Again this has implications for social philosophy. Human beings are at the top of the evolutionary chain. They, therefore, make a far greater impact upon their environment than other species,

and this is a fact which one should not lose sight of.
5. The science of thermodynamics is primarily the science of energy transformations. It seems to have little or nothing to say about matter. This is presumably because at the highest theoretical level, matter is simply seen as a form of energy. Einstein's equation reads $E = mc^2$.

Yet as Georgescu-Roegen shows, this is not really correct:

First of all, *mass* is not *matter in bulk*, which alone is a factor of macroscopic phenomena. Also even particles with a mass at rest (such as the proton or neutron without which there is no matter) cannot be produced in a stable form from energy *alone*. . . . [31]

adding in a footnote, 'At least not at temperatures developed after a small fraction of a second following the Big Bang.'
This leads people, according to Georgescu-Roegen, wrongly to claim that:

'Energy is the Ultimate Raw Material', sometimes referred to as the 'energetic dogma'. He says this view is shared by even the most famous physicists. He cites one of them, Glen Seaborg as saying that we shall be able to 'extract, transport, and return to nature when necessary all materials in an acceptable form, in an acceptable amount, and in an acceptable place so that the natural environment will remain natural and will support the continued growth and evolution of all forms of life. . . . [32]

If the energetic dogma is correct, then complete recycling is possible, and 'All we need is to add sufficient energy to the system and we can obtain whatever material we desire.' [33]
Georgescu-Roegen wishes to argue that matter matters. For work to be performed, not only do we need free energy but we also need 'matter arranged in

some definite structure.' In the process of producing work, not only does most of the free energy become bound energy, but so does a good deal of matter become disordered, degraded or dissipated, and no longer available for useful work. There is not only energy entropy but also material entropy. Material entropy too is increasing all the time and will eventually reach a maximum. The earth, relative to the rest of the universe is, as we have seen, a closed system. All the material (which we, human agents, and other non-human agents transform in our activities) are already here on the earth. And matter and energy can neither be created nor destroyed according to the First Law.

Of course, matter can be recycled, but one must always remember that there is a price to be paid. To quote Rifkin's and Howard's example:

> suppose we extract a chunk of metallic ore from beneath the earth's surface and fashion it into a utensil. During the life time of that utensil, metal molecules are constantly flying off of the product as a result of friction, and wear and tear. Those loose metal molecules are never destroyed. They eventually find their way back into the earth. But now they are randomly dispersed throughout the soil and are no longer in a concentrated form to perform useful work, like the original chunk of metallic ore. A way might be found to recycle all of these randomly dispersed metal molecules but only at the expense of an increase in entropy in the process. A mechanical device would have to be assembled to recollect the metal molecules and an energy source introduced to run the machine. Since the machine itself is made out of metallic ore from the earth, it would be losing its own metal molecules to friction and wear and tear even as it is recycling the other random metal molecules. At the same time, the energy used to run the recycling machine would also end up increasing the entropy. [34]

Recycling can never, therefore, be 100 percent

efficient, although, doubtless, there is room for improvement, in our existing methods of recycling chunks of discarded matter, like old cars and cardboard boxes. It is somewhat fanciful, however, to think that we can recycle all the molecules of metal and other bits of matter, which are continuously being thrown off into the surrounds through friction, wear and tear.

Georgescu-Roegen proposes a new law to cover the behaviour of matter, which can be variously formulated as 'A closed system cannot perform work indefinitely at a constant rate' or 'In a closed system, available matter continuously and irrevocably dissipates, thus becoming unavailable' or 'Complete recycling is impossible'.

He emphasises that for the purpose of coping with the problems of entropy, we must keep energy entropy separate from material entropy, and not regard matter simply as a form of energy. Energy is, he says, a homogeneous thing but matter is not:

> it exists in numberless forms, each with its characteristic properties. Otherwise the Mendeleev table would have no relevance. This being so, it seems hardly possible (at this time) to embrace the entropic degradation of matter into a single formula for all cases. [35]

6. In conclusion, let me sum up the relevance of the principles of ecology, the non-linear paradigm of causation embedded in the science of ecology, and the laws of thermodynamics for social/moral philosophy. The first two inform us, human agents, that the consequences of our activities, based on EST, of transforming energy and matter, can drastically degrade and even bankrupt the ecosystems in the world. Such ecological degradation and bankruptcy, therefore, render our present civilisation and its core values unsustainable in the long run, and can have very undesirable effects on human agents as well as other non-human agents. The latter, *via* the First Law, in-

forms us that we can neither create nor destroy energy and matter, only transform them; it follows that a civilisation like ours, based on ever increasing consumption (see Chapters Three and Five), which uses up, in many cases, non-renewable forms of energy and matter, is not viable in the long run. A viable sustainable civilisation must be based on renewable forms of energy and matter. The Second Law tells us that our human transformations of energy and matter, inevitably, increase entropy and disorder. But this increase is not worrying only if it can be compensated for by the capacity of the ecosystems, to recycle and re-absorb the side products of our transformational activities. But our understanding of the science of ecology has already made us aware that this crucial capacity, on the part of ecosystems to recycle and re-absorb, is not unlimited and infinite.

It may be appropriate to quote what two ecologists have written about the relevance of ecological knowledge, if not wisdom, to the crisis:

1. Whatever is done to the environment is likely to have repercussions in other places and at other times. Because of the characteristic problems of ecology some of the effects are bound to be unpredictable in practice, if not in principle. Furthermore, because of the characteristic time-dependence problem, the effects may not be measurable for years — possibly not for decades.
2. If man's actions are massive enough, drastic enough, or of the right sort, they will cause changes which are irreversible since the genetic material of extinct species cannot be reconstituted. Even if species are not driven to extinction, changes may occur in the ecosystem which prevent a recurrence of the events which produced the community. Such irreversible changes will almost always produce a simplification of the environment.
3. The environment is finite and our non-renewable resources are finite. When the stocks run out we will have to recycle what we have used.
4. The capacity of the environment to act as a sink

for our total waste, to absorb it and recycle it so that it does not accumulate as pollution, is limited. In many instances, that limit has already been passed. It seems clear that when limits are passed, fairly gross effects occur, some of which are predictable, some of which are not. These effects result in significant alterations in environmental conditions (global weather, ocean productivity). Such changes are almost always bad since organisms have evolved and ecosystems have developed for existing conditions. We impose rates of change on the environment which are too great for biological systems to cope with.

5. In such a finite world and under present conditions, an increasing population can only worsen matters. For a stationary population, an increase in standard of living can only mean an increase in the use of limited resources, the destruction of the environment and the choking of the environmental sinks. [36]

(The points raised under (5) will be discussed in Chapters Five and Six.)

If the above is correct, the fundamental implication of the combined sciences of ecology and thermodynamics for social/moral philosophy must be that we have (a) to alter our technology from ES̲T to EST; (b) to give up ever increasing consumption of energy and matter, whether renewable or non-renewable.

It is the failure to appreciate these implications which has led to the present crisis facing our industrial civilisation. Indeed it is a civilisation predicated upon ignoring the principles of these two sciences, as if the very opposite of what they maintain holds true. But, while those who initiated it three hundred odd years ago could well claim ignorance as grounds for exemption for responsibility, those today, who either fail to give them due attention or deliberately turn their backs on them in order to carry on business as usual, have no such excuse.

The denial that social/moral theories can be rationally assessed by the four checks I have listed at the beginning of Chapter One, and especially the latter three, has led to the construction of theories or philosophies which could be said to be irrelevant, because they are fantastic. A fantastic social/moral theory may be defined as one, which ignores or violates the check of facts, the check of empirical/scientific assumptions and the check of the problem.

I have elsewhere maintained as an example of a fantastic theory that held by Nozick, which is a liberal social/moral theory. (I leave it an open question whether all extant liberal theories are fantastic.) Nozick's theory would be an adequate and appropriate social theory if its presuppositions obtain, and are true. (Being presuppositions they are not articulated by him — I have articulated them in an effort to make sense of what he is trying to say and to do.) Its presuppositions include that (i) human beings do not have distinct stages, from infancy and dependency, to independent adulthood, to dependent senility, (ii) we all arrive fully grown as mature adults into the world, (iii) such adults are necessarily perfect in their equipment to deal with the world, that they are always fit, healthy with all the endosomatic organs intact, with a corpus of knowledge and information about how to cope with the world, (iv) there is no overlap of generations, that is to say, while some are being born, others are reaching maturity, and yet others are dying, etc.

Nozick recommends two principles of distribution, which he considers to be just. To simplify, these are: (1) that agents are entitled to acquire goods (what he calls holdings) through their labour (a Lockean view — see Chapter Six, section 1 for further elucidation); (2) that agents are entitled to holdings which they might not themselves have acquired under (1), but which they have received under a (free and willing) transfer from other agents who have. However, a moment's reflection would show that not all agents are in a position to acquire holdings under (1), as some of them are too young, others too weak, diseased, handicapped, or senile to do so. Nor are all agents lucky enough to receive any holdings under (2).

This means that a good many agents will be left with nothing, if these two principles, alone, were in operation.

But in Nozick's presupposed world, this unfortunate consequence of his theory, would not occur, as it seems falsely to imply that all the agents are borne mature, fully-grown, able-bodied, in possession of the appropriate information, skills and wherewithal to acquire holdings through their labour. In such a world, too, it seems reasonable for such agents to transfer to another the fruits of their labour, if and only if they so wish, as personal gifts. In such a world, the principles of justice he advocates would, then, work and constitute a relevant solution to the problem of distribution facing such agents.

Nozick may get out of the charge that his theory is fantastic, but only at the expense of his acceptance of its major implication, that is, that a good many agents might get very little or nothing under his schema, through no fault of their own. The young, the sick, the handicapped, the aged, those born to parents who are themselves not fully able-bodied, not possessing the appropriate skills and information in order to acquire a good many holdings through their labour, those without fortunate (personal) beneficiaries and patrons, as we have seen, are all left out. Such a theory of justice, if it can be called that, violates the distributive value of equality. (See Chapter Nine.)

However, such a theory which professes to tell us how we ought to live under the type of social arrangement recommended by it is beside the point, as those presuppositions do not hold in the world you and I occupy. It will, therefore, not solve the problems of distribution, which face us human agents, in our particular kind of world, as the model of 'human' agency and existence, presupposed by it, bears no resemblance to actual human agency and existence. One significant feature of human existence, as we have seen in Chapter One, section 3, is the overlap of generations, of the processes of birth, growing, ageing, dying occurring simultaneously, as well as the fact that many if not all the actions of existing generations, could have profound consequences for the well-being of yet non-existent generations. Any adequate solution to the problem of distribution must necessarily take into account these messy complex facts of human life.

In a similar manner, those social/moral theories constructed in ignorance of, or not in accordance with, the sciences of thermodynamics and ecology, are equally fantastic. This in effect means the dominant social philosophies of today, whether represented by the first world of liberal representative democracies allied to (bourgeois) capitalism, or by the second world of the people's democracies allied to (state) capitalism. The major social philosophies, since the seventeenth century, have been such fantastic theories. It is time to rethink them, and if necessary, to jettison them, in favour of one which is not fantastic.

CHAPTER THREE

ECOLOGICAL SCARCITY

1. Another way, as we have seen, of putting the implications of the principles of ecology, the non-linear model of causation embedded in that science, and the laws of thermodynamics for social, moral theory, arrived at in the last chapter, is to say that there is scarcity of both low entropic energy and matter in a closed system like our planet, earth. Let us explore this further and call it ecological scarcity [1] or low entropy scarcity. In particular, it is necessary to try to meet the arguments of those who challenge the existence of such scarcity.

From the point of view of defending the notion of ecological scarcity, it makes sense, as it is commonly accepted, to divide energy and matter into the renewable and the non-renewable. Let us start then by examining the most important form of renewable energy, that is, solar energy. Because of its renewable nature, we have seen how some people have argued that there can be no real scarcity of energy, since ultimately the sun is our source of energy supply, and so long as the sun exists in its present form more or less, we need not worry about its eventual run down and demise in the distant geological future.

It is of course true that ultimately life on earth depends on the sun. We know that without the warmth and the light provided by solar energy, photosynthesis would not take place. Without photosynthesis, a good deal of organic life as we know it today would collapse. However, it may not be so obvious that other essentials of life (including human life), such as the oxygen in the air for breathing, and water, are equally dependent on the sun.

Take water.

The ecological significance is severalfold. In addition to its obviously important role in constituting some 20 percent of the weight of organisms, it is the significant medium for biological activity. Further, it is an agent of geological change, eroding in one place and depositing in another. It is also thereby an agent of nutrient distribution, a role which is augmented by the great variety of chemicals it carries as dissolved salts and gases. Finally, but of fundamental significance to ecosystems, is water's role as an agent of energy transfer and utilization. The large amounts of energy involved in converting ice to water (80 gcal/gm), of raising water temperature (1 gcal/gm/ degree) and vaporizing water (536 gcal/gm) make water a tremendous factor in ameliorating wide changes in temperature that would otherwise accompany the variations in incoming solar radiation. [2]

The hydrological cycle is effected by an interchange between the earth's surface and the atmosphere *via* evaporation and precipitation. 23 percent of the total solar energy intercepted by earth goes into this. Most of it is used to turn water into water vapour. The wind then drives the water vapour until it eventually con- denses, and falls back to the earth's surface as rain or snow. The cycle is a steady-state one, the total precipitation is balanced by the total evaporation.

It is true that as far as solar energy is concerned, it is in theory unlimited, and for human purposes may be regarded as renewable. It is, therefore, more of a flow than a stock. (See Chapter Six for further discussion of this distinction.) Unfortunately, however, it is also true that the rate of its arrival on earth and its pattern of distribution are fairly restricted. The sun shines only part of the time during the day; for those parts of the world beyond the equatorial belt, it shines for fewer hours and less strongly during the winter months. As a result, plants in those parts only grow, by and large, in the spring and summer. Over the years, humankind has developed methods of storing and preserving food to tide over the non-growing season.

To tap and harvest the solar source of energy in a concentrated form to do work, like drive machines, would mean evolving a technology which at the moment is in some ways still experimental. In this field of research, there are two different outlooks — those who favour using the sun in a 'passive' manner for space heating, cooking, for instance, through relatively small localised units of production, [3] and those who have grandiose visions of erecting satellite mirrors and platforms in space, [4] or those who speak of the solar-hydrogen-economy [5] to provide large scale, immensely concentrated energy to nurture the industries as we know them to be.

On the modest version, solar energy could not conceivably be seen to sustain the kind of industrial civilisation already in existence, and on the sort of scale it now functions. On the grand and ambitious version (even if we were to overlook its mere experimental, if not speculative, nature at present), its achievement would bring, in its train, certain problems which are, to say the least, not easy to overcome, such as the increase in the world's temperature, through ever increasing use and consumption of energy (see section 4). The scarcity of energy is, however, not the only relevant concern, the scarcity of low entropic matter is equally significant; indeed, such scarcity coupled with the overcoming of the scarcity of low entropic energy (even if successful) could in turn lead to environmental degradation and hazards (see section 4).

From the above discussion, one can see that relying on solar energy as a renewable form of low entropic energy to carry on business as usual appears to be less than satisfactory or realistic.

Another renewable form of fuel, the direct technological capture of solar energy apart, is biomass.

Plants through photosynthesis transform and concentrate the sun's energy in their cells. These could be used to produce fuel. However attractive this proposal may appear, one must not forget the basic principle that renewability itself is not both a necessary and sufficient condition for overcoming scarcity. It is only a necessary condition, for the renewable form of energy could well, like biomass, compete with equally urgent calls upon other scarce resources. To grow sugar cane for fuel requires land, for a start. Apart from suitable terrain itself being limited, land is also needed for growing food and for housing, just to mention two other essentials of human existence. So although renewable, it nevertheless remains scarce.

Moreover, because of the Entropy Law, as every farmer knows, the land cannot remain just as fertile through continuous cultivation. Plants absorb minerals and other goodness from the soil, as we have seen. Sooner or later, these ingredients become depleted. Soil is also blown away, scattered by non-human and human agents alike. To replenish the soil, it must either be let to lie fallow (thus increasing scarcity), or one must add fertilisers to it from an outside source. If the fertilisers are organic and natural, their availability ultimately depends on the rate of conversion by the sun, the wind, ice, rain, bacteria, etc. in breaking down bits of organic matter like fallen leaves and stalks, human and animal manure, and inorganic matter, like rocks. To produce twelve inches of topsoil takes a thousand years, it has been calculated. Today, agriculture in the economically 'developed' countries relies on inorganic fertilisers which themselves require low entropic energy and matter to produce, not to mention that they are derived, in the main, from scarce non-renewable matter.

One must not forget too that plants take time to grow. Genetic engineering could, of course, produce varieties in which the growing period is reduced; but even genetic engineering could not perform miracles so that plant growth and maturity become almost simultaneous. Moreover, such varieties may only produce the desired outcome if a lot of resources (again such low entropic energy and matter themselves being in short supply) were pumped into nursing them. The so-called 'Green Revolution' — the miracle high yield rice and wheat strains — is a case in point. It exacts a price in terms of a massive input of fertilisers and water (the latter too is in short supply — see below for further comment). Such strains may also not be as hardy or disease or pest resistant. As a result, more herbicides and pesticides may have to be used to protect them. These in turn produce adverse effects on the environment.

The rate at which one turns biomass into fuel must above all be compatible with the goal of avoiding soil erosion. Soil erosion may be caused by failure to replant as well as excessive replanting without re-plenishment. Managing a renewable stock of this kind is not easy, even with our improved understanding of how ecological systems work. Our preindustrial fore-bears also tried to manage such a fuel source but, in the end, they failed — they caused extensive de-forestation, thereby causing soil erosion which in turn led to a shortage of wood. As a substitute, they then turned to coal which became the fuel eventually of the new industrial civilisation (although it is true that the first industrial revolution was based on the power of the water mill).

As for the non-renewable forms of energy, fossil fuels — of which coal and petroleum are the most obvious examples — by and large sustain our present industrial civilisation. These are themselves, of course, stored-up solar energy. To use them up is to use up capital — once gone, forever gone. The tremendous progress achieved in the last two hundred years of our industrial civilisation is based first on coal, then also on oil.

The total amount of these fuels which exist in the earth's crust may be much more than the amount which we will ever be able to extract. This is because if the fuels exist in inaccessible places, or not in a sufficiently concentrated form, complicated and ex-pensive technologies will have to be developed to get at them. This is precisely what happened in the case of off-shore oil exploration and production.

Our concern here, however, is not so much with money and the market, but with the thermodynamic reality behind them. The rise in price of a commodity fuel is after all not simply due to a rise in demand but also to its ecological scarcity, and, hence, the fact that higher costs of production are involved to get at less accessible sources of the fuel. To drill a well in a Texan suburban backyard costs much less naturally than to drill in the North Sea. More energy and matter will be used up and, correspondingly, more entropy, waste and pollution will also be produced. There may well then come a point where the net yield of energy, [6] that is, the gross yield minus the amount of energy and matter used in producing the fuel, is insufficient to justify extraction; indeed, it could get so bad that there may even be a net loss.

But if matter really matters, then we need to worry not only about scarcity of energy, but also scarcity of matter, such as minerals. To produce cars, microwave ovens, etc., we need not only a source of energy, whether based on coal, oil, uranium, biomass or whatever, but also metals, wood, plastic, and so on with which to construct factories, other buildings and the machines themselves. To simplify matters, let us just briefly look at the scarcity of minerals.

Minerals are by and large non-renewable. But some people have, of course, denied that this is so. It seems that, in the main, they rely on the thesis, already examined in the last chapter, that it is feasible (always given the right technology or the sun's ability in the very long run) to recycle the molecules thrown off by chunks of metal, and scattered to the four winds through friction, wear and tear. This, as we have seen is somewhat fanciful, if not (physically) impossible, according to Georgescu-Roegen.

Or they use the argument, already referred to in passing, that there is always more available than budgeted for by the thermodynamic or ecological pessimists, even if it is true that the resources are not strictly speaking infinite and inexhaustible. The sea bed, for instance, contains huge and practically endless amounts of manganese nodules, which could provide us with a source for non-ferrous metals. But this argument forgets that the entropic costs may be very high indeed. However, the question of entropic cost will be examined in detail later — see section 4.

Some experts have predicted that, at the current rates of consumption, half of the world's metals considered to be useful now, will have been exhausted within seventy five years or even less. [7] By early next century, copper, gold, antinomy, bismuth and molybdenum will have become really scarce. The US itself by the middle of the next century will have used up its extractable amounts of the following — tin, commercial asbestos, columbium, fluorite, sheet mica, high-grade phosphorus, strontium, mercury, chromium and nickel. [8]

So far we have looked at the minerals. But increasingly, advanced technologies rely also on non-metallic materials. One of these is helium which plays an indispensable part in nuclear technology, both the breeder reactor as well as the proposed thermonuclear fusion reactors of the future, in electricity transmission by superconducting power lines, and so on. Yet helium is a scarce material. At the moment, it is obtained through extraction from natural gas. It is conceivable that it could also be obtained by liquefaction from the atmosphere, but only at a very large cost, both in money and thermodynamic terms. No suitable substitute (which itself is not scarce) is in sight. Yet some experts have said that the demand for helium is likely to exceed supply (without resorting to liquefaction) within the next 100 years. [9]

Of the numerous forms of matter, one which is indispensable to nearly all industrial processes is, of course, water. But not any water will do. Sea water is plentiful enough but without further treatment to remove excessive salt from it, it is not of great use. Relatively pure water has so many competing uses that any technological innovation, which relies on heavy use of it, would naturally present problems that are not easy to overcome. We are able in certain parts of the world to tap stores of underground water which have collected over geological time. But this source of water, like fossil fuels, must count as non-renewable stock. One cannot, therefore, rely on it forever more.

In its renewable form, its renewability is, however, dependent on many other natural processes, such as tree growth, which are themselves under threat from industrial pollution. Moreover, an ever-increasing demand for it would lead to the danger of outstripping the capacity of the ecosystems to renew it.

It is impossible in a book like this to go through every minor or, indeed, major form of low entropic energy and matter, which enters into the industrial processes of production today. The above instances are mere illustrations of the problems, theoretical and practical, which we realise must face our industrial civilisation, once we understand properly the implications of the principles of ecology and the laws of thermodynamics.

2. Moreover, the problems mentioned above in the last section are greatly exacerbated by the fact that the world's economies are predicated on the axiom of growth (see Chapter Six), and that the rate of growth is exponential. So we need urgently to understand the implications of exponential growth for ecological scarcity. Very briefly, it may be defined as follows: 'A quantity grows exponentially when its rate of increase during a period of time is a fixed percentage of the changing size of the quantity.' [10]

Its basic idea may be readily grasped *via* the notion of compound interest. £100 deposited with a bank or building society at 10 percent interest *per annum* (if left untouched) would have doubled itself at the end of seven years. With simple interest, at the same rate, the doubling takes place at the end of ten years. A quick formula to use for calculating doubling times is to divide the annual rate of growth into 70. If the annual rate of growth of an economy is 2 percent, the economy would have doubled by the end of 35 years.

The point may also be made even more vividly by imagining a lily pond growing in a fish pond of a certain size. (This is often cited in the literature.) Suppose the lily to double its size every day. In 30 days, the lily would have covered the entire pond. As a result, the fish dies. On the 28th day of growth, the lily pond would have covered, however, only a quarter of the pond. By the 29th day, half the pond. By the 30th day, the whole pond. The dramatic change from half to the whole of the pond all within 24 hours drives home the impact of exponential growth upon finite resources. What appears as a large, though manageable problem at one moment, may be turned into a total disaster in a very short span of time seemingly quite unexpectedly.

As far as the world's non-renewable mineral resources are concerned, given exponential growth and a high absolute demand, there are then two things to bear in mind:

(1) even if we assume that the entire earth contains nothing but minerals and that all of it is potentially extractable, it still remains true that the total would be exhausted within a relatively short period.

At a current 3 percent growth rate in the use of ten leading minerals, we would literally mine the equivalent of the entire world's weight within several hundred years. That is not a very long time when one stops to realize that human beings have been on earth for over $3\frac{1}{2}$ million years and that the earth itself has existed for 4 billion additional years. [11]

(2) 'The time for concern about the potential exhaustion of a resource comes when no more than about 10 percent of the total has been used up.' [12] This means now, rather than later, or we will be like the farmer who seems surprised to find his fish dead, having been suffocated by the exponentially imperialising lily.

3. The example of helium mentioned earlier raises a general point. A substitute for something scarce may itself be scarce. The scarcity, in other words, is absolute not relative, a fundamental point to grasp. A similar distinction is sometimes made by economists in terms of Malthusian and Ricardian scarcity. Malthusian scarcity is absolute scarcity while Ricardian scarcity is said to be relative scarcity. [13]

Malthusian scarcity has been much reviled by Marx, at least in the form put forward by Malthus originally. But perhaps Marx had confused two things — the fact that absolute scarcity exists, and the solution that Malthus endorsed to cope with it. Malthus thought nothing could be done by human intervention to alter the outcome of excessive reproduction, which is famine, hunger, disease and death. However, to revile Malthus for the former is to execute the messenger for bringing the bad news. But it would be right to criticise Malthus for implying that altering existing distributive patterns of resources, changing one's mode of production and consumption as well as the rate of reproduction itself (that is, through deliberate human intervention) could not make a difference to the outcome. That would simply be fatalism. (See below for qualification.)

Malthus in that famous essay of his — *Essay on the Principle of Population as it affects the Future Improvement of Society* — published in 1798, held that as human reproduction occurs at an exponential or geometric rate while resources, such as the production of food in a limited space, grows at best at an arithmetic rate, then there are bound to be more mouths than there is food to feed them. Death through disease, famine and war (what he calls 'negative checks') would eventually bring the population back to equilibrium.

However, it is held that in the later editions of the essay, he went on to qualify that original pessimistic thesis somewhat, to the extent of admitting that 'positive checks' might become available, such as higher standards of prudential behaviour on the part of the labouring classes, presumably obtained through better education and improved living conditions, brought about by economic growth which would recognise the wisdom of curbing reproductive activities and, hence, ward off the terrible potential outcome of over-population.

But while this qualification may do justice to Malthusian scholarship, it does not really touch the point that I am interested in emphasising, namely, that what Malthus is saying is that there is absolute scarcity — space for food is physically limited, and so is one's ability ultimately to improve food productive capacity because of the Entropy Law. Indeed, desperate attempts (which try to ignore the Second Law) to increase food production, brought on by population pressure, would simply bring on, more quickly, soil erosion and desertification, which, in turn, means that the soil would produce even less than it did before. We can today see this tragic process at work in many so-called fourth world countries. [14]

Ricardian scarcity understood as relative scarcity amounts to saying (1) that while there is scarcity of a particular resource or resource of a particular quality, there is never absolute scarcity, for (2) there is always available the same resource even if of a lower grade, (3) even if that resource, of whatever grade and quality, runs out, there is always available a substitute which itself is not scarce.

While prime agricultural land is pretty limited and runs out, poorer land would, and could, be brought into production, illustrating (2) above. While wood ran out as a general fuel, coal took its place; if coal and oil were to run out, then some other fuel resource would become available, like nuclear energy, illustrating (3).

It presupposes the possibility of substitutibility. Substitutibility in turn presupposes the availability of an appropriate technology to deliver the alternative resource to the productive process. Marshy land before it can be brought under the plough has first to be drained. This requires the availability of the technology of drainage. To harness the energy, that comes through splitting the atom, obviously requires a nuclear fission technology.

Increasingly, economists and politicians and many scientists themselves naturally pin their faith on science and technology to guarantee substitutibility. It is said that while the industrial revolution of the nineteenth century leaned on science and technology, it was not led by them. But the industrial civilisation of the twentieth century is of a different character — science and technology are intrinsic to the industrial processes, determining their very nature and their direction.

On this view, the process begun in the seventeenth century towards progress, will be carried even one stage further. Progress consists of humankind controlling Nature and subordinating it to human purposes and ends. (See Chapter Eight.) Progress becomes near total in the twentieth century when science and technology allow human beings to do what they like with Nature. Indeed so thrilled and exhilarated are some people by this vision that, paradoxically, it leads them to say that the human species is increasingly less and less dependent or, indeed, even no longer dependent upon Nature. To quote one such view: 'Man has probably always worried about the environment because he was once totally dependent on it.' [15]

Another pair of influential economists writes:

Advances in fundamental science have made it possible to take advantage of the uniformity of energy matter — a uniformity that makes it feasible, without preassignable limit, to escape the quantitative constraints imposed by the character of the earth's crust. A limit may exist, but it can be neither defined nor specified in economic terms. Flexibility, not rigidity, characterizes the relationship of modern man to the physical universe in which he lives. Nature imposes particular scarcities not an inescapable general scarcity. Man is therefore able, and free, to choose among an indefinitely large number of alternatives. [16]

But such optimism is misplaced for it flies against

the First and Second Laws of thermodynamics (as well as Georgescu-Roegen's Law of Matter Entropy). As far as energy is concerned, one can substitute a renewable resource under pressure, like wood, for a non-renewable resource like oil and *vice versa*. As far as matter is concerned, we might one day substitute, say, silicon, which is relatively plentiful for copper, which is not. This, however, cannot be used to support the view that we become less and less dependent on Nature, or that there is no absolute scarcity of low entropic energy and matter.

If we can neither create nor destroy energy and matter, but only transform them, then it remains true that we can never liberate ourselves from a dependence on Nature, no matter how sophisticated our tools of transformation might have become. With their help, we might be able to make use of substances which are relatively plentiful in supply. But it is sheer illusion and fantasy to believe that, as a result, we are are no longer using, or using less, resources provided by Nature. Substitution can put off the day of having run out but not abolish absolute finitude itself.

Moreover, the more sophisticated our tools and technologies, the more, not less, low entropic energy and matter we might have to use in the substitution process, and thus in the end create more entropy and degradation. To labour an obvious point — to burn bits of firewood or cow dung lying about to cook a meal uses much less energy and matter than relying on a bottle of gas, as a source of fuel for cooking. The production of the latter, as well as the cost (not monetary, but the entropic cost) of transporting it to the site of use, overall, therefore, produce greater entropy. When firewood becomes unavailable and one has to resort to bottled gas, the substitution, relying on a relatively sophisticated technology, is often more entropic, not less.

Another example may be taken from modern technologised agriculture:

> If we look at farming from the standpoint of calories of food crop delivered to the American

table compared to calories of energy expended in the form of fuel, electricity, chemicals (including pesticides as well as fertilisers), energy tied up in the manufacture of farm tools, transportation devices, supermarket refrigerators, etcetera, etcetera, we come to the appalling conclusion that the American food system devours 9 times as many calories as it produces. Instead of being the most efficient system, it is energetically by far the least efficient system of agriculture that has ever existed or that we can imagine. [17]

Furthermore, as Georgescu-Roegen, Daly and others point out, it is not the homogeneity of matter-energy that:

makes for usefulness, but precisely the opposite. It is nonuniformity, the differences in concentration and temperature, that makes for usefulness. If all materials and energy were uniformly distributed in thermodynamic equilibrium, the resulting 'homogeneous resource base' would be no resource at all. There would be a complete absence of potential for any process, including life. . . .(T)he economist's notion of infinite substitutibility bears some resemblance to the old alchemist's dream of converting base metals into precious metals. All you have to do is rearrange atoms. But the potential for rearranging atoms is itself scarce, so the mere fact that everything is made up of the same homogeneous building blocks does not abolish scarcity. Only Maxwell's Sorting-Demon could turn a pile of atoms into a resource, and the entropy law tells us that Maxwell's Demon does not exist. [18]

4. Let us explore further the entropic cost of the kind of technology which the majority of today's theorists celebrate as the liberation of our dependence on Nature, as well as the cause of the abolition of absolute scarcity and finitude.

To achieve these ends, they often fall back on what

is sometimes dubbed 'the burn the rocks and dredge the sea' policy. But this strategy forgets, as we have seen above, that the less concentrated the matter or energy as it occurs naturally, the more matter and energy must be used to collect them into a useable quantity. Take a more familiar example first. Suppose the precious beads of a necklace had been scattered, as the bag which leaked the broken necklace was being carried from Land's End to John O'Groats. To reconstitute the necklace by finding and gathering up those beads would in principle be possible, but it would require an excessive expenditure of energy and matter to do so. Suppose the chosen method consist of scooping up all the surface material lying on the path over which the bag travelled, and then using a device to sort out the beads from the rest. The rest constitutes waste. To get hold of all the beads again would create an enormous amount of waste.

The same happens when one proposes to get at scattered bits of metals embedded in the earth's crust in order to concentrate them in a usable form. It has been calculated that 'the ratio of unusable waste to useful metal in granite is at least 2000 : 1, so that the mining of economic quantities of metal from rock or seawater will very quickly burden us with impossible quantities of waste.' [19]

Four problems at least present themselves immediately to the naive mind: (a) where will one park the waste? (b) while all this mining especially of the earth's crust is taking place, what alternate sites are there for all the other activities normally carried on, like farming, housing, building factories, etc? (c) even if, very conveniently, the mined areas are not used for habitation and other productive activities, mining destroys the ecological systems already established — even cosmetic landscaping (unsatisfactory from the ecological point of view) would in turn cost a tremendous consumption of further energy and matter (d) mining of land requires an excessive amount of water, and water is all too scarce, with numerous other competing demands upon what is available.

But above all, there is another form of waste one

must bear in mind — heat as waste. All industrial processes produce waste heat. If we consider the amount produced by the consumption of electricity in one country alone, we can begin to see the enormity of the problem.

> Even if we ignore the waste heat from power stations, that produced by the actual consumption of electricity will quickly call a halt to growth. For example, in the US in 1970, heat from that source amounted to an average of 0.017 watts per square foot, and Claude Summers has calculated that if consumption continues to double at the present rate, within 99 years, after 10 more doublings, the average will be 17 watts per square foot — compared with the average of 18 or 19 watts the US receives from the sun! Clearly, well before this point energy consumption will be limited by the heat-tolerance of the ecosphere. [20]

One of the consequences of changes in heat, which might only alter the global temperature by as little as one or two degrees Celsius, is said to be sufficient to bring about quite drastic changes in climate, such as the onset or the end of ice ages. If the production of man-made heat were to reach the equivalent of one percent (at 5 percent growth rate, this would take 200 years) of the absorbed solar flux, this would increase the global temperature by that critical one degree Celsius. As a result, the present climatic patterns would change, with severe consequences for agriculture, for population and so on.

It is essential to realise that no technological miracle could deflect this. To quote Ophuls:

> It is important to reiterate that *there is no possible technological appeal from this heat limit*, for it is a consequence of the fundamental laws of the universe. This has not prevented people from trying, but all such efforts are doomed to thermodynamic futility. For example, some propose to divert sunlight from the earth with satellite mirror arrays or

bands of particulates in upper atmosphere, but this would significantly reduce photosynthesis (and thus crop production) and grossly alter the climate. Others propose to gather up the heat and pump it into space, but even assuming we had a technology capable of performing such a thermodynamic miracle, so much energy would be expended in the process that we should be worse off than when we started. [21]

For this reason, the availability of a virtually endless supply of energy (which some people believe nuclear fusion technology might allow us) might not be an unmixed blessing. Limitless energy used to burn the rocks and dredge the sea, in order to extract scattered and dispersed minerals, could in turn cost severe ecological disruptions both known, and as yet unknown.

The biosphere (the system which includes all living things, the air, water, soil, etc. which is their habitat) can absorb and cope with waste but only if the quantity and the rate is low enough without causing undue disruption, as we have seen. But modern technology which is, by and large, ecologically insensitive, tends to overload the system. Take the marine ecosystem as an illustration. Fish excrete waste. They also die. All this together with organic detritus are converted by bacteria to inorganic products. These in turn form the basis of food for algae which the fish eat. The ability to absorb and recycle the waste enables the system to be stable. But modern farming technology can destroy stability and undermine its self-regulatory mechanisms. Artificial fertilisers are pumped into the soil to sustain the high yield. The soil itself and the plants cannot, and do not, absorb all the nutrients which then get washed away, and are eventually carried into rivers and coastal waters. They, together with other detritus like human waste, encourage excessive aquatic plant growth. When these die, the bacteria required to break them down may not be sufficient, as the bacteria have to compete for oxygen with a greater quantity of other organisms. If the disruption goes on for long enough, the oxygen would have become so depleted that the bacteria would die. With their death, so would the algae and the fish die.

As already mentioned in the last chapter, another danger to the biosphere posed by modern technology lies in the increasing production of synthetic substances as substitutes for scarce natural ones. Natural substances took a long time to evolve; at the same time it is likely that there evolved solvents, so to speak, for them. If there were no enzyme capable of breaking down a particular type of molecule, how could the basic cyclical processes of life, growth, death and decay have carried on? But Nature is not prepared for the introduction of synthetic substances. They cannot be broken down. They accumulate as the undigested waste in the ecosystems, thus eventually disrupting, and even destroying them.

Nearly always modern technology itself has no satisfactory solution for this problem that it has created. A vivid example of this is raised by the disposal of nuclear radioactive waste. No one really knows what to do with it. And when technology does propose a solution, it may produce in its wake other problems with equally undesirable ecological (not to mention sometimes political) consequences. One of the elements produced by the nuclear breeder reactor is plutonium-239. It is the most toxic substance ever made by humans in quantity. One pound of plutonium, dispersed as fine particles one micron in diameter, could cause 9 billion lung cancers. It has a half-life of 24,000 years.

5. So far, then, one may sum up the main implications of ecological scarcity for social philosophy as follows:
I (a) we may begin to answer the question of endurance a little more fully — in the last chapter, we have established that the faster the rate at which low entropic energy and matter are used up, the shorter the period of human existence in the eventual history of the species;

(b) the finitude and eventual depletion of low entropic energy and matter are not overcome by technology; on the contrary, technology which itself uses a massive amount of low entropic energy and matter and, hence, in turn produces an even greater increase of high or positive entropy, hastens the rate of depletion.

Such technology appears to be characteristic of our present civilisation which I have called ecologically insensitive technology (EST). EST overloads the biosphere and ecosystems, disrupts, destabilises and if unchecked, destroys them. It is incompatible with their so-called carrying capacity. Following Vogt, one may define carrying capacity as follows:

C = B : E. C stands for *carrying capacity* of any area of land — its ability to provide food, drink, shelter to the creatures that live on it. B stands for *biotic potential*, or ability of the land to produce plants for shelter, clothing, food etc. E stands for *environmental resistance*, or the limitations that any environment, including the part of the environment contrived and complicated by man, places on the biotic potential. The carrying capacity is the resultant of the ratio between the other two factors. [22]

II (a) it follows then that, conversely, should we want human existence to continue within a stable framework for as long as possible, it would be wise to adopt a type of technology which is ecologically sensitive (EST), which does not exceed the carrying capacity of the biosphere and the ecosystems.

No technology, however ecologically sensitive, can overcome the finitude of low entropy scarcity itself. It is only a question of the relative speed of depletion (and its effect on the capacity of the ecosystems to cope with the waste which comes from the activities of depletion, and to renew themselves by breaking down the waste and re-absorbing and recycling the broken down components) that we humans can hope to control. The imperative we ought to follow is:

divert resources to developing EST rather than E$\underline{S}$T, and the corollary, that of two or more competing technologies, choose that one which is more ecologically sensitive than its rivals.

Our present civilisation based on E$\underline{S}$T has so far lasted roughly three hundred years. But it is impossible for it to last for very much longer, even if one were to assume the most optimistic assumptions with regard to technological innovations, if the understanding, given to us of Nature by the sciences of thermodynamics and ecology, is correct. Attaching an actual date to its eventual demise is neither here nor there. [23] It would, however, be safe to say that its total span would be a relatively short one compared to the entire span of human existence which preceded it.

(b) we need to change to a different type of civilisation, so that the transition would be as little traumatic and disruptive as is possible, under the circumstances. A very rapid transition (even if it were possible) is bound to be more painful. Moreover, to change in a context of no choice, where one's options have already been narrowed or destroyed, is less optimal than to change when a range of options still remains. The time to work towards change is, therefore, not later, but now.

CHAPTER FOUR

HUMAN AGENCY AND ITS EXTERNAL
RELATIONS

1. The last two chapters gave an outline of the bio-physical foundation of life, including human life, and tried to answer the question of endurance of human society. But this chapter will try to fill out the other fundamental issue in social philosophy, about how human life is to be conducted within an enduring framework.

The issue about the conduct of human life traditionally in social/moral philosophy is understood to have two aspects: (1) the problem of interpersonal conduct — how one human agent ought to behave to other human agents — the domain of the public; (2) the problem of the agent her/himself — what sort of person ought one to be? — the domain of the private.

A third aspect which this study is equally interested in is often, if not universally, ignored — (3) the exchange between the human agents and their material environment. The approach of this study is to argue that the three aspects are interrelated (the ecological non-linear model of relationship referred to in Chapter One), that they can and do affect one another, and in turn they affect the question of endurance itself. Nevertheless, it will also argue that a proper understanding of (3) will cast light on (1) and (2) above, and enable us to arrive at a conception of interpersonal conduct, and of the self and how it ought to develop, which can be said not to be arbitrary but rationally justifiable.

This chapter then, based on the arguments of the last two, explores further two of the three aspects mentioned above, namely, (1) and (3) which together constitute the domain of external relations for human agency. Aspect (2) will be developed in Chapter Seven.

To do this, one needs first of all to give an account of what it is to be a human agent in order eventually to show how such human agents in their activities relate to the world of Nature, which is bounded by ecological scarcity, and whose boundaries of possibilities are governed by the laws of thermodynamics and the principles of ecology. This involves advancing a definition or account of human agency which cannot be said to be a purely verbal definition, or to be arbitrary and whimsical.

For this, one requires a real definition, as opposed to a linguistic, lexicographical or persuasive definition, which are all ultimately verbal. Verbal definitions can be dismissed or ignored. It is open to anyone or group of language users to give an alternative rival verbal definition. A dominant contemporary view of philosophy says that definitions are all verbal and, therefore, are no more than linguistic fiats. This is but a version of the Humpty Dumpty account of meaning — words can be made to mean what the user wants them to mean.

On this interpretation, to take an extreme instance, the term 'human agent' could, if one so wishes, be defined to mean an entity without a body. Thus defined, one could go on to construct a social philosophy which does not have to take into account the laws of thermodynamics, as such 'human agents' could presumably 'act' without incurring entropic costs. But such a social philosophy is what I call a fantastic theory, a theory which has no application to the world you and I occupy; as a result, it cannot solve the problems which face us and, therefore, can be (rationally) ignored.

But how are real definitions generated? They are generated by reference to the check of facts and the check of empirical/scientific assumptions and claims.

(See Chapter One.) So I propose the following real definition of human agency which I maintain is in accordance with commonly accepted facts and empirical, scientific assumptions and claims. An entity X counts as a human agent if and only if:

(i) X has desires, inclinations, emotions, such as, X wants to sleep, to cry;

(ii) X consciously entertains thoughts, purposes, goals — these are generally expressed as, X wishes s/he could be warm, X would be happy if s/he could lose a few stones in weight through exercise or dieting;

(iii) X has (some) knowledge of the causal sequences that obtain in the natural world (and indeed in the social world), and can foresee (to some extent) the impact of her/his behaviour upon the existing causal scene;

(iv) X has capacities, for instance, for feeling pain, for acquiring skills and information;

(v) based on (i), (ii), (iii) and (iv) above, X formulates intentions, plans, both long-term and short-term — for instance, X resolves to teach her/himself Italian so that s/he could read its literature in the original, X intends to buy a new coat this winter as the existing one is too tatty;

(vi) X has the power of choice — X can choose to spend a free Wednesday afternoon going for a walk in the country or playing tennis at the club;

(vii) X wants to execute her/his intentions into action;

(viii) X suffers frustration if intentions cannot be translated into action.

(For those philosophers who find the notion of a real definition obscure or unacceptable, the point I wish to make can be made in a slightly different way. I could perhaps simply offer the eight propositions above as statements, which are true and which enter into my account of human agency. Of course, there are other statements which are also true but which I have not bothered to mention, such as 'X has two legs (arms)', 'X has a brain of a certain size and complexity', etc. But although not directly mentioned, one could say that they are presupposed by my account of human agency and, therefore, not incompatible with it. For instance, 'X has a brain of a certain size and complexity' is presupposed by sub-theses (ii), (iv), (vii) and (viii). My aim here is not to give an exhaustive list of such true propositions, but to select the most salient of them for the purpose of constructing a social philosophy, which recognises the existence of absolute or ecological scarcity.)

I can immediately think of two objections to some of the eight propositions above. With regard to (ii), some Freudians, for instance, maintain that not all thought is conscious. As a more complete account of human agency, I can add that qualification without undermining my enterprise. I would, however, wish to object to the more extreme thesis that all thoughts are unconscious, in the sense that they are all rational-isations. There are well-known philosophical dif-ficulties with this theory which I do not need to rehearse here.

With regard to (vi), some philosophers have argued that there is no freedom of the will. It is a mere illusion that we do. I do not wish to explore here the metaphysical issues involved in free will. For my pur-pose, I need only emphasise, from the phenomenologi-cal point of view, that we enjoy freedom of the will is real enough. Moreover, not only do we all believe in it as a matter of fact, but we necessarily do, whenever we act, that we have the capacity for choice. In other words, human agency, which involves action, and, therefore, choice between actions, is unintelligible unless free will is assumed.

There are, of course, other implications which flow from the definition offered above which I do not in-tend to pursue in this study, for example, do foetuses count as human agents? etc. — themes more appro-priately raised in a study on medical ethics.

Let me enter a caveat here. The account of human agency given here for the moment is what may be called a static account. The dynamic aspect will be explored in Chapter Seven where aspect (2) mentioned earlier will itself be examined.

2. To explore aspects (1) and (3) more thoroughly, one needs to concentrate at this stage of the argument on sub-theses (v), (vi), (vii) and (viii), which enter into the real definition of human agency. What these sub-theses amount to saying is that human agents must act. As it stands, this is an innocuous assertion, which no one might wish to dispute. Yet not enough attention has been paid in social philosophy to the consequences which flow from this fundamental axiom, truism though it be.

One must then urgently raise the questions, 'What is it to act?' and 'what is required in order to complete an action successfully, that is, to execute intention into action?'

Unfortunately, from the entropic point of view, there are no actions which do not require low entropic energy and matter for their successful execution. (Hillel Steiner uses the term 'material components of action'. [1]) Even acts of day-dreaming are no exception. The act of eating requires food or nourishing substances. The act of writing requires a quill, pen, ink, a typewriter, a word processor, and so on. Even the act of standing still requires the availability of a bit of space.

In other words, whether it be a very simple, elementary action which contributes to the bare survival of the agent, or very elaborate actions which agents engage in to secure other goals, bare survival apart, actions are necessarily expressed through a material medium. Some of these actions are performed with parts of our own bodies, such as our voice box, our arms and legs. These organs we are born with are sometimes called endosomatic instruments, without which we cannot accomplish certain sorts of acts. Let us call this class of actions endosomatic actions.

But endosomatic actions cannot be regarded as an exception to the rule that all actions require low entropic energy and matter. First they presuppose an entity which is alive. To be alive, one must be sustained by nourishment, protection from the weather, etc. Second, they require, at the very least, availability of space, which is itself absolutely scarce and is subject to a variety of competing demands. Third, like the act of plucking with bare hands a ripe nut from a tree, it means the availability of a certain type of low entropic matter, such as edible nuts.

Most human actions, however, depend on tools or exosomatic instruments. Let us call this class of actions exosomatic actions. Human agents, more than any other animal, devise tools and implements to capture and transform low entropic energy and matter, to serve ends and to execute intentions they have formulated into action. The history of human civilisation is the history of such transformations. From this perspective, there is no pre-history. Pre-history, perhaps, is just a misnomer for that very long period of human existence, before human agents had developed written languages and a class of scribes to write down their story, or to that also very long period of existence when human agents were hunters and gatherers, and had no need yet to resort to a sedentary mode of existence based on cultivation.

Exosomatic actions, unlike endosomatic actions, make even greater claims upon low entropic energy and matter. First, these enter into the making of the tools themselves. Second, the tools are then used to transform other sources of low entropic energy and matter in order to execute certain goals and intentions into action. The last two chapters have already established that these two stages also themselves produce an increase of entropy; the amount depends on the kind of tools being fashioned, and the purpose to which these implements are in turn made to serve.

For the purpose of illustrating aspect (3), one can draw the following diagram:

tools (technology)	to perform actions
produced through use of low entropic energy/ matter	using up in the process low entropic matter
↓	↓
emission of high entropy	emission of high entropy

114

ox/plough (tools)	to plant wheat
plough requires wood ox requires grass	plants require topsoil, water, nutrients, sun's heat and light
↓	↓
decay of plough cow dung, eventual death of cow	gases produced in photosynthesis

tractor (tool)	to plant wheat
metals, fuel to make make steel, fuel to convert steel to tractor	specially genetically engineered strains; soil enriched by chemical fertilisers; pesticides and herbicides for proper growth; plenty of water, sun's heat and light
↓	↓
heat, other chemical waste, eventual decay of tractor	gases produced in photosynthesis, unabsorbed nutrients which pollute rivers, etc.

This exchange between exosomatic actions and Nature has consequences which need explicit commentary straightaway. When we, present human agents, pre-empt through the use and consumption of low entropic energy and matter, and, thereby, increase entropy in the universe:
(1) we are competing with other agents, plants and animals, for access often to the same resources — an obvious example is when we drain a swamp in order to cultivate cereals for our food, we destroy the habitat and, therefore, the lives of its numerous organisms. Such destruction may in turn have repercussions elsewhere, which may be detrimental to the well-being of some other species as well as to our

own;

(2) the increase of entropy may turn out to disrupt or destroy other forms of life not, perhaps, in the immediate vicinity of our action but elsewhere and some time later. Economists call these 'externalities'. The use of DDT and detergents come readily to mind as examples; [2]

(3) through overloading the biosphere and the ecosystems with waste, this could well rebound on the human agents themselves and their potential actions. In Chapter One, we have seen how the depletion of the ozone in the atmosphere could have undesirable consequences for us. If we produce carcinogenic substances which neither we nor Nature have a way of rendering safe, then sooner or later, we might die increasingly of cancer or, in some cases, even suffer genetic mutations of a harmful sort.

The above analysis of exosomatic action and its impact on the environment bears out the inappropriateness of the linear model of causation and affirms the appropriateness of the loopish or ecological model discussed in Chapter Two.

3. The above discussion also brings out that a non-linear, ecological model of causation has a very significant implication for morality. Social philosophies can usually be divided into those which proclaim that human agents are essentially selfish or egoistic, and those which proclaim the opposite, that human agents are essentially altruistic (and perhaps that their selfishness is a form of corruption). But if it turns out to be true, that our actions interact with our environment in the intricate manner illustrated above, then the usual dichotomy made between egoism and altruism becomes less sharp. If we do not respect life and its multifarious manifestations, and be very sensitive about them (suppose such an intrinsic respect may be said to be a form of altruism or lead to altruistic behaviour towards them), then sooner or later, the lack of altruism could injure ourselves, the human species — sometimes the very agents who initiate the selfish

actions, but usually those who live after them or elsewhere. To pursue a lifestyle which is compatible with
ecological requirements involves a lifestyle, which is at
once selfish and altruistic. [3]

For most of human existence, the two have been
intimately linked. So-called 'primitive' peoples have a
deep respect for Nature, its various processes and its
multifarious forms of life. But they also, of course,
killed some of these forms of life in order to live.
However, they usually did not kill in such a way as
to destroy them needlessly. In the kind of balanced
lifestyle that they lived, one could say that they behaved, at once, both altruistically and selfishly.

In their relationship to one another, as human
agents, they displayed a similar balance. For instance,
in hunter/gatherer societies (before the emergence of
'the big man' as distributor), anthropological evidence
tells us that this was so. When a group of hunters
made a kill, the booty was shared equally amongst all
members. On the surface, it may strike us moderns as
pure altruism, but this is not entirely so. The policy
of equal distribution ensures a steady supply of protein. If there were no sharing out, those unsuccessful
in a hunt might have to go without for a long time.
It might also prompt people to overhunt. Overhunting
could in turn lead to ecological instability and disruption. We can represent the *raison d'être* of their
practice as follows:

ensures no overhunting; prevents ecological disruption which in turn secures i. survival of the individual — selfishness; ii. survival of the community — altruism	shares for all not only for the suc-cessful — altruism steady and constant supply of protein in the future for the now successful hunter — selfishness

Their implicit understanding of the intricate
interdependence between human actions and their
environment does not permit what we now see as an

unbridgeable (or near unbridgeable) gap, between selfishness and altruism, between the self and others. It is not appropriate, given this complex causal nexus, to draw such dichotomies.

Contemporary civilisation gives us the illusion, as we saw in the last chapter, that our actions are independent (or at least increasingly so) of Nature, because of the very powerful exosomatic tools (technologies) we have developed and fashioned. At the same time, the introduction of the institution of money, not simply as a medium of exchange, but as an ontological substitute for low entropic energy and matter (see Chapter Six for further discussion on the theme of the accumulation of money as capital, which takes the place of the direct accumulation of natural resources), reinforces the illusion that a single individual could achieve survival, and flourish, not only independently of Nature, but also of other human beings. As a result, the selfish/altruistic aspects of human behaviour become sharply dichtomised, with a resultant emphasis on the selfish dimension, at the expense of the altruistic one, in contemporary civilisation. This has become so entrenched in modern thinking that theorists proclaim that human beings are essentially selfish, and other such certainties.

But as we have seen, our type of civilisation will probably occupy a very small stretch of the entire history of human existence. It has so far lasted at most four hundred years and will probably last as long again (the precise span is not important and relevant). Such a civilisation, based on the exploitation of non-renewable resources by means of EST, does not bode well for the endurance of human society as such. One must, therefore, change gear, so to speak, and return to a mode of existence which recognises the intricate interdependence between human agents and their environment. (I am not suggesting, of course, that we return to a hunter/gatherer lifestyle; that is not possible, anyway, given that the earth today is not what it was in the days which supported such a mode of existence.) This interdependence once restored, the sharp dichotomy between selfish and altruistic behaviour, between the self and others, will also become muted. The social arrangement, we would adopt, would be such that our policies are at once selfish and altruistic, and the conception of well-being for the self will also be a conception, which includes inextricably the well-being of others, both human and non-human.

Under the impulse of selfishness and individualism, our society encourages human agents to consider the morality of their actions from the perspective of what the costs and benefits are to the individual, here and now, without considering the costs and benefits to other agents, both human and non-human, not merely here and now, but elsewhere and in the future. (John Maynard Keynes once said that in the long run we are all dead — if he meant by this the death of the individual, then the time span to be reckoned with is no more than the average life of a human agent. But if so, then Keynes could not be serious about the problem of endurance.) This raises the problem of the free rider and the tragedy of the common. I maintain that these are really two aspects of the same problem, and illustrate very clearly, indeed, what happens when we overlook the intricate connectedness between the consequences of how an agent acts and their implications for other agents, human and non-human, that is, the relationship between aspects (1) and (3), what I have called the domain of external relations of human agency.

Let us first look at what Garett Hardin has called the problem of the tragedy of the common. [4] His example is of a group of herdsmen rearing cattle in a pasture open to all.

As a rational (in the sense of maximising his own benefits while minimising his own costs) being, each herdsman seeks to maximise his gain. Explicitly or implicitly, more or less consciously, he asks, 'What is the utility *to me* of adding one more animal to my herd?' This utility has one negative and one positive component. 1. The positive component is a function of the increment of one animal. Since the herdsman receives all the proceeds from the sale of the additional animal, the positive utility is nearly +1. 2. The negative component is a function of the additional overgrazing created by one more animal. Since, however, the effects of overgrazing are shared by all the herdsmen, the negative utility for any particular decision-making herdsman is only a fraction of -1. Adding together the component partial utilities, the rational herdsman concludes that the only sensible course for him to pursue is to add another animal to his herd. And another. . . . But this is the conclusion reached by each and every rational herdsman sharing a commons [sic]. Therein is the tragedy. Each man is locked into a system that compels him to increase his herd without limit — in a world that is limited. Ruin is the destination toward which all men rush, each pursuing his own best interest in a society that believes in the freedom of the commons. Freedom in a commons brings ruin to all. [5]

One can readily think of other examples to illustrate the same point — overfished fisheries around the seas of the world, the hunting to extinction of the bison in America, and so on.

Notice here that Hardin, in common with most contemporary theorists, defines 'rationality' in terms of egoism. It is simply assumed to be axiomatically true, that to be rational, is to act to further one's immediate self-interest. But as I have tried to argue in Chapter One, this axiomatic assumption is unwarranted. Even within the confines of egoism, it is not obvious why it offends rationality to equate it with a conception of enlightened self-interest; and certainly, there is nothing *prima facie* objectionable to equating rational conduct with conduct, which includes altruistic considerations.

The free rider is a person who behaves typically in the following way: imagine four of you wishing to go to London. One of you had or could borrow a car which, however, was none too reliable. The chances of it breaking down *en route* and, hence, of having to push it to get the engine going again were pretty high. Suppose, nevertheless, all four still thought it worth your while to risk that. Further suppose that the car did break down. It then occurred to one of you, who knew more about matters of mechanics than the others, that if two people were to push as hard as they could (the third controlling it at the wheel), the engine would restart. The fourth then could simply pretend to push. Utility would thus be maximised because the objective of reviving the engine would have been achieved, but minus the disutility involved, through the absention on the part of the fourth person, plus the further utility accruing to the abstainer of arriving in London, unsweaty, looking fresh and crisp. The abstainer is the free rider.

Very briefly, one can define the free rider as someone who consumes the good produced without contributing to it, in the absence of any morally relevant difference between her/himself and the producers, except in respect of her/his desire to consume without any effort of production. In other words, the free rider is what is normally called a moral parasite.

Many moral philosophers today hold that the notion 'morally relevant difference' has no content other than what the agent chooses to count as a morally relevant difference. If so, one could not condemn the free rider, since s/he is simply fastening on her/his unwillingness to contribute, while being eager to consume the good produced by others, as constituting a 'morally relevant difference' between her/himself and others. But is this account correct? I maintain not, and that the notion itself is not based on individual whim or arbitrariness, but on another notion, which could be said to be capable of objective determination. That notion is causal relevance. What counts as a morally relevant difference must satisfy causal relevance.

To illustrate this, let us go back to the car pushing example. Suppose it only takes two people to restart the engine, with a third controlling the car at the wheel. Also suppose the fourth redundant person turns out to be someone who is very weak, having just recovered from a major illness. The weakened condition would constitute a difference which is causally relevant to the outcome, as her/his contribution at best would be a marginal one, quite apart from the deleterious effect to that person's health which may arise from the exertion.

To labour an obvious point, what counts as causally relevant to the outcome depends on the activity concerned. Imagine that a hole has to be dug, for some reason like collecting water for cattle. One member of the group has a broken arm. The broken arm is of causal relevance as someone with only one good arm, given the spade as an instrument, could not dig at all or not efficiently even if s/he were to try. But if the good to be achieved were the control of flood waters by turning on and off certain switches, then a broken arm cannot be said to be causally relevant — one can manipulate switches with one hand only. So strictly speaking, what counts as causally relevant depends, not only on the nature of the activity and the type of good to be achieved, but also on the technology, the tools involved.

Abstention from contribution is morally permissible if a causally relevant difference obtains; and the abstainer, then, is not a moral parasite or a free rider. However, the desire simply to be a free rider cannot be said to be a causally relevant difference. The free rider is, therefore, a moral parasite.

In the examples I have cited so far, I have only imagined one member of a group to be tempted to a free ride. But in a society where everyone is potentially a free rider, as it must be assumed under the impulse of selfishness and extreme individualism, the moral parasites bring about the tragedy of the common. But to see the link more clearly, one has to look at the so-called logic of collective action under universal egoism.

4. Mancur Olson [6] has drawn our attention to it in his influential book. Put very briefly and in outline, his thesis can be interpreted to say that the tragedy of the common is bound to occur in large groups

(whose members are rational egoists), though not in small groups. He defines a small group as consisting of no more than the size of a committee, the average size of a committee being probably six or seven persons.

To see why this is so, one has first all to introduce the notion of a 'collective good' or a 'common good'. (In the literature inspired by rational egoism, the latter term is not normally used, but as far as I am concerned, they amount to the same thing.) For good measure, I will also introduce the notion of a 'collective bad' and I will often equate the avoidance or the elimination of a collective bad as the attainment of a (corresponding) collective good.

A collective good [7] is distinguished from a so-called individual good in the following ways:

a. an individual good, like knowing how to read and write, or a piece of steak, is appropriated, used or consumed by the individual. (If you choose a pair of shoes as an example, of course, more than one individual can use it, but by its nature not very many, and not more than one at a time, if you assume that the shoes have to be worn during waking hours, and people go to sleep more or less at the same time.) A collective good, it is said, if it were available to one, by its very nature, is available to all. Clean air, public hygiene, safety and health, law and order, external defence are sometimes cited as examples;

b. an individual good can be causally produced or achieved by the effort of a single individual. It is conceivable that an individual could raise a cow, which is then slaughtered to provide the piece of steak. More commonly, it is assumed that the money cost of a piece of steak is within the capacity of an individual to earn by working, whether it be for an hour, a week or a month. A collective good, however, is such that its production from the causal point of view can only be brought about by the contribution, if not of everybody in the (big) group, but of a very large majority of it. (For the sake of the argument, let us suppose it requires 90 percent contribution or cooperation.) In the example of public hygiene, an immunisation programme does not require every child to be immunised, say, against whooping cough to be successful, but a large majority of them has to be;

c. moreover, in the case of the collective good, the contribution of each individual is infinitesimally small and imperceptible, so that withdrawal of any single contribution considered in isolation could not be seen or said to undermine its achievement in causal terms. We can illustrate this point by looking at drops of water falling on a rock, eventually creating a hole in it. Any one drop of water on its own could not be said to make a difference to the outcome. Similarly, any single act of crossing a beautifully kept lawn considered in isolation could not be said to create perceptible defacement.

A collective good is, therefore, a good which satisfies (a) that it is in the nature of such a good that it be enjoyed by all in the community, and not confined to one or a few, (b) that it requires the effort of the majority in the community causally to bring it about, (c) that the contribution of each individual to its production is infinitesimally small and imperceptible, when considered on its own in isolation from other acts of contribution. (a), (b) and (c) jointly constitute the necessary and sufficient conditions for the generation of a collective good.

In our society which assumes that everyone, as a rational egoist, is trying ideally to be a free rider, the logic of free riding leads to either (a) failure to attain a collective good, or (b) production of a collective bad, that is, the tragedy of the common. Parasites can only thrive when others at large are not parasites. Logically, everyone cannot be a parasite. Yet in a society motivated by rational egoism, everyone is determined to act as a parasite. Everyone hopes to be able to enjoy the collective good in question (or the avoidance of a collective bad) by relying on the contribution of others, while abstaining oneself. In such a situation the collective good can never come about; instead a corresponding collective bad will ensue. That is why, Olson says, in large groups collective goods will always remain latent (unless other measures are brought to bear on the situation).

In a small group, Olson holds that the following can happen:

(i) the contribution of each is less imperceptible and, therefore, may be more readily identifiable in causal terms. If it literally takes three people pushing the stalled car as hard as each could, with the fourth at the wheel, before the engine would start up again, it would soon be obvious that someone might be cheating. In any case, the car would not budge until the cheater puts her/his shoulder to the grindstone;

(ii) he also implies that the collective good of a small group may not satisfy criterion (b) listed in the logic of collective goods above — that is to say, it is of a type that could be singlehandedly causally brought about by one person. Assuming that the good is of sufficient significance to that individual, s/he could set about procuring it regardless of the others not contributing. In the car example, if what is required to be done to get it moving is to change a punctured tyre, then one person could conceivably do the job, even though it could be done more quickly or with less effort, on the part of the sucker, if the others also helped. But once the car gets going again, the others, who have not helped, could still continue the journey, unless s/he sees fit to rush off without them as a kind of just desert. But this sort of example is not really the same as a collective good, whose nature is such that no one individual or a small group of individuals could on its own produce the good in question. In any case, Olson's qualification about small groups has no relevance to issues in social philosophy, for they are all matters which involve *ex hypothesi* very large groups.

To get results with large groups, it is held that there are two methods — the carrot or the stick. Those who approve of the former accuse those who advocate the latter as 'Stalinists'. The carrot approach stays firmly within the rational egoistic framework. An example to illustrate this: inner city congestion (a collective bad) at peak perods brought about by commuters, usually with one person only at the wheel, driving from the suburbs and dormitory towns into the city centre to work. Each commuter reckons that if s/he were to abandon the car for public transport, such an act in isolation would make no difference to the outcome. And in any case, as a rational egoist, one hopes that others in sufficient numbers would do so, but not oneself. Hence the inevitable collective bad of congestion. Banning cars except for certain essential vehicles, or only permitting those to enter if all seats are occupied, or making cars pay a heavy toll for entry, would be to use the stick or coercion.

One should, instead, tempt drivers to leave their cars behind, by dangling carrots before them so that in their egoistic calculations they would conclude that the benefits to them of using public transport would outweigh the costs of not using their cars. It was in this spirit, that some years ago, the then Manchester Transport Authority ran specially appointed luxury coaches, complete with a bar and bunny girls to serve drinks, in order to seduce business executives living in one of the expensive suburbs to ride in them.

For the sake of the argument, let us suppose that a trade union, through collective bargaining, could be said to produce collective goods for its members, like better safety and health conditions at work, better pension rights and sick leave, etc. Those who advocate a closed shop policy are then said to be advocating the stick or coercion. Instead, the carrot approach tries again to dangle individual goods like price concessions in certain shops, cheaper insurance premiums, holiday packages, etc. should one join. Suppose the annual subscription is £40. If the rational egoist were to do some calculations on the back of an envelope, s/he would realise that if during the year one were to buy a carpet or a freezer at these concessionary prices, one would be saving more than the £40 required for membership. It would then pay such an individual to join the union. There is then no need to use coercion to run a closed shop, provided sufficient goodies are made available to tempt sufficient numbers of people to join. This would still leave room for some people to be free riders. But within the individualistic egoistic framework, there is nothing morally reprehensible about free riding.

However, on the whole, in spite of the general abhorrence of coercion in the achievement of collective goods, theorists of rational egoism and individualism, nevertheless, endorse the use of coercion by the state in order to procure certain collective goods, namely, internal law and order and defence against external enemies. Either such theorists do not believe that sufficiently ingenious and attractive carrots could be devised to get sufficient numbers of the citizenry to volunteer contributions, or they believe that these collective goods are so important that it is justified to use coercion to achieve them; or both of these reasons. If this were so, then it shows that the use of coercion to achieve collective goods is never justified, cannot be held by rational egoists as an absolute truth. Every departure can, and must, be argued for, on its own merits. So, even for the rational egoists, the use of coercion to achieve collective goods like the prevention of ecological degradation and disruption cannot, therefore, be ruled out of court *a priori*.

5. The internal incoherence of rational egoism (as embodied in the free rider problem), with regard to collective goods, may be brought out by considering Kant's Categorical Imperative, at least when it is applied to the category of perfect duty to others.

It may not be easy to see what Kant means by the Categorical Imperative. But an attempt should still be made. Kant's category of perfect duties to others may provide an access to what he is trying to get at. The Categorical Imperative is taken to imply that for any course of action an agent proposes to carry out to count as valid, the universalisation of its maxim must not lead to contradiction. Consider the issue of the morality or otherwise of tax evasion. Citizen A proposes to withhold taxes, on the grounds that s/he could further her/his own interests in that way. The maxim of the action then is: I will do that which would advance my own interests best. According to Kant, citizen A, before carrying out this course of action, should pause and try to universalise the maxim of the action — what would happen if everyone tried to withhold taxes in order to augment and further their own respective interests? The public purse would be empty, and even services like law and order would collapse. In other words, the general interest or the common good would be harmed. Citizen A, no more than citizen B, or citizen Z wants chaos and anarchy. Each wants to enjoy the benefits of law and order provided s/he can be a consumer without being a producer (in the absence of any relevant difference between oneself and others). The agent is, at one and the same time, maintaining: (i) that s/he wants the common or collective good to be sustained, (ii) s/he does not want to contribute to its maintenance. Universalising the maxim of the proposed course of action would make the agent realise that to want (i) and (ii) simultaneously involves inconsistency. The individual can only attain the end embodied in the maxim of her/his action by claiming the privilege alone for her/himself. The maxim cannot be universalised and, at the same time, the end be achieved. The agent could only achieve both (i) and (ii) provided that s/he becomes a free rider. Herein lies the contradiction. [8]

Kant is normally celebrated as a thinker of the Enlightenment as well as of the individualist tradition. But curiously, Kant's Categorical Imperative (at least in the context of perfect duties to others) may be said to have been inspired by a theorist usually considered to be anathema to individualism, namely Rousseau. [9] One knows that Kant was, indeed, greatly influenced by Rousseau. [10] His otherwise spartanly furnished study was reputed to have one decoration hanging over his desk — a portrait of Rousseau. Rousseau's distinctive contribution to social philosophy lies in his notions of the 'common good' and the 'general will', notions much reviled for their metaphysical obscurity, if not rejected as outright nonsense. Yet it is not too strained to interpret Rousseau's insights in terms of the problem raised by the tragedy of the common, [11] of the free rider with regard to the achievement of collective goods or the avoidance of collective bads.

Suppose we equate the common good with the sum of collective goods. And collective goods are to be defined in the way proposed by Olson *apropo* large groups. (However, on the Rousseauesque model, there is no need to postulate, unlike the form implicitly adopted by Hardin or explicitly adopted by Olson, that human agents are necessarily rational egoists. All that one needs postulate is that individual agents could be tempted to act selfishly, not that they ought always to act egoistically. This model presupposes the commonsensical view of human beings that they sometimes act selfishly, sometimes altruistically, that they are capable of acknowledging that they ought not to act egoistically in certain circumstances.) There is then nothing mysterious, or sinister, or metaphysical about the conception of the common good. Rousseau has defined the general will (as opposed to the will of all) as that which is directed to the attainment of the common good. On the revised terminology, this amounts to saying that the general will is that will which is directed to the achievement of collective goods or the elimination of collective bads.

The will of all is merely the sum of individual wills, says Rousseau. Applied to the tragedy of the common, the will of all refers, then, to the resolution (and attendant execution of their respective resolutions) of each herdsman to add one more sheep to their respective flocks. End result of the will of all — degradation of the pasture, such that it can no longer support any sheep at all, or many less than it could before the additions to their herds, that is, ruin for all. The will of all leads inexorably to the production of a collective bad.

The collective good, in this instance, is the continuity of the pasture's capacity to sustain the optimal number of sheep. The collective good requires restraint on the part of a sufficiently large number of herdsmen not to contribute to the undermining or disruption of the carrying capacity of that ecosystem. It could tolerate some free riders from the causal point of view. But as we have seen, when all of them attempt to free ride, under the will of all, this leads inevitably to disaster.

The production of the collective good is Janusfaced. It is at once selfish and altruistic. It benefits the individual contributors as well as those who may not have contributed (like the small number possessing morally relevant differences from the others which it could causally tolerate), and future generations of herdsmen, by acts of restraints. These acts are not, however, merely acts of self sacrifice and, therefore, pure altruism, for by doing so, their own livelihoods may be secured, as well as those of their posterity. Benefiting posterity may in turn assume both selfish and altruistic dimensions, for the welfare of their children and their grandchildren could enter into the conception of happiness of the very individuals who perform the acts of restraint, as I have argued in Chapter One. The pursuit of the collective (common) good enables us morally and conceptually to transcend the sharp dichotomy between promoting the interests of the self and the interests of others. Conversely, the failure to pursue the common good injures both the self and others.

Now we have seen that the production of collective goods usually does not require 100 percent co-operation. From the causal point of view, it can tolerate a minority of non-contributors. We have also seen that within the framework of egoism and individualism, (a) one cannot distinguish between the free rider and other non-contributors, such as the person with a broken arm with regard to digging a hole with a spade, (b) nor are there intellectual resources morally to condemn free riders as parasites. But within the framework advocated by this book, I have argued that it is possible to distinguish genuine non-contributors, who are not moral parasites, from free riders, who are, by relying on the notion of causal relevance. Let us explore further how the free rider may be morally censured and criticised within a framework, which is non-egoistic and non-individualistic.

The free rider may be said to violate the conception of justice as fairness. To behave fairly is (a) to adhere to a rule, which all could assent to and which it would be rational to assent to, the rule here being, in the absence of relevant differences, all consumers must be producers; (b) not to abrogate it by making an exception of oneself to the rule (in the absence of any relevant difference), for the sole purpose of self-aggrandisement at the expense of others. Violating (a) and (b) constitutes unfair and unjust behaviour. Unfair behaviour subverts the moral harmony and consensus amongst the community of agents.

It also at the same time subverts the integrity of the self. To bring out this point, it may be difficult to avoid the so-called dualistic picture of the self, with reason as the nobler side and selfish appetites as the baser component. Reason argues that it is right to consent to the rule of the co-incidence of production and consumption, and that it would be unfair to violate it. But the base appetite of selfishness tempts one to override the dictate of reason. By giving in to the temptation, one becomes a slave to appetite. Reason, however, could show, as we have seen, that there is a contradiction and, hence, irrationality involved in the logic of free riding. If everyone were to have a free ride, the collective good would fail to be brought about — there is, therefore, a contradiction between one's intention to enjoy the collective good and the means proposed to execute that intention into action, for the very means, proposed and acted on by everyone, would subvert the very intention of enjoying the collective good in question.

If one were to push the dualist imagery a little further, one would begin to see what Rouseau might have meant by that notorious phrase 'to force someone to be free'. A slave is not a free person. Historically, some slaves had not wanted to be free. The law of emancipation in that sense 'forced' them to be

free. In an analogous way, the moral rule or law —
do not behave unfairly or one ought not to behave
unfairly — and the criticisms that follow upon its
violation (the moral sanction) force the free rider to
abandon the path, which would lead to the domination
of reason by appetite.

Freedom here means free from being a moral parasite, free to act morally and rationally. The moral
rule, like the legal rule, while guaranteeing freedom
with one hand, also lays down constraints and restraints with the other. (This point about legal freedom will be examined in greater detail in Chapter
Nine.) The legal rule, which guarantees the freedom
of a person of sound mind, over the age of eighteen,
to marry without parental consent, entails that parents
are unfree to interfere with what their grown up offspring propose to do by way of marriage. Analogously, the moral rule, while guaranteeing freedom for the
self to follow the dictates of reason, entails that the
self is unfree to follow the dictates of base appetite.
Unlike the legal sanction which takes the form characteristically of physical coercion, the moral sanction
acts in two ways, (a) *via* the conscience of the individual, and (b) more publicly, *via* the criticisms of
one's community.

Sometimes, the moral sanction may be reinforced by
the legal sanction. We have seen that physical coercion, in ensuring the procurement of collective goods,
cannot be ruled out *a priori*. If the collective good in
question can be shown to be very important and urgent (as important and urgent as law and order and
external defence), if it can be established that a substantial minority, and not merely an insignificant
minority, is tempted to a free ride, then it could be
argued that legal coercion may be justifiably used to
procure compliance. This need not rule out, however,
education in the sense of trying to get would-be free
riders to see and appreciate the moral point of the
rule. A complete internalisation of the rule by all
members of the community would render the legal
coercion unnecessary. This is, of course, what
anarchists mean by a society without the need for

law. But complete internalisation by all members at all times may be unlikely. What is more likely is success with regard to the majority, but insufficient success with regard to a significant minority.

6. The difference in approach to the problem of achieving collective goods, as presented by the free rider's egoism and Rousseau's common good and the general will, can be linked to another issue, namely, the thesis about the accumulation of the unintended consequences of individual acts. Here we can see a theory of individual responsibility being opposed to a theory of collective responsibility with regard to these so-called unintended consequences. (But this section will deal with the first thesis, leaving the second to the next section. Moreover, the former also raises the problem of the threshold effects, an issue I have, however, already dealt with in Chapter Two.)

The thesis about the accumulation of the unintended consequences of human actions could be spelt out as follows: suppose agent A decides to take a short cut through a beautifully kept lawn because he is in a tremendous hurry. Such an act of lawn crossing, taken on its own and in isolation from other acts of such crossing, would produce an infinitesimally small and imperceptible amount of damage to the lawn. But suppose other agents, B to N, without collusion and quite independently of one another, also decide to take a short cut because they, too, are in a hurry. Suppose further that these acts of crossing are suf-ficiently large in numbers and in sufficiently close frequency, such that the grass is not able to regen-erate itself each time damage is produced through these individual acts of crossing. In due course, the lawn will be defaced. The defacement has been bro-ught about by the accumulation of the unintended consequences of individual acts of lawn crossing. If the individual agents were to be interviewed, they would each avow that their intention is simply to take a short cut, and not to deface the lawn. Indeed, they might even be appalled by the defacement.

The accumulation of the unintended consequences of individual acts of lawn crossing has, in this instance, produced a collective bad, that is, the defacement of the lawn. (One could, of course, take the alternative view, that the creation of the path as a short cut is a collective good. This then becomes a case, where the creation of a collective bad could, on some occasion, also involve the creation of a collective good. One would then have to balance the one against the other, the defacement of a beautiful lawn against the utility of the path. But for the purpose of this discussion, I will stick to the simpler case, where the defacement of the lawn as a collective bad will be considered.)

The defacement of the lawn, produced *via* the accumulation of the unintended consequences of individual acts of lawn crossing is a collective bad because it satisfies the criteria earlier described in the characterisation of such a bad. It satisfies (i) that if it is brought about, it affects not one, or some, but all in the community; (ii) that it does not require 100 percent contribution, but say, 90 percent contribution from the causal point of view for its generation; (iii) that a single contribution, on its own and taken in isolation, produces only an infinitesimally small and imperceptible amount of damage. From this discussion so far then, one may legitimately conclude that the thesis about the accumulation of the unintended consequences of individual actions coincide in significant ways with the thesis about the characterisation of collective goods/bads and their causal generation.

The thesis about the accumulation of the unintended consequences of individual acts is usually said to emerge originally from the writings of Adam Smith and other classical economists of the Scottish Enlightenment. Smith's dictum about the 'invisible hand' of the market, creating benefits for all, is often cited. When an individual agent buys a good, s/he hopes to buy as cheaply as possible; when an individual sells a good, s/he hopes to sell it for as much as possible. These acts are motivated by egoism. Yet the overall unintended consequences of these selfish acts lead to a beneficial outcome for one and all — the market, for instance, is said to create more wealth in society from which all can benefit. In other words, what Smith is saying is that a collective good — greater wealth in society from which all benefit — can be produced by everyone (or nearly everyone) acting essentially self-ishly; the collective good is simply the product of the unintended consequences of each of these selfish acts.

This, then, seems to contradict the analysis of the last section which holds that collective bads, rather than collective goods, are the inexorable outcome of egoism. On Olson's analysis, collective goods could never be generated in a society of rational egoists (without resort to coercion or some kind of carrot, if not stick), only collective bads, these having been defined as the absence of corresponding collective goods.

Smith's thesis can be criticised from at least two aspects:

(a) the collective good created by the market may not be a genuine collective good — it is simply not true that the greater wealth created benefits everyone. While no one might wish to dispute that greater wealth in a society is a good, one might, nevertheless, wish to dispute that it is a collective good, as it violates the rule which says that a collective good, if available to one, is available to all. Those in society who cannot be said to benefit are, for instance, those who are made redundant and unemployed through technological innovations, which the market and capitalism require in order to maximise profits, those who, through exposure to dangerous chemicals and other health hazards at work, suffer debilitating diseases and, indeed, even painful death. Moreover, those who benefit do not derive equal portions. A few derive a very large share while the majority gets the remainder. Greater (total) wealth is an aggregate which says nothing about how it is to be distributed. It could be so distributed that, either not everyone in the community benefits, or benefits to the same extent.

Historically, in the earlier phases of capitalist development in the West (as has been alluded to in Chapter One), genocide was practised especially in the

135

north and south American continents, slavery of African peoples occurred in order to provide the necessary labour to develop the American continents, once its indigenous populations had been substantially wiped out by deliberate killing, or through disease as a result of contact with white men. (See Chapter Nine for further discussion of all these points.)

(b) the greater wealth generated has been presented as an absolute good or gain by the simple procedure of not counting certain costs, that is, entropic costs, which are discounted as 'externalities'. But if these costs were to be included, which they must, then the debit or cost column could well outweigh the credit or benefit column. Far from selfish acts of maximising profits leading to a collective good, on this more conscientious analysis, it leads to a collective bad.

Some critics, as a result, propose that it is closer to the truth to say that Smith's invisible hand guiding society under capitalism is really a malevolent 'invisible foot'. Each agent is simply concerned and preoccupied with the problem, 'How can I improve my profits?'. Profits (in money terms) could well be increased in each case by introducing, say, a new technology which has, however, the effect of creating more waste, both physical and psychical. But this waste, at least the physical variety, is then simply dumped into rivers or released into the atmosphere at large. (The psychical waste, in the form of depression, ailment, even suicide is also left unaccounted for in the ledger books.) The will of all, that is, of each entrepreneur acting in the way just outlined, of each consumer conniving at such a way, leads then to environmental degradation through a cumulative process; the collective bad is indeed the accumulation of the unintended consequences of individual acts of profit maximising.

This way of looking at Smith's claim is, then, in accordance with Olson's analysis and its fundamental conclusion, that is, that under rational egoism (in large groups), collective goods would not emerge. The logic of rational egoism is such that even if such goods are perceived to be worth achieving, it could not be produced. On the contrary, the logic of rational egoism compels each agent to act in such a way as, cumulatively and necessarily, to generate collective bads, that is, the absence of corresponding collective goods.

We have also seen, however, that in a framework other than that of rational egoism, collective goods may emerge (without resort to coercion), though not invariably so, under very favourable circumstances. These include successful internalisation by all members of the community of the moral rules of fairness discussed earlier, successful dissemination and assimilation of relevant information by the members (such as, what would happen if nothing is done to curb the emergence of collective bads), and so on. But when conditions are less than favourable, which is often the case in the real world, coercion may be justifiably used to procure collective goods, thus eliminating collective bads. Coercion may be exercised in the form of moral coercion and/or legal coercion. Both may be regarded as forms of collective action, to secure collective goods and to prevent collective bads from emerging. (Anarchists and Marxists have their own respective objections, of course, to the view of legal coercion as a form of collective action to achieve collective goods, but it would be beyond the remit of this exercise to examine them.)

7. As we have seen, within the framework of rational egoism, the individual entrepreneur does not directly and deliberately intend any disastrous ecological outcome. Such outcome is simply the accumulation of the unintended consequences of individual acts of improving profits, of being competitive, trying to avoid bankruptcy, or not being squeezed out of business altogether, etc. An individual entrepreneur would even claim that he has no choice but to reduce the unit cost of his production. (See Chapter Six for further discussion on this point.) But to do so, typically, involves the introduction of a new technology which,

though more 'productive', may also be more polluting. And he would further claim that he cannot afford, without going out of business, to introduce measures to reduce the level of pollution. As each entrepreneur would argue and act in the way just outlined, the accumulation of the unintended consequences of each of these acts of reducing the unit cost of production would lead inexorably to the generation of ecological degradation.

This then presupposes a theory of individual responsibility. The elements underlying such a theory include:

(a) the distinction between deliberately and directly intending X and indirectly or obliquely intending X;

(b) the distinction between what can be foreseen by the individual and what can be foreseen according to the corporate body of knowledge obtaining in society at any one time;

(c) an individual may be held responsible only for an act and its consequences, which s/he foresees and directly intends. (This view seems to assume, too, that an individual has no responsibility not to remain in ignorance, and that those who know, have no responsibility to remove ignorance, by transmitting information and acting on it.)

Such a theory of responsibility seems to be more plausible and adequate in that area of human conduct which is traditionally dealt with by the common law (in this country), such as how to determine responsibility in the law of murder, of assault, etc. A defendant, it could be argued, should be charged with first degree murder, only if (i) s/he deliberately and directly intends to kill another (that is, malice aforethought); (ii) if s/he foresees the death as a practical certainty.

It seems reasonable to exempt someone from responsibility for the crime of first degree murder, if the individual agent in question (a) did not, and could not, foresee that shaking and slapping a very small child violently, especially on the head, could lead to death (because the agent is severely subnormal), (b) did not really mean (deliberately intend) to kill an old

138

lady by yanking hard at a coin metre box in the cellar of the house s/he was burgling, and in so doing, unfortunately, spring a leak in the elderly gas pipes, which eventually caused the death of the neighbour, when the gas seeped into her living room (from the cellar next door), where she was watching television. This would seem to be reasonable, even if the agent could foresee that in such circumstances, it was possible (but the statistical probability is not very high) for such leaks to occur.

But one should not extrapolate from such a limited legal context to cover all cases of responsibility. It seems to be particularly inappropriate to apply to a context of the elimination of collective bads or the generation of collective goods. Collective goods/bads, let us recall, are enjoyed or suffered by one and all; they cannot be causally produced by the effort of a single individual or a small group of individuals; the contribution of each is infinitesimally small and imperceptible. None of these conditions is satisfied by those cases of death or injury dealt with by the common law. Its theory of responsibility implies, instead, that the bad is confined to an identifiable individual or individuals; it is deliberately brought about; it is caused by a single identifiable individual, or in some cases, more than one identifiable individual.

On the theory of individual responsibility extrapolated from the common law of murder, no individual contributing to the production of a collective bad could be held responsible, as (a) such an indiviudal does not deliberately and directly intend the bad outcome; (b) such an individual has not singlehandedly (in causal terms) brought about the bad in question; (c) in some cases an individual could even claim that s/he did not foresee the bad that would be produced by his/her action and other similar acts.

What is needed is, therefore, an alternative theory of responsibility which may be called a collective theory of responsibility. The elements of such a theory would include, first of all, distinguishing between different senses of wanting or desiring X that may be involved, in deliberately intending X and obliquely/indirectly intending X.

To want to do X (and to intend to do X) involves wanting in the sense of striving to do X, the achievement of which will bring fulfilment in accordance with sub-theses (vii) and (viii) referred to, in the real definition of human agency earlier, in this chapter. It is in this sense that frustration would occur if one cannot do what one wants and intends to do — call this want, $desire_0$. An agent, for instance, may $desire_0$ to go ice-skating on a cold frozen afternoon, whereas another agent may $desire_0$, more than any thing else, to read a novel.

An agent who $desires_0$ to see a film or a play may have to queue for half an hour in order to get a ticket. Queuing for half an hour may not be $desired_0$ by the agent, but, indeed, may be looked upon as an inconvenience. But a rational agent who $desires_0$ the end, X, must also desire the means, Y, to achieve the end. Call this means/end sense of desiring, $desire_1$. Imagine an agent who says s/he $desires_0$ A; then having gone through the various means by which A could be attained, s/he decides not to adopt any, and can give no further justification why they are unsatisfactory or objectionable. We will have difficulty in understanding such an agent to be rational. This is because agency requires the execution of intention into action. The agent must choose a means to carry out A; if all the possible means are unacceptable to the agent in some way and the agent cannot, therefore, act to achieve A, then such an agent suffers frustration — sub-thesis (viii) in my real definition of human agency. $Desire_1$ is, therefore, entailed by sub-thesis (vii) of that same definition.

Sometimes, of course, the means may also be $desired_0$ instead of simply being regarded in a neutral fashion, or as an inconvenience to be suffered by the agent. Take an agent who loves trains and to travel in them. Suppose s/he $desires_0$ to get to destination X but the means to get to X, that is, by train, is both $desired_0$ and $desired_1$.

But often, the means available or chosen, has consequences which are themselves not $desired_0$. However, as they are the inevitable consequences, the side effects of the means chosen to achieve the end, then as an extension of the principle, whoever desires$_0$ the end desires$_1$ the means to achieve the end, we can say, whoever desires$_1$ the means desires$_2$ the side effects of the means. These are sometimes said to be indirectly or obliquely intended.

The undesired$_0$ side effects may not be foreseen by the one single individual agent concerned; but it does not necessarily mean that they are unforeseen by others according to the body of knowledge extant in a society. (Of course, what is so far unforeseen, relative to the best available extant knowledge, cannot enter into any theory of human action or responsibility. Moreover, the body of knowledge available is itself not static.)

When applied to the generation of collective bads, the undesired$_0$ side effects of the means chosen to achieve the desired$_0$ end, as we have seen, are imperceptible when confined solely to those produced by a single act in isolation from other similar acts of adopting the same means, that is, desiring$_1$ a certain means Y to obtain a desired$_0$ end, X. A theory of collective responsibility must necessarily therefore:

(i) apply to all who intend to adopt Y (which is desired$_1$) to achieve X;

(ii) extend to the side effects of Y which are undesired$_0$ but desired$_2$;

(iii) as these are foreseeable (corporately);

(iv) as these foreseeable effects work cumulatively;

(v) as these effects affect everyone, it would be unfair for anyone (in the absence of causally and, therefore, morally relevant differences) to exempt her/himself from responsibility;

(vi) as the avoidance of the collective bad (or the generation of the corresponding collective good) is not, and cannot be, causally brought about by the effort of an individual or a small group of individuals, we must act collectively, using both the moral and legal sanctions (and, indeed, even the religious sanction for those who believe in them);

(vii) as responsibility implies the power to choose

141

(sub-thesis (vi) in the real definition of human agency) as well as the Kantian dictum ' "ought" implies "can" ', those responsible for the production of the collective bads ought to choose an alternative course of action (and according to the arguments of this book, there is an alternative to the collective bad of ecological degradation), which would avoid the undesired$_o$ consequences in question.

8. The main conclusion of this chapter may be put as follows:

(a) human agents are entities or beings with purposes and intentions, goals and aims which they want to execute into action;

(b) in executing intentions into actions, especially exosomatic actions, such beings must bear in mind that these require substantial inputs of low entropic energy and matter (which is ecologically scarce), and involve the output of high entropy, which would be produced at such a rate and quantity, that the ecosystems cannot cope with it;

(c) such agents ought, then, to be reminded that in the exchange with Nature and the material environment, they should adopt at least a mode of production, which is in keeping with ecological sustainability;

(d) this is neither a purely selfish act nor a purely altruistic act. It is both at once. In worrying about the livelihood and well-being of other agents, human and non-human, one is worrying about one's own livelihood and well-being. In protecting the livelihood of others, one is simultaneously protecting one's own. In this way, one can transcend the two polarities of morality, selfishness on the one hand and altruism on the other, a confrontational dichotomy mistakenly foisted on modern civilisation;

(e) in our relationship with other human beings, one must behave justly and fairly, for the violation of just and fair rules of behaviour under the impulse of egoism, will inevitably bring about the production of collective bads, of which ecological degradation and bankruptcy is a glaring example. Adherence to rules

of justice and fairness itself is also not wholly
altruistic, as through it, one achieves one's own well-
being as well as the well-being of others, both human
and non-human;

(f) in the real world, the elimination of collective
bads or the achievement of corresponding collective
goods, more often than not, can only be brought about by collective action through moral and legal
coercion;

(g) but collective action presupposes a theory of collective responsibility, not the standard theory of
individual responsibility which underpins the common
law.

In very brief summary: the interdependence between
one part of Nature and other parts, the interrelation
between the actions of individual human agents and
of these and their environment, therefore, can give us
guidance as to how to behave to others, and in this
way, to ensure the endurance of human existence and
society, as well as the endurance of other non-human
agents and non-living processes. (a) to (g) above constitute answers to the questions in social philosophy,
which at the beginning of the chapter, I have said,
make up the domain of the external relations of human agency.

CHAPTER FIVE

RATES OF REPRODUCTION AND CONSUMPTION

1. Human agents, through their actions, both endosomatic and exosomatic, can affect the ecological systems and their sustainability in three main ways, *via* (a) their mode of production, (b) their rate of reproduction, (c) their rate of consumption. But it is important to realise that overloading of the biosphere and ecosystems, depending on the rate with which low entropic energy and matter is used up (with corresponding increase of high entropy), is determined by these three factors as an ensemble, rather than the rate of each, taken separately, and then aggregated.

If the latter were true then the rate of increase in entropy in principle can be controlled by decreasing the rate of either (b) or (c) or altering (a) respectively, or even changing only two out of the three factors. But as we shall see, the matter is not quite so simple. An effective reduction may be brought about only through a change simultaneously of all three.

Controlling population (that is, the rate of (b)), on its own, may not have the desired effect, as the entropic demand per person and, therefore, the total entropic demand of the society, depends very much on (c), the rate of consumptiom, as we shall see. (To rely on population control exclusively could also lead to a position which may be called ecofascism — see Chapter Nine, section 2.) Reducing the rate of consumption on its own, while reproducing at an even higher rate, might again end up by not achieving the target. Retaining the rate of reproduction and the rate

144

of consumption, while lowering the entropic costs involved in the productive processes (that is, changing the mode of production and its technology), may reduce some overload, although it remains doubtful as a claim. Reducing the rate of consumption (in the first world), while holding the rate of reproduction constant, may also have some effect.

Different types of economy may, however, require different combinations of these strategies in order to achieve the greatest reduction in their demands on the ecosystems in the world. For instance, first world economies could achieve it most effectively by altering (a) and (c) in particular, while holding (b) more or less constant; third and fourth world economies by altering (b) (even while increasing (c) as some of these countries display a level of poverty which fails to meet genuine human needs — see Chapters Nine and Ten). But the maximum effect, world-wide, and in the long run, would only be achieved by holding constant the rate of (b) and of (c), once the latter has either been reduced in the case of the first world economies to a level that can be said to meet genuine human needs, or raised to reach such a level in the case of the third and fourth world economies, and by changing from EST to EST under (a) in the case of first world economies, and not being seduced to adopt EST in the third and fourth world economies.

So far I have touched on (a) but aspects of it will be further explored in Chapter Six. I have also raised *en passant* (b) in Chapter Three. In this chapter, I would like to look at this further and also to consider some aspects of (c) — its other aspects will be examined in Chapters Six and Seven.

2. In human history, apart from slaves who do not own their own bodies, the rate of reproduction has been very much a by-product of the sexual impulses of individuals. This, however, does not mean that human agents through the ages, have made no attempt to control their population growth, or to practise customs which have the effect of doing so. An in-

stance of the latter is the practice of not weaning children, of even up to five or older, in some cultures. Abortion and infanticide, usually of girls (this sex discrimination may itself rest on the knowledge that the rate of reproduction depends more on the number of women reaching the age of fertility than on the number of men reaching such an age), as well as contraceptive devices of various kinds have been used to bring down population. This is an acknowledgement that population, if left unchecked, could wreak havoc on the supply of food and other resources.

If what Malthus says is correct, that while human beings are capable of reproducing at a geometric rate, resources at best increase at an arithmetic rate, then overpopulation is bound to lead to ecological disorders. Whenever new land has been brought under cultivation through new technology or conquest, people have tended to use the extra land to support new mouths, rather than solely to increase the rate of consumption. This could partly be because many of the methods of population control have severe physical and/or psychical costs — abortion in the absence of medical hygiene could be lethal, and infanticide must be a measure of last resort. Others might not have been particularly effective anyway.

Malthus drew the conclusion that disease, famine, death and poverty were pretty endemic to human existence. [1] But the situation might not be as bleak as that. This is not because one disputes the fact of Malthusian or absolute scarcity (there is no running away from the reality that low entropic energy and matter is finite and limited), but because given our better understanding of the exchange between human agents and the material environment, of improved technologies of contraception and abortion, not to mention improved chances of infant survival, we have the means now to limit the rate of reproduction, such that it is consonant with ecological sustainability. However, to say that we have the means, does not imply there are not immense problems in practice to achieve the end.

The world cannot sustain an indefinite exponential rate of growth in the human population, no more than it can sustain an indefinite exponential increase in the rate of consumption, as we shall see. It is said that if present trends continue, the world's population would be as follows:

1	to 2 billion	1850-1925	75 years
2	to 3	1925-1962	37
3	to 4	1962-1975	13
4	to 5	1975-1985	10
5	to 6	1985-1993	8

or

0.75	to 1.6	1750-1900	150
1.60	to 3.3	1900-1965	65
3.3	to 7+/-	1965-2000	35

It has been calculated that 'If replacement is achieved in the developed world by 2000 and in the developing world by 2040, the world's population will stabilise at nearly 15.5 billion (15,500 million) about a century hence, or well over four times the present size.' [2]

It is possible to regard population increase leading to Malthusian conclusions as another instance of a collective bad. The individual couple may well arrive at the calculation, that an additional child to them might lead to more benefit than cost. Their own addition, taken singly, would make no perceptible difference to the outcome of ecological instability. That outcome is, therefore, the accumulation of the unintended consequences of individual acts of additional procreation.

If this account is correct, it, then, indicates that a family planning policy as conventionally conceived is not the same as a population control policy. Indeed, if the former were conscientiously carried out, it could in some cases have effects the very opposite to those of trying to reduce or stabilise the population. It works usually on the simple-minded slogan, 'every child a wanted child', used as a caption underneath a picture of a happy family (usually father, mother, 2 children, a boy and a girl). Every couple who works out that it pays, on a cost/benefit calculation (including psychological costs and benefits), personally to have an additional child, be it the second, third, fourth, etc. and has one, the couple in question no doubt wants and welcomes such a child. Similarly, every couple which decides on personal grounds to have only 1 child (or none at all) also satisfies the slogan, 'every child a wanted child'. But the total effects of these personal decisions added up could mean either an undesirable overall increase in population or decrease in population.

To rely on a family planning policy of the kind described to achieve the desired end of population control is, at best, a hit or miss business, depending for its success on a fortunate and fortuitous conjuncture of factors and circumstances, which does not, however, obtain in all cases of its application.

This, then, in turn, raises the question whether coercion in some circumstances may not be justified to avoid the collective bad. Those who disapprove of coercion tend to argue, analogous to the carrot approach discussed in the last chapter, that the best way to achieve the goal of curbing reproduction is by raising the standard of living of individuals so that in their cost/benefit calculation, bearing another child costs far more than whatever benefits s/he brings to the parents. Raising the standard of education of women in particular, it is held, would make such women, on the whole, less inclined to produce a large number of children, as this would, and could, have the effect of keeping them out of paid outside work and a career. Moreover, to bring up a child till s/he becomes independent, and able to earn a livelihood costs a lot more in a society, where the standard of living is higher. This view is called the 'demographic transition thesis'.

The developed affluent first world has already gone through this stage or is going through it in some cases. Some of the more advanced ones in the league might even be showing a rate less than that required for the reproduction of its existing population, such as in the Scandinavian countries. The crucial issue is, how can it be made to hold in the developing world? How can the standard of living in such countries be improved so that the birth rate would then fall, as a consequence of individual couples calculating, that it would not pay them to have more than one or two children?

The standard answer lies in the 'dribble or trickle down' theory of economic growth. As the industrialised developed world increases its growth (exponentially), the benefits would filter down to those below at the next level of development, and so on.

Unfortunately there appears to be a fatal flaw in this argument. (I will be examining it at greater length in the next chapter.) If there is absolute or Malthusian scarcity of low entropic energy and matter, the faster the rate of growth in the developed world, the less in the end is there for the others. At best, there might be crumbs for some of the others. Those who deny this bleak prospect may deny Malthusian or absolute scarcity, of course. But in Chapter Three, we have already seen that this denial makes no sense in the face of thermodynamic reality.

Moreover, the examples of success usually cited do not appear to support the thesis. Japan did not wait for economic growth to reduce her birth rate automatically and spontaneously, so to speak. Japan deliberately and consciously pursued (and still does) a policy of population control, falling back at one stage, extensively and liberally, on the use of abortion. Even Britain and Western Europe were not a simple case of affluence leading automatically to birth decline. Some historians point out that the increase in wealth over the last 400 years was preceded by a dramatic reduction in population caused by the Black Death — it could be argued that population reduction is conceivably a necessary condition for the improvement to follow.

It is also the case, as actual examples show, where economic growth appears to have arrived in a developing country, yet the hoped for effect does not seem to take place. Brazil from 1964 onwards was one such case. Herman Daly writes:

> But what of the demographic transition thesis that
> fertility falls as income increases? For one thing,
> the real income of the masses hardly seems to be
> rising at all, and for another the thesis itself may
> be just wishful thinking. Rising per-capita income
> may be as much the result of lowered fertility as
> the cause, and the expectation that a process that
> took place over centuries in Europe will be repeat-
> ed in the Third World in a matter of decades in-
> spires skepticism. . . . A lowering of fertility will
> take a long time at best and may never take place
> if governments sit back and wait for some auto-
> matic transition to occur as a by-product of eco-
> nomic growth. . . .It is a fact that illiteracy has
> declined with economic growth, but on the basis of
> that commonplace no one invents a 'literacy tran-
> sition thesis' and counsels Brazil not to waste
> money on MOBRAL because economic growth will
> automatically induce literacy! [3]

The demographic transition thesis may have put the
cart before the horse. A drop in population in a
country already overpopulated may be a prerequisite
for a rise in the level of wealth, rather than a rise in
the level of wealth is a necessary and sufficient condition for a fall in the birth rate. (Incidentally, those
who do not accept that a country, or the world, as a
whole, could be said to be overpopulated, usually cite
as evidence that the amount of food grown and,
therefore, available is sufficient to feed the numbers
that exist, if properly distributed. Now while this
claim may be true, this does not settle the matter, as
human agents need more than the about-to-go rancid
butter stored in the EEC butter mountains, or the
beef, or the grain or the skimmed milk (of late containing an unacceptable level of caesium in it) given
as hand-outs in order to thrive and to flourish. They
also need, to say the least, clean water to drink, a
decent roof over their heads, education, land to till,
tools to till with, etc. etc. In principle, the existing

food available in total in the world today is no doubt sufficient to prevent famine and hunger. But immediate salvation from such ills could hardly be said to rid the world of problems arising from over-population.) This may be so for several reasons:

(a) as noted earlier, a rise in the level of wealth could simply be used up by producing more people, in the absence of any conscious policy of limiting the population. This is the feature referred to about the logic of generating a collective bad — a man and a woman finding that their income has risen might conclude that they could afford to have yet another child. Each couple similarly placed, deliberating and resolving, would lead to the collective bad, that is, of having used up the increase in wealth in society to create a situation, in which everyone would be worse off than even before the increase in the level of wealth;

(b) to talk about an increase in the level of wealth in a soceity is to talk about an aggregate, but it says nothing about how that increase is distributed within that society. Most (real) societies, if not all, are highly unequal societies.

As Daly shows in the Brazilian example, the increase due to economic growth in the north-east region of the Brazilian economy had been shared very unevenly. He writes:

In 1960 the poorest 80 percent of the population received 46 percent of the total national income, while in 1970 they received only 37 percent. Correspondingly, over the same period the share of the richest 20 percent increased from 54 percent to 63 percent, while the richest 1 percent increased its share from about 12 percent to about 18 percent... But is the Brazilian majority getting worse off absolutely as well as relatively? Between 1960 and 1970 the *absolute* income of the lowest 80 percent taken as a whole increased by 8.4 percent, while that of the richest 20 percent increased by 55.4 percent. For the richest 1 percent the increase was 103.2 percent. Within the large category of the

poorest 80 percent, there were no doubt many people (especially in poor areas like the northeast)
whose absolute real incomes did not rise at all, or
actually declined. . . .the falling purchasing power
of the real minimum (actual inflation has been
greater than the anticipated inflation used in calculating the minimum wage adjustments) suggests that
many of the poor are getting worse off absolutely)
[4]

In other words, for the demographic transition
thesis to work, it is not enough to rely solely on
economic growth — a necessary condition might include a distribution of that growth in such a way that
the poorer classes, who are already the more prolific
reproducers, could be said to have their standard of
living raised. But as we shall see (in Chapter Nine),
those who rely on economic growth alone to set the
world right are also those who tend to use it as a
substitute for redistribution *à la* Robin Hood, and use
it, as the Brazilian example shows, to redistribute *à la*
Matthew.

If reduction of population especially in the poorer
parts of the world cannot be achieved through economic growth (even if economic growth were capable of
being achieved for all of them, which is doubtful),
then there is no alternative but to face up to the
possibility of using other instruments for population
control, such as the law.

But before examining this in detail, a more general
point will first be made. Those who do not favour
direct intervention with the rate of reproduction by
society, through its legal system, tend to evoke liberalism to condemn it. To couch it in terminology
now particularly fashionable, they say, it is to violate
the fundamental human right to procreate as the individuals see fit. Procreation presumably is considered as
falling into Mill's category of self-regarding actions
rather than his category of other-regarding actions.
Yet it may surprise those who rely on J. S. Mill as
the founding father of (classical) liberalism, or are inspired by his philosophy, to know that Mill himself

did not see the act of procreation as falling into the self-regarding sphere. Instead, he favoured interference on the grounds that to have as many children as suits oneself is a matter, that clearly has harmful implications for others.

He wrote:

The laws which, in many countries on the Continent, forbid marriage unless the parties can show that they have the means of supporting a family, do not exceed the legitimate powers of the State: and whether such laws be expedient or not (a question mainly dependent on local circumstances and feelings), they are not objectionable as violations of liberty. Such laws are interferences of the State to prohibit a mischievous act — an act injurious to others, which ought to be a subject of reprobation, and social stigma, even when it is not deemed expedient to superadd legal punishment. Yet the current ideas of liberty, which bend so easily to real infringements of the freedom of the individual in things which concern only himself, would repel the attempt to put any restraint upon his inclinations when the consequences of their indulgence is a life or lives of wretchedness and depravity to the offspring, with manifold evils to those sufficiently within reach to be in any way affected by their actions. When we compare the strange respect of mankind for liberty, with their strange want of respect for it, we might imagine that a man had an indispensable right to do harm to others, and no right at all to please himself without giving pain to any one. [5]

Mill cannot be accused of being inconsistent; rather he is consistently applying that famous distinction of his. Mill seemed to show greater awareness of the entropic problems made upon the environment and other agents through excessive fertility, although he did not quite put the point in this way. What Mill's careful examples in detail show, is that the class of self-regarding actions might not be as large as his programmatic enunciation of the two spheres of actions at first sight appears to be. This is, of course, not to say that the class of the self-regarding acts is a null class.

To use the law to control behaviour is, of course, ultimately to use coercion. But it is not often realised that, even within a coercive framework, the law in theory has a choice in the methods it could use to procure compliance. The penal sanction (that is, sending non-compliers to prison) is the ultimate one (and for this reason, the law is basically as well as characteristically coercive). Nevertheless, the penal sanction is only one out of several methods. We are familiar with one such alternative, namely, the use of fine. A less familiar one is the use of reward. Unfortunately, as Bentham has argued, this method is of limited application and, hence, cannot be the characteristic method of the law. [6] An example to illustrate this technique — the legal sovereign instead of threatening those (if caught) who obstruct the course of justice with punishment, could offer a reward to those, who report the whereabouts of a felon. The law too can dangle carrots on occasion if it thinks it wise or effective to do so.

To secure a fall in the birth rate could well be one of these occasions. As a matter of fact, states which have pursued a direct policy of population control have tended to use legal rewards rather than legal punishments. In other words, instead of throwing people into prison should they fail to comply, such states have used inducements and preferential treatment of those who do comply. For instance, the compliers and their child(ren) would be given priority in nursery places, in housing, etc., whereas those, who fail to comply, might have no access to additional subsidised good and services for the child(ren) they have, over and above the number considered desirable. This does mean that the non-compliers are being penalised, although not by way of incarceration. So although there are costs involved, this method is still preferable to one in which non-compliers are straightforwardly thrown into prison with no positive incentives for compliers.

(Incidentally, it seems that people have less qualms about the state using legal inducements to underpin their population control policy, when that policy is concerned to raise the birth rate rather than to decrease it. So-called liberal critics have not been known to raise their voices against states like France, whose generosity towards 'familles nombreuses' is designed to increase the number of 'citoyens', that they are using legal techniques to do so. [7] Of course the followers of Monsieur Le Pen might object, but on the quite different grounds, that such generosity merely encourages non-Gallic, Muslim citizens to be prolific in their procreation, thus producing an increase in the wrong kind of 'citoyens'.)

Similarly, such states, on the whole (the Sanjay Ghandi episode in India being an exception), have not resorted to compulsory sterilisation or abortion. Instead, other agencies and organisations (some sponsored directly by the state and others not) have resorted to counselling, to advice, to putting social pressure to bear on those who do not immediately see and accept the point of population control. While resorting to such methods may be considered to be undesirable to those who wish to see reproduction entirely as a matter of individual right and freedom, nevertheless, it must be borne in mind that the urgency of the goal could be argued to override such breaches, as Mill had done; indeed, Mill had gone one step further, as the quotation shows, that he simply did not think that the question of reproduction is one which falls into the domain of individual freedom. [8] As such, interference by the state and society may be justified.

2. Those who believe that economic growth (usually brought about by the (bourgeois) capitalist market system) is the panacea for all social ills deny, of course, the existence of Malthusian absolute scarcity. But (bourgeois) capitalists are not the only ones who subscribe to the desirability of economic growth without too many questions asked about its eventual viability.

Marx, too, in spite of some awareness of the entropic problems involved in production and consumption, nevertheless, on the whole denied Malthusian scarcity. (Marx's conception of the good society would be looked at, in greater detail, in Chapter Eight.) This then is another instance of ideology triumphing over science and common sense.

It is true that Malthus accepted the bourgeois capitalist system. Marx then inferred that if that system were replaced by another, then poverty would not necessarily result, even if the fertility rate were left uncurbed. Malthus might have run several things together which should have been distinguished. But Marx too (and Marxists) appeared not to have seen that distinctions have to be made.

These are: first, the capitalist relations of production itself, which is really about the legal ownership of the resources of production; second, that mode, when used to generate economic growth in order to promote the maximisation of profits; third, the entropic costs involved, given the absolute scarcity of low entropic energy and matter on the planet earth, in promoting economic growth; fourth, the entropic costs being exacerbated by a technology which is, on the whole, EST.

The third is a fact of nature and exists irrespective of whichever technological mode of production one adopts. But as shown in Chapter Three, the technological mode chosen can hasten or retard the rate of depletion of natural resources and the corresponding rate of producing pollution, and hence, either sustains or undermines the stability of the biosphere and the ecosystems — an EST hastens ecological bankruptcy but an EST avoids it.

Marx deplored the following things: (a) the profit motive which is the driving force behind (bourgeois) capitalism; (b) the endemic inequality between labour and capital in the capitalist relations of production which assign the legal ownership of the factors of production and their ensuing products to the capitalist class; (c) the ensuing unequal distribution of economic growth generated as between capital and labour. But he did not doubt the denial of absolute scarcity; nor did he question economic growth, itself based on the predominantly EST mode of production.

But to deplore and change the inequality endemic in the capitalist relations of production in favour of labour is a matter of redistribution, which on its own (without altering other ends and means, such as the goal of ever increasing growth, and the means of EST so far relied on by industrial civilisation to achieve growth) need not, and does not, alter the rate of depletion of low entropic energy and matter and its corresponding rate of increasing pollution, and most certainly cannot alter the fact that low entropic energy and matter are limited and finite. (See Chapter Six for further discussion.)

If the fertility rate were left unchecked, but there was redistribution in favour of the labouring masses, then poverty would be relieved, it is true, but only in the short term. This is what the People's Republic of China discovered, to her cost, in the early years of the Revolution. [9] Malthus' insight, shorn of its (bourgeois) capitalist dressings, would remain valid. As the fertility rate rises exponentially, the entropic demands, made by uncurbed fertility, would sooner or later (indeed sooner rather than later) take its toll. What is required is more likely to be, at least, a combination of redistribution and population control, a combination of techniques which neither the first nor the second world could afford to ignore.

3. As we have seen, a reduction in the population in absolute terms, while very significant, by itself does not necessarily decrease the demand for low entropic energy and matter. It could even rise if it is accompanied by an increase in the level and rate of consumption. This fact may be brought home by comparing two countries — India and the USA.

By all accounts, India is overpopulated but has a low *per capita* consumption. The USA is not considered to be overpopulated but it has one of the highest per capita consumptions (if not the highest) in the world. If the number of people were multiplied by per capita consumption, then it is not obvious that India as a country is making as great an entropic demand upon the earth's finite store of resources as the USA. Experts have worked out that one American child in his/her lifetime consumes 50 times as much as an Indian child and, hence, makes 50 times as much demand upon the limited supply of low entropic energy amd matter in the world. This *per capita* consumption is sometimes expressed in 'Indian Equivalents'. [10]

Assuming for the sake of the argument that the population of India at the moment is 800 million and that of the USA is 250 million, using Indian Equivalents, one could say there are living in the USA the equivalent of 250 x 50 = 1.25 billion Indians. Looked at from this point of view, it is not obvious that reducing population growth in India is the only urgent issue on the agenda. Reducing the rate and level of consumption in the USA is just as urgent, if not more urgent, as the figures show.

Another statistic which boggles the mind is that the amount of energy used in the summer for air conditioning alone in the US is equivalent to the total annual energy (used for all purposes) in the People's Republic of China, which is said to have a population of at least 1 billion people, or nearly a quarter of the world's population, as compared with the fact that the USA population is a mere 6 percent of the world's total population. The USA is responsible for consuming half of the total use of natural gas and 30 percent of the oil use.

United States energy consumption is equivalent to 400 people working full-time for each member of the population. In other terms, we average 40 horsepower per person at all times. Of course, the use of energy is horrendously inefficient — for example, we use a car capable of 180 horsepower to move one person. This is even more extravagant than the pharaohs of ancient Egypt, since it corresponds to 2800 slaves carrying one individual. [11]

It brings home the fact the USA is a profligate user of energy. It is said that the Scandinavians manage to attain a similar standard of material comfort as the Americans but use less energy in doing so. If this is true, then the Americans are inefficient as well as profligate. The following story told about Nixon when he was in the White House amply illustrates the points. Nixon says he loves an open fire, but the only time he could enjoy one in the White House was in the summer. One's puzzlement is removed when further informed that the White House, like most buildings in that country, is heated to a very high temperature in the winter months, so high that people strip to their shirtsleeves to be comfortable. Conversely, in the summer months, it is cooled to such an extent that a fire is called for. It is no wonder that developing countries can be cynical when urged by first world governments, international organisations (usually dominated by 'experts' from the affluent first world itself) and academics to curb their population, whilst affluent countries are not required to curb either their reproduction or their consumption. Indeed, as we shall see, such affluent countries are urged instead to consume even more, so that poorer nations can benefit from the 'invisible hand' of growth.

But consumption and depletion of energy is only one element; other equally scarce and non-renewable resources are also involved in the increasing rate of consumption of first world economies and, hence, their growth.

The earth is fast running out of almost every major nonrenewable mineral necessary for the maintenance and growth of the highly industrialized economies. Each year the US economy alone uses nearly '40,000 pounds of new mineral supplies per person for our power plants, transportation, schools, machine tools, home, bridges, medical uses and heavy equipment.' America is chiefly responsible for gobbling up the remaining stock of the earth's precious minerals. According to the US Department of the Interior, the US economy produces or imports 27 per cent of the world's bauxite production, 18 percent of the world's nickel. In order for the rest of the world to reach a par with the American standard of living, it would have to consume up to 200 times the present output of many of the earth's nonrenewable minerals (this assumes a doubling of the world population between now and the early part of the twenty first century). While catching up with the US standard of living is the goal of most developing nations, it is obviously a pipe dream [12]

as long as the US and other advanced economies are gobbling up the world's resources in order to fuel their own (exponential) growth.

It is often made out, contrary to the truth, that the only villain in the drama of poverty, disease, famine, underdevelopment is population growth in the underdeveloped world. It is not. But neither should one fall into the other trap that redistribution from rich to poor is all that is required. Redistribution must also be accompanied by the developed economies cutting back on its consumption, reducing its rate. Underdevelopment is the other side of the coin of development. The solution to the problems of the kind of lop-sided world we live in, where underdevelopment in most economies goes hand in hand with so-called spectacular development in some others, is not single but multi-track.

CHAPTER SIX

ECONOMICS AT ODDS WITH ECOLOGICAL SCARCITY

1. It might be handy to look at the relationship between economics and ecological scarcity by, first of all, considering economic thinking in its more familiar form, that is, as (bourgeois) capitalism. From this, one can then proceed to show in what ways economic thinking, in so-called non-capitalist socialist form, may depart from the presuppositions of the former.

The beginnings of bourgeois economic thinking could be found in John Locke, although as a science, it was not formulated till a century or so later by members of the Scottish Enlightenment (at least if we confine it to British thinkers only). From the point of view of the Entropy Law, it could be argued that Locke makes two significant contributions, which are presupposed by standard economic thought. This, however, is not to say that Locke maintains these explicitly, but to say that they can be constructed out of his thoughts, without straining them.

First, Locke assumes that for practical purposes natural resources, that is, low entropic energy and matter, are boundless and unlimited. He could perhaps be forgiven for his optimism, as he lived at a time, when European exploration and colonisation, especially of the New World, was afoot. Admittedly, Europe itself might be old, even exhausted but this was more than compensated for by the 'discovery' of new lands with their seemingly infinite riches. But this optimistic spirit remains undimmed even though today, the riches of these 'new' lands, too, are at the point of near

161

exhaustion. Geographical discoveries are replaced by technological discoveries as the basis of contemporary optimism. Attention, for instance, is turned to Antarctica, where technological innovations of a more and more powerful kind could soon make it yield up its goodies. And when Antarctica is exhausted, there is always space itself to colonise.

Not only does Locke assume that natural resources are limitless, he also assumes that they are more or less of equal grade and quality, so that no matter how much an individual may appropriate for her/his own use, there will always remain more of similar quality for others. He said: 'there was still enough and as good left; and more than the yet unprovided could use.' (The Second Treatise in *Two Treatises on Government*, 1690, par. 33) This would be an admirable principle of distribution if the world were, indeed, boundless in its provision of uniform, low entropic energy and matter. But alas it is not.

Some theorists, today, when they apply Locke's principle are fond of using the example of a well. One should not take so much water from it as to leave others with nothing, or with some, but not as good in quality. This is a particularly unfortunate example as wells run dry, if the replenishment rate is less than the withdrawal rate of their content. Indeed, some wells draw upon a virtually non-renewable supply, such as artesian wells. But even if one dry well could be replaced by drilling another equally well stocked, this still does not mean that those users who have consumed the water of the first well have left as much and as good for those who come after. For drilling itself requires the expenditure of low entropic energy and matter. It could also be that the water in the second well is buried much deeper, or in more tricky geological strata than the first, so that greater entropic costs will be incurred than in drilling the first well itself.

An alternative interpretation of Locke's principle, which is more in keeping with the Entropy Law, is to say that according to it, one should not appropriate so much, and at such a rate, that the resource could not be renewed. This would hold, however, only for renewable stocks. But what about non-renewable resources? On this reconstruction, Locke had nothing to say about the latter. Or could it be that Locke wrongly assumes that all resources are renewable? But anyway, this more ecologically sympathetic interpretation is not available to Locke because of another thesis he also holds.

This may be called the thesis of the ontological substitution of money for low entropic energy and matter, and is, in my opinion, one of the most important elements which enters into the formation of capitalist thought, although it is not usually seen as such.

The examples that Locke relies on, to illustrate his implied principle of distribution mentioned earlier (that is, as much and as good left for others), concerned edible organic things like apples, nuts, etc. These things rot as Locke has pointed out. His paradigm of natural resources is organic matter which eventually rots. As such, it would be very reasonable for an individual to appropriate as much as s/he could consume before the food rots. (He was, of course, speaking in those days when there was no refrigeration, or deep freezing or canning. However, he did seem to have overlooked methods of curing, pickling, and so on, which were in use at the time.) There is hardly any point picking more and more nuts and storing them in vast barns indefinitely. (Of course, Locke could not have anticipated EEC butter and beef mountains, wine lakes, and so forth.) When confined to foodstuffs, the Lockean principle makes sense — the natural process of putrefaction would ensure that there would be, as much and as good left, for others. In such a context, accumulation beyond one's requirements to sustain oneself makes no sense (as even the EEC, in its heart of heart, knows in spite of today's advanced technology for delaying putrefaction).

Locke seems then to realise that food is not a satisfactory kind of capital as it cannot be accumulated indefinitely, since it rots. Ever increasing accumulation must be of something which does not rot, and that constitutes capital. Money, he says, does not rot. Therefore, the introduction of money into society and its economy transforms radically the nature of society and its economy.

Accumulation of this non-putrefying object on the part of the individual can now be limitless and go on for ever, the accumulation process having been emancipated from the workings of Nature. A new principle of distribution appears — accumulate as much as you can and indefinitely, regardless of whether there is much left for others. In any case, money is inexhaustible; so there is no need to worry that others would be left without — all others need to do is to work as hard as oneself to accumulate it. As for the 'as good' bit, money is a uniform thing; so the question does not arise. (Again, Locke had not anticipated that some currencies are more desirable and sought after than others.)

Now money had been in existence in most societies long before the arrival of capitalism in Europe. So it cannot be the mere existence of money that Locke has in mind. What he has done is to give money a new function and a new legitimation, through using it as an ontological substitute for natural resources. Before capitalism, money existed mainly as a medium of exchange. Some societies may support a small merchant class and others a larger one, which indeed regard money and its accumulation as capital. It is only when money is given its other function by theorists like Locke, the function of capital whose essential nature is to be accumulated and maximised (*via* the profit motive), and is allowed to invade most (if not all) forms of human relation, that a society may be said to be a capitalistic one.

In Locke's days, the principal forms of money were gold and silver coins. Now, it is true, gold and silver do not rot in the way that apples and bread rot. But even gold and silver, to be tiresomely pedantic, are subject to entropic degradation through wear and tear. More seriously, gold and silver as low entropic energy and matter are finite and exhaustible. Even the seemingly endless looting of South American gold and silver had to come to an end.

Even in Locke's day, money did not manifest itself solely in solid, tangible bits of metal. There were promissory notes (what we now call cheques) of one kind or another. Promissory notes would be cashed. But that is one more step which lengthens the chain between the real things and resources like flour, eggs, fruit, clothes, shoes, doors, coal, oil, uranium, etc. and the money with which we pay for these things. The introduction of paper money, or what we now call plastic money, or what is rapidly emerging in the financial international markets controlled by an electronic system of communication called 'hot' money, and so on, adds yet more complicated links to an already long chain. So long and complex have the strands of the chain become that one tends to overlook the base, that is, the real things containing low entropic energy and matter, which have been transformed by the process of production for use and consumption, and simply fasten on to this metaphysical entity (now you see it, now you don't) called money, which was introduced originally as a medium of exchange and as a facilitator to create more wealth, that is, real things like food, shelter, etc.

But the means seems to have become the end; the end drops out of sight. Worse, the end — wealth measured in terms of real things like food and shelter — is replaced by a new conception of wealth, that is wealth as money. Wealth is no longer understood as having tasty, nourishing food to eat, a warm house to live and relax in, to be healthy, to live in surroundings which are non-polluted and aesthetically pleasing, etc.

These real things which constitute (dare one say 'real') wealth are, no more and no less, than things which require a supply of low entropic energy and matter. Money has usurped the place of these real things because money has become a substitute for them. But money cannot be a real substitute. [1] To think that it can, and that it is, is to confuse one ontological category with another. Money is not real and does not exist in the same sense as low entropic energy and matter in the form of houses, clothes, trees, fish, wheat, clean air, can be said to be real and exist. These are subject to the laws of thermodynamics and the principles of ecology. They are, therefore, finite and limited, even though it is true that some forms of them are renewable under carefully nurtured circumstances.

But money as such is not subject to the laws of thermodynamics. That is why to run the world on the assumption that capital is essentially money is to try to defy the Entropy Law. Textbooks in economics may piously remind their students that capital is really plants, raw materials like factories, uranium, oil, etc., but the people who really matter, that is, people at the centre of power, who actually run nation states and their economies, hold that speculation on the stock exchange, and other forms of paper, or electronic transactions, are as genuine and valid, indeed, more so, as a form of wealth creation as building houses and sewers.

But such a world would sooner or later come a cropper. We would end up with a society which is very 'wealthy' in money terms (per capita annual income is so many thousand dollars or pounds), but which is poor in terms of a healthy environment to live in (radioactive fallouts, acid rain, poisoned rivers), in terms of the food we ingest (full of hormones, additives, tasteless to boot, but good only to look at with a long shelf life — why? — because in this way paper 'wealth' could be maximised), in terms of the stress people suffer through compulsive eagerness to earn more money.

The so-called affluent first world is already facing such a situation. Money can, of course, be used to protect its owners to some extent from the side effects of 'wealth'. But even they cannot totally escape from radioactive pollution when nuclear power stations go nastily wrong, or from the wear and tear of the human body and psyche endemic in fierce competition for yet more 'wealth'.

So, at the very beginning and core of modern

Western European civilisation is the severance of the economic process from its thermodynamic reality. Locke as a founding father is instrumental, indeed, even pivotal, in causing the severance. Without it, capitalism as we know it today, could not have come about. Locke has given money a new legitimation by incorporating it into the very essence of the capitalist process of accumulation. The restless nature of capital seeking indefinite growth and increase would not, and could not, be compatible with its resting on something that is by its very nature limited and finite. It has to be anchored to something equally capable of infinite and indefinite expansion.

It has taken roughly four hundred years for this fundamental axiom to be worked out to its logical conclusion. In Locke's days and up to the nineteenth century, indeed, even the beginning of this century, money as the ontological substitute for low entropic energy and matter did not manifest itself in quite so blatant a form. Eighteenth and nineteenth centuries entrepreneurs, by and large, built their wealth on things like canals, bridges, railways, clothing material like woollen and later cotton, cars, etc. But in the last half of the twentieth century, entrepreneurs who are the most admired tend to be the asset strippers, those who conjure up dramatic and spectacular improvements in paper profits, like magicians who conjure up rabbits out of thin air. As the creation of this 'wealth' is not subject to thermodynamic reality, it is possible to increase it indefinitely and at any pace whatsoever, the only limit being the ingenuity of the entrpreneur-cum-magician to fool the gullible public who, too, wish to increase their 'wealth' as money.

The physiocrats [2] who (amongst other themes) believed that wealth lay in the land, in agriculture, never formed part of mainstream economic thought, and are regarded by economic historians to be a curiosity and an aberration. They did not hold, like the orthodox economic tradition, that manufacturing and commerce were the way to progress, at least for the France of their time. But obviously, the industrial civilisation, headed then by England, was increasingly leaving agriculture behind as the focus of economic growth.

On the interpretation advanced by this study, Locke's contribution to economic theory is just as important as his contribution to political theory. He is indeed the embodiment of bourgeois thought, an account of which could not be said to be complete without referring to that very important part of it, that is, economic thought. Locke did not ignore it.

2. The early development of the new economics coincided with the rise of modern science in Europe in the seventeenth century. Again, like Locke's contribution, the spirit of that science provided an essential philosophy for that economics, and in so doing, harnessed itself irrevocably to the economic processes of production. And like Locke's contribution, too, as we shall see, it is in the twentieth century that we can see more clearly than ever before, the inextricable link between science and technology on the one hand and the economic processes of production on the other.

Scientific achievements in the seventeenth century were so spectacular that it led people to regard the centuries that had preceded it as benighted, even dark. Darkness consists of being dominated (1) by supernatural entities, like gods and their commands, and (2) by Nature. The human will would only become triumphant by shaking off superstition and by learning how to dominate Nature, instead of Nature dominating us. This, the new science would do, for with it in place, we no longer need to fall back on supernatural entities and their doings to explain how Nature works; and in turn our scientific understanding of how Nature works will also enable us to conquer Nature. So progress or Enlightenment consists of dominating Nature through science. Man becomes the master of his environment. As such, he can make Nature do as his will dictates.

And what does his will dictate? As Locke has told

us, it is the indefinite accumulation of money as capital and as 'wealth'. So science, its understanding and its technology could be used to subdue Nature to create more 'wealth'. The technological industrial civilisation transforms natural resources (that is, low entropic energy and matter provided by Nature) into commodities which can be bought and sold and owned, so that profits might be maximised and money as capital and 'wealth' accumulated.

What we have here as constituting progress and modernity are the congruence of three ideas:

1. the logic of capital whose essence is that of accumulation and maximisation;

2. the logic of industrialism based on science and its technology which is, by and large, ecologically insensitive;

3. the logic of economic thinking based on improving efficiency and productivity.

None of these three ideas is anchored in thermodynamic reality. We have seen that this is so with the logic of capital in the last section. In Chapter Three, we have also seen how it is the case with the logic of industrialism as practised in the last four hundred years, in the sense that the entropic costs of the EST are not taken into account, as long as the EST is being harnessed to the maximisation of profits and the accumulation of capital. So the restless spirit of capital, necessarily seeking more and more profits indefinitely, finds a perfect ally and reflection in a philosophical attitude of dominance and hostility to Nature, generated by the new science and technology. (For further discussion about the notion of the dominance of Nature, see Chapter Eight, section 6.)

In the earlier periods of our industrial civilisation, science and science-led technology played less of an intrinsic role. It was true that industry incorporated and generated many new technologies, but quite often these were craft-based. Indeed, some of the most productive innovations (in the economic sense) were made by people with little or no education, never mind a scientific one. An outstanding example is George Stephenson. In spite of earnest self-improvement at reading and writing after he had made good, Stephenson could not be said to be very good at such literary skills. And he certainly knew no physics and chemistry, a fact considered so astonishing in every way that he could not be credited with having invented what we now call the Davy lamp — the honour was claimed, and claimed acrimoniously, by Davy himself, an eminently well-educated gentleman and a fellow of the Royal Society, who accused Stephenson of being a cheat and a liar. [3] It was only with the theoretical breakthroughs in chemistry in the nineteenth century that the growth and survival of industries became led by, and inextricably propelled by, the growth of science. Today, it is increasingly obvious (except to those who suffer from a near-fatal dose of short-termism) that the continuance and the lifeblood of industrial civilisation depends on breakthroughs in fundamental science and its induced technologies. It is this which inspires, as we saw, the optimistic confidence of those who believe that we have not only conquered Nature as the Enlightenment thought we should, we are also on the verge of emancipating ourselves from Nature, having reached the dizzying heights of being 'less and less dependent' on Nature. However, such optimism is misplaced.

We will now look at 3. One of the most commonly and popularly entertained view about the subject of economics today is that it is the science of studying scarcity, how to allocate scarce resources, and, therefore, how to develop criteria for what counts as an efficient allocation of such scarce resources. (Perhaps Lionel Robbins' influential *An Essay on the Nature and Significance of Economic Science*, 1932, could be said to be one of the sources of this conception.) [4]

At first sight, this may look a promising start as it claims to be concerned with the problems arising out of scarcity. However, the scarcity it appears to have in mind is not so much the kind of scarcity this essay is concerned with, namely, ecological scarcity. We have already seen that orthodox economists deny that there is Malthusian or absolute scarcity. [5] At best, they are talking about Ricardian or relative scarcity.

But for most purposes, when economists grapple with the problem of the allocation of scarce resources, they are really talking about the relative scarcity of money, that is to say, unfortunately, it seems always to be the case that any agent or group of agents, at any one time, has a limited amount to spend, so that if the agent were to spend it on X, Y, Z, then there would be none left to spend on A, B, C which the agent would also like to have. So it is said that there has to be a trade-off — the agent must decide whether s/he wants X, Y, Z really more badly than A, B, C. Furthermore, to help such decision-making, the agent must also work out how many or how much of X s/he would get with that amount, as opposed to how many or much of A could be procured with the same sum, and so on. How much of X or A one could buy, at any one time, with a certain sum of money, economists tells, is dependent on the law of supply and demand. If there are more Xs in demand than supply, the price of Xs will rise and you get fewer Xs for the stated sum. If there are more Xs than there is demand for them, then the price drops and one gets more Xs for the stated sum.

So what is or is not cost effective depends on the price of certain things at any one time. The price of X also depends on the price of the ingredients which go into the making of X, which themselves depend on the law of supply and demand, and so on.

But at no time in this very long chain of price determination do the entropic costs of the production of the Xs, their components and sub-components appear directly in the accounting columns. This is because most of these costs have been deliberately discounted, that is, ignored. Economists, as we know, call them externalities, the cost of which in entropic terms, is not borne by the producer. At best, the law of supply and demand may hint at the thermodynamic reality behind the cost of production — for instance, the decline in supply of A and its corresponding increase of cost may be acknowledged to be caused by ecological exhaustion or imbalance. But for the purpose of determining efficient allocation of scarce resources, that is, of a limited amount of money, at any one time, it is not necessary to probe behind the law of supply and demand to the thermodynamic reality behind it. What is an efficient allocation is, therefore, one which is simply confined to a comparison in money terms. In money terms, today, the price of a unit of energy based on oil is cheaper than the price of a similar unit based on, say, wave power. On this criterion of efficient allocation, one should spend the money on oil and condemn the alternative as inefficient, even though it must be obvious that while the former is non-renewable, the latter is renewable, and that sooner or later, we need alternative renewable forms of energy of which wave power is only one.

The same reasoning obtains behind the current notion of productivity. One technique of production is more productive and, therefore, more efficient than another if one can produce a unit of X for less in money terms. If it turns out that human beings cost a lot to hire, then one way of improving productivity is to use machines, instead of human beings, if the machines could in the end reduce the unit cost of production. In agriculture, immense productivity has arisen through using tractors, combine harvesters which replace human beings, as well as liberal doses of pesticides and herbicides, which are spread not by human beings, but by a helicopter instead. But the fact that this mode of production requires in total a far greater input of low entropic energy and matter and produces a far higher output of entropy than more traditional methods for every ton of wheat produced, say, is not considered to be relevant to the notions of efficiency and productivity.

Such discounting of entropic costs is necessarily misleading. Some call it 'short-termism'; others call it instant gratification. The combination of the three logics, the one reinforcing the other, that is, through synergism (the sum of each acting on its own would not have produced quite so devastating effects as when they act in concert with one another — see Chapter Two for further discussion on this point), have created a situation of entropic degradation and

172

exhaustion which ought to alarm orthodox economists, even if it does not, as a matter of fact, do so.

3. The contemporary obsessive preoccupation with economic growth is entailed by the logic of capital. Its restless nature dictates that new investments must be made, the turnover in volume must be swift and large, people, plants and methods which are no longer considered to be cost effective must be abandoned and scrapped. Above all, its restless nature dictates that an entrepreneur must keep one jump ahead of his competitors in order to survive. All this makes for economic growth. (But there is another aspect to economic growth which is an entailment of capitalism, which will be dealt with in Chapter Nine, namely, capitalism also relies on it as a substitute for redistribution from the rich to the poor.)

By acquiring a swift turnover, by being concerned with volume, it necessarily uses up, at a correspondingly increasing rate, low entropic energy and matter, which in turn, necessarily increases correspondingly the rate of positive entropy in the world. The GNP of a country is expressed in terms of X number of tons of steel produced in a year, Y number of barrels of oil extracted, and so on. A country with X-n tons of steel, Y-n tons of oil production has less economic growth and is, therefore, less wealthy than the first economy. An economy with more economic growth may be more 'wealthy' than another, but it may also mean that that country suffers more ecological degradation than the other. Japan, usually considered to be a modern economic miracle, pays for it in terms of her ecological degradation (not to mention psychic costs — children there are known to commit suicide at an alarming rate because of the pressure put on them to be competitive) — the poisoning by mercury suffered by those who ate the fish caught in Minimata Bay, which received the industrial effluence of the area, is but only one striking example amongst others. [6] Many other countries pay for theirs through, for instance, pollution of rivers like the Rhine, acid rain, and so on.

An increase in the GNP is often taken to constitute economic growth. But the GNP is simply a measure of the monetary transactions involved in the production of goods and services in any one year in an economy. Critics of this measure of economic growth tirelessly point out, time and time again, that it is hardly a satisfactory yardstick of wealth as well-being of the society, for (i) it says nothing about services and goods performed and produced without payment, (ii) entropic costs are ignored, (iii) and if they are taken into account, such as in some anti-pollution measures, these goods and services are in turn considered as part of economic growth (and by implication of well-being), (iv) goods and services are indiscriminately recorded whether these be drugs, arms, prostitution or education. [7] In view of these limitations, it is not right to read into the notion of growth that it is necessarily a good thing, as an indicator of well-being of the society concerned. Yet the notion has come to be uncritically understood in this way, even though it may not have begun life as such under Keynes.

Economic growth is exponential growth. (An economy is considered to be in a bad state if it shows little or no growth for the year.) But even if growth is at a very modest rate of 2 percent per annum, this would still mean that the economy would have doubled itself in 35 years. Without the benefit of indulging in a detailed calculation, it is already blindingly clear that indefinite economic growth for every economy is (physically) impossible, unless once again, one falls back on the unfounded optismistic assumption, even science-fiction assumption, that science and technology would enable us to become eventually independent of Nature and her finitude.

4. If economic growth, as an entailment of the restless spirit of capital, requires swift and large turnover in the production and consumption of goods and services, then it follows that the rate of consumption

will also increase exponentially. This, indeed, is the way in which advanced capitalist economies (in the first world), by and large, operate. In the earlier days of capitalism, growth could take place by way of ac- cumulating capital goods. But as accumulation of capi- tal goods reaches a certain level, growth tends to take place *via* the production of consumption goods. Also in its earlier stages, possession was foremost. But in more mature capitalist economies, while possession is still central, nevertheless, consumption is just as sig- nificant. After all, most people cannot hope to own more than the house they live in and, at best, a few shares here and there, but everyone could be persuad- ed to buy endless pairs of shoes, handbags, clothes, etc. and to change the car every two years or so.

Several methods and institutions have been evolved to stimulate consumption. They include the following:
(1) the use of advertisement whose sole purpose is to lure the onlooker to buy the good regardless of its intrinsic qualities, or whether the buyer would have any need for it, through a whole array of psychologi- cal techniques, such as flattery, sexual fantasies, gla- mour and subliminal appeal;
(2) built-in obsolescence;
(3) the dictates of fashion;
(4) 'keeping up with the Joneses'; [8]
(5) the doctrine of 'the more the better';
(6) the doctrine of infinite insatiable wants;
(7) the doctrine of consumer sovereignty.
I will comment mainly on the last three items, for together they provide the philosophical foundation for the others.

The fifth seems to assume if X is a good thing, then the more Xs there are, the better it necessarily is. If a pair of shoes is a good thing for someone without any, *ipso facto*, a further pair is also a good thing, so that in theory the thousandth pair of shoes you may want, is as good a thing as the one pair you want (indeed 'need' — see Chapter Ten on the distinction between want and need), when you do not have any. (In practice, of course, economists tell us that this does not happen, for given a relatively limited amount of money in one's pocket, individuals have to trade-off the fifth pair of shoes against the tenth new suit for the season, and so on.) One could make a very good case for possessing more than one pair of shoes, of course — a pair of town shoes for the office, a pair of evening shoes for parties, a pair of warm boots for the winter months, a pair of wellingtons for when it rains. But there is a limit to this kind of justification. In terms of use and need, it seems impossible to justify the doctrine of the more the better.

Yet so deeply seated is this view in economic thinking that economists have even used it to define the very concept of efficiency itself. For instance, Okun starts off with an innocuous definition of efficiency as 'efficiency means getting the most out of a given input', and then goes on to say:

> This concept of efficiency implies that more is better, insofar as the 'more' consists of items that people want to buy. . . .I, like other economists, accept people's choices as reasonably rational expressions of what makes them better off. To be sure, by a different set of criteria, it is appropriate to ask skeptically whether people are made better off (and thus whether society really becomes more efficient) through the production of more whiskey, more cigarettes, and more big cars. . . .Are there criteria by which welfare can be appraised that are superior to the observation of choices people make? Without defense and without apology, let me simply state that I will not explore those issues despite their importance. That merely reflects my choices, and I hope they will be accepted as reasonably rational. [9]

But his shorter definition of efficiency does not bear out the longer detailed account. 'The more the better' is just not the only implication. To try to get the most out of a given input is value-neutral as between two possibilities — (a) more of the output is a good thing as understood by Okun, or (b) the less input the better without necessarily implying (a). [10] For the use and need of a particular society, for instance, we can imagine that only one item is required, like a plutonium bomb-making plant. (For the sake of the argument, let us grant that one such bomb is a necessity for preventing wars.) But such a society would still be interested presumably in using methods, which cut down the use of materials in manufacturing the product, that is, to lower the entropic cost of production. But it does not mean that the more bomb-making nuclear plants the society has, the more bombs it makes, the better off the society is. But alas, some societies have, indeed, bought Okun's account of efficiency, thus leading to an indefinite multiplication and proliferation of, not only shoes and handbags, but also nuclear arms.

This doctrine of 'the more the better', again, has come to full flowering only in the twentieth century. In earlier periods, it was not built into economic thinking. Indeed, quite the opposite axiom was invoked, namely, the principle of diminishing marginal utility. There is a cut-off point where more of the same thing is no longer a good thing, but becomes even a bad thing. The first meal that a hungry person eats after a whole day without food is a jolly good thing; if pressed to eat another straightaway, it is less of a jolly good thing; come the third, fourth helping, it becomes a jolly bad thing. As Bentham would say, utility would start to decrease instead of increase. In other words, the more the worse.

It is this which guides one to allocate rationally and efficiently scarce resources including time, which is existentially scarce. Suppose in the Lockean paradise, I have just collected enough food for a very large meal which I then proceed to consume. Having done so, I do not need to spend the rest of the day collecting more food as I would not get any utility out of yet another meal. Instead I can spend the time drawing in my cave. As I have not done any for some time, I will derive a lot of pleasure from it. New economic thinking may scorn this principle of allocation. But without it, it is difficult to see how one can talk of an efficient allocation of scarce resources.

Without it, indeed, one is left with Okun's the more the better. But the more the better would lead us to allocate resources to produce more and more of the same item in question. How could this be considered as an efficient allocation, to produce more and more toothbrushes, more and more cars, more and more computers? A world populated entirely by more and more of these objects would be an insane world.

In actual fact, of course, economists have not really ditched it, much as they profess to have done so in their theoretical pronouncements. When they say that there is a trade-off between 'more of Xs' and 'less of Ys', given the relative scarcity of money, at any one time, faced by an individual agent, an individual, as Okun says, is simply presumed to have made a more or less rational choice when he opts for more Xs and less Ys. But if pressed beyond the mere choice and the presumed assumption of rationality, an individual agent, uncorrupted by current economic theorising, would justify the choice by saying 'I have already 2Ys — two new coats this season. I don't need yet another one for the moment, but I can do nicely with having the walls of the house repointed.' (Suppose for the sake of the argument, one wall, an X, costs the same as Y, a new coat.) To justify the choice, thus, is to rely on the principle of diminishing marginal utility. Another four coats are counter-productive of utility. So the resource is directed to something urgently in need of satisfaction which, therefore, produces far greater utility. But, as we shall see below, this commonsensical way of justifying choices rationally is officially denied, and considered to be conceptually incoherent by contemporary economic, as well as philosophical theorising.

The principle of diminishing marginal utility, apart from providing a criterion of rational allocation, also requires a more equal rather than a less equal distribution of scarce resources. Giving all ten meals, for instance, to one hungry person produces less utility than giving one meal to ten equally hungry persons. [11] This egalitarian implication alarmed Bentham

greatly when he realised it. Although he never formally ditched it, it is true that he introduced numerous
other principles, which had the effect of attenuating
and even overruling it. [12]

Those who came after Bentham had even less use
for it and proceeded to undermine its relevance to the
issue of distribution further by arguing that it is an
incoherent notion. Neo-classical economic thinking
tries to show that (a) the principle at best applies
only to wants, like food, but not to all wants; (b)
intertemporal comparison of utility makes no sense —
the individual at time t_1 whose utility total at that
moment in time stands at n units cannot be compared
with the same individual at time t_2, to determine
whether a further allocation would add, or detract
from the n units of utility; (c) interpersonal comparison of utility also makes no sense — we cannot
say that the person given the third mink coat would
get less pleasure from it, than the person who gets a
woollen coat, when she has none. For all we know,
the mink coat recipient derives infinitely greater
satisfaction or utility than the recipient of the woollen
coat. (This is tied up with the doctrine of consumer
sovereignty which will be looked at soon.) The mink
coat recipient may be a connoiseur of fine objects.
The egalitarian implication of the principle of diminishing marginal utility is, hence, replaced by the
Brahmin principle of allocation. [13]

Theses (a) and (c) above will be looked at in the
comments that follow. So let me examine thesis (b)
here first. If what it says it true, namely, that intertemporal comparison of utility makes no sense, then it
entails the denial of the continuity and identity of the
agent as an individual. An individual agent necessarily
endures over time (a certain portion of it, as human
agents are mortal). It possesses a memory (see Chapter
Seven for further discussion of this criterion as a
criterion of identity), its metabolism takes into account what it has eaten, drunk, absorbed, expelled
over time. To deny continuity and identity of the agent is unintelligible. The denial entails the absurd
view that the individual agent is no more than what

it is, at any moment in time, and that there are as many different individuals as there are successions of such moments in time. This atomistic image is so radically fragmented as to make no sense. Having drawn the reader's attention to it, I shall leave it, however, as to explore it further will take me too far from the purpose of this study.

The axiom of 'the more the better' ties up very neatly with Locke's thesis of ontological substitution. The principle of diminishing marginal utility may be true, as we saw, if one has in mind things like food, drink, clothing, sleep and even sex (except for 'Olympic gold medal' sexual athletes, even sex must pall if done to excess, one presumes, contrary to what contemporary Western culture presupposes.) But food, drink, clothing are real things, that is, they are embodiments of low entropic energy and matter. However, Locke tells us that that is not what we are after — it is the accumulation of money. Excess money does not make us retch in the way excess of food and drink does. As money is not subject to any of the biophysical laws which underwrite human existence, excess of money does not create any disorder or destabilisation. Hence the more the better. This together with the inculcation of the value that satisfaction and pleasure are to be derived, primarily if not solely, from the possession of money and through it, ever increasing consumption, one secures a society geared to economic growth and all that it entails.

Once the principle of diminishing marginal utility has been ditched, this simultaneously opens the door wide to an implication of Locke's axiom of ontological substitution, namely, that we are creatures of infinite insatiable wants. No matter how many of these wants may have been satisfied, there are always others lying ahead crying out to be fulfilled. It follows that there can never be contentment, that enough is enough. This is celebrated as an aspect of Man's Faustian nature and of the Enlightenment project of progress. The restlessness of the human spirit in its search for something which lies always one step beyond the horizon becomes distorted, so that it is the counterpart of the restless nature of capital itself, in its endeavour to accumulate more and more profits indefinitely. One is not satisfied with just one mink coat; one wants another. One is not satisfied with two mink coats, one wants something else, a house with three bedrooms but six bathrooms, perhaps, and so on. Infinite desires and wants, with their entailment of permanent existential dissatisfaction, mesh in with the necessity for endless accumulation, through economic growth, through an ever increasing rate of consumption.

Daly correctly points out [14] that Okun slides from 'the more the better' thesis to the doctrine of consumer sovereignty. This doctrine assumes (a) that the individual is the best judge of her/his interests; (b) interests are identical with wants and preferences; (c) wants and preferences themselves *simpliciter* are rationally chosen; (d) wants and preferences, thus expressed, are a measurement of welfare/happiness.

The four assumptions taken together imply a tautology, namely, that by definition, whatever an individual agent wants/prefers constitutes rational choices, which embody her/his interests, welfare or happiness. It is, therefore, empty of content. Should an individual want to inject heroin, then injecting heroin is the rational thing to do and necessarily is in her/his interests, welfare/happiness.

This tautology is but an entailment of the contemporary thesis in the philosophy of value, that values cannot be rationally justified. They are subjectively, irrationally or non-rationally chosen, albeit sincerely. [15] Sincerely choosing or committing oneself to a value, a course of action, makes that value or course of action morally correct or right. If someone sincerely commits her/himself to injecting heroin (on this philosophical view, sincerity is measured in terms of actually carrying out the action in question), then such a mode of existence must be morally correct. We each then create our own universe of morals; there are as many moral universes as there are individual agents, and each of them is essentially and necessarily right.

Okun's comments in the latter part of the quotation cited earlier reveal this philosophical stance.

The official ditching of the principle of diminishing marginal utility plus this philosophical tenet of value irrationalism or non-rationalism in contemporary liberalism can be said to provide in part, if not *in toto* the ideological foundation for mature capitalism, in the first world, in the last half of the twentieth century. A consumer, who wants a tenth mink coat, wants it as urgently and as badly as a consumer, who wants an ordinary warm coat, because the extant one is too tattered to provide warmth for another winter. A consumer may want junk food or junk television programmes. In every case, the consumer is necessarily correct in her/his judgment that it is the best. So long as consumers vote with their money to buy A, A must be a good thing, regardless of the intrinsic qualities of A or the purpose (or the lack of) to which it may be put. This is what is meant by the doctrine of consumer sovereignty. To question it is to challenge the ideological sanctum of advanced mature twentieth century capitalism. Hence, Okun's refusal to stray into such possibly treacherous depths.

So, to summarise the points raised so far in the foregoing sections. These are:

(1) beyond a certain level of the accumulation of capital goods, the restless nature of capital seeks growth *via* ever increasing rates of consumption;

(2) this is theoretically supported, by drawing out to its logical conclusion Locke's axiom of the ontological substitution of money, which does not obey the Entropy Law for real things which do, by the related doctrines of the infinite insatiability of wants, of 'the more the better', and of consumer sovereignty which, in turn, are supported by the philosophical thesis of value irrationalism or non-rationalism or subjectivism;

(3) science and technology (by and large, ES̲T) by subduing and conquering Nature play an inherently indispensable role in bringing about progress as understood in terms of (1) and (2) above.

5. Now let us turn our attention to the standard alternative economic arrangement available today. This has been (or at least claims itself to have been) much influenced by Marx. It is irrelevant to pursue here the issue, whether states which call themselves socialist or communist are, or are not a true reflection of Marx's thinking. All that one needs do in this more limited context is (a) to see if some of the main themes of Marx are reflected in such economies (without necessarily denying that there may be other equally central themes ignored by them); (b) to explore, of those reflected, whether they have any presuppositions and consequences (which follow from these presuppositions) in common with their rival, so-called bourgeois economic thought.

According to Marx, as we saw in Chapter Five, to be on the way to transcending capitalism, one must alter the capitalist legal relations of production — the means of production must no longer be owned privately by the capitalist class, but taken into public or common ownership. Now state ownership might not be the only form of public ownnership possible of the means of production, but it could be said to be a form. Contemporary socialist economies, by and large, go in for state ownership. A corollary of state ownership is a centrally planned economy. It could be that Marx himself did not have in mind state ownership as either the only form, or the only desirable form of public or common ownership. But if so, it appears that he never made that explicit, or explicit enough, for those who claimed to have been influenced by him to realise that state ownership is not alone compatible (or indeed it could even be incompatible) with his conception of socialism/communism.

Whilst Marx was entirely against the capitalist legal relations of production, which embody an unequal relationship between labour and capital, he was full of admiration for the energetic explosiveness of capitalism to produce goods. The perversion of capitalism (and hence also its inner contradictions) lies precisely in its ability to expand its productive capacities, but in its inability to ensure that they will be produced to meet human needs, instead of maximising profits. The way forward, then, is to try to create a type of social arrangement, which can capture the productive capacities typical of capitalism, but without embracing its perversion. Public ownership of the means of production is, then, the means by which this end may be achieved, that is, to ensure that ever increasing productive capacities are devoted to meeting genuine human needs, not to serve the goal of profit maximisation.

Marx was as much an heir of the Enlightenment as the thinkers he castigated. He too accepted that progress consisted of abolishing superstition through a scientific understanding of the universe which, in turn, would also enable us to control and dominate Nature, making Nature serve human ends and purposes. However, Marx did qualify the latter by occasionally reminding us (especially in his earlier works), that human activity (labour) could not entirely abolish or transcend Nature itself. [16] But Nature is, nevertheless, made subordinate to the human will and its purposes by transforming her. And the transformation is done by means of science and its EST.

Again, one could point out that Marx was well aware of the drawbacks of technology and its dehumanising effects. He drew attention to alienation caused by reliance on machines. Machines would come to dominate us instead of serving our ends. His genuine worry, however, seemed confined to the threat posed by technology to us, human wills, and not so much with the threat it poses to Nature and through Nature, ourselves and other beings. His concern could be said to be homocentric, rather than a wider preoccupation about the exchange between human agents and Nature, with all that it entails in entropic terms. He, therefore, appeared to have embraced the technology of his day (indeed he could even be credited with having anticipated computer technology) which, of course, was and is predominantly EST.

Now, one may be tempted to defend Marx by saying that he could not be expected to know what we now can see (except in the case of those who do not wish to) so clearly, the ecological degradation around us. This might provide some mitigation. Marx did know (*via* Engels, if no other source) the devastating effects of the Industrial Revolution, not only in human terms, but also in ecological ones. But in keeping with his analysis, he traced the degradation to the capitalist legal relations of production. He wrote:

> Capitalist production. . .disturbs the circulation of matter between man and the soil, ie., prevents the return to the soil of its elements consumed by man in the form of food and clothing; it therefore violates conditions necessary to the lasting fertility of the soil. . . .Moreover, all progress in capitalist agriculture is a progress in the art, not only of robbing the laborer, but of robbing the soil: all progress in increasing the fertility of the soil for a given time is a progress toward ruining the lasting sources of that fertility. The more a country starts its development on the foundation of modern industry, like the United States, for example, the more rapid is the process of destruction! Capitalist production, therefore, develops technology, and the combining together of various processes into a social whole, only by sapping the original sources of all wealth — soil and laborer. [17]

He implied that the same technology, married to another set of legal social relations of production, would no longer exploit both soil and labourer. But this might not be the case. It might no longer exploit the latter but it could still exploit the former. Moreover, he even toyed with a conception of socialism which might not have relied on EST. But in the end he rejected it as utopian. (See Chapter Eight.) By so doing, he seemed to have thrown his weight behind the standard technology to exploit Nature to serve human needs. In this sense, Lenin's dictum that 'Communism equals socialism plus electricity' was what the Bolshevik Revolution was about, is not far off the mark.

Marx too was preoccupied by the fetishism of

money. Could this be used as evidence that he was challenging what I have called Locke's axiom of the ontological substitution of money for low entropic energy and matter, that is, real things like topsoil, clean air, unpoisoned food, etc.? I do not think entirely so.

Marx was keen to show up the perversity of capitalism. Money fetishism is part of the perversion, the accumulation of money becomes an end in itself and masks its legitimate function as a medium of exchange for real things, like food and shelter, to meet genuine human needs. Marx's challenge to Locke is, therefore, more limited and confined than might at first sight appear. He was not really concerned with its implication about the severance of economic or productive activities from its thermodynamic, ecological base. For Marx too, like Locke and many others, assumed that natural resources are inexhaustible, that there is no Malthusian absolute scarcity, only Ricardian relative scarcity. The creative energies of capitalism were (and are) being channelled to exploit these bountiful (but infinite) riches to serve Mammon and to create inequalities between classes, so that the genuine human needs of the labouring classes cannot be met, whilst the capitalist class appropriates the surplus value of labour-power. We need to change that, said Marx, so that science and technology, in transforming the boundless bounty of Nature, could be used to serve the needs of all.

In other words, Marx did not see natural resources as a problem in the productive process. The conflict between labour and capital constituted, in his analysis, the real problem. Once the shift towards labour has been made, by altering the capitalist legal relations of production to one of the public (common) ownership of the means of production, all would be well. And he implied that the other elements might remain intact more or less. We have seen that EST remains in place. But other things that will remain in place once the perversion has been removed also include, as we shall see, the doctrine of economic growth, of ever increasing rate of consumption (in meeting genuine human needs?).

Under the capitalist legal relations of production, economic growth is required (a) to maximise profits, (b) to avoid the painful issue of redistribution from the rich to the poor, as it is used as a substitute for it. Marx was, of course, against both of these objectives. The maximisation of profits for its own sake is a form of perversion. A less unequal distribution rather than a more unequal distribution (to put it minimally) was favoured by Marx, and hence his argument against the capitalist legal relations of production as one embodying profound inequalities between capital and labour. But economic growth, not thus harnessed, could be quite acceptable. It is, then, used simply to meet the genuine needs of all agents.

But indefinite economic growth is only necessary to meet genuine human needs, if these needs are assumed to be ever expanding and growing. Otherwise, given sufficiency of need (see Chapter Ten), economic growth beyond a certain point becomes irrelevant and meaningless. But Marx, belonging to the same Faustian tradition as most of his critics, saw an infinite expansion ever upwards, as being in keeping with the image of Man soaring ever and ever upwards in a God-like fashion. So long as the technology is available, Man can and will transform Nature to serve his will. By assuming infinite and ever expanding needs (unlike most of his critics, he wishes to distinguish, and implies that it is possible to distinguish, between wants and needs), he appears to have rejected as definitively as those who assume infinite and ever expanding wants, the notion of sufficiency and, by implication, the principle of diminishing marginal utility.

If so, Marx must also endorse the standard concepts of efficiency and productivity. Productivity is standardly understood as productivity of labour. Productivity of labour means the following: X number of workers can produce Y number of units (of whatever good or service) per hour; however, if a new technique or a new piece of technology is introduced, then half the number of workers can produce the same output per hour. Productivity is said to have doubled.

Of course, viewed in another way, productivity of labour is just redundancy of labour. Historically, those made redundant found jobs elsewhere, sooner or later. Hence, a permanent increase in unemployment was not said to be an issue. When agricultural labour was made redundant through improvement in agricultural productivity, it picked up employment in the manufacturing industries that were expanding; later, when manufacturing labour was shed through an increase in manufacturing productivity, it was channelled into the expanding service industries. Today, the service industries are themselves shedding labour owing to an improvement in productivity (by courtesy of so-called information technology). It is not so obvious where the unemployed will go from here.

Efficiency, as we have seen, is standardly defined as more output for a given input, and not as the same output for less input. The former emphasises the desirability of the output; hence, Okun's the more the better. Historically, the greatest output has been achieved through the use of EST whose entropic costs (externalities) are not included in the input cost. On the whole, in the history of modern economic management, efficiency in this sense is 'primarily the result of attempts to increase the output from the environment rather than produce a given input more efficiently'. [18] It is important to remind ourselves, that the EST employed, achieves what scientists call a second-law efficiency of only 10 to 15 percent.

Second-law efficiency is the ratio of the least available work that could have done the job to the actual available work used to do it. It is addressed to three questions:

The concept is task-oriented rather than device-oriented. The more usual concept of efficiency (first law efficiency) is device-oriented. Of the total amount of available work put into a device, what percentage comes out in the desired, useful form? There remains the further question of whether another (perhaps not yet invented) device could theoretically give the same useful output with a smaller input of available work. And what is the least input of available work that could accomplish the task without violating the second law? [19]

The alternative definition of efficiency mentioned earlier, as same output for less input, would, therefore, be in keeping with the concept of second-law efficiency. So paradoxically, 'efficiency' on the standard interpretation is really not all that efficient.

Because of the endorsement of the doctrines of economic growth, of an ever increasing rate of consumption to cope with ever expanding human needs, of the standard definitions of productivity and efficiency, all underpinned by the axiom of the inexhaustibility of natural resources, Marx and Marxists have seen their alternative system of production, based on public ownership of the means of production, as a competitor to that system of production which involves capitalist legal relations of production. Indeed, many believe that it can be a more efficient system (the standard interpretation of efficiency) for a variety of reasons. In practice, it might not have appeared to be so in actual socialist economies, for these economies, unlike those in the first world, have to devote economic growth, first of all, to the accumulation of capital goods. But once a certain level of such accumulation has been reached, then it ought to be able to deliver consumption goods in the way capitalist economies are able to do. If it does not, then, like Gorbachev, one should do one's best to make it do so by removing bottlenecks and other obstacles in the system. Deng and his colleagues in China nurse the same ambition.

In section 2, I said that the concepts of progress and modernity rest on the congruence of three ideas: (1) the logic of capital, whose essence is that of accumulation; (2) the logic of industrialism based on science and EST; (3) the logic of economic thinking based on efficiency defined as more output with given input. Could Marx be said to accept these three ideas? Quite uncontroversially, he could be said to endorse (2) and (3). But what about (1)? A word of warning to begin with — the discussion of this issue should not be turned into a purely verbal matter, or to be debated as one.

I have, so far, tried to identify the capitalism condemned by Marx by referring to its legal relations of production, that is, a system where the means of production are legally owned by the capitalist, together with the products that are created, through the purchase of labour-power as a commodity. I then distinguish this kind of productive system from Marx's alternative by referring to a different set of legal relations of production where the means of production are publicly or commonly owned, including state ownership as a possible (if not standard) type of public ownership. I further argue that Marx (a) wanted the productive system not to serve personal greed but to meet genuine human needs of all agents, which the system he was criticising could not do, (b) wanted to abolish exploitation based on the unequal relations between capital and labour. It is this kind of capitalism that he wished to transcend. Let us call this bourgeois capitalism.

This then leaves open the question whether Marx at all challenged the logic of capital as a process of accumulation of producer goods, consumer goods, etc., whose essence is to grow and enlarge itself continuously? (This sense of capital has nothing to do with the legal relationships of production, whether the means of production are publicly owned or privately owned by the class of capitalists.) [20] It could be no. If he endorsed (2) and (3) and their implications as he appeared to do, then it is not easy to see how he could reject (1). Without (1), you cannot have (2) and (3). The ever increasing rate of consumption to meet ever expanding human needs, using science and EST to dominate Nature in meeting these needs, requires ever accumulating capital, including money as a form of capital. (Indeed, socialist economies have a job trying to increase that most desirable form of it, that is, hard currency.) In this sense of capital, its logic is as much a part of bourgeois capitalism as it is of its most serious competitor to date. That is why some commentators of the left have characterised existing socialist economies as embodying state capitalism. This recognises, then, that there is an underlying commonality between the two forms. This commonality includes the logic of capital as a never ending process of accumulation, that is, to see capital as a flow, not as a stock. (See next section for further elucidation of this point.)

Even if it is true that Marx himself never approved of state capitalism, it remains the case that existing socialist economies can be said to be forms of state capitalism. Such states certainly embrace the logic of industrialism and the logic of the standard conceptions of efficiency. That is why it is not at all surprising that such countries exhibit similar problems of ecological degradation. They too are part of the industrial civilisation, part of progress and modernity. So they, too, must pay the same thermodynamic and ecological price. In other words, we are all facing the same crisis and the same set of problems, which no amount of political and ideological shouting from either side can conjure away. (Indeed, the realisation that we are, may be seen in the sympathies, nowadays, displayed by the one side following a major technological disaster in the other — witness the lack of *shadenfreude* except in the case of a few unthinking hawks, when, for instance, the Challenger spacecraft blew up and when the Chernobyl nuclear power station went astray.) What is required is a radical rethinking of how we ought to organise human existence, given the understanding we have, today, about the complexities in the exchanges between human economic productive activity and the material environment.

6. A small, but hopefully growing, band of non-orthodox economists (some of them have even stopped regarding themselves as economists) argues that the way forward is a type of economic theory and practice which is in keeping with thermodynamic and ecological reality. This amounts to a repudiation of

the three logics referred to above. Capital as a process of accumulation should not and need not be endless. Beyond a certain level (which the first world has most certainly already surpassed by a long chalk), it should not be allowed to increase. Our industrial civilisation, based on a mechanistic paradigm of explanation, a linear model of causation and a technology which is EST would have to change. The ecological model of non-linear causation cannot be ignored in scientific as well as social thinking; an alternative technology which is EST will have to be developed. This does not mean that one turns the back on science to embrace mumbo-jumbo or mysticism of one kind or other. But it does mean we can no longer, as our forebears did, and most of our contemporaries still do, believe that progress lies in dominating Nature through science (based on a mechanistic linear paradigm of cause and effect) and its EST, making it serve our human ends at all cost. An EST is a technology which is consonant with the principles of ecology, the laws of thermodynamics, including the concept of second-law efficiency. As such, it will have to ditch the standard concepts of efficiency and productivity. It will have to reject the doctrines of economic growth (beyond a certain point) and ever increasing rates of consumption.

Some of them have called the new economics 'steady-state economics' [21], others 'space ship economics'. [22] Of the great economists of the past, only J. S. Mill, according to Daly and others, had the foresight and clarity of vision and moral courage to embrace it. He wrote:

I cannot. . .regard the stationary state of capital and wealth with the unaffected aversion so generally manifested towards it by political economists of the old school. I am inclined to believe that it would be, on the whole, a very considerable improvement on our present condition. [23]

Daly himself defines a steady-state economy as follows:

an economy with constant stocks of people and artifacts, maintained at some, desired, sufficient levels by low rates of maintenance, 'throughput', that is, by the lowest feasible flows of matter and energy from the first stage of production (depletion of low-entropy materials from the environment) to the last stage of consumption (pollution of the environment with high-entropy wastes and exotic materials). It should be continually remembered that the SSE (steady-state economy) is a physical concept. If something is nonphysical, then perhaps it can grow forever. If something can grow forever, then certainly it is nonphysical. . . .The steady-state perspective seeks to maintain a desired level of stocks with a minimum throughput, and if minimizing the throughput implies a reduction in GNP, that is totally acceptable. [24]

Its chief features entail, therefore:
1. the rejection of capital in the form of the accumulation of producers' goods, consumers' goods, human beings as necessarily ever increasing, because on its view capital is not a flow but a stock. Whilst flows can accumulate endlessly, stocks can have a definite limited size;
2. the rejection of the GNP, on the grounds that it is a flow and not a stock (the GNP is no measure of well-being in any case);
3. the clarification of three important concepts which have to be distinguished:

Stock is the total inventory of producers' goods, consumers' goods, and human bodies. . .and may be thought of as the set of all physical things capable of satisfying human wants and capable of owner- ship. Service is the satisfaction experienced when wants are satisfied, . . .Service is yielded by the stock. The quantity and quality of the stock determine the intensity of service. . . .Service is yielded over a period of time and thus appears to be a flow magnitude. But unlike flows, service cannot be accumulated. It is probably more accurate to think of service as a psychic flux. Throughput is the entropic physical flow of matter-energy from nature's sources, through the human economy, and back to nature's sinks, and it is necessary for the maintenance and renewal of the stocks. [25]

The size of the stock is to be chosen in accordance with its being consonant with the stability of the biosphere and its ecosystems, and a conception of sufficiency. (On the latter, see Chapter Ten, section 4.) Service is the final end of economic activity; throughput, an entropic flow, is the cost, which is incurred in the production of artifacts (as stock) which in turn yield service.

Although the SSE is necesarily incompatible with economic growth for its own sake, it is not incompatible with development. However, development itself may have limits. For instance, while one can improve second-law efficiency in the design of our technology, efficiency could never be 100 percent. We should design the stock to slow down the rate of wear and tear, to make it do as much work as possible, but it will eventually wear out all the same. However, within that thermodynamic parameter, there is plenty of room for development.

Daly says, as service is not about a physical flow but a psychic one, it may grow in the sense that there is no limit to the amount of service or psychic satisfaction one gets from a given stock. But this, as he also points out, may not be entirely so. The principle of diminishing marginal utility presupposes that, subject to a small range within which individual differences occur, the human organism has a certain kind of physiological, neurological system such that it is unlikely that psychic satisfaction can grow indefinitely. No matter how intensely satisfying listening to Wagner may be to Wagnerian devotees, such a devotee could not listen to his music all the time non-stop. The human system needs rest from any one given activity after a certain length of time. If fed on the same fare, the person feels bored sooner or later. There is a level of sufficiency, which an individual

discovers, at which s/he would settle for anyone activity or object, from which s/he derives satisfaction.
If this is so, indefinite economic growth may not be
necessary, irrespective of whether it makes sense as a
notion.

CHAPTER SEVEN

CIVILISATION, ITS CONTENTS AND ITS DISCONTENTS

1. Civilisation is necessarily based on the repression of some inclinations and the expression of others. The crucial question is always: which inclinations ought to be allowed expression and in what ways, and which should be repressed, or reshaped and rechannelled? A short answer to this question is to say those deemed desirable by any one society would be allowed expression, while those deemed undesirable are to be repressed, or if not repressed, at least redirected so that they find expression in some other more desirable or acceptable form.

Those who hold the meta-ethical view of philosophical relativism or irrationalism about the justification of values will put the emphasis entirely on the word 'deemed', for apart from the individual or society in question simply deciding (sincerely) these are desirable values for expression and manifestation, those are undesirable values and destined for repression, there is nothing more that one can say about their justification.

But this book assumes a different meta-ethics. Discourse about the justification of values is just as critical and rational as other forms of discourse deemed unproblematically critical and rational. On this view then, one can justify one set of values and not another by citing evidence, which can be said to be objectively determinable — that is, it can be discovered to be true or not, independent of the wishes, feelings, convictions of the person citing the

196

evidence, and that it is not the mere existence of these subjective elements, which render the evidence either true or false. These are logically irrelevant to the issue of the correctness, adequacy or otherwise of the values involved. [1]

Our present civilisation (dating from the seventeenth century), as the foregoing chapters show, amongst other things, celebrates and encourages the expression of selfish inclinations, to the extent of even denying that human beings are capable of altruistic ones — the pursuit of 'wealth' as money, the possession of goods and command over other agents through them, the rapid consumption of goods, etc. It represses altruistic inclinations, the desire of seeking satisfaction in activities other than the pursuit of wealth as money, the possession and consumption of material things. Above all, it celebrates competition and represses co-operation.

But such a set of values (ecologically insensitive values, ESV for short) is not consonant with the laws of thermodynamics and the principles of ecology. A social, moral theory embodying such values, which are at odds with so established and fundamental a science as thermodynamics, must be judged, therefore, to be wrong, inadequate, misleading and, indeed, even fantastic. These values should then be discouraged. An alternative set (call it ecologically sensitive values, ESV for short), more consonant with thermodynamic and ecological reality, ought to be celebrated. A new type of social arrangement, reflecting ESVs, ought to replace the existing social arrangement which embodies ESVs.

2. The question about civilisation endorsing some values whilst rejecting others has two aspects: (a) the endorsed values enable human agents to negotiate conduct with one another, not to mention the exchange between such conduct and its material environment; (b) the endorsed values will also determine the moral identity and integrity of human agents. They will inform the way in which such agents formulate their

ends, purposes, intentions and, hence, the execution of their intentions into action — see sub-theses (i), (ii), (iv), (vi) in the real definition of human agency in Chapter Four.

In other words, the endorsement of ESVs enables us not only to act correctly as far as the external relationships with one another and Nature are concerned, and to yield an answer, as we saw, to the issue in social philosophy about endurance. These may also be said to be related to the question 'What is the good society?'. But it also enables us to cope with the other crucial question in social philosophy raised in Chapter Four, 'What sort of person ought one to be?' Now is the time to look in detail at how this latter question is answered by reference to ESVs.

One must first of all go back to those ESVs of ever increasing possession and consumption, and of the derivation of satisfaction mainly, if not solely, from such possession and consumption. There is no need to labour the obvious, that such values will eventually beggar us all because of their entropic costs. However, there are other aspects which are not so obvious and, therefore, need further exploration, namely, (i) their psychic costs, apart from their entropic ones, (ii) the psychic costs being entailed by their essential competitiveness, (iii) competitiveness in turn entails incoherence. Hence a theory of the moral identity and integrity of the self, based on such incoherent values, must itself be incoherent.

The origin of this incoherent theory of the self may be traced back to our old friend Locke. Based on Locke's writings, two theories of the self, not one, may be constructed. Those who study Locke's epistemology as part of a course in the history of modern philosophy or the philosophy of mind will be aware that he is said to hold a theory of self-identity in terms of the continuity of memory. I am the same person as the one who yesterday chopped down a tree in my garden, because my present memory is continuous with the memory of that said person, and, moreover, includes the event of the tree chopping. Should I suddenly suffer amnesia for all the memories from childhood right up to the tree chopping event of yesterday, then I cannot, on this theory of memory continuity, be any longer the one and the same person. This theory may run into certain difficulties such as whether one can identify memories without referring to the body. If we cannot, then it looks as if Locke is not altogether right in saying that the identity of the self is given solely in terms of its memory. But this is not the theory, which is the ancestor of that theory of the self which embodies ESVs.

The second theory that can be reconstructed is more familiar to those who study Locke, not so much in a course about the history of modern philosophy (which is primarily the history of modern epistemology from Descartes onwards), but to those who study Locke in another course usually taught in another department, called the history of modern political thought or theory. (This usually starts with Hobbes.)

In brief, this second theory may be reconstructed as follows:

(1) individuals, through their labour, may legitimately appropriate certain things which are commonly available such as apples, nuts, fallen branches and twigs from trees, etc. — these are the fruits of their labour of picking or harvesting. Or individuals, through their labour of planting and nursing a tree, are also entitled to the fruits of their labour;

(2) but as we saw in the last chapter, the thesis of the ontological substitution of money for real things profoundly alters the scene — money can be accumulated indefinitely. This entitles us to appropriate more things as we accumulate more money;

(3) as a result, the appropriation and possession of these things is less and less connected with the original idea of legitimate appropriation as the fruits of one's labour. In some cases, one might just have inherited the money from a remote relative one had never seen or even known about. In other cases, one could have won it in a football pool, or the stock exchange, to name but two extreme possibilities;

(4) we possess arms, legs, eyes, ears, voice box, that

is, endosomatic organs. One's identity could be said to be affected if suddenly one finds oneself (through accident or illness) minus an arm, a leg, an eye or speech — one sees oneself then as a handicapped person. So it is clear that one's personal identity depends very much on the possession or the lack of our endosomatic organs. But many of the things that we can possess through the accumulation of money are tools or instruments, which may be considered to be extensions of our endosomatic organs, like a microphone, a car, a newspaper, a microscope etc. These are our exosomatic organs. (See Chapter Four.) Just as our endosomatic organs form part of our self identity, so it is held our exosomatic organs are also part of our identity. On this view, a person who has five houses, several old masters, numerous gold and diamond mines is, therefore, a very different person from the pauper he was before he owned these things Possession is an extension of the self. To lose one's personal possessions is to lose one's personal identity, in part at least, if not totally. To deprive an individual of his possessions, his exosomatic organs, is as harmful as depriving him of his endosomatic organs.

The two theories of identity are logically very different types of theory. The first is based on the possession of something, namely, memories which are internal to the agent. The second is based on the possession of something, namely, material goods which are external to the agent. On the first, it makes no sense to deprive someone of her/his memories (even if it is technologically possible to induce amnesia through making the person swallow amnesia pills) in order to give them to a third party. It makes no sense to talk of redistributing memories. (I leave aside the issue of brain transplant.) But on the second, it clearly makes sense to deprive someone of her/his material possessions to give to a third party.

Possession of memories is not logically identical to the possession of material things. Whilst Locke's theory of memory continuity seems an appropriate criterion to use for determining identity in most contexts (when emended to include the presupposition that identity of memory is mediated by identity of the body), his theory of the continuing possession of material goods does not appear to be an appropriate criterion for determining identity, except for the special context it might have been designed to justify, namely, to resist the redistribution of material possessions from those, who have, to those, who have none.

Moreover, the first theory conflicts with the second in the sense that a person, though deprived of most of her/his material goods, would still retain the memories of those events which so far constitute one's identity, including the event of being deprived of one's material possessions. On this criterion, the person remains the same person as s/he was before the deprivation. The second theory denies this, which is counter-intuitive. It appears to be a case of special pleading. Moreover, unless personal identity is predicated on the first theory and not the second, it makes no sense for a deprived or disinherited person to feel aggrieved and to attempt to reclaim the lost goods. On the second theory, at most what Locke could do was to condemn a change of identity as wrong through depriving the person of her/his material possessions, on the grounds that any change of identity, through the adding or subtracting of material external goods, is wrong. But if so, the enrichment of an individual (suppose it is possible to do so without prior deprivation of another) must be just as wrong.

I am, of course, not denying that the loss of material possessions can have a pretty traumatic effect on some people, from which indeed they might never recover. For instance, a millionaire who lost his fortune overnight through the Wall Street crash and found himself in very reduced circumstances could suddenly lose his youthfulness, or even kill himself in a fit of depression, whereas before, he was full of bonhomie. But to admit this is simply to admit psycho-physical causation, and the role played by the great value attached to material possessions in the society in question. If great value is put by society on giving children very expensive toys at Christmas and on birthdays, then a child who never receives such gifts could feel very deprived and rejected, so much so that her/his personality and identity may be shaped around this fact of deprivation. However, to say that this could affect a child's personality and identity is not the same as saying that one could lose one's identity through the loss of memories.

It is possible to deprive someone of an arm or leg — torturers apparently do and have done so throughout a lot of human history. Today, with advanced medical technology, it is even possible to redistribute such endosomatic organs by giving them to someone without. But ethicists have argued that such redistribution is morally unacceptable (except voluntarily and without endangering life or impairing it — donating a kidney is all right because one could live conceivably with only one such organ but donating a leg is more difficult to justify), even if technologically feasible, on the grounds that forcible deprivation amounts to an assault on the person and her/his bodily integrity. Mutilation through force amounts to slavery. A slave does not own her/his person. A master may do what he likes with his slaves legally. But in a non-slave society everyone is supposed to own her/his own person, including her/his own body. Hence, to permit mutilation against the person's will is to revert to a form of slavery.

But this analogy with slavery cannot be extended to removing, even against the person's will, some of one's material possessions, although this has not prevented some theorists of late arguing that taxation is indeed a form of slavery. Slaves are human beings who satisfy the characteristics which enter into the real definition of human agency as given in Chapter Four. What is objectionable to treating slaves as chattels is precisely that it deprives them of their exercise of human agency, in all but the most trivial contexts. It is to treat them as if they were material objects.

The argument behind the thesis that taxation is a form of slavery is actually the view that no (legal) coercion should be used, through taxation, to procure collective goods (this has already been looked at in

Chapter Four), and that redistribution from the rich to the poor is neither necessary nor desirable in society, based usually on the defence that economic growth is a far better substitute.

3. If the answer to the question, 'What sort of person ought one to be?' lies in (a) a person who always advances her/his own interests; (b) a person who regards the height of virtue to lie in the accumulation of money as 'wealth'; (c) a person who derives satisfaction from the possession and consumption of material possessions which money can buy, then such a conception of personal identity and integrity leads to certain contradictions.

We have already seen in Chapter Four how (a) involves contradictions. Not everyone, logically, can be a successful free rider, although everyone can try to be one. To try to succeed, however, is not the same as to achieve success. Successful free riding is essentially a minority preoccupation; hence, to be a successful free rider is to be a moral parasite. So I need not labour the point here.

It might look at first sight that no logical difficulties arise by exhorting everyone to regard the accumulation of money as 'wealth' to constitute the highest virtue. As we have seen, under the Lockean thesis of ontological substitution, money is infinite and inexhaustible in theory, as it does not obey the laws of thermodynamics, not being a physical thing. So everyone can have a shot at accumulating as much as possible. However, not even Lockean economists themselves wholeheartedly swallow the Lockean axiom of ontological substitution. The process of accumulating money does not altogether, and totally, exist at a level, which has transcended the world of thermodynamic reality. (Ironically, the monetarist is desperately trying to put Locke's genie back into the bottle after having released it with such glee.) Even they know one cannot literally eat money. One can only eat real things like a piece of beef or a plate of lentils. One can only ride in, or on, real things, like a bicycle, train or car. Economic growth cannot simply be the growth of money. It must ultimately mean an increase in the number of beefburgers, of cars, of shoes produced, consumed or used. This brings us then to (c).

The laws of thermodynamics and the principles of ecology tell us that low entropic energy and matter out of which we fashion real things like beefburgers and cars, thereby producing entropy, waste or pollution, is not simply relatively scarce, but absolutely scarce. Its rate of depletion is also immensely hastened by an ever increasing rate of consumption under economic growth which is exponential growth. The imperative of economic growth cannot, therefore, be a universal precept for the simple reason that there is not enough of low entropic energy and matter to go round, and that the capacity of the biosphere to act as a sink is finite and not unlimited. Herein lies one contradiction — urging us all to act in a way when it is physically not possible for everyone to do so. The 'everyone' here refers minimally to everyone alive today in the world; maximally, it refers to future generations as well.

When we think of shoes and clothes as items for possession and consumption, it is perhaps not so obvious that these are in limited supply. But if we take high quality diamonds in the form of tiaras, the point might become more obvious. Or again if we take prime agricultural land. Or houses occupying desirable sites with scenic panoramic and unobstructed views. However, the real point to grasp is that even mundane things, like clothes and beefurgers, given their ever increasing rate of consumption, would cause ecological bankruptcy, if left unchecked. Indeed, the insatiable desire for more and more beefburgers (even when for the moment this desire is confined, by and large, to North America) seems already to be playing ecological havoc in large parts of South America, where the rain forests have been, and are still being cleared, to turn them into pasture land for beef cattle. Natural fibres alone cannot keep pace with the ever increasing demand for clothes. Synthetic fibres have been developed, using non-renewable ingredients derived from oil.

If any item, call it X, is in limited supply, and people are urged to possess and consume X, then this necessarily becomes what game-theorists have called a zero-sum game, that is, a game with winners and losers. The winners of such a game tend to be much smaller in number than the losers. The top winners in the zero-sum game of ever increasing possession and consumption of goods are those who, by and large, belong to the first world, but they constitute a minority in the world's total population.

Such a zero-sum activity in turn combined with (a), that is, the morality of egoism can but lead to never-ending and ever more intense competition. (Competition is endemic to all zero-sum games.) If satisfaction in life is to be derived from being a winner in this kind of competition, one must put in never-ending efforts (i) to become a winner, (ii) to stay being a winner. The psychic costs to the individual agent must then be immense, to the losers as well as to the winners.

The losers naturally become certified as failures in spite of their efforts to win. Having endorsed the central ESVs of their society and internalised such values, they write themselves off as well as being written off by their neighbours.

Whilst the losers may sink forever into a morass of worthlessness, the winners must forever be vigilant in maintaining their foremost positions. They cannot afford to slacken or rest. The psychic costs as well as physical wear and tear must be very high indeed.

Moreover, the whole point of this kind of zero-sum game is precisely that nobody should be content with what s/he has got, for the entire emphasis is on ever increasing possession and consumption. Satisfaction is not derived simply from the possession and consumption of goods even at a certain high level (in absolute terms); for this would entail the notion of sufficiency which it specifically denies. No level may be said to be high in an absolute sense. To every 'high' level, there is always a higher level towards which one must strive. To have a comfortable warm house to live in is not enough; one should strive to have two or three, each one grander than the last. To be a millionaire is not enough, for one should always strive to be a two million millionaire and so on. Compared with the latter, the former is, indeed, a very 'ordinary' millionaire. As the goal post is forever moving ahead of one's effort and achievement, this Faustian search for satisfaction is, therefore, always one step ahead of the seeker. In other words, it is never truly achievable. Like Achilles and the tortoise, Achilles will never catch up with the tortoise because a gap will always develop between the two. It is, therefore, a holy grail which by design and conception, one will never attain, or obtain so fleetingly that in the very next moment, it has vanished from one's grasp. Herein lies another contradiction. One is urged to chase something that cannot logically exist and endure for more than a fleeting moment. It is as if one has been told to make it one's lifetime's work to square the circle.

4. So far I have been considering the kind of zero-sum game in relation to ecological scarcity. It is now time to look at it from the point of view of another type of scarcity, namely, existential scarcity. One's time is necessarily more or less dedicated to the central preoccupation of acquiring more and more. As a result, there is very little time left to use, to enjoy, to derive real satisfaction from the material goods one manages to accumulate.

We have but twenty four hours in a day of which, let us say, ten to twelve must be devoted to sleeping, eating and other bodily functions. This leaves at best half the number of hours for other activities. If most of that itself is used up in the struggle to stay afloat or keep ahead, then pretty little is left for the activity of getting the most out of what we already possess, never mind cultivating and nursing human relationships. Having worked hard, let us say, to acquire a Palladian mansion, the owner might well find that s/he has no time to live in it and to enjoy it.

Moreover, as one's continuing success in accumulation enables one to acquire yet more possessions, these ever increasing possessions clamour for what time there is available to be appreciated in their own rights. During that limited spare time, one could choose either to spend in one's Palladian mansion or on one's luxury yacht, but not both.

Time, for us mortals, constitutes existential scarcity. It is absolutely scarce like low entropic energy and matter. Death for us is annihilation of time. But death is not something we can escape. At most we can slow down the processes which eventually lead to death. In this way, we buy more time. It is true that by buying more time in this way, the owners of material possessions may find more time to enjoy their possessions. But paradoxically, the central imperative in this kind of zero-sum game requires ever increasing effort with all that it entails for the wear and tear of the body and the psyche. Such an ethos and lifestyle, far from slowing down the processes leading to death, often hasten them. Herein lies another contradiction.

Given that time is existentially scarce, then the only sense of satisfaction permitted by such a zero-sum game is the satisfaction to be derived from the *mere* legal ownership of the goods, and from conspicuous consumption of them, that is, the mere fact that others know that you own the highly desired goods in question. It is the satisfaction, in other words, derived from things as status symbols.

Such satisfaction is not the satisfaction to be derived from appreciation of the objects in their own rights. Such serious and proper appreciation, as we saw, minimally requires time, if not understanding of what they stand for, how they work and what they are capable of doing. To appreciate an old master, one must at least sit still in front of it and look at it with attention, not once and for all, but over periods of time. To appreciate it as a masterpiece, one must acquaint oneself with some knowledge about art traditions, techniques, the history of art, and so on. All this requires yet more time.

The satisfaction based on things as status symbols panders to human vanity. One could argue that vanity is not necessarily an evil because one could harness that vanity to serve other worthwhile ends. I have no wish to criticise the more general defence of vanity. What I say here is more limited — the vanity in the case under discussion does not appear to advance any defensible ends. It beggars Nature and those of us who are losers; it beggars the winners themselves in terms of the psychic costs involved, and prevents them from deriving true satisfaction from things.

This pernicious account of the source of satisfaction is a variation of the second Lockean theory of identity based on the possession of material goods. A person's worth is measured by what one possesses. A person's worth is determined by the number and types of status symbols s/he can lay claim to. To deprive a person of her/his status symbols is to deprive her/him of worth. But as we have seen, this kind of 'worth' is pernicious. So we ought not to build a theory of personal worth, of personal identity and integrity, on such a conception. As its perniciousness centres on (a) its essential competitiveness, (b) its psychic costs both to winners and losers, (c) its entropic costs and all that that entails, (d) its interference with the satisfaction that can be derived form a proper appreciation of objects and from cultivating and nourishing human relationships, an alternative account of worth which enters into a more adequate theory of personal identity and integrity must avoid these pitfalls. Only ESVs would do.

5. A theory informed by ESVs would direct human agents to seek satisfaction not from the ever increasing possession and consumption of material goods which are scarce, but to direct us to seek satisfaction in activities which are not dependent necessarily on ever increasing possession and consumption *per se*. All activities, in so far as they are performed by human agents, as we have seen, necessarily involve

material objects. So I am not advocating anything so silly as that we should engage in activities which involve no ecologically scarce goods. There are no such activities. The theory proposes something quite different — that we should seek satisfaction and worth in activities which consume as little of these scarce goods as possible, that we should, on the whole, prefer those activities which make less entropic demands rather than those which make more.

To cultivate and nurture human relationships is presumably one such activity, much neglected today in the rush to chase the logically and physically impossible goal of ever increasing possession and consumption of material goods. Talking and listening to people, conducting conversations, etc. require time which of course is existentially scarce. But once we have liberated ourselves from the pernicious goal set by contemporary civilisation, then we would have more time to devote to this surely very important aspect of human existence.

Many activities which *per se* do not require the possession and consumption of many material objects have become so, by having been transformed into industries. And if they themselves have not been so transformed, they have been displaced by such leisure industries. Traditionally, singing, dancing, for example, were popular ways of spending leisure. Playing games too. But nowadays, games are no longer primarily activities from which people derive pleasure by participating in them themselves. They have become spectator sports — spectators derive pleasure from watching others who are professionals, backed by big money. Such sports are hence high-powered industries.

My aim here is not to give details of such transformations and how to 'deindustrialise' them, but to make the point that we need to get back to an ethos of active participation in activiites carried out with the minimum gear, and to turn our back upon those which extol satisfaction through passivity and mere possession.

The point made above requires one to distinguish between the logic of the pursuit of external goods and the logic of internal goods. It is obvious what external goods are. They are material objects, and I have explored the logic of their pursuit just now. But what are internal goods? A very brief answer is to say that they may be summed up under the more familiar notion in social philosophy of self-development.

Suppose I wish to develop myself musically and would like to try to play the flute. The whole point of the exercise is not to own a flute, or the harpsichord or whatever instrument involved, but to make use of it and, through the object, to acquire a skill which I hitherto lack, and to develop a capacity which I may possess. When I have learnt how to play the flute, be it tolerably or exquisitely, I would have acquired an internal good.

Another example. Suppose I would like to learn Spanish. Learning a language requires access to some material goods and services, like learning to play an instrument — books, possibly nowadays a cassette player and tapes, a teacher. When I finally have acquired either a tolerable command or a perfect command of Spanish, I have acquired an internal good.

From the examples cited so far, one may deduce that internal goods have the following characteristics:

(a) their acquisition requires access to some external material goods (and services), although usually they are pretty modest;

(b) the external goods are simply means to achieve the end of self-development and self-enrichment;

(c) while, on the whole, internal goods make less demands on external goods, nevertheless, they tend to make excessive or, at least, considerable demand on time and effort, for these goods often turn out to be forms of knowledge and skills; as such, they augment the agent's store of both knowing that and knowing how;

(d) it follows from (c) that internal goods become a part of the person in the same way that memories are part of one's person;

(e) their acquisition *per se* does not involve a zero-sum game; it is essentially non-competitive and can, therefore, be co-operative; there are no losers; all may be winners.

Let me comment first on (c) and (d). Skills and knowledge are indeed part of one's memory. They are stored in the brain. However, once acquired, they may also attenuate and sometimes even become lost like memory about events, which happened in one's life. But while, on the whole, we do not know much about why we remember some things vividly, others only faintly, and yet others not at all, we do know how skills and knowledge can be retained once acquired. They require exercise. In this sense, someone may be deprived of her/his skills and knowledge by not being allowed to exercise them. But usually faded skills and knowledge could also be revived and resuscitated once the opportunity arises.

But like memory of events, it makes no sense to deprive someone of her/his skills and knowledge, and literally redistribute them to another, in the way one can deprive someone of her/his external goods and give them to a third party. In other words, the logic of internal goods fits better with Locke's first theory of personal identity than his second theory.

It also follows that the usual charge of baseness of motive made against those who argue for redistribution in order to remove inequalities, namely, that it is born out of envy, does not really apply. On the contrary, a theory of personal worth and identity, based on the ever increasing possession and consumption of external goods, could motivate one to be envious of those who have more, and could move such a person, under the competitive impulse, to try to deprive those who have more by hook or by crook. A theory of personal worth and identity based on the acquisition of internal goods would not lead to envy of others, at least for their material possessions, as its central value is not the possession and consumption of external goods *per se*. External material goods only enter into the calculation as a means to enable agents to acquire internal goods. In some contexts, redistribution may be required to ensure that agents have access to external goods in order to develop themselves, it is true, but that cannot be said to be based on envy as a motive.

Internal goods are not alienable in the way external goods are alienable. Historically, a major source of envy lies in the desire of the have-nots to possess the material goods of the haves. The emphasis, in the ethical ethos I am proposing, rests, however, on the acquisition of internal goods. This then would remove one of the most powerful historical sources which sustains the motive of· envy. Although it is admitted that envy cannot be said to be logically misplaced with regard to non-alienable internal goods, it might, nevertheless, make one wonder about the point of being really envious of someone who, through effort and time, can speak five languages or who can ice-skate beautifully. It might prompt admiration instead, which is more morally appropriate. Envy develops more naturally in contexts where differential possession of material goods prevails, within an ethos, which celebrates such possession. But once the shift in ethical perspective has been made, there would be less inclination on the part of agents to envy others even for goods which are not alienable, and where the person who envies, cannot logically enrich her/himself, in any way, by such envy. Instead, they might spend time and energy enriching themselves by acquiring internal goods of some kind or other from which they can derive satisfaction, self-respect as well as respect from others.

Envy of those who possess internal goods would have to find expression in violent forms. They would involve mutilation or death of the agent. Suppose I play the violin like an angel. Since the only way you can deprive me of my skill is to chop off my hands, this amounts to an assault on my person. Or if you are really so possessed of envy you might kill me. But not even such drastic measures could enrich you personally. Transfer of skill and knowledge is not achieved through mutilation or death of those agents who have them. It can be effected through labour and the time consuming process of teaching and learning. Moreover, paradoxically, transfer of skills and knowledge actually proliferates them; it creates a greater pool of skills and knowledge than exists before. If wealth and worth are to be defined in terms of self-development, in acquiring skills and knowledge, in developing capacities one possesses, then for much less entropic input, we could create a lot more wealth. The extant pool of external goods at any one time can only be redistributed, but not increased, without a vast input of low entropic energy and matter. But for the acquisition of many internal goods, though not all, the only entropic cost involved may be the existence of a human agent with the relevant skill and knowledge and another existing agent willing to learn. The only other cost is time. Wealth creation in this way can, therefore, be very economical in entropic terms.

Internal goods are only scarce goods in the sense that their acquisition depends on the availability of material things as means to their achievement. But as they are generally also time-consuming to achieve, being complex in nature, existential scarcity itself imposes a limit on the number of internal goods one could acquire at any one time, or over a lifetime. Moreover, as many of them make only very modest demands on external material goods whilst at the same time managing to produce a lot of satisfaction in the long run, in spite of the arduous nature initially of the activity, they are unlikely to produce ecological bankruptcy, which the pursuit of ever increasing possession and consumption of external goods inevitably involves.

Internal goods are not scarce in the sense that the rewards of a competitive zero-sum game are necessarily scarce. Such a game, as we know, necessarily entails many losers as well as a few winners. But acquiring a skill or knowledge on my part does not prevent someone else, who is similarly interested, from acquiring the same skill or knowledge and to the same degree of proficiency. The reward, that is, the achievement of the skill or knowledge, can be enjoyed not necessarily by one person or only a small group but by all those who are interested and who possess the capacity. It is true that it would not be possible for the stone deaf to try to acquire the skill of playing a musical instrument, or those born blind to try to paint. But this does not mean that the stone deaf could not try to paint and the blind to play the trumpet, should they be so interested.

Acquiring an internal good involves no competition with others. There can be as many winners as there are willing agents. It is true that some agents will develop the skill to a higher level of perfection than others. But this need not induce a sense of failure and worthlessness in those who are not so good. Indeed, individuals can exercise autonomy by choosing for themselves the level of perfection which they regard as constituting sufficiency. For instance, while I might not wish to be able to play the violin as well as Paganini (even supposing I can), this does not mean that I might not wish to learn to play the instrument to a level of perfection somewhat beneath that of the sublime. When I have reached such a level of proficiency and sufficiency, I might then wish to allocate my time, not to perfecting any further my violin playing, but to learning how to cook instead.

As a non zero-sum game, there is plenty of room for co-operation. Once I have reached, say, the level of perfection to which I aspire, there is no reason why I should not then help others to achieve similar heights. In enriching others, one is not diminishing oneself. Far from it, further satisfaction may be derived from the fact that one has enabled others to acquire excellence. In enriching the self by acquiring a certain excellence, one is also enriching others in the sense that by one's example, others could be inspired to try to reach similar heights. In a non zero-sum game, there is no necessity to polarise egoism against altruism.

In summary, one can say that the pursuit of internal goods is superior to that of external goods because it is non-competitive, non-divisive and on the whole incurs less entropic costs as well as less psychic costs.

The psychic costs incurred by the competitive ethos lies primarily in the losers' certification as failures, and in the continuous pressure on the winners not to be left behind. As the former involves no preordained losers, at a stroke, that source of psychic cost does not apply. It bears repeating that although we cannot all hope to be Einsteins or Mozarts, it does not follow (i) that we might not be good at something other than theoretical physics or music, (ii) that we cannot each settle for a certain level of excellence as sufficient for our own conception of self-development.

Suppose I have an exaggerated idea of my artistic capacity. In spite of hard effort, I now know I would never go far. Naturally, I am disappointed. There is some psychic cost incurred when I realise that I am a failure in this field. But this disappointment is hardly likely to induce a sense of total failure and worthlessness in me, because a civilisation which promotes the pursuit of internal goods simply celebrates excellence of any kind (subject to the restriction of harming others and that the entropic costs be not too great), at whatever level of perfection, and would not, therefore, certify me as a failure.

Empirically, it would be difficult to envisage a normal agent (one, for instance, who is not so brain damaged as to be reduced to a vegetable) who does not possess the capacity for some degree of excellence in one or more activities, be it joke telling, gardening, making bookshelves, polishing furniture, writing poetry. Failure and its heavy psychic cost are (a) endemic in a type of social arrangement which celebrates success only in one or two clearly defined activities, tolerating little or no deviation, and (b) where there is a built-in very small success, but overwhelmingly large failure rate. But in a society devoted to the acquisition of internal goods, neither limitation obtains. Consequently, empirically, the psychic costs through failure would be minimal or, at least, much less than they are in contemporary competitive civilisation.

However, I am aware that autonomy on the part of the individual to attain a certain level of excellence, in any one activity, could lead in some cases to disutility outweighing utility, so to speak. Indeed an individual who sets his/her sights too high could incur frustration and even suicidal depression, if not actually attempt suicide itself. So the agent, far from deriving overall satisfaction from the activity, derives overall dissatisfaction and misery. Clearly, when such counter-productive results occur, it would no longer be morally acceptable to insist that the agent continue in such unrelenting pursuit of excellence. In cases like this, the right thing to do is to counsel less intensity or, indeed, giving up such a demanding activity altogether for one which is less so. In other words, the pursuit of excellence, though an admirable moral ideal which in principle and in practice can give meaning and satisfaction to life, nevertheless ought not to be pursued to such lengths as to cause mental and psychological stress which may lead to a nervous and/or physical breakdown. The pursuit of excellence is meant to be encouraged in the context of developing a whole and harmonious being; a neurotic, suicidally depresssive person is hardly a whole and harmonious being.

6. All capacities on this view are worth developing so long as they do not damage others. Naturally, the capacity on the part of some people for indiscriminate sexual satisfaction and excitement through rape could not be allowed expression, as has been argued. But should someone wish to perfect her/his capacity for miniaturist writing, like transcribing the whole of the Lord's Prayer on something the size of a postage stamp, there is no reason why such a capacity should not be allowed expression. I might not find such a preoccupation attractive myself, but that is beside the point. Diversity can be celebrated. Some may derive satisfaction from chess playing, others embroidering, etc. There is no need to distinguish between the arts and the crafts, between so-called intellectual activities and non-intellectual ones and regard the one as superior to the other. They are all equally acceptable provided they are not so simple-minded as to make little or no demands on the mind, body or both. Uniformity in activities is not part of the logic of the

pursuit of internal goods. Far from requiring conformity in aspiration, it actually encourages and promotes the development of all sorts of excellences. There is no one activity which is singled out for universal emulation such as football or whatever, or the making of money as endorsed by contemporary civilisation. Only those activities are discouraged which demand excessive consumption of low entropic energy and matter, and which injure others.

To cultivate skills and excellences is to develop certain capacities in ourselves. It is to stretch our potential. It is therefore in keeping with that tradition in moral/social philosophy which celebrates the ideal of self-development. Strangely enough, this ideal cuts across the usual ideological divide, for those passionately in its favour include not only theorists one associates today with the 'left', such as Rousseau and Marx, but also J. S. Mill, who is usually claimed by the 'right' as one of them. (One could argue, of course, that Mill, being eclectic, borrowed ideas indiscriminately and did not attempt or succeed, even if he did try, to make a coherent whole of them. But I have no wish to follow up this question of Millean scholarship here.)

To cultivate skills and excellences necessarily involves activity, not passivity. It involves the exercise and the stimulation of various faculties and organs (endosomatic tools) we possess, including the brain. As a result, such an agent is more alert in both mind and body. (Admittedly, purely intellectual skills stimulate the mind more than the body, but nearly all other skills involve both.) It involves effort and is arduous. But it would be a mistake to infer from its arduous nature that human beings do not derive satisfaction from it. On the contrary, as a matter of fact, [2] complex activities and skills, which require the most effort, are precisely those which pay off best by way of satisfaction in the long run. Initially, the costs may be heavy. But as a long term investment, they may pay off handsomely. By contrast, things which require no or little effort, no activity but passivity, like watching a programme on television, may give instantaneous satisfaction, but that satisfaction evaporates as soon as the show is over.

If one cares to use Bentham's felicific calculus to illustrate the difference, it may be formulated as follows: passive spectator pleasures score less than active pleasures on the whole along the dimensions of fecundity and duration. It is conceivable that the latter, while it lasts, might yield very intense pleasure. But this pleasure is instantly consumed, leaving usually no residue to generate further pleasure in the future, without further input. That is why in an age when people, by and large, depend on spectator (passive) pleasures to while away their leisure, such as watching television, the programmes must literally be on twenty four hours a day, for the pleasure will last only so long as one is watching them. But when one has acquired a skill, the skill lasts one's lifetime, can give immense satisfaction (not only to oneself but also to others) whenever it is exercised, as well as leading one on possibly to other activities, which in turn give one satisfaction. (As an illustration of the last possibility, take gardening. If one produces beautiful flowers, this could lead to an interest in other skills, like flower arrangement, drying flowers for display, etc., all immensely pleasurable activities.)

The emphasis on activity is in keeping with my account of the real definition of human agency, when human agency is looked at not merely from the static point of view, but from the dynamic point of view. Sub-thesis (iv) specifically asserts that such an agent has capacities for acquiring skills, information and knowledge. As an agent acquires these, this in turn affects one'e range of desires, inclinations, emotions, purposes, goals and, hence, the formulation of intenttions and plans, both long term and short term, that is, sub-theses (i), (ii), (v).

Before an agent learns how to bake a perfect 'Black Forest' cake, such a person could not entertain seriously the intention of baking one as a surprise for a friend's birthday; nor can such an agent think of opening a small bakery selling fancy cakes. The acquisition of new skills and knowledge enlarges one's options. Things, which were not possible, may begin to look feasible.

It is not possible to determine *a priori* what capacities an agent may or may not possess. For quite often, capacities can lie dormant and, therefore, unsuspected for years until opportunities or circumstances make the person realise that s/he has a certain potential. We have heard of Grandma Moses, who at a very advanced age, discovered that she could paint and, indeed, paint so well that she could even sell her pictures. Or of widows, who had never shown any interest, never mind ability, in running a business, suddenly found themselves in charge of one upon their husbands' unexpected death. Through accident or force of circumstance, they suddenly discover that they possess talents which no one, least of all themselves, has ever suspected to exist. Women in general are said not to have the capacities to do all sorts of things, such as drive tractors, pilot aeroplanes, and so on, until a shortage of male labour caused, say, by a war, would, all of a sudden show that they do have such capacities after all. But, of course, promptly the war is over, women are dispensed with in such jobs, and once again are said no longer to possess such capacities.

Self discovery or self exploration in this sense, the achievement of the self through the acquisition of skills and knowledge is, therefore, an open-ended dynamic process. Only death terminates it. Hence education in this broadest sense should also be an open-ended process. Any social arrangement which ignores this large empirical fact and assumes the opposite must, therefore, be judged to be inadequate, if not grossly wrong.

7. A theory of human development which says crudely that genes are the ultimate determinant of what we are is too simplistic. Similarly, a theory of human development which says that the environment is the ultimate determinant of what we are is equally simplistic. Human development (like the development of

all biological organisms) is epigenetic.

The two crude theories understandably enough start from the causal postulate, that if differences obtain between two entities, it follows that they were either different from the outset, or that they have been exposed to very different environmental conditions. But this binary interpretation is in keeping with the linear model of causation. Either A causes X, the effect, or B causes X, the effect. As a result, it overlooks a third possibility, which is more relevant to the issue of development, namely, that development is the outcome of the interacting processes between what is 'there from the outset' and environmental conditions. And it is more in keeping with the non-linear model of causation. Each separately is a necessary condition, but the interactions between them are both necessary and sufficient conditions, that is to say, developmental processes are epigenetic events. But to put it this way is already grossly to oversimplify matters as an example will show.

Take the very beginnings of the development of an human agent. 'What is there from the outset' is the fertilised egg (that is, the embryonic genetic substrate), no more and no less, which contains information relating to structural order or various levels of organisation, as well as information to execute certain dynamic activities, such as cell division (that is, the predetermined or preprogrammed mechanisms).

According to Lovtrup, the following takes place:

When, after fertilization, the formation of the embryogenetic substrate is completed the predetermined mechanism embodied in the centriole enters into action, answering for the embryogenetic process of cell division. Gradually also the other predetermined mechanisms begin to function, with the result that cell diversification and morphogenetic processes take place. As development progresses, various kinds of interaction occur between the embrygenetic processes and between the latter and the substrate. All these changes are obviously not preformed. If they were predetermined, it would be impossible to change their course, and the well-established existence of this possibility excludes the application of this epithet. Under these circumstances it appears unavoidable that *everything, without exception*, which happens in the embryo after fertilization must be classified as *epigenetic events*. . . .The embryogenetic processes are continuously affected by the substrate and by the other processes, and may be changed by external influences. [3]

(One should bear in mind that in talking about the process of embryogenesis, the environmental influences in question refer to the internal environment residing in different parts of the embryo as well as the uterus, in the case of the mammal.)

When we talk of human development, we do not normally have in mind the process of embryogenesis. We normally at best start with the birth of the foetus. But biologically speaking, this is not correct. Ontogenesis includes pre-neonate, neonate and post neonate development. If the former is epigenetic, so are the latter.

At birth, 'what is there at the outset' is, therefore, not simply genes as the individual is already the outcome of an intricate series of epigenetic events. What happens after birth depends on further intricate series of epigenetic events which may only very crudely be portrayed as interactions between 'what is there' and the environment. [4]

'The environment' is itself just an umbrella term to refer to a whole host of variables which could be acting upon the individual agent, interacting with 'what is there', ultimately shaping her/his development. At each stage of interacting, the 'what is there' has altered, so that 'what is there' in the individual overtime is to be conceived in dynamic, not static terms. If the epigenetic account of development is correct, then the genes *versus* environment or nature/nurture controversy is much too crudely and simplistically conceived and, hence, is misleading, even false. [5]

One very important variable in 'the environment',

so to speak, which helps shape the development of an individual in these on-going causally intricate sets of epigenetic events, must be the dominant values of the society in question — those which the civilisation celebrates and allows expression and those which it disapproves of and represses. Adults in charge of growing children, adults who run key institutions and establishments have all more or less successfully internalised the approved values as well as the rejection of the disapproved values. Transmission to the younger generation and reinforcement in adults of these values take place simultaneously.

Another important point to bear in mind is that 'what is there', not being something static as has been pointed out above, may not only have dimensions added to it but may also have aspects subtracted from it. Which of these two alternatives takes place depends on the availability or the lack of opportunities in 'the environment'. As I have already mentioned, skills, knowledge, information acquired could become rusty, if not totally lost, unless one keeps exercising and calling upon them regularly.

It is just as important to remember that how an individual reacts to 'the environment' depends on her/his developmental history. The 'same environment', therefore, does not necessarily elicit the same response given different developmental histories.

However, the central message of the above for social philosophy lies in this — a necessary condition for the maximisation of self-development in individuals must be (i) the provision of an environment which encourages such a development by elevating it to a central dominant value in society, (ii) by ensuring that the resources necessary for such development (always subject to the criteria (a) that the activity should not harm others and (b) that by and large activities incurring less entropic costs are to be encouraged) are accessible to individuals.

8. The pursuit of internal goods is said to constitute a morality of production or the artistic mode of

production, while the pursuit of external material goods is said to constitute a morality of consumption. [6]

Kamenka argues that the writings of the early Marx support a morality of production or the artistic mode of production, and that for Marx a truly human society is a society of artists. [7]

It must be pointed out at once that in this context, 'artists' and 'the artistic mode of production' do not refer to actual flesh and blood artists, that is, people who paint, sing, dance, act, those we commonly call artists. It refers instead to the idea of art and the artist, in particular, to an attitude or frame of mind embodying certain values which infect the way in which the activity is carried out. As such, the concepts of the artist and the artistic mode of production can be used to characterise any one who prosecutes her/his activities in a certain way — the person in question could be a scientist or a cook, a ballet dancer or a house painter and decorator, an academic or a carpenter.

The artistic mode of production is characterised as follows:

(1) there are no external ends to which the activity is subordinated, such as reward, fame, honour etc.;

(2) the artist strives to create an object which is dictated by the laws of art peculiar to the object, and not by laws dictated from outside the activity by non-artistic or even anti-artistic ends (in so far as (1) and (2) are violated, art becomes degenerate and artists prostitute their art);

(3) artist and material are part of a single process of production so that interaction between the two is not governed by externally imposed means to an end, but is simply part of the activity which is the artist's end;

(4) in so far as it is an activity which is not merely constrained by aesthetic goals, it displays ethical qualities — *qua* artist, s/he needs not look upon others as hostile rivals and competitors but rather as mutually inspiring:

(5) an activity which enables the individual to

transcend her/himself and her/his individual ends —
to dedicate the self to something larger than private
limited ends, to an ideal or movement which one is
helping to sustain and enrich. In this way, conflict
between individual and social demands may become
muted and less polarised.

As examples of the violation of the artistic mode
of production, let me cite the following. Vance
Packard gives an instance of it, although he does not
present it in the idiom I have used. In order to procure a high turnover of product use, manufacturers
have taken to designing their products with a certain
'death date', also called, 'built-in obsolescence'. But it
appears that some engineers are both uneasy and reluctant to co-operate with management to pervert
their designing skills in order to serve the extraneous
end of maximising the firms's profits. [8]

In contrast, some painters and decorators may put
on only one undercoat of paint when the job to be
done properly calls for two such layers. Research scientists under pressure to get prizes, promotions, to be
the first to get the findings published, have also been
known to 'cook' their data. This perversion of the
artistic mode of production in the pharmaceutical
industry, when conducting tests for new drugs, is,
sometimes, called 'graphiting', which includes claiming
that patients exist when they are already dead, and
other gross violations of truth. The temptation to cut
corners is of course immense. I do not wish to claim
that one never engages in it in any way in one's
activities. What I am emphasising is the relevance of
the artistic mode of production as an ideal, which
ought to guide and inform our activities even if it
does not often, and always, do so, unfortunately.

The main differences between the artistic or productive morality and the morality of consumption may
be schematised as follows:

Artistic morality
(logic of internal
    goods)
	Morality of consumption
	(logic of external
	    goods)

(a) worth comes from	worth comes from pos-

the activity indulged;
(b) spontaneous and mutual co-operation between producers is possible in a non-zero-sum game;

sessing, consuming things; in a zero-sum game where participants are fighting for the same scarce goods, co-operation is impossible; it emphasises egoism, leading to conflict, competition;

(c) each producer produces to his own satisfaction — goal is not something that if one achieves it, one thereby deprives others of it;

the goal involves the acquisition of goods, material and psychic, whose nature is such that more to one, then less or none to others;

(d) envy is misplaced; it makes no sense to be envious when what the other has is not something s/he could be deprived of; the achievement forms part of one's personal identity which cannot be appropriated by another.

envy is not misplaced for it makes sense to deprive the successful of what they have and to appropriate them.

9. The conclusions of this chapter may be summarised as follows: the central values of civilisation ought to be ESVs, not E$\underline{S}$Vs. A lifestyle of ever increasing orgiastic consumption, relying on economic growth using E$\underline{S}$T to exploit Nature, should therefore be replaced by a lifestyle of frugal consumption using EST, sufficient to meet genuine human needs, including the need to excel, but which ought not to be perverted to become the 'need' to get ahead of others and to acquire status symbols. In other words, while the former is a genuine human need, the latter is not. The need to excel should take the form of self-development, of adopting the artistic mode of

production. (On the point of genuine human neeeds, see Chapter Ten for detailed discussion.)

A lifestyle of ever increasing consumption is morally wrong and unacceptable because:

(i) it degrades and bankrupts the biosphere and eco-systems;

(ii) at the same time, it benefits only a small minority of the existing human population at the expense of the majority, who not only does not participate in the cornucopia, but also has to suffer the costs of the benefits enjoyed by the few in the form of poverty, ill health, malnutrition and degradation of their environment; moreover, it is just not physically possible for all to participate in such a lifestyle;

(iii) such a lifestyle based on the possession of material external goods and its logic is, therefore, a zero-sum, divisive, competitive game, necessarily with few winners and many, many losers;

(iv) the imperative to win, to succeed within such a lifestyle cannot be a universal precept for, logically speaking, if there are winners there must be losers in such a game; the imperative as a universal precept must be recast as the imperative to try to win, which acknowledges the existence of failure; such an imperative may lack universal support once its implications are fully realised;

(v) moreover, the winners also pay a price, this time in the psychical and physical wear and tear involved in the process of staying a winner;

(vi) it also cheats posterity of a decent life because it leaves to posterity an ecologically degraded and near bankrupt earth.

A lifestyle of frugal consumption is morally commendable because:

(a) it does not degrade and bankrupt the biosphere and ecosystems;

(b) it is physically and conceptually possible for all existing human agents to participate equally and fully in it;

(c) such a lifestyle, based on the acquisition of internal goods and its logic, is a non zero-sum game and there is room for co-operation;

226

(d) the psychic cost in practice is very much less, as no normal agent is so bereft of capacities that s/he could not develop one or more of them and perform reasonably well in some chosen activity, and in this way earn satisfaction and self respect as well as respect from others; (bear in mind that (i) any chosen field of activity would do provided that it does not harm others, and is not extravagant in entropic costs, (ii) the emphasis on the pursuit of excellence is conducted within a context of developing a whole, harmonious person, not a neurotic one;

(e) it also does not cheat posterity, for it ensures the handing on to future generations an earth, no worse off in terms of ecological degradation than when the existing generations find it; indeed there is even a good chance of leaving the earth in better shape, ecologically speaking, for our children and grandchildren. (See Chapter One for a discussion of this point.)

CHAPTER EIGHT

WORK AND THE TWO SOCIALISMS

1. The artistic mode of production, which has been characterised in the last chapter, is intended not merely to answer (1) the question 'In what way(s) should we derive satisfaction in life?', but that in answering it in the way outlined, it has profound implications for other questions, equally crucial in social philosophy, namely, (2) how should we organise work (to provide for the needs we have for food, shelter, reproduction including the need for nurturing of the young etc)?, and (3) how should we organise leisure which we also need?

There are two profoundly different conceptions of socialism [1] depending on how the latter two questions are treated. The first of these may be called the cornucopic or expansive version of socialism (essentially subscribed to by Marx and by most people who call themselves socialist). The other may be called the ascetic version which Marx eventually rejected as a form of utopian socialism, and could be conveniently associated with the name of Charles Fourier. [2] For Marx questions (2) and (3) ultimately remain separate issues; work and leisure are separate domains of life. For Fourier, (2) and (3) become integrated. The price for integration is the ascetic version of socialism. Marx refused to pay the price, opted for the cornucopic version. The price for him is to maintain the distinction between work and leisure.

The question then arises — which is the more coherent version and more compatible with thermodynamic/ecological reality? I will argue that Fourier's is. (However, this need not be taken to imply that I approve of everything that Fourier has written and the specific concrete details of his proposed social arrangement.) It is superior to Marx's in its general direction of arguments for the folowing reasons: (a) that the ascetic version is an implication of the way we answer question (1), namely, that we should find abiding satisfaction in life in the artistic mode of production; (b) that that answer itself is dictated by our understanding of the laws of thermodynamics, of the existence of ecological (absolute) scarcity of low entropic energy/matter and of existential scarcity (time). In other words, if we take these entropic implications seriously, then Fourier's version of socialism, in principle, far from being utopian as Marx had thought, becomes paradoxically more realistic, and Marx's version looks (together with its mirror image, bourgeois capitalism) increasingly utopian. Perhaps 'utopian' is not quite the right word to use — a utopia usually refers to an ideal state of affairs which, because of the tawdriness of human nature, we cannot achieve. Marx's vision of the good society is not so much utopian as a physical impossibility — it is therefore a fantasy which is incapable of being sustained in thermodynamic and ecological terms, just like bourgeois capitalism.

2. The philosophy of work or labour itself assumes a significance in the history of Western European thought from the seventeenth century onwards which it did not have before, and is a reflection of the changing conditions under which production was taking place in the transition from late feudalism to incipient capitalism.

Capitalism requires labour power to be sold as a commodity. The labour power that is sold to the capitalist under the terms of a contract is put to work in return for wages, but also to generate profits on behalf of the capitalist. It is part of the logic of capital to increase its accumulation *via* the maximisation of profits. Maximisation of profits usually entails cutting back the costs of production. Costs of production could be reduced in a variety of ways, but historically included (i) paying as little wages to the workers as one could get away with; (ii) spending as little as possible on the actual work place in terms of aesthetics, health and safety; (iii) making workers work as long hours as one could get away with; (iv) making workers work continuously with as few breaks as it is possible to get away with during the hours of work; (v) simplifying the production process, breaking up a complex operation into parts in order to increase productivity; (vi) replacing labour wherever possible with machines to push up productivity (but at the cost of throwing labour on the scrap heap of unemployment and redundant skills.)

Under such conditions, it is not a wonder that labour has come to be seen as a curse. But the curse having been inflicted, ideological resources must be marshalled in order to render it acceptable, if not palatable. The Bible at this point is conveniently co-opted to render the curse merely as a consequence of original sin. Adam and Eve, having eaten of the forbidden fruit, were cast out of paradise (where they did not have to work — paradise is paradise because (a) the resources to sustain a good life are not scarce, but infinite and inexhaustible; (b) the resources are readily appropriated without the intervention of hard boring work). God said to the pair: 'In the sweat of thy brow, thou shalt earn thy bread'.

The wages of original sin apart, the dire threat of hunger (or today's equivalent, the hassle of obtaining, and the difficulties of living on, supplementary benefits) through refusal to do the kind of work demanded by capitalism, or through unemployment, made work on these terms a necessity. It is within such a context that the so-called Protestant work ethic has risen. If we all wanted work, we could find work — work is only unavailable to those who are not prepared to take less wages, put up with worse conditions at work in terms of aesthetics, health, safety, the lack of control of the production processes, etc.

230

[3] Those who remain unemployed deserve their fate. To eat, one must work at all cost. Work, even though a curse, is a necessity. One should never evade work if one wants to retain pride and dignity, and not be relegated to the class of scroungers and/or the undeserving poor.

Work on this view necessarily involves pain, and is therefore something one would avoid if one could. But because one must eat, one wants to avoid being labelled a scrounger, or one wants to become rich, one must work. In the hands of Mises, the thesis is presented as follows: labour is disutility as it involves effort. But the disutility of labour is overcome because agents prefer the produce of labour to the satisfaction derived from leisure. On his view, an agent would never perform an action if s/he were satisfied or contented. 'The incentive that impels a man to act is always some uneasiness' [4] — be it hunger, fear, desire for money, power or status.

This is the so-called instrumental view of work or labour. Labour which is necessarily painful is a means to an end, considered to be desirable or pleasurable, such as earning money, which in turn is a means to other desirable ends, like buying goods or gaining leisure. There is no way in which the dichotomy between desirable or pleasurable end and painful means could be overcome. [5]

On this kind of view, work is waged work. Unwaged work either does not count at all (like housework, work in looking after the young and the old by the family), or it falls into the leisure domain. What after all is the difference between decorating someone's house for a wage or payment and decorating one's own outside work hours? The first counts as work, the second as not-work. All DIY activities are not-work, even though, in essence, they are no different from those very activities for which cash transactions are made.

This gives a clue to realising that the thesis, that work is inherently painful and to be avoided if one could, may be suspect. Wielding a paint brush when one is being paid to paint someone else's walls involves no greater effort, pain or discomfort than wielding one in painting one's own. However. to do the first, one needs the threat of hunger, fear of the workhouse to impel one to do so. To do the second, it is not obvious what the stick is or the carrot for that matter, unless one makes the implausible assumption that all DIY activities are carried out, because of the motive of status-seeking to impress one's neighbours. But if neither stick nor carrot operates, then, strictly speaking, such activities would never take place, if Mises is to be believed. But they do.

Some of the socialist thinkers grappled with this problem, the nature of work under capitalism which has become a curse. It inspired them to conceive of an alternative social arrangement in which work does not have to be a curse, and the dichotomy between work and leisure becomes eroded, if not totally transcended. Fourier's attempt is one such. It would be a mistake to see his vision of the good society as a simple sentimental return to rural nostalgia. Indeed, his is one of the most radical conceptions of the future possible, based, in many ways, on a prophetic anticipation of the critical problems which now face us in the form of ecological crises and potential bankruptcy.

To understand more fully what Fourier and others are doing, one must go back to clarifying some matters raised by Mises' thesis of work. His thesis masks two possible senses of the notion of 'painful' work. The first sense is embodied in the notion of work as a curse because it has become increasingly alienating under the requirement of the capitalist mode of production. Work has become fragmented, simplified, mindlessly boring; management has taken over the conception (involving mental or brain power) of the production process leaving the worker with its mere execution (involving only repetitive physical motions). All this amounts to the loss of control of the production process on the part of the workers. (This first sense gives rise to the problem whether there can be another way of arranging work, which is not alienating, provided one gives up bourgeois capitalism, whose aim is the maximisation of profits for private gains. This in turn raises the problem whether substituting the legal relations of bourgeois capitalism for those of public ownership of the instruments of production, and meeting genuine human needs for private gain, are enough to overcome alienation at work, without also giving up some of the other crucial presuppositions of bourgeois capitalism — on these points see the sections which follow in this chapter.)

The second sense seems to equate 'painful' with whatever involves effort. As work necessarily involves the expenditure of energy and therefore effort, work then is *ipso facto* 'painful'. But this is a misleading and false identification. As we have seen, under the artistic mode of production, work as such, involving effort, indeed even great effort, may be joyfully and spontaneously engaged in. It is work in the first sense which is painful and hence to be avoided if one could possibly help it.

By eliding the two senses, Mises implies that the opposite of work (which is effortful and, therefore, necessarily 'painful') is leisure which is to be then understood as a state of passivity involving no effort, as slumping, literally doing nothing with the mind blank and the body at rest. That is why on Mises' view, it would follow that workers after work hours are to be given leisure in the form of mindless passive distractions and entertainment. It would also explain why workers, contrary to the implication of Mises' view, engage in DIY activities after work hours. This kind of leisure involves effort but it is work which is under the control of the worker, and hence is the opposite of work under alienating conditions, which render it painful and to be shunned if one could do so.

Socialist thinkers try to argue for a type of arrangement where work is not painful in the first sense, and to challenge work as being 'painful' in the second sense. In this way, they hope to transcend the dichotomy between work and leisure.

3. Charles Fourier was born in 1772 in Besançon (eastern France) and died in 1837. His father was in the clothing trade but family fortunes declined. As a result, he did not inherit his father's business but was forced to earn a living which he did, also in the clothing trade as a kind of travelling salesman as well as clerk. His former work took him to other parts of the country especially to Paris where the deficiencies and inadequacies of 'civilisation' hit him hard and full in the face. (To Fourier, 'civilisation', that is, bourgeois civilisation was a dirty word; it did not stand for progress, as the Enlightenment thought, but for irrationality and brutality.) His heart was clearly not in his work, which was as a mean cog in that sordid division of 'civilisation', called commerce. He was taken up with the vision of building a New Jerusalem which would be the very antithesis of bourgeois civilisation. But the originality and the radical nature of the good society he proposed was due in part, if not wholly, to the fact that he was an autodidact and outside the mainstream of (and indeed directly opposed to) Enlightenment thought of his time.

Like all Frenchmen, however, he paid his respect to Descartes, even though he thought little or nothing of other thinkers past and present. He was inspired, he said, by the Cartesian method of doubt. His methodology consisted in the main of what he called the methods of absolute doubt and absolute deviation — by which he really meant that no received idea or opinion, no assumption or presupposition should escape his critical scrutiny, with the possibility, therefore, of eventual rejection of all of them. Because of this, his critics accused him of sheer intellectual arrogance and indeed even of dogmatism. But yet with hindsight, given what we know today about the ravages caused by 'civilisation' to the earth's fabric, to the human psyche and the burdens imposed on it, Fourier's insights seem remarkably prescient and testify to the intellectual courage he possessed in formulating thoughts (although his most radical work, *Le Nouveau Monde Amoureux*, had to be hidden from the world for fear of further ridicule and total repudiation by the intellectual establishment of his time, and was only published in 1967), which ran so much counter to the dominant philosophy and ideology, not only of his lifetime, but even today.

Fourier divided 'civilisation' into four branches — production, distribution, commerce and consumption. He traced the evils in each domain. But the horrors of 'civilisation' were first brought home to him in the domain of commerce. His sojourn in Paris made him realise that it is one of the roots of poverty. He was fond of saying that there are three famous apples in the world to which he would add a fourth. We all know about the apple of Paris and Helen, of William Tell and of Newton. To these, he would add Fourier's apple.

In Paris, he noticed that one apple was sold for fourteen sous. In Besançon, one could have bought one hundred apples for fourteen sous. From this simple observation, he concluded that middlemen (those engaged in commerce) formed a parasitic class which was not truly productive. On the whole, it lived off deceit, dishonesty, usury and was dedicated to self-aggrandisement at the expense of the producers as well as the consumers.

However, Fourier was not a 'loony lefty'. He realised that there was a legitimate place for commerce in an economy. The act of buying and selling itself is innocent, provided (a) the goods are well-made and (b) the prices honest. Unfortunately, most of the goods sold in 'civilisation' were shoddy goods sold at an inflated price.

On this point, Fourier could be said to have anticipated the arguments put forward today by critics of our society, like Vance Packard. Fourier even gave instances of what we now call built-in obsolescence in products.

The system of production was based, said Fourier, on wage-slavery and not on co-operation. As a result, there were both exploitation and alienation. Again, these are themes which loomed large in the writings of Marx who was much influenced by Fourier in his earlier period, even if he, in the end, rejected the

French philosopher's solution to the problems of exploitation and alienation.

But the systems of production and distribution were also wasteful. So was consumption. He cited numerous cases of transportation, storage facilities, fuel consumption which were dealt with in a fragmented way and, therefore, inefficiently. The fragmentation came primarily from the fact that 'civilisation' organised people in 'isolated, incoherent households'. For instance, instead of having a large efficient oven for baking in a neighbourhood, there would be as many ovens as there were households. This is actually part of a wider attack on the bourgeois family, on patriarchy and on the subjugation of women in Fourier's totality of thought.

His critique of bourgeois civilisation led him to the following conclusions:

(1) such a 'civilisation' celebrates acquisitiveness, egoism and destructive competition;

(2) it correspondingly represses co-operation, finding satisfaction in doing things well and joyfully, instead of in possession of material goods;

(3) it also viciously represses the sexual instinct in all ways except through the rigidly enforced institution of monogamy.

In this last, one can see why Fourier was so well aware of the persecution which could, and would be visited on his head, were he to publish his thoughts on the matter. One could say, here, he anticipated Freud, not only in the main thesis that the libido is the key to human understanding but also in the mechanism of defence that Freud later identified, such as that of sublimation. Fourier realised that not all so-called 'instincts' could be allowed expression. But since total repression is bad and leads to neurosis and ailment, the damaging 'instincts', like that of sadism, should be channelled into creative rather than destructive activities — would-be torturers could, through sublimation, be guided to become useful citizens (or Harmonians) as butchers and surgeons.

In his good society, there would be no outcast and, therefore, no frustration and humiliation. Groups which 'civilisation' discard as useless or leprous could be found a place, such as the old, the handicapped, those with powerful sexual drives, those with little or none, and so on.

The old, for instance, could be given a respected role by being counsellors to the inexperienced and those with problems. They could be psycho-therapists, social workers, citizen advisers all rolled into one.

The way to deal with the libido is not to force it into the procrustean bed of official monogamy but to tie it to authenticity. People should be free to choose to adhere to different rules of sexual conduct — to be faithful to one partner or not to be. In this way hypocrisy is dissolved.

All socialists advocate some form of social minimum below which no-one ought to fail. But no socialist would go as far as to advocate a sexual minimum. Fourier did. The sexually unattractive, the not so charming or forward might end up with no sexual gratification. [6] Instead of such frustrated persons turning to prostitution at best, their needs might be provided for by those who fell from grace, that is, those who chose to adhere to the rule of fidelity but yet gave in to temptation, and became inauthentic. As penance, they could (instead of saying so many Aves — Fourier was keen to borrow and adapt Catholic institutions to serve different ends in his good society) provide sexual services for the rejected and the despised. They could thus redeem themselves as well as give joy to those in need.

4. There are two twin pillars to Fourier's good society which he called Harmony. One is liberation from sexual repression, and the other liberation from what we now call the Protestant work ethic. Work need not be a curse; it need not be something one performs either through fear of hunger, or through the psychological compulsion to work. [7] It could be something done spontaneously, willingly and joyfully in surroundings which are pleasing, aesthetic, delightful, under conditions which are not alienating. One

needs to transcend the dichotomy between work and leisure, so that work is leisure and leisure work.

Work that is freely chosen to suit one's temperament and interest is work that, by and large, will be done spontaneously and without the need of threats. As much as is possible, that should be the principle of allocation of work — someone who loves to do the accounts would not be happy if s/he has to scrub out the stables; *vice versa*, someone who loves animals would not be happy as a bookkeeper. Work done in the company of friends and lovers, he said, would also add to the pleasure. As much as is possible, work teams should be self-selected.

At this point, the critic is bound to raise the inevitable objection — who will do the filthy dirty work? No-one would elect to do that surely? To this Fourier had a reply. First of all, it is not obvious that what one calls dirty work is so to everyone. Children delight to play in mud and in what we adults call dirt. Why not harness the little hordes to perform such tasks like muck spreading? (Exploitation of children occurs in 'civilisation' where children's labour is sold as a commodity. In Harmony, as well as in most other cultures preceding our present one, children, like adults, contribute according to their ability.)

Of those truly unattractive unpleasant jobs which everyone shuns, it is always possible to arrange to do them by rotation. No matter how nasty and boring, if one knows that it is a temporary undertaking, it becomes more bearable. Such work in 'civilisation' degrades the worker only because the worker has to do it for the rest of her/his life; moreover, s/he has to bear the humiliating label and status that go with it, and suffer low pay and other disadvantages to boot.

But again the critic raises other objections. Admittedly, agricultural and horticultural work could conceivably be handled in the way proposed for his commune. But surely factory manufacturing work is not amenable to such an arrangement? So whatever plausibility there might be in Fourier's ideas lies in his vision of the rural, and could have no relevance to an industrialised society. This brings us to the crux of the matter — does Fourier's type of socialism necessarily reject industrialised civilisation, itself based on science and EST to exploit and dominate Nature?

Before attempting to answer this general question, let me first say something about Fourier's answer to the question about the place of manufacture in Harmony. He did not reject the relevance of manufacture altogether. Instead, (a) he recognised that the method of manufacturing products could be unattractive and boring in most of its processes; (b) in so far as one must have manufactured products, one must make sure (i) that they are genuinely useful, (ii) that they are well-made to last as long as the state of one's technology permits. At a stroke, one cuts down on the volume of boring unattractive work, saves resources and reduces waste and pollution.

Critics charge Fourier with irrelevance. They maintain that as someone writing in France even before industrialisation had properly reached the country, what could he have to say about a kind of society he never experienced? It was happening in England, of course. So his rejection of industrialisation, by and large, rested on his Gallic prejudice against Albion. But to say this is unnecessarily to trivialise Fourier's contribution to social thought. It seems to me his insight consists of trying to articulate a form of social arrangement, which avoids the evils of a mode of production based on the logic of industrialism, using science and EST to dominate Nature and to exploit her to serve human ends, especially the end of ever increasing possession and consumption of material external goods.

For Fourier, 'civilisation' is objectionable because, as we have seen, it (a) celebrates egoism, competition, divisiveness while repressing other inclinations and preferences; it urges agents to find satisfaction in status-seeking through the acquisition of external goods and their consumption;
(b) (a) entails the 'Protestant work ethic' — (i) work itself is so organised and devised that it becomes a

curse; (ii) those who are successful in this zero-sum game, nevertheless, are compelled to work further and harder so as not to lose their place in the queue or, indeed, through an impoverished and distorted psyche, to lack the resources to do anything else; (iii) the majority has no choice but to submit to the curse of work in order to keep hunger and other humiliations at bay; (iv) yet others work in order to qualify to be successful;

(c) this in turn reflects the instrumental view of work — (i) work which is a curse has to be endured, in order to realise the desirable end of being regarded as successful through possession and consumption; (ii) work which is a curse has to be endured, in order to reach the desirable end of leisure, not having to work; (iii) but (i) interferes with (ii), as the zero-sum game of success ensures that no-one could pause to relax and enjoy the fruits of his/her work. (I have argued in the last chapter that as time is existentially scarce, this absolutely scarce factor on its own would render it impossible for agents to do anything other than own objects as status symbols);

(d) as mere accumulation and consumption recognise no level of sufficiency but increase indefinitely, and must so increase, to serve as status symbols, the gratification of this central impulse in 'civilisation' is bound to lead to waste;

(e) this, combined with the Enlightenment project of progress which aims to use science and its EST to dominate Nature and exploit her in the way outlined, inevitably leads to a rape of Nature and a destruction of the earth's fabric.

Conversely, Harmony could avoid these evils of 'civilisation' through the crucial recognition, that satisfaction in life (in Chapter Ten, I will argue that this is a genuine need for the self to excel and to do well) is to be derived not through the destructive (both psychically and ecologically) goal of ever increasing possession and consumption of external goods, but that it should be rechannelled to a goal which is both psychically liberating, as well as ecologically sustainable, that is, to transcend the Protestant work ethic, so that work no longer would be a curse that has to be endured both by the successful, the would-be successful and the unsuccessful alike, so that it could be co-operatively carried out, so that it is no longer necessary to seek leisure (which is the other side of the coin to the curse of work) because work itself is pleasurable, creative and joyfully undertaken.

Such human motivation would lead to a lifestyle which is more at peace with Nature, and hence more ecologically sustainable, and at the same time, less psychically devastating. If manufactured products are no longer required to play their role as status symbols, but only as useful products to meet certain needs, then as we have seen, Fourier argued, less room would be needed to accommodate the manufacturing sector. Yet it is primarily, though not solely, in this sector, that the unsustainable ecological demands are made.

Once we have divested ourselves of the possession of manufactured goods beyond the level of meeting needs, what else is there in the main to sustain human agency? Food. While manufactured goods can be made to last as long as the state of technology permits, food, by its very nature and also given our human metabolism, is not manipulable in the same fashion. We have to eat roughly three times a day (this point will be explored at greater length in Chapter Ten.) Once consumed and digested, food becomes faeces and cannot directly be re-used. Hence the need for a constant, steady and renewable supply of food. But if food is eaten for sustenance and not for conspicuous consumption, then there is a limited amount we can eat at any one time. Our work then to produce food, said Fourier, may be conducted in a more relaxed way, and may even be punctuated by feasts and other celebrations.

Fourier wrote:

Let us refute. . .a strange sophism of the economists who claim that the unlimited increase of manufactured goods constitutes an increase in wealth. This would mean that if every individual could be made to use 4 times as much clothing as he does, society would quadruple the wealth it derives from manufacturing work. Nothing of the kind! The economists are wrong on this point just as they are wrong in desiring an unlimited increase in population or *cannon-fodder*. In Harmony real wealth is based: 1) The greatest possible consumption of the different kinds of food; 2) The smallest possible consumption of different kinds of clothing and furniture. . . . [8]

As such, the production of food is central to the endurance of society, in the sense that food is continuously being used up and, hence, must be continuously renewed. This sense of centrality does not deny that houses and clothes are also central — houses and clothes can, however, be made to last more than one occasion of use but food cannot; but they are, of course, necessary for survival. Hence Fourier's emphasis on agriculture and horticulture. Whilst manufacturing may be said to be peripheral in this sense, agriculture cannot. In other words, Fourier was implicitly criticising the trend that was obviously taking place in the England of his time and which he must have observed, of turning agricultural labour and land into manufacturing labour and use. Today's critics of 'civilisation' agree too with Fourier that we need (a) to wind down the manufacturing sector, and (b) to return the surplus to the land, so that agriculture can stop being an industry, which relies on excessive use of chemicals and machinery, which combine to create ecological disturbances; instead, it should become, once again, labour intensive using more technologically benign methods to nurse the plants.

Agriculture in modern times has become peripheral to the economy under 'civilisation', crucially because it has become agribusiness, using the methods of science and its EST. (For instance, in the USA, the working population in the agricultural sector of the economy fell from 50 percent of total employment in 1880 to 4 percent in 1970.) But as Fourier was well aware of the drawbacks of an exploitative science and its E$\underline{S}$T, he was farsighted enough to reject its application to the domain of agriculture. To be ecologically sustainable, in other words, it would not do (in spite of the temptation of so-called productivity through energy-intensive techniques) to use massive chemical pesticides, herbicides, fertilisers, etc. Faeces and other organic waste must be returned to the earth; fields must be left fallow to recover fertility; plants which are nitrogen fixers must be grown in the fields; companion planting must be practised, and so on. Machines which lead to the destruction of hedgerows, there by causing soil erosion, might have to be forsworn; other machines which cause the earth to impact might also have to be given up. All this probably implies a more labour-intensive type of farming. Moreover, it has to depend on the flow of solar energy and not on the non-renewable stocks of fossil fuels and their derivatives.

As Georgescu-Roegen and Ophuls point out, it means the kind of farming — organic, not monoculture, labour-intensive — typical of so-called traditional farming upon which progress has poured scorn increasingly for the last two hundred years at least.

To quote Ophuls:

A mode of agricultural production that gets only a one-to-five or, worse, a one-to-ten return on its energy input may make economic sense in the short run, but it is ecological nonsense in the long run, unless energy is super-abundant and ecologically harmless, which is not the case. Moreover, despite what technologists and spokesmen for agribusiness say, there is a real possibility of breaking the vicious circle of technological addiction in agriculture and shifting back towards an agriculture based on dilute but renewable and nonpolluting solar energy, but informed by a high degree of scientific understanding and biological sophistication. With care, very high yields could be obtained for millennia from such an agricultural technology. Some of the principles and techniques of ecological farming were suggested in the preceding chapter.

Ironically, many of them resemble earlier farming
techniques that we have scorned as primitive and
inefficient — combined forestry and grazing, controlled cropping of game animals (game ranching)
instead of cattle-raising in tropical areas, fish ponds
that turn wastes into protein, mixed farming instead
of monoculture, crop rotation and the use of both
animal manure and 'green fertilizer', substitution of
labour for herbicides and pesticides, and so forth.
Especially if they are brought up to date with modern science, these techniques are highly productive
(on a per-acre basis they can outproduce industrial
agriculture), *but only when human labor is carefully
and patiently applied.* Thus farming that is both
productive and ecologically sound seems very likely
to be small-hold, horticultural, essentially peasant-
style agriculture finely adapted to local conditions
(especially in the tropics). It should be obvious that
many of the developing countries are well posed to
make the transition to this modernized version of
traditional agriculture. Except for the excessive use
of insecticides and chemical fertilizers in some
areas, the agriculture of China, Taiwan, Korea,
Ceylon, Egypt and others is already close to this
mode, and has high per-acre yields to show for it.
By contrast, the United States and some other developed nations (Japan is a major exception) appear
to face a great deal of 'development' in order to
change over to this style of agricultural production,
so that the transition would be socially painful. The
back-to-the-land movement notwithstanding, how
many Americans would willingly return to family
farming? [9]

Fourier, were he alive today, would find nothing to
disagree with in Ophul's assessment. In other words,
his insights on this matter were too far ahead of his
time and he was written off as not quite right in the
head. Like the physiocrats, his plea that the economy
(and life itself) should primarily be based on agriculture and horticulture, and not manufacture, were
ignored as the industrial civilisation tore ahead at that

time to base its economic growth and wealth on manufacture, using an exploitative science and its EST.

Now we seem to have come full circle. Today's critics of industrial civilisation realise, like Fourier, that the exponential growth of manufactured goods is both ecologically unsustainable and destructive. So contemporary critics (or Jeremiahs to those who believe that economic growth at an exponential rate is both physically possible and a conceptually coherent goal), like Fourier, argue that (i) we should limit the production of such goods by ensuring that only useful ones (to meet needs) are produced, that these useful goods are produced by an EST and not an EST, that they are made to last as long as possible; (ii) that we should return to the less polluting, less demanding in ecological terms, more efficient (in terms of net energy yield), organic, labour-intensive agriculture.

Fourier saw with great clarity that exploitative science and its EST (in conjunction with the profit motive or greed) could only lead to debasement of both food and manufactured goods. He wrote:

Indirect depravity of the sciences. Progress in the sciences of chemistry, to cite just one example, only serves to plague the poor by providing commerce with the means to debase all commodities: bread made out of potatoes, wine squeezed from logwood, sham vinegar, sham oil, sham coffee, sham sugar, sham indigo. All our foodstuffs and manufactured goods are adulterated, and it is the poor man who suffers by this chemical cheapening: he alone is the victim of all these mercantile inventions. They could be put to good use under a system of truthful relations, but they will become increasingly harmful until the close of civilization. [10]

Is this not precisely what the critics of 'civilisation' today are saying? How prophetic indeed is Fourier. It is true today that the poor are worse off — survey after survey show that their diet of predominantly pre-packaged, processed convenience food is less nutritious and less healthy than what the richer and better informed middle classes live on. They also buy the shoddy, mass-produced goods which, again, the richer could afford to discriminate against.

Fourier's attitude to Nature ran directly counter to that of the Enlightenment. Whilst to the latter it is a hostile force to be subdued, overcome and 'humanised' no matter what the cost, to Fourier it is essentially benign and generous, if not abused. So long as our needs are modest and our numbers not too many, Nature could meet them without undue stress and strain. We can live in harmony not only with Nature but also with ourselves. Hostility to Nature is rooted in hostility amongst human agents, in greed, egoism, acquisitiveness and competition. Once liberated from such vices, we can be co-operative not only with fellow human agents, but also co-opt Nature in a non-aggressive, non-destructive, non-exploitative way to meet our genuine human needs.

In other words, if Fourier's vision is a socialist one, it is a socialism which rejects the logics of capitalism, of industrialism and of economic growth. It is an ascetic socialism, that is, one which is sufficient but frugal in material possession and consumption but paradoxically rich in spirit — in the possibilities of self-development, in the achievement of internal goods.

It is important to recognise that Fourier should be seen as advocating the artistic mode of production. Such a mode, as we saw in the last chapter, is an attitude and a way of conducting activity, no matter what the activity may be. It could be growing pears, milking cows, playing the flute, doing a scientific experiment. Such a mode which embodies the ethical spirit does not imply that the activity conducted under such a spirit is necessarily simple, easy or effortless. Part of the misunderstanding of Fourier lies precisely in this. He is made to look idiotic through implying that the activities he regarded to be central, those pertaining to agriculture, horticulture, husbandry are simple-minded non-demanding activities which could not begin to compare with other activities central to 'civilisation'.

However, to conduct an activity, any activity under the artistic mode of production, is to be engaged physically and mentally with it. For instance, to look after animals properly means, amongst other things, getting up in the middle of the night at lambing time to help them give birth if necessary, to round them up at all hours when the weather gets too severe, etc. It involves observing them closely to see if they might not be suffering from incipient infection, disease of one sort or other. The life of a shepherd(ess) conducted under the artistic mode requires infinitely more effort than when animals are simply kept under battery conditions and controlled by electronic gadgets, under the mode of consumption for gain and for the sake of productivity. Yet the hard work that is involved, nevertheless, gives one abiding satisfaction which comes from the knowledge that it is a job well done. So even though getting out of one's warm bed in the middle of a very cold spring night is intrinsically unpleasant, nevertheless, the good husbandry person would willingly and spontaneously do so to assist a difficult birth or to look for a lost lamb. Such a person does not need the threat of wages lost or the whip or the incentive to get rich to do so.

It is for this reason that Fourier was so scornful of the formal freedoms guaranteed by the kind of democracy which we, today, call liberal representative democracy. Formal freedoms have nothing to say about the liberating of the libido from crippling repression and hypocrisy, and of the agent from the Protestant work ethic. Instead, Fourier talked about bicompound freedom, a freedom which was based, in his analysis, on the emancipation from the two crucial kinds of repression under 'civilisation'. The democracy he implied had more in common with what political theorists, today, call participatory democracy, [11] of which democracy at the work place is an essential ingredient. Harmonians met every evening at the Exchange to discuss and determine for themselves the schedule of work in all aspects for the morrow (and presumably also to plan for the future needs of the community). This, for Fourier, was more meaningful a type of democratic process than casting a vote every few years at an election to produce a group of decision-makers, which enjoys (at least under the revised democratic theory [12]) *carte blanche* power to decide how they please, with little or no accountability, till the next election comes round.

5. In order to understand Marx's attitude to the theme of work or labour and his conception of socialism/communism, it is necessary not only to examine Fourier's thoughts, but also Saint-Simon's. For while Fourier provocatively rejected the logics of industrialism and exponential economic growth, Saint-Simon, one could say, was (is) the patron saint of our industrial civilisation. He was fired with enthusiasm by the prospect of organisation in large-scale industries and was hailed as the prophet of the age of organisation and technology. The main features of his ideas may be summarised as follows:

(a) every man has the right to work or to demand employment.

(b) society has no room for the idle, privileged rich, the nobility, the soldiers, the priests and those who live off their unearned incomes without taking part in the productive process.

(c) the producers in society are, on the one hand, the managers, the industrialists and the bankers and, on the other, the workers. The former he called 'les industriels' who plan and control society using science and technology to increase material prosperity, and to promote the welfare of the class that is the most numerous and the poorest — 'la classe la plus nombreuse et la plus pauvre' — a kind of meritocratic *noblesse oblige*.

(d) he believed that men are unequally endowed with talents. This, combined with the principle of functional differentiation according to talents, would yield a hierarchical society. The élites are the technocrats:

> In the Saint-Simonian world outlook, organic in-
> equality among men, inequality in the social hier-
> archy, and difference of social function were
> natural and beneficient. . . .Born unequal in their
> faculties, men required a society in which each was
> allotted a function 'according to capacity' — this is
> the true meaning of the famous slogan of the
> Saint-Simonian cult. [13]

Status, power, income are to be determined by function, by the individual's capacities to contribute to the
production process. The right to property is to be
confined to those who could put it to good purpose.
(His disciples, especially Bazard, advocated the abolition of inheritance of property — property on death
would pass on to the state.)

He was no lover of democracy — neither of the
kind we now call liberal representative democracy,
which Bentham was fighting for, nor the kind that
Fourier recommended. The Revolution of 1789 bred in
him a deep suspicion of the masses. Democratic rule
is based on ignorance, not knowledge. The élites —
the financiers and the captains of industry — are the
natural leaders of the industrious poor, for whom they
have a duty to rule and to plan the economy.

(e) Saint-Simon's real insight lies in the realisation
that organisation is the key to the development of
industrialisation based on science and technology. That
is why he is, *par excellence*, the philosopher of the
age of organisation and of the triumph of the industrial revolution. 'The philosophy of the eighteenth
century was critical and revolutionary; that of the
nineteenth century will be inventive and organization-
al.' [14]

For Saint-Simon, a political and social message lies
in the notion of organisation. It is the answer to
instability and disorder — 'The necessary and organic
social bonds [were to be found] in the idea of industry.' [15] An organisation is a whole which is greater
than the sum of its parts. The whole determines and
orders a rational arrangement of the functioning parts.
It requires that some parts be subordinated to other

parts. This implies direction, authority and control. The principle of function, says Wolin, is the principle of legitimation. Organisation implies hierarchy. But the masses are not interested in either liberty or equality, only in material prosperity, of which there would be plenty when Nature is exploited systematically through science and its EST. Once that is given them, they would become loyal supporters. The industrial order in delivering the goods will ensure stability, integration and unchallenged authority. [16]

(f) this order is guided by principles which are both 'necessary' and 'true', based on 'the nature of things' and so are 'independent of human will'. Scientific laws take over from men and, hence, the disappearance of the political element. Men would no longer dominate men — the substance of politics — but would together subdue and dominate Nature. Politics would be reduced to a minimum of 'establishing a hierarchy of functions in the general action of man on nature', and to remove obstacles to 'useful work'.

(g) organisation enables the conquest of happiness by satisfying desires. A whole society, organised and united in exploiting Nature by its methods and its technology, would end all frustration. Desires can grow indefinitely and be satisfied continuously. Finitude is a source (indeed the only source) of frustration.

One can see from the above characterisation that two powerful themes are central to Saint-Simon's social philosophy — the logic of industrialism and the logic of exponential economic growth, both rendered possible for the first time in human history by exploiting Nature through science and its technology. Socialists (with the exception of those who, I argue, opt for the ascetic version) and capitalists alike take both seriously. In *Capital* Marx said: 'In Modern Industry man succeeded for the first time in making the product of his past labour work on a large scale gratuitously. . . .like the forces of nature.' [17] It is true that Marx did not buy some of the other themes of Saint-Simon's social philosophy, but he seemed to have no qualms in the end co-opting the two just mentioned.

6. As this work is not concerned with Marxist scholarship, I will just confine myself to making some remarks about the general thrust of Marx's thinking, in particular, with regard to the theme of work as productive activity and its related theme of overcoming alienation in work.

It does look as if Marx seemed to have changed or, at least, modified his views on these matters as his thoughts matured. His earlier works show a pronounced influence by Fourier (and also by Schiller), to such an extent that in the *German Ideology* Marx said, that the socialist (communist) mode of production would enable one 'to do one thing today and another tomorrow, to hunt in the morning, fish in the afternoon, rear cattle in the evening, criticise after dinner, just as I have a mind. . .without ever becoming hunter, fisherman, shepherd or critic.' [18]

It is sometimes remarked that this sounds remarkably like a Germanic analogue of the vision of life on a summer's day in Fourier's Harmony. Mondor, one of the relatively richer Harmonians, enjoyed the following lifestyle on a typical day of his existence: he would have eaten five meals, attended Mass, two public functions, a concert (or ball), and spent an hour and a half in the library. He would have performed eight tasks — in the morning, he would hunt, fish, garden and tend pheasants; in the afternoon, he would spend his time at the fish tanks, the sheep pasture, and in two different greenhouses. Finally, just before supper, he would attend a session at the Exchange to plan activities for the following day.

In the margin of the manuscript of the *German Ideology*, Marx and Engels indicated another set of activities: 'cobbler in the morning, gardener in the afternoon, and actor in the evening'. This seems to resemble the lifestyle of Lucas, a relatively poorer Harmonian — in the morning, Lucas would look after the stables, garden, barnyard, the vegetable plot; in the afternoon he would do forestry work, irrigation and manufacture; in the evening, he too would attend the session at the Exchange, followed by entertainment.

To overcome alienation, work instead of being

boringly the same must be varied. To overcome fragmentation and to become a whole person, one must
be able to engage in a variety of activities. Both of
these, Fourier tried to accommodate, and so did Marx,
in so far as he followed Fourier. The passage cited
from the *German Ideology* just now is preceded by
the following:

> as soon as the division of labour begins each man
> has a particular, exclusive sphere of activity, which
> is forced upon him and from which he cannot es-
> cape. He is a hunter, a fisherman, a shepherd, or a
> critical critic, and must remain so if he does not
> want to lose his means of livelihood; whereas in a
> communist society, where nobody has one exclusive
> sphere of activity but each can become accomplish-
> ed in any branch he wishes

Like Fourier, he was in favour of abolishing the division of labour as minute specialisation of tasks.

However, in the *Grundrisse*, Marx accused Fourier
of being like a coquettish shop girl ('grisette-like
naiveté') in dealing with a serious and profoundly
significant matter. 'Attractive labour' *à la* Fourier is
an illusion, and so is the freedom that goes with it.
Members of Harmony would be working most of the
time in order to achieve and maintain the social minimum that Fourier guaranteed them. By repudiating
technology, science and organisation altogether,
paradoxically, Marx argued, men would have to labour
so hard for so much of the time that the integration
between work and play, labour and leisure, that Fourier envisaged, would not be able to take place. The
arcadian bowers of bliss are illusory havens and
heavens. Human beings should not hold science and
technology at arms' length as Fourier recommended.
Instead, socialist human beings should wholeheartedly
embrace them, and tame and harness them, to serve
genuine human needs.

One can see by this stage Marx (and Engels) had
virtually accepted, in spite of earlier doubts, Saint-
Simon's logics of industrialism and exponential

economic growth to meet ever increasing desires and needs. But Marx (also Engels) is wrong (i) in assuming with Saint-Simon that science and its EST in exploiting Nature could cope with ever-increasing desires, and to use means which are exhorbitant in their demands on low entropic energy and matter, and prolific in their generation of waste and pollution, to meet human needs; (ii) in reading into Fourier the mistaken view that the artistic mode of production necessarily involves no hard time-consuming work. Marx wrote: 'Really free work, for example, composing, is at the same time precisely the most damned seriousness, the most intense exertion.' [19] As I have argued, this is not something that Fourier would wish to deny.

It is precisely because of Fourier's realisation that exploitative science and its technology would not be ecologically sustainable, that an ecologically sustainable mode of production requires intensive labour, that he, paradoxically, worked out a different work ethic from that of the Protestant one. I have argued that the artistic mode of production, the achievement of internal goods, embodying a morality of co-operation, repudiating acquisitiveness of external material goods, can be fulfilling, satisfying, spontaneous, exhilarating and indeed joyful in spite of having to work hard. Work informed by a different ethical spirit, operated under non-alienating conditions, need no longer be shunned as drudgery. Presumably Marx himself, in both his practice and theory in his earlier works, celebrated the artistic mode of production. He undertook his vast projects in just such a spirit. No one would wish to deny that Marx put in long, arduous and strenuous hours both at the British Museum and elsewhere; nor would anyone wish to deny that he must have got tremendous satisfaction out of his lifelong projects. They were all spontaneously and willingly undertaken, in his case, often, in spite of the threat of hunger.

Indeed if Marx took seriously the view that the truly human society was a society of artists, then he should have come to the same conclusion as Fourier.

But along the way, Marx appeared to have been seduced by Saint-Simon's logics of industrialism and of economic growth, based on the (economist's) concepts of productivity and efficiency. (See Chapter Six.) He, therefore, ended up by accusing Fourier of having misunderstood industrial civilisation and the Industrial Revolution.

By *Capital* III, Marx was claiming that the struggle to wrest a living from Nature under any mode of production (whether capitalist, socialist, or savage) belongs to the realm of necessity.

The realm of freedom actually begins only where which is determined by necessity and mundane considerations ceases; thus in the very nature of things it lies beyond the sphere of actual material production. Just as the savage must wrestle with Nature to satisfy his wants, to maintain and reproduce life, so must civilised man, and he must do so in all social formations and under all possible modes of production. With his development this realm of physical necessity expands as a result of his wants, to maintain and reproduce life, so must civilised man, and he must do so in all social formations and under all possible modes of production. With his development this realm of physical necessity expands as a result of his wants; but, at the same time, the forces of production which satisfy these wants also increase. Freedom in this field can only consist in socialized man, the associated producers, rationally regulating their interchange with Nature, bringing it under their common control, instead of being ruled by it as by the blind forces of Nature; and achieving this with the least expenditure of energy and under conditions most favourable to, and worthy of, their human nature. But it nonetheless still remains a realm of necessity. Beyond it begins that development of human energy which is an end in itself, the true realm of freedom, which, however, can blossom forth only with this realm of necessity as its basis. The shortening of the working-day is its basic prerequisite. [20]

First of all, a relatively minor point. Unlike the nineteenth century, today's anthropological evidence suggests that the 'savage' or really the hunter-gatherer did not have to work as hard in terms of hours alone to get a living as industrialised people do. They probably worked the equivalent of our three working days a week. 'Progress', far from always making it easier for us to obtain the things in life to sustain us, makes it actually harder. [21] We have to work longer hours to earn our keep. Coming to times nearer to our own, not even the medieval peasants had to work as hard as industrialised people. They had more feast days and holidays. They did not have to do night shift, having to work so-called unsocial hours all the time. Instead, by and large, they ceased work when the sun disappeared below the horizon. The winter months were not quite as hectic as the sowing and harvesting seasons. Neither the hunter-gatherer nor the medieval peasant had to put up with grisly conditions at their work place, where production line discipline demanded, and still demands, that to pause, 'even for a pee', requires that one obtains permission first from the foreman. As for their caves and hovels, they could be better, but certainly no worse, than urban slum tenements for the operatives, or the shacks of urban squatters in many of the cities of third world economies today.

Next, as we have seen in an earlier chapter, Marx saw it necessary to remove only the legal relations of production under (bourgeois) capitalism, as they are for him the basis of exploitation and of a class divided society. But he saw no need to depart from the other assumptions of capitalism, apart from making sure that the fruits of exploiting Nature, through science and its technology, are equally divided amongst agents based on needs, instead of unequally retained in the hands of the capitalist class.

It is the retention of these other assumptions which made it necessary for Marx to repudiate Fourier, and to accept the dichotomy between labour and leisure as something impossible in principle to supersede. The shortening of the working day has since been accomplished in the advanced industrial economies of the first world. Unfortunately, the leisure available has become dominated by the leisure industries.

The Marxist solution would work if its fundamental assumption were correct, namely, that science and technology could render ecological (that is, absolute) scarcity into relative scarcity, an assumption also shared by bourgeois capitalism. But alas it is false. As a result, a cornucopic version of socialism, which could claim to be less wasteful, more efficient in meeting human needs than bourgeois capitalism is equally false. The Faustian aspiration of proliferating desires and, hence, needs is a dream.

The implied Marx's analysis of need is a deeply troubled one. On the one hand, unlike bourgeois capitalist theorists, Marx would like to say that there are genuine human needs which could be distinguished from mere wants and desires. The latter may be frivolous and, therefore, need not be met; but the former are urgent and should be met. Clearly market allocations often (if not invariably) fail to meet them in the case of most people. So another type of allocation, which makes sure that they are met, must be installed. On the other hand, Marx appeared reluctant to recognise that genuine human needs (as will be argued in Chapter Ten) have a natural sufficiency (so long as the genuine human need to excel is not tied up with the ethic of sheer acquisitiveness and ever increasing consumption of external material goods). As such human needs are not infinitely growing and limitless. If they are not, neither do we need to exploit Nature through science and its EST to meet them. The needs are rooted in our human capacities. But we have a choice to meet these needs — a rational society, which understands the implications of the laws of thermodynamics and the principles of ecology for human (and other) existence, would choose to satisfy them in ways which do not bankrupt the ecosphere and the ecosystems.

Sufficiency of needs together with an ecologically sensitive choice of the satisfiers to meet the needs would, however, add up not to a cornucopic version of socialism (what bourgeois capitalism and consumerism can do, we can do at least as well if not better), but an ascetic model which is frugal in its entropic demands upon Nature, but which at the same time could be liberating in spirit through the achievement of internal goods. As such, there is no need, as Marx did, to regard Nature as basically hostile to our human ends. There is no need to 'humanise' Nature at all cost — instead we can live a fulfilling life within the constraints imposd by Nature *via* the laws of thermodynamics and ecology, without abusing and destroying Nature and, hence, our species, as well as other species.

Marx thought that technology (namely E$\underline{S}$T) was neutral with regard to alternative forms of social arrangements, and assumed that both bourgeois capitalism and socialism are equally compatible with it. His doubts about the alienating potentials of technology were not so much about E$\underline{S}$T itself as any one established form of it. He warned in a letter to Annenkov (18/12/1846) that any form could restrict not only the quantity of products but importantly, and to the point, the quality of human needs it satisfies. [22]

A sympathetic interpretation of Marx's view on technology is that put forward, for instance, by Mészáros who argues that alienation may never be totally superseded, and that the solution lies in achieving an ever decreasing trend of alienation in a technologised socialist society. He writes:

(1) that no *a priori* safeguards and assurances can be given for a practical supersession of alienation, since the issues involved are themselves inherently socio-historical; (2) that there are some *dangers* of alienation which are inherent in the reifying *potential* of certain instruments and institutions of human interchange; (3) and that no achievement in this respect (however radical and important) can be considered an *absolutely* definitive (permanent) 'Aufhebung' of all possible forms of alienation. [23]

A less sympathetic interpretation would say, that his enthusiasm for EST, makes it impossible really to supersede alienation. After all, the phenomenon of alienation arose precisely (though not entirely) because work has become technologised. Before the arrival of modern science and its EST, work might be hard, arduous, backbreaking, but it was not necessarily alienating (except for slaves who did not own even their own bodies, and serfs who had to work some of the time for someone else.) But under EST, in particular, machines become the master; machine production requires that jobs become over-simplified and in that way over-specialised. EST either renders human skills redundant or renders them fragmented through increasing division of labour, and reduces human intelligence to the level exhibited by machines.

In the end Marx offered amelioration and not any attempt to transcend the dichotomy posed by the realms of necessity and of freedom. In other words, he basically held an instrumental view of work — work is a curse but it is necessary to endure the curse in order to achieve the desired end, that is, of leisure where one could then develop oneself in ways not allowed by the curse of work.

Amelioration includes (1) job enrichment, enlargement and rotation; (2) using robots to do the most boring jobs, so that humans could be mainly concerned with the preparation and planning of the entire productive process; (3) better technical and scientific education, so that workers would understand the whole process of production of which their own is a part; (4) a greater part in the management of the productive process.

To conclude, with hindsight, it is difficult to share Marx's wholehearted scorn for Fourier and his (implied) enthusiasm for what Saint-Simon stood for. However, it was not Fourier's insights which were co-opted by mainstream socialist thought. The second world is inspired, by and large, by Marx's conception of cornucopic socialism. China, belonging to the third world, is in a somewhat more non-orthodox position. On one interpretation of what is happening today in

China, one could say that the two conceptions — the ascetic and the cornucopic — are each struggling for ascendancy, with sometimes the one winning and the other trying to re-assert itself.

Marx and Engels did not bestow their scorn only on Fourier, of course. They also spent considerable energy ridiculing the so-called 'true socialists', who, in the main, showed an affinity to Fourier's view of work and Nature. The whole of the second volume of *The German Ideology* is devoted to that task. A group of German thinkers round about 1840, which included Ludwig Feuerbach, articulated a conception of socialism (and communism) which called for a return to a 'natural' order. Amongst other things, they argued that (1) human beings are themselves part of Nature; (2) that Nature forms a unity of life; (3) that humans should live in harmony with Nature, like all the other forms of life, which are part of the whole that is Nature.

As for thesis (1), one of them had written:

Did not man too spring from the primeval world, is he not a child of nature, like all other creatures? Is he not formed of the same materials, is he not endowed with the same general energies and properties that animate all things? Why does he still seek his earthly happiness in an earthly beyond? [24]

To which Marx and Engels responded:

The *same* general energies and properties which man has in common with '*all* things' are cohesion, impenetrability, volume, gravity etc., which can be found set out in detail on the first page of any textbook of physics. It is difficult to see how one can construe this as a reason why man should not 'seek his earthly happiness in an earthly beyond.' [25]

This remark betrays Marx's and Engels' unquestioned acceptance of classical physics as the paradigmatic science, and its associated mechanistic paradigm of explaining the universe in all its workings.

As for thesis (2), the same author wrote:

'gay flowers. . .tall and stately oaks. . .their satisfaction, their happiness lie in their life, their growth, their blossoming. . .an infinite multitude of tiny creatures in the meadows. . .forest birds . . .a mettlesome troop of young horses. . . .I see' (says 'man') that 'these creatures neither know nor desire any other happiness than that which lies for them in the expression and enjoyment of their lives. When night falls, my eyes behold a countless host of worlds which revolve about each other in infinite space according to eternal laws. I see in their revolutions a society of life, movement and happiness.' [26]

And

'Nature as the basis of all life is a unity which proceeds from itself and returns to itself, which embraces the immense multifariousness of its phenomena, every individual life, exists and develops only through its antithesis, its struggle with the external world, and it is based upon its interaction with the totality of life with which it is in turn by its nature linked in a whole, the organic unity of the universe. . . .The individual life finds, on the one hand, its foundation, its source and its subsistence in the totality of life; on the other hand, the totality of life in continual struggle with the individual life strives to consume and absorb it.' [27]

To the intricately interrelated ecosystems and niches which these paragraphs appear to celebrate, Marx and Engels retorted by way of the image of 'nature red in tooth and claw'.

Man could also observe a great many other things in nature, eg. the bitterest competition among plants and animals; he could see, for example, in the plant world, in his 'forest of tall and stately oaks' how these tall and stately capitalists consume the nutriment of the tiny shrubs. . . . [28]

They tended to read social Darwinism into Darwin's evolutionary thesis.

As for (3), the 'true socialists' believed that 'Man can therefore only develop in and through the totality of life.' [29] One does not wish to defend all the theses that these 'true socialists' had held. But of the three mentioned above, it is not obvious why they should be dismissed so readily out of hand. Admittedly, their view was articulated, as Marx and Engels said, in a 'belletristic and poetic', hence almost romantic manner, and not in terms of today's understanding of ecology and thermodynamics. However, Marx and Engels were able to disregard totally their conception of socialism because, although in the 1844 Manuscripts Marx came close to the vision of these 'true socialists' (note, though, that *The German Ideology* was written between 1845 and 1847), in the end, they accepted the logic of exponential economic growth and the logic of industrialism based on science and EST, which would enable human agents to dominate Nature, to make Nature do what we will in order to meet our ever increasing desires and needs.

7. This may be an appropriate place to examine more carefully the concept of the domination of Nature by science and its EST. I have argued that both cornucopic socialism (which may also manifest itself as state capitalism) and bourgeois capitalism share the view that Nature ought to be dominated by human agents, through science and its technology, in order to serve human ends and desires at all cost, even at the cost of abusing and degrading Nature. The ascetic version of socialism, however, rejects this common assumption. But in the extant literature on the subject, such views do not emerge clearly. On the contrary, in some Marxist-oriented inquiry, the notion

of the domination of Nature is quite differently perceived and correspondingly analysed. This difference may be traced to my earlier argument that although Marx repudiated the legal relations of production which underpin capitalism (bourgeois), engendering an inherent inequality between labour and capital and exploitation of the former by the latter, Marx did not repudiate the exploitation of Nature by human agents through science and its EST. As a result, Marxist-influenced theorists have concentrated on interpreting the domination of Nature, as we shall see, as simply a mask behind which exploitation of human agents takes place under (bourgeois) capitalism. I will use the work of Leiss to illustrate these points. [30]

Leiss correctly points out that although the notion of the domination of Nature is normally traced to Francis Bacon, it has actually altered somewhat through the last four hundred years since Bacon first articulated it. He rightly holds that the concept, both in its own right and as a piece of ideology, is much more complex than meets the eye. As for the latter, he holds that the concept is simultaneously both transparent and obfuscating. It is transparent in the sense that man's domination over Nature, through his possession of superior technological capabilities, is meant to benefit all mankind. It is in Bacon's words 'to relieve the inconveniences of man's estate'. In reality, however, this unfortunately is not so, and has never been so. The reference to 'Man' and 'Mankind' obscures the historical truth that the beneficiaries have not been all human beings but only some human beings.

Leiss writes:

Considered abstractly, the level of domination over nature in any period is the same for all men, that is, it represents a stage of development attained by the human race as such. In reality, of course, the material benefits derived from the mastery of nature have always been distributed unjustly; but equally importantly is the fact that, however accomplished this human mastery becomes, the antagonisms of a class-divided society make it impossible for men to bring their productive system (of which mastery over nature is a part) under their control. This possibility emerges for the first time in a classless society. [31]

And again:

If the idea of the *domination* of nature has any meaning at all, it is that by such means — that is, through the possession of superior technological capabilities — some men attempt to dominate and control other men. The notion of a common domination of the human race over external nature is nonsensical [32]

(at least in a class-divided society under bourgeois capitalism).

In other words, the abstract (and hence ideological) idea of the whole human race dominating Nature for its benefits is used to mask a political domination of some men (a few) over other men (the majority). The domination of Nature through technological superiority is used to enforce a political superiority, both within a state through class divisions, and between states on a global scale. And for good measure, one could also add, that political superiority in turn is used to reinforce technological superiority.

We have increasingly come to use the composite notion 'science and technology' in talking about the domination of Nature. But in Leiss' opinion, there is a danger in lumping the two together; for he wishes to distinguish between scientific rationality and technological rationality. He characterises the former as follows:

Modern science is supposed to represent domination over nature in a unique and highly developed form. Thus we must ask: what is the meaning of this mastery with reference to scientific nature? To employ Bacon's phrasing once again, we may say that modern science expresses its mastery over nature in that it 'takes off the mask and veil from natural objects, which are commonly concealed and obscured under the variety of shapes and external appearance' and deals with the 'secrets' embedded in its hidden structure. From the viewpoint of science the nature given in sense perception masks the underlying uniform structure of matter, and modern science's mastery consists in penetrating this disguise and identifying the characteristics of the structure. Considered from the opposite angle — from the viewpoint of life in the familiar world — the mastery of science is manifested in its ability to cast a 'veil of ideas' (*Ideenkleid*) over the nature experienced in everyday experience, that is, to treat the phenomena of nature as if they were purely mathematical geometrical objects. The scientific understanding of nature strives for the elaboration of a theoretical system in which all the axioms implicit in its conceptual foundation (the mathematization of nature) — or to put the point in more familiar terms, all the laws of nature have been fully unfolded, tested, and unified into a coherent picture. The idea of internal harmony, order, and regularity among the occurences and behaviour of natural phenomena, together with the notion of the universal applicability of the laws which govern them, act as heuristic principles of the intellectual disciplines that work with scientific nature: disharmony and internal inconsistencies are signs of flaws which should be eliminated, in the theoretical structure or in the experimental techniques, not in nature itself. These and other elements constitute the rationality of the scientific methodology arising out of the mathematization of nature, a rationality that has proved itself decisively in practice. [33]

He maintains that such a conception of scientific rationality and methodology is irrelevant to the so-called domination of Nature. The villain of the piece is technological rationality. He says:

I have tried to show that nature *per se* is not the object of mastery, that instead various senses of mastery are appropriate to the various perspectives on nature. If this proposition is correct, then the converse is likewise true, namely, that mastery of nature is not a project of science *per se* but rather a broader social task. In this larger context technology plays a far different role than does science, for it has a much more direct relationship to the realm of human wants and thus to the social conflicts which arise out of them. . .scientific rationality and technological rationality are not the same and cannot be regarded as the complementary bases of something called the domination of nature. [34]

And: '. . .caught in the web of social conflict, technology constitutes one of the means by which mastery over nature is linked to mastery over men.' [35]

In one sense, Leiss is right to say that mastery of Nature through the conception of scientific rationality does not necessarily involve domination; mastery of nature in this context means the understanding of Nature. This is the explanatory goal of science. However, the understanding of Nature through scientific theories, providing explanations of natural phenomena, has never been the sole and only aim of scientific methodology even as conceived in the seventeenth century. He has hinted at one other related aim, both intellectual and practical, in his account of scientific rationality quoted above, namely, the goal of prediction.

Scientific theories have to be tested *via* the predictions they could be made to yield. But at the same time, such predictions could often be of use and relevance to what he has called the 'realm of human wants'. For instance, if a theory in geology can, not only explain geological phenomena (enabling us thus to understand Nature), but also enables one to predict precisely where a particular type of phenomenon could be located (such as oil), then such a theory is both intellectually satisfying as well as practically relevant.

But, unfortunately, not all theories satisfactory from the explanatory viewpoint may be equally successful from the predictive viewpoint, especially that of yielding very accurate and precise predictions like 'oil will be found here at a depth of so many feet'. Geology, as well as many other theories, including the theory of evolution, cannot satisfy this symmetry. (Such theories could at best make very rough and general predictions — for instance, the theory of evolution could predict that the ratio between black and white moths in a population would change, if the habitat of the population changes in certain ways, but it could not predict the precise ratio by any means.) Conversely, some theories may be successful predictive devices but hopelessly inadequate as explanatory constructs.

But there is still another goal associated with the scientific method from its very beginnings in the seventeenth century, and that is the goal of control. Control requires something stronger than mere prediction. The latter gives one minimal control, if you like, but not maximal control. For instance, a set of meteorological theories might enable one to forecast the onset of a tornado. As a result, one could evacuate people from the areas. But such a theory has nothing to say about how to prevent the occurrence of the tornado. Control in the maximum sense requires that a theory be able to identify those conditions which, altered or removed, would make a difference to the outcome. Such a theory is again considered to be more deeply intellectually complete as well as relevant to the 'realm of human wants' than a theory which merely enables one to predict and/or explain phenomena.

If this is true, then Leiss' dichotomy between scientific rationality and technological rationality breaks down somewhat. Even a 'pure' scientist would have intellectual interest in developing a theory to such a stage that it could have implications for and applications to the control of phenomena. However, this should not be interpreted to mean that what a theory and its associated technology render possible, one should automatically translate into action. The crucial question pertaining to social/moral values then arises — 'ought one to use such a theory/technology to achieve certain social goals?' This is what is meant by the social responsibility of science, a responsibility not only of the scientific community but of the entire civilisation, indeed, human community.

The second point of dissent concerns a matter which has already been raised in the first chapter, namely, that his conception of scientific rationality rests implicitly on classical physics as the paradigm of the sciences, and on the mechanistic paradigm of scientific explanation. While not wishing whatsoever to denigrate the contributions of either to scientific advance, exhaustive concentration on them, however, would produce needless distortions. This enterprise (together with others) tries to draw attention to at least one other equally fundamental science, namely, thermodynamics and to the science of ecology, and the paradigm of non-linear causation which is implicit in ecological explanations. As I have already dealt with this issue, I will not labour it any further.

Finally this book deals with a crucial meaning of the concept of human domination of Nature by science and its EST which Leiss appears not to have discussed seriously except to raise *en passant*. A conception of science based on the mechanistic paradigm, on a linear model of causation and a technology which is ecologically insensitive, and which is not in keeping with the laws of thermodynamics, dominates Nature in a very physical sense. That is why some writers have even been tempted to talk about the 'rape of nature'. Indeed Bacon, as pointed out by Leiss himself, uses an imagery to describe man's interaction with Nature which is in terms of political domination, conquest and weaponry. Bacon talked of 'the victory of art over nature' (by art here he meant techniques and technologies) — 'For you have but to follow and as it were hound nature in her wanderings, and you will be able, when you like, to lead and drive her afterwards to the same place again.' (*The Advance of Learning*, Works, IV) and also '"experiments in the mechanical arts deal with nature under constraint and vexed; that is to say, when by art and the hand of man she is forced out of her natural state, and squeezed and moulded." (*The Great Instauration*, IV)'. [36] Leiss comments on Bacon: '(For Bacon) human art and knowledge are weapons with which men compel nature to do their bidding.' [37]

But to this crucial issue (at least central and crucial to this outline of social philosophy), Leiss has devoted at best two paragraphs in his otherwise penetrating book. In connection with Hockheimer's account of the revolt of nature, he adds:

> In the interval since Hockheimer first presented this notion a related aspect of the problem has been recognised: in a different sense the concept of the revolt of nature may be applied in relation to ecological damage in the natural environment. [38]

One could say, in other words, that Leiss' account of the concept of the domination of Nature is in the best Marxist tradition. Like Marx, he correctly draws attention to (1) the endemic inequality that (bourgeois) capitalism embodies; (2) to the necessity to remove such inequality, together with its consequences, exploitation and poverty amongst the many. Writing in the latter half of the twentieth century, he also points out the failure in the Marxist hope of liberating humankind in the manner Marx had outlined; moreover, that the socialist countries today, in spite of their undoubted achievements in many areas, nonetheless turn out to be a betrayal of Marx.

However, he too does not challenge the physical violence done to Nature herself endemic in the science and its EST of our industrial civilisation, and fails to see it as a crucial source of social conflict. Indeed it is the availability and practice of such a science and its technology which sustains social conflict, at least as a necessary, if not both a necessary and sufficient condition. By treating Nature in this physically violent fashion, one also moulds human agents in the direction of conflict, competitiveness, egoism and violence itself.

In abandoning such a violent way in our interaction with Nature, we can at the same time lower the level of conflict in relationships between ourselves, and nurture those capacities in us which would render us in turn less competitive, less egoistic and less prone to violence, and at the same time remove inequalities which stand in the path of self-development for all. Harmony with Nature, that is, with other non-human agents which form part of Nature, could lead to greater harmony amongst human agents as well as inward peace and calm in the human agents them-selves.

The cornucopic version of socialism, however, im-plies the notion of the domination of Nature in the sense that (i) a minority of people uses superior tech-nological capacities to dominate the majority; (ii) as such it is bound up with inequalities and social con-flict in so far as the latter is focused on competition for the satisfaction of human wants. The ascetic ver-sion accepts the above but goes beyond it to assert that the kind of science and technology championed by contemporary industrial civilisation through the notion of progress from the seventeenth century on-wards leads to the domination of Nature in a very real, literal and physical sense of doing violence to Nature — the rate of change and the quality of change inflicted upon Nature upset the biosphere and the ecosystems to such an extent, that they can no longer repair and regenerate themselves. In impo-verishing and even destroying Nature in this way, we impoverish and are in danger of destroying ourselves, including future generations, that is to say, we are endangering the survival of the whole human species as well as other species and things which form part of Nature.

8. In the light of the foregoing sections, it becomes obvious that there are three currents running through Marx's and Marxist writings, which should be identi-fied and separated: (1) the critique stemming from the

insight about how work historically has been transformed to become a curse under capitalism; [39] (2) the critique stemming from the insight that the legal relations governing the capitalist mode of production embody deep inequalities and are, therefore, exploitative; (3) admiration for and the celebration of industrialism, based on using science and its EST in exploiting Nature to serve the ends of human agents (although not of all of them admittedly).

We have seen how Marx implied that he could retain (3) so long as the new social arrangement he advocated, abolished the unequal and exploitative legal relations of the capitalist mode of production. By so doing, Marx arrived at a cornucopic version of socialism. By so doing, Marx might also well succeed in ending exploitation of the many by the few, but he had overlooked that cornucopic socialism would, nevertheless, involve ruthless exploitation of Nature by all human agents.

Marx's view chimes in with the dominant tradition in Western thought which sees human beings as the rulers of the world. In its Biblical form, it says that God made Adam and Eve to His own image and gave them dominion over all His other creatures and creations. I have already traced this oversight to the fact that Marx appeared not to have appreciated enough the implications of two senses of capital that have to be distinguished — namely, capital as defined by the legal ownership of the means of production, and capital as defined as ever increasing accumulation. This understanding of Marx appears to have been the one taken, by and large, by theorists and activists in countries which consciously claim to be Marxist, or to have been influenced by his ideas. Such an understanding pays scant attention, if at all, to (1), the critique of work as a curse. This is because to overcome work as a curse turns out to be incompatible with retaining the notion of capital as ever increasing accumulation and admiration for industrialism.

There is at least one thinker who regarded himself to have been profoundly influenced by Marx but who did not 'buy' this interpretation of Marxism. That

270

theorist is William Morris, and it might pay us to examine his work more closely, not so much for the purpose of settling the matter at a purely verbal level, whether it would be right to call him a Marxist, but in order to see whether transcending work as a curse entails not only transcending the unequal exploitative legal relations of capitalism, but also rejecting (3), thereby rejecting the ruthless exploitation of Nature by humankind, and the cornucopic version of socialism favoured by Marx and Marxists in general.

But before looking at Morris, let me first go back to the critique of work as a curse. Such a transformation historically under capitalism was (is) required in order to maximise profits (or to increase capital). The means adopted to achieve this end has been (and is) to increase productivity, that is, to improve efficiency understood as reducing the unit cost of production. In turn, to achieve these sub-ends, the following means are used: (a) increasing division of labour based on the simplification of the operations into which the work process is divided; (b) replacement of inefficient human beings by efficient machines; (3) replacement of less efficient machines by more efficient machines.

These means and sub-ends, euphemistically referred to as the 'productivity of labour', in reality amount to (i) redundancy of labour, (ii) deskilling of labour, which in turn means (iii) the work process being broken up into simple, mindless, repetitive, boring operations whose rhythms are set by (iv) the pace of the machines in an environment of noise and filth created by machines and other operations, so that (v) workers become no more than machines themselves, or the mere adjuncts to machines. Assembly-line production in a factory is the acme of such efficiency and productivity; in other words, it is also the symbol of the degradation of labour, of work having become a curse.

Historically, as we know, the surplus arising from the 'productivity of labour' in the agricultural sector was diverted to the manufacturing sector. In turn, the surplus arising from the 'productivity of labour' in the manufacturing sector was/is diverted to the service sector in the economy. However, the idea of factory-machine-manufacture itself represents more than simply a stage in the development of capitalism. It represents something more, being the embodiment of capital's control over the productive process which is total. A product manufactured by machines tended by humans in a factory, as opposed to a natural product, is *ex hypothesi* an artifact made to the capitalist's will and his specifications. (It is different from a traditionally produced artifact which is the work of artisans and craftsmen.) A natural product is subject to the vagaries of climate, season, soil and other factors beyond the control of the capitalist. In principle, with the help of science and its technology, the ingredients which enter into the manufacture of the factory product could be assembled from all quarters of the globe, thus escaping the constraints of local scarcity, weather and other limitations.

Not only is scarcity of matter and energy no longer a problem, existential scarcity is also no longer a constraining factor. A factory can be put to work twenty four hours a day, three hundred and sixty five days a year. To be maximally productive and efficient, plants should operate all the time non-stop. Machines, unlike human beings, which are natural beings, can be so constructed that they can operate continuously without rest, till they grind to a halt and are then replaced. Human beings, who are needed to tend the machines or to work as adjuncts to the machines, can be made to work in shifts, unnatural though it might be for human beings to work when it is time to sleep. In this way, existential scarcity is overcome.

The idea of turning Nature into a factory, of transforming natural products into factory-machine-manufactured products, is a tempting one, and a challenge which has been eagerly taken up. In northern climes, vegetables, like lettuces and tomatoes, will grow only in the summer. But as 'manufactured' products in factories like greenhouses, they become available the whole year round. Cows naturally lactate when they have had calves. Under factory conditions of milk production, cows are injected with hormones so that their milk yield can be a continuous one. Farms have become factories. Every step in the production process can now be controlled and rendered uniform, so that the consumers can be guaranteed manufactured products which are identical in size, shape, weight, colour, texture, taste (or more likely, lack of taste). Agribusiness is but another name for farms having become factories. Hens become egg-laying machines, and cows milk-yielding ones.

The factory-machine-manufacturing mode of production clearly is the antithesis of the artistic mode of production. (See Chapter Seven, section 8.) Hens kept under battery conditions, where they are not allowed to see daylight, to flap their wings, to fly about, that is, to live a natural life, could hardly be said to be cared for, looked after and reared under the artistic mode of production. As far as animals are concerned, as they are sensate creatures like ourselves, a denial of their capacity for movement may be said to constitute cruelty — for further elaboration on this point, see Chapter Ten, section 2.

However, farms only became full-blown factories as the twentieth century wore on. But by the time of William Morris (1834/96), it was obvious that the factory-machine-manufacturing mode of production had replaced the artistic mode of production in the manufacture of artifacts. As we shall see, Morris' objection to our industrial civilisation lies precisely in the replacement of the artistic mode of production as exemplified and embodied in the work of the artisan and the craftsman by the factory-machine-manufacturing mode of production.

It is therefore not surprising that both Fourier and Morris who reject the idea that there is no alternative to work as a curse also reject (1) the central place occupied by the factory-machine-manufactured product in our civilisation, (2) industrialism itself based on the exploitation of Nature using science and its EST, thereby rejecting (3) the cornucopic version of socialism. It is not an accident that Fourier relegated factory-machine-manufacture to a peripheral place in his good society, and Morris rejected it altogether in favour of craft manufacture. In the case of Fourier, by advocating factory-machine-manufacture of only those items which are necessary and useful but made to last, one cuts down the volume and importance of this sector and, hence, the time spent under such conditions of work. In the case of Morris, by advocating that craftsmen and artisans manufacture only what is necessary and useful, but beautifully made and made to last, one dispenses altogether with the degrading and humiliating conditions of work as a curse. In the case of both, agriculture, horticulture and husbandry should not be subject to the idea of factory production whatsoever. In advocating such choices, they consistently and joyfully accepted the ascetic model of socialism. The artistic mode of production has nothing to do with increasing productivity and efficiency in order to maximise profits or increase capital; as such it does not lend itself to the cornucopic version based on the ever increasing production and consumption of material goods by all human agents.

Marx, on the contrary, as we saw, was lured by the vision of seemingly infinite abundance. Once rid of the unequal and exploitative legal relations of the (bourgeois) capitalist mode of production, Nature herself could be exploited to serve the genuine needs of all human beings. The domination of some men over many men is replaced by the domination of Nature by all human agents. Unfortunately, he seemed to have overlooked that the attainment of cornucopia, which is at the expense of Nature, may not be sustainable indefinitely. It is also secured by the factory-machine-manufacturing mode of production (in all spheres of production). In his good society, it might be possible to remove some of the worst excesses of work as a curse as he himself had indicated, but it would in no way be possible to alter its essential character. Indeed, that essential character must be maintained if the desired goal — cornucopic socialism — is to be achieved.

With William Morris, the artistic mode of production acquires another dimension, namely, the aesthetic one. His aesthetic sensibility was deeply offended by the handiwork of capitalism. Buildings of architectural worth and beauty were torn down in order that developers could make profits erecting ugly soulless blocks. This led him to found The Society for the Protection of Ancient Buildings. However, running a pressure group like that soon made him realise that art is not something autonomous and separate from the rest of society, especially its economics and its politics. Therefore, the preservation and maintainance of the arts cannot be effective without a radical restructuring of society. He wrote: 'Both my historical studies and my practical conflict with the philistinism of modern society have *forced* on me the conviction that art cannot have a real life and growth under the present system of commercialism and profit-mongering.'

Morris began by being a bohemian and an aesthete, associating with Burne-Jones, Rossetti and other Pre-Raphaelites. But his love of art drove him consistently towards both practical politics and attempting a theoretical understanding of capitalist society. In this latter endeavour, he was helped by Hyndman who introduced him to Marx's writings. As Marx has said, capitalism turns everything into a commodity. Art, too, has become a commodity. Its commodification is, therefore, its corruption. Art, then, is no longer produced under the artistic mode of production. Aesthetic qualities are no longer integral to the product. It has become simply one commodity amongst others to be bought and sold, subject to the laws of the market. As such, it has lost its integrity and hence its beauty.

When he married and wanted to furnish his home, he found that the products available on the market were so poor and ugly that he had to manufacture his own if he wanted anything decent. To do this, he had in the end, almost single-handedly, to revive the numerous arts and crafts which had already died under the pressure of factory-machine-manufactured cheap and shoddy goods. But alas, yet again, he was to discover that the production of beautiful objects under the artistic mode of production by craftsmen and artisans, within a capitalist structure, simply meant that he was producing luxury items for the rich who could afford them, while the majority who could not had to put up with shoddy things. So he became even more convinced that tinkering with the system was no answer. For art to be given back to the people (to everyone that is, not only to some), a radically different society had to come into existence.

Morris concluded that capitalism is evil because (1) it destroyed art and craft, the artisan and the craftsmen who embodied the artistic mode of production; (2) factory-machine-manufacture could only lead to shoddy goods for the masses while the rich could enjoy expensive, exclusive luxury products; (3) by so doing, work has become joyless and a curse, and workers suffer alienation (although it is true that Morris himself did not use the term); (4) moreover, shoddy goods by their very nature must be replaced at a rapid rate — the volume turn-over must then lead to the destruction of the environment; (5) many of them, as well as most of the luxury goods for the rich, are neither useful nor beneficial to society. The latter, for instance, serves as status symbols and not objects to be used and appreciated in their own right.

In contrast, the good society must restore art to its rightful, central place in human existence — 'Art one day will be won back again to our daily labour' (*Art and Socialism*); 'Art is man's expression of his joy in labour' (*Art under Plutocracy*). [40]

Art should not be an adjunct to life, as represented by a painting on the living room wall. Art embodies creativity. Human beings are artists. And as we have seen, the artistic/creative spirit is not expressed in merely one particular type of activity, namely, art in the narrow sense, but is something that informs all activities. So in Morris' case, one can say that his interest in art in the narrow sense led him eventually to the broader theme of art as joy in labour. Hence for him, the decorative arts perform two essential functions — to give people pleasure in things 'they must perforce *make*' and to give pleasure to people in things 'they must perforce *use*'. Pleasure in making and pleasure in using things enable us to be whole and creative again. In a society where neither luxury nor shoddy goods are produced, what is produced (to meet genuine human needs) can then be produced under non-alienating conditions.

It is sometimes said that Morris, like Ruskin, Carlyle and Arnold who were all deeply affected by medieval civilisation, was just invoking a kind of medieval romanticism and nostalgia. But this charge is not fair. To Morris, the artisan and the craftsman do not simpy embody a reactionary quaintness, but the artistic mode of production which is central to the good society he envisaged. In this he differed not only from those who wished to restore the feudal past, but also from Marx who was contemptuous of the artisan mode of production, calling it at times 'craft-idiocy'. This, as we know, is in keeping with Marx's celebration of industrialism but, at the expense, in the end, of taking seriously his own critique of work as a curse. Morris, on the other hand, emphasised the centrality of restoring joy to labour. He, therefore, saw the artisan as the embodiment of non-alienated work — the worker is in charge of the work process, from the conception of the product to its execution, working at a pace and in a manner dictated by its conception, as well as by the nature of the material and its requirements.

Morris, while enamoured of the workmanship typical of the medieval guild, was distinctly repelled by the hierarchical nature of medieval society. His New Jerusalem was an equal society. It is said that he owed his egalitariansim to his other abiding interest, Norse civilisation.

The distinctiveness of his social vision may then be seen to lie in his attempt to weave together at least four different strands and influences into his conception of socialism:

(1) the aesthetic dimension from his association with the Pre-Raphaelite Movement;

(2) Marx's writings, which made him fully aware why

art under capitalism as a commodity must be corrupt and degenerate;

(3) the medieval craftsman and artisan which he saw as the embodiment of non-alienated work, the artistic mode of production;

(4) the egalitarianism of the Vikings.

In *How I Became a Socialist*, he presented his vision of the good society as follows:

A condition of society in which there should be neither rich nor poor, neither master nor master's man, neither idle nor overworked, neither brain-sick brain workers, nor heart-sick hand workers, in a word, a world in which all men would be living in equality of condition, and would manage their affairs unwastefully, and with the full consciousness that harm to one would mean harm to all — the realisation at last of the word COMMONWEALTH.

And finally to the point whether Morris could be labelled 'Marxist'. He certainly owed to Marx at least the following points: (a) the consequences which arise from the commodification of art; (b) his critique of work as a curse under the factory-machine-manufacturing mode of production; (c) the intrinsic inequalities built into the legal relations of the capitalist mode of production. However, if one interprets Marx, as I do, as being more concerned in the end with simply removing the perversion of (bourgeois) capitalism by advocating the common or public ownership of the means of production, while retaining and celebrating industrial civilisation itself, based on exploiting Nature by using science and its EST, then Morris is clearly not a Marxist. By concentrating on Marx's critique of work as a curse, he consistently and systematically arrived at a vision of the good society which is very different from that of Marx — an ascetic or frugal model of socialism, not Marx's cornucopic model, a form of socialism which does not ruthlessly exploit Nature to meet ever increasing needs.

CHAPTER NINE

REDISTRIBUTION
EQUALITY AS THE DISTRIBUTIVE VALUE

1. It is commonly held that growth and redistribution
are mutually exclusive. If you have the former, you
can dispense with the latter. This is because growth
automatically raises the standards of living of all
groups, or classes in society, and of all societies in a
world-wide context. Hence it can be seen as a substitute for redistribution within society and between
societies, rendering it redundant and unnecessary.
However, if the former turns out to be a mirage,
then one may have no choice but to fall back on the
latter. Although this view is by and large correct, it
may still be too simplistic. One needs to explore more
carefully what these notions may mean, and the relationships between them.

On the whole people are agreed on what economic
growth means as used standardly in the literature. It
is that which is given (annually) by an increase in the
GNP. Critics of the latter, of course, point out, as we
saw, how unsatisfactory the concept is as a measure
of well-being or welfare, and argue for the need to
construct alternative conceptions of wealth and well-
being. [1]

But what does redistribution mean? As it has not
been carefully scrutinised so far, let us examine it
first. Both the proponents of the doctrine of economic
growth and many of its opponents (as well as most
ordinary citizens) assume that redistribution means,
taking from those, who have (more), to give to those,
who have not (or less). Let us call this the Robin

279

Hood Principle of redistribution. Indeed, one could argue, that in order to make sense of the view, that economic growth may function as a substitute for redistribution, then redistribution must imply the Robin Hood Principle, or at least imply that the growth or 'wealth' generated must be distributed in such a way, that all of it, or most of it, does not go to those who already have more.

However, that is not the only interpretation of the concept and indeed, historically, as we shall see, another meaning is at work, which sees not so much economic growth and redistribution being mutually exclusive but mutually reinforcing. Redistribution, on this alternative understanding, means taking from those who have little (or less), to give to those who have more — this may be said to be a version of the Matthew Principle, that is, to those who have, more shall be given. In other words, redistribution may take place in the direction towards greater equality or towards greater inequality. The Matthew Principle is in the direction of the latter; the Robin Hood Principle is in the direction of the former.

The Matthew Principle may be divided into two sub-varieties — (i) the benign form where it is simply the case that to those who have, more will be given, to those whose who have less, less will be given; (ii) the malign form where it is the case that wealth will be transferred from those with little or less to those who have more or the most.

One of the most spectacular uses of the Matthew Principle of redistribution, in its malign form, to engender growth, in the history of modern economics is, of course, the enclosure laws in Britain, especially those in the eighteenth century. Economic growth demanded that the land be concentrated in the hands of the landowners. The common was traditionally available to the villagers to graze their animals, to collect fuel to augment their produce from tilling the soil. But to promote an efficient sheep farming industry to provide wool for the expanding woollen industry, such lands were enclosed, that is, the law ordained that the common, from then on, belonged to the landowners, and were no longer available for use to the people of the village. This had the effect of undermining the latter's livelihood, and they then had no choice but to drift to manufacturing employment, and sell their labour, or to become paupers to be kept on the rates. Dispossession was required in order to bring about progress as economic growth.

On a global scale, one could also say that the growth of the cotton industry, which formed one of the foundations of wealth in nineteenth century Britain, relied on American cotton, which until the abolition of slavery, used slave labour. The prosperity of some British ports and cities in the eighteenth century was partially, if not wholly, founded on the slave shipping trade. It was also made possible by the export of such goods to British India and other parts of the Empire, thereby virtually ruining the native cottage textile industry in those countries. Slavery, dispossession, unemployment and impoverishment of large numbers of peoples in different parts of the world were required to fuel economic growth in the history of the first industrialised country, and other countries (which today form part of the first world), which followed the British footsteps of industrialisation and colonialism. [2]

Today on the global scene, the same principle also appears to be at work. For instance, it is held that economic growth in the first world would be facilitated if, and only if, the prices of raw commodities, like rubber, tin, oil, uranium and so on, which are predominantly the products of third world countries, are kept low. Cartels like OPEC which try to raise prices have not notably been successful, although they might create quite a nasty shock to first world economies for a short period of time. Through depletion of their non-renewable stocks of oil, rain forests, etc., such third world countries could be said to be subsidising first world economies.

So the Matthew Principle, in its malign form, may be seen to be at work both in the past and now, *intra* state and *inter* states. However, the Matthew Principle, in its benign form, may be implied by those who hold the 'trickle down' theory of redistribution. Historically, it is best illustrated by the post Second World War boom in first world economies. It held true, by and large, for about 30 years (say, from 1945 to 1973), for all classes in these economies enjoyed a rise in their respective standards of living, and indeed, even wealth. At one stage poverty was even believed to have been eliminated, and when its existence was rediscovered, it was characterised as 'relative deprivation'. But even if it be granted that during this period, all might be said to have benefited, those who benefited most were those with more, not those with less, and those, with the most, are also those, with the most capital.

This is because under the legal relations of (bourgeois) capitalist production, the law decrees that the product belongs to the owners of the capital and not the workers. The workers claim wages. They could ask for an increase in wages and/or in pensions. But even with growth, there is no guarantee that the owners would see fit to grant a rise. Whether they do depends on a combination of factors, including the bargaining powers of the unions to which the workers belong, the law of supply and demand in the industry at the time, and so on. And even with growth (in a particular industry), there is no guarantee that the workforce might not be reduced rather than increased, as the decision to hire more or to fire some depends also on the state of technological possibilities. Management, in pursuit of lowering the cost of production, could invest in new technology which requires fewer people to operate it, rather than hiring more hands by buying more of the extant, but less productive machines.

As such, capitalists are bound to do better than workers. This law would only not hold true in cases where the capital owned is minute, and those, who have only their labour to sell, can command very high fees. In the case of the latter, they soon accumulate capital, sometimes very substantial amounts indeed. But on the whole, the sellers of labour do not and cannot command exceptionally high fees or wages. It follows then that those who benefit most from economic growth are clearly those who already own capital. Economic growth, while it may benefit the average worker to some extent, necessarily benefits those who have more (that is, those already with substantial capital) than those who have less. In other words, the trickle down theory is very apt in cases where it obtains — those at the top get the cream, those at the bottom get the dregs. The principle operating in (bourgeois) capitalist systems, which governs distribution, is one of inequality.

On the analysis advanced, the Matthew Principle of redistribution, either in its malign or benign form, indeed, underpins economic growth, although theorists, sympathetic to the notion of economic growth, imply that only the benign variety is involved and required. The general argument for the benign form coincides with the standard conservative justification for the institution of private property, namely, that its existence and the rewards for it, are necessary for the creation of wealth. This assumes that (a) private property is a more efficient means of wealth creation than other extant alternatives; (b) it would only remain effective if there are sufficient rewards for the investment of such capital; (c) however, the owners of such wealth must also entertain *noblesse oblige* to those who have not.

I do not wish to examine (a) more carefully here, as it would take me beyond the immediate task. (b), however, is germane to my argument, that for bourgeois capitalism to work, the rewards must remain sufficiently high. This is particularly so in an era of international capitalism, where capital could not be persuaded to stay within a particular national boundary, unless the inducements, in its calculation, are large enough to tempt it to stay.

But the argument is in constant danger of taking on the malign form: today, in this country, it is held that for the economy to prosper, businesses must reinvest, and top business men must be given incentives to pursue plans vigorously, which would lead to growth. Incentives would take the form of fiscal generosity towards corporations and their executives. But paying Paul generously, however, might well mean robbing Peter to make up for the deficit. [3]

In other countries, particularly in third world economies, multi-national companies are tempted to invest there not only because of lower wages, fewer holidays, but also less stringent regulations governing the health and safety of the workers, the safety of the product, as well as the protection of the environment. All these add up to reduced costs in production, and hence more profits. The endangered health, poverty of third world peoples and the degradation of their environment are the price paid for the 'wealth', created under economic growth. The recent disaster in the Union Carbide plant in Bhopal, India, is a perfect illustration of this kind of malign redistribution à la Matthew.

'Wealth' creation or growth is concerned with the aggregate, with the total increase in the GNP of this year, compared with that of last year. As such, it has nothing to say about how the total increase is to be distributed within the society.

Take the following simple example. Suppose two brothers till x acres of land. This year, it happens that the rain came at the right time and in the right amount. The sun too shone at the right time to ripen the grain. As a result, the harvest is double that of last year. We know that there has been growth, but from it, we cannot infer how, as a matter of fact, it would be distributed. To know the latter, we have to find out what rule, or rules, of distribution would be applied. It could be that the older brother would take the total increase over last year's harvest, the younger brother get none. It could be the two brothers would share out equally between them. It could be that whoever has more mouths to feed, gets more of the surplus. The two could conceivably decide by throwing a coin — heads, I take the lot and tails you do, and so on.

Economic growth is strictly speaking neutral as to how the increase in the size of the cake is to be distributed. Left on its own, there is no reason to expect the poor to benefit. In Chapter Five, we saw that in Brazil, economic growth (before the present crisis) has not benefited the poor. On the contrary, their standard of living has gone down in absolute terms. This shows that there is nothing automatic about the trickle down theory, working in the way the theory says it ought, that is, to raise the respective standards of living of all the classes in a society. To achieve that, governments have to intervene to ensure that the wealth generated under growth does dribble down to all the layers, as the theory says it should.

The above discussion shows that the most important factor which determines how growth is to be engendered, and then distributed is the intervention of the law in *intra* state situations (see section 7 for further discussion on the role of the legal system in distributing and guaranteeing such rights and freedoms), and the joint intervention of the law, and the might of the gunboat in *inter* state situations. The gunboat was, of course, very obviously used in the nineteenth century at the height of European imperialism. However, even today, its presence is felt. In the last forty years, one could cite Suez as an instance.

In the first world economies, the benign instantiation of the Matthew Principle in the last hundred years or so is due to deliberate legislative intervention. The post World War Two construction of the welfare state is an obvious example. In other words, without conscious attempt by the state to use legislation to transfer wealth from the rich to the poor, the wealth generated under growth would not necessarily and automatically flow or trickle downwards. Theorists, who advocate the trickle down theory, are really advocating a particular type of politics to go with the growth, which makes it possible to transfer some of the wealth generated to the worse off. In other words, they favour narrowing inequalities to some extent. Otherwise, given the built-in polarisation of (bourgeois) capitalism, growth would simply increase inequalities, not decrease them.

The trickle down theory is, in other words, not so much an empirical thesis about wealth distribution as envisaged by its proponents, but a normative theory which makes sense, and works only, when it is underpinned by a particular type of political prescription.

Philosophically, the most discussed theory of distributive justice of late is that of John Rawls. [4] Rawls' work has been subjected to a variety of interpretations, and a whole industry of commentaries has grown up around it. I do not wish to add much more to the extant body of comments, except to point out that I see his theory as a type of benign interpretation of the Matthew Principle. He gives several formulations of the so-called difference principle. On page 60 of his book, it is formulated as: 'social and economic inequalities are to be arranged so that they are both. . .reasonably expected to be to everyone's advantage. . . .' On page 15 and elsewhere, it is rendered more specifically as 'social and economic inequalities. . .are just only if they result in compensating benefits for everyone, and in particular for the least advantaged members of society.'

As such, it tacitly recognises that a politics of redistribution is required to complement the doctrine of economic growth. But the distributive criterion he advocates may accommodate a wide range of possibilities, from maintaining gross inequalities (subject to the least advantaged deriving some crumbs from them) to narrowing inequalities to a substantial extent, which is in keeping with economic growth itself. But if it turns out, that those who support the trickle down theory of growth, are likely to argue that narrowing inequalities to a substantial extent is not consonant with growth, because the inducements for capital would not then be high enough, then it looks as if Rawls' theory (at least on this interpretation) might have to be content with only a small decrease in inequalities at best.

In the light of the discussion above and in earlier chapters, the arguments against the doctrine of economic growth as a substitute for redistribution (that is, *à la* Robin Hood) may be summed up as follows:
(a) as economic growth, measured by the GNP, is an

aggregate, it says nothing about how the 'wealth' generated ought to be distributed. It is in keeping with (i) a small minority of people, namely, the owners of capital getting most of it, (ii) a much larger group of people benefiting from it. For (ii) to occur, usually active legislation is required to transfer the 'wealth' from those who already have more to those who have less; left to economic growth alone, the inbuilt inequalities of capital would ensure that (i) rather than (ii) happens. Moreover, even (ii) is compatible with the existence of a significant minority who are not in employment, and may, therefore, be unable to participate in the increase of wealth through a rise in wages, in pension provisions, in tax allowances, etc. In other words, the trickle down theory *intra* state, even if it does work to some extent, does not work automatically, but in conjunction with the political objective of redistribution *à la* Matthew in the benign sense;

(b) *inter* states, the trickle down theory works even less well, as there are no morally and legally recognised effective mechanisms to transfer wealth from rich countries to the poorer ones. Left to the unequal economic bargaining powers of states, the theory merely ensures that first world economies grab the lion's share of the world's non-renewable stocks of raw materials, at a price dictated by them, in order to fuel their own exponential economic growth.

The fact that such economies are doing that, as well as destroying almost beyond repair what is in principle renewable, like soil, in some third and fourth world countries (and elsewhere), is not considered worrying, only if one has unbounded faith in technology overcoming scarcity, through the principle of substitution. For any scarce X, a Y could be found, through technological manipulation, which would do duty for X, so that there is never absolute scarcity. But we have seen that this is flawed, for the simple reason that we cannot create nor annihilate energy and matter, only transform them. They can only be transformed to become objects of use to us provided there is a supply of low entropic energy and matter. These, however, are precisely the very items which are absolutely scarce.

Moreover, the technology itself is E$\underline{S}$T which, in the process of substituting Y for X, produces an inordinate amount of waste which could easily, and does overwhelm, the ecosphere and upset ecosystems in the world. The capacity to absorb and recycle waste is itself absolutely scarce.

And even more tellingly, as the technology gets more and more E$\underline{S}$T and sophisticated, the less likely are the poorer nations of the world able to afford it, even if substitutions are available. Once again, there is nothing to trickle down. And as the Green Revolution shows, in many countries, it has the effect of dispossessing the poor farmers of their land. The poor and the dispossessed will only inherit the waste, not in a trickle, but in generous abundance. This, then, is the Matthew Principle of redistribution, in its malign form, at work;

(c) in any case, exponential economic growth, as a prescription for all the economies of the world, is clearly a physical impossibility. It can at best only work for a few and for a limited run. But what morally entitles the few to enrich themselves at the expense of the resources in the world, and of the overwhelming majority of their fellow human beings? May they not be assigning to themselves a privilege which cannot be morally justified? And is it this which causes them to delude themselves and others into believing that economic growth for all is physically possible, and a panacea for all social ills?

(d) economic growth cannot be a substitute for redistribution *à la* Robin Hood, as that principle runs directly contrary to the Matthew Principle, both, in its benign and malign forms, behind the doctrine itself. The Robin Hood principle has nothing to do with economic growth as such, but with the straightforward transfer of resources from the rich to the poor.

2. We have seen that economic growth, without the

conscious implementation of a particular policy of redistribution aimed at removing inequalities to some extent, could on its own lead to a polarisation of inequalities. In the same way, one should also realise that ecological scarcity (the other side of the coin to ever-increasing economic growth), without a conscious implementation of a policy of redistribution *à la* Robin Hood, could lead to a pattern of distribution *à la* Matthew in the malign sense. Schnaiberg [5] has raised three possibilities:

(1) there is continued production expansion — such a future society to be both increasingly authoritarian and unequal;

(2) it is business as usual — in such a society, although there is reduced production expansion, there is also expansion of present inequalities;

(3) there is a change to technology suitable for conditions under ecological scarcity; such a future society will decrease consumption and production, while also reducing inequalities.

This schema is helpful in clarifying the directions a society could possibly develop under ecological scarcity. However, it fails to mention another possibility. His ecological synthesis should perhaps be subdivided into two types — what he calls the Left Social Distribution, and the other, an Extreme Right Distribution. But I shall borrow the terms 'ecosocialism' and 'ecofascism' to designate the two sub-types.

The more radical form of ecosocialism may be characterised as follows: EST, less machine and capital intensive, more labour intensive production, much decreased commodity consumption and production, increased equalities not only in the so-called standard of living, but also very importantly, in the control of the work processes, deciding what is to be produced and how it is to be produced, not to mention the removal of inequalities in other areas of existing unequal power relationships.

A more radical form of ecofascism may be characterised as follows: EST, less machine and capital intensive, more labour intensive production, much decreased commodity consumption and production overall, but with inequalities in the standard of living between groups, authoritarian control of the work processes by the dominant group, ordering the weaker groups to carry out its will, which may be in accordance with the ecological requirement of less commodity production and consumption, of minimising the consumption of low entropic energy and matter, and the production of high entropy. Carried to extreme, it may even become a slave-owning society, with the slave masters driving the slaves to fulfil their vision of a society, which recognises ecological scarcity.

No theorist writing at the moment could be said to satisfy the characterisation above. However, it has been said that the basis of a form of ecofascism may be detected in the writings of some theorists like Garrett Hardin and Paul and Anne Ehrlich. This charge is traced to their neo-Malthusian views on population, their zero-population-growth doctrine.

The exclusive emphasis on it to cope with ecological scarcity has led them to advocate a triage strategy, with regard to the issue of providing aid to the third and fourth world economies. Aid from the first world should be confined to countries which are serious about population control, and indeed are making progress in the matter. Countries which are not should be abandoned as hopeless. Their lobbying along these lines have led to the formulation of US policy, such as the US Agency for International Development, which sees as the key to the saving of 'civilisation', the prevention of rapid population growth in the third and fourth worlds, whilst ignoring the issue of social injustices, of blatant economic and other inequalities, which exist between the first world on the one hand, and the third and fourth worlds, on the other. [6] This seems then to lead to the charge that ecological scarcity requires that the poorer peoples in the world carry the burdens and sacrifices of not drawing upon the supply of limited and finite resources, through decrease in their reproduction. This then is a kind of *inter* state ecofascism, it is alleged.

As to *intra* state population control, an analogous ecofascist line may be developed. The poorer groups, which may or may not coincide with ethnic groups, but in many cases do, within a society, could also be required to decrease their rate of reproduction, as a means of coping with ecological scarcity.

To avoid ecofascism in any form, one must therefore (a) not pursue the single track prescription of population control, particularly only of the weaker and the poorer groups within a society and in the world; population control must be across the board; [7] and in any case it must be pursued in conjunction with other policies, such as the reduction of consumption and production by the most well-off, and hence a transfer of wealth from the rich to the poor; (b) in other words, the removal of social, economic, political inequalities in the direction of greater and greater equality must be made.

This then places a great burden on the notion of equality, its meaning, its analysis and its implications. As many theorists have denied that it is meaningful, we must next urgently look at it.

3. There are infinitely different rules of distribution. One may categorise them in different ways. For instance, one can say some are rational principles, and others are pretty arbitrary. Classic candidates for the former are the principle of deserts or of needs. Arbitrary ones could be tossing a coin, or a theory of entitlement which gives only to those, whose names contain no more than three letters of the alphabet, or only to men (or women), or only to white people (or black people). [8]

But the broadest category, which concerns us here, is that between principles of equality or inequality. We have seen that the demand of economic growth, under bourgeois capitalism, endorses a distributive principle of inequality. But this book, like some other critics of economic growth and its attendant ecological bankruptcy, endorses a distributive principle of equality. But before arguing for the validity of such a principle, and to explore it at greater length, there is, however, another more fundamental issue to be looked at, namely, why do we need a distributive principle at all, be it one of equality or inequality?

A social/moral theory, to be coherent, requires a distributive value as well as (for want of a better term) what may be called a substantive value(s). The latter tells us, what the theory regards to be the central good(s) to be aimed at, in the good life, and the good society. For example, industrial civilisation, under (bourgeois) capitalism, regards the accumulation of money as wealth, the ever increasing possession and consumption of material goods as the central values of the good life, and the good society. The burden of this book is to establish the central good to be the acquisition of internal goods, that is, of self-development under the artistic mode of production.

But a theory, which tells one only about the substantive value, is not complete. It must also tell one how that good is to be distributed — is it to be made available to all, or is it to be made available only to a few? (Bourgeois) capitalism, as we have seen, tacitly, if not openly, endorses a distributive value of inequality, that is, through the Matthew Principle of redistribution, in its benign or malign forms. Moreover, as we also have shown in the last chapter, the substantive good it advocates cannot by its very nature be available to all. Being a zero-sum game, there are bound to be lots of losers but only some winners. The alternative conception of the acquisition, not of external goods but internal goods, by contrast, is logically capable of being made available to all. Given that such acquisition makes sustainable demands on low entropic energy and matter, it is also physically possible for everyone to acquire such goods, which is not the case with the ever increasing possession and consumption of external material goods.

A substantive value(s) is not the same as a distributive value. The latter operates upon the former, as the mathematical operator ÷ operates upon a number. They are not the same kind of value, logically speaking, just as ÷ and 10 are not logically speaking the same sort of entity — 10 is a number while ÷ is an operator. The second cannot be put on the same level as the first.

From this, it follows, that two commonly held views are wrong:

(a) that it makes sense to say that a social/moral theory postulates only one central value, be it money, freedom, happiness, etc.

(b) that it makes sense to choose between more of freedom/personal wealth and less of equality, or more of equality and less of freedom/personal wealth.

A trade-off between two things is strictly speaking possible only if the two things are of the same logical type. It makes sense to say that I choose to have less money in my pocket, but more public services like hospitals provided *via* taxation, for money is the means of procuring such services. It makes sense to say that I choose to have less money in my pocket, but more leisure time by declining to take on another job, even if I could have got one. (Here one is referring to the role of money as a medium of exchange, and not as an ontological substitute for real things. In its latter role, money and real things, like hospitals and leisure, are not of the same type.)

Those who claim that they prefer more personal wealth and less equality are really saying they prefer a type of social arrangement which permits gross substantial inequalities in personal wealth to occur, rather than a type of social arrangement which permits less inequalities, or little inequality in personal wealth, to occur. In other words, they are saying (a) personal wealth is a (substantive) good, (b) that this good be distributed more unequally, rather than less unequally.

A theory, according to this understanding, must therefore contain at least two values, one of which must be the distributive value. As a matter of fact, contrary to rhetorical denial (in some cases), all social/moral theories do presuppose a distributive criterion, either one which endorses greater inequalities, or one which endorses less inequalities. Why should this be so?

This is because of the obvious fact, that human agents are distinct and discrete individuals, each occupying a certain portion of space and time. [9] As distinct and discrete individuals, human agents have so evolved that each has her/his own nervous system, brain and other set of organs.

From this certain obvious inferences follow:

(a) I cannot eat on behalf of another human agent. If you are hungry, you must have food. The mere fact that I have just eaten, or are famished, is irrelevant to your hunger;

(b) I cannot see on your behalf (or perform any of your bodily functions on your behalf);

(c) I cannot feel your pain — if you sit on an ant-hill, you are the one bitten by the ants and suffer the pain, not I;

(d) I cannot appropriate your memories (see Chapter Seven). One talks of sharing memories with another. This only means that the parties concerned participated in the same events, but the memory of each is integral to the identity of each agent.

The 'cannot' in the four propositions above is at once empirical and conceptual. It is a contingent empirical fact that my nervous system is not plugged into yours, that I cannot feel your pain, your hunger, your desire for sexual intercourse. (There is, one is told, an exception to this general rule. There have been recorded instances of monozygotic twins who, though far apart, could share each other's pains — for example, if one twin is having labour pains miles away, the other twin, who is not even pregnant, could feel similar pains.) But this empirical contingent fact is so basic and fundamental, that it enters into the very concept of identity, and integrity of the self. This will remain so, even if technology one day renders it possible for all human agents to be clones, so that they will be similar in height, temperament, etc.

However, similarity should not be confused with identity. Such clones may be similar, but, nevertheless, remain separate and discrete, so that they will not be identical with one another. As D. H. Munro says, 'to give two treats to one twin is not the same as to give one treat each to both'. [10] If clone A feels hungry, it is pointless and irrelevant to give two portions to clone B, who is also feeling hungry, but none to A.

The former remains hungry so long as s/he has nothing to eat, irrespective of how the latter, as a matter of fact, has eaten (or not eaten).

Needless to say, it follows that if all human agents were all plugged into the same nervous/physiological system, so that if one feels pain, the rest automatically does, if one feels cold, the rest does, and so on, then the question of distribution does not arise, or arises, not in the way it does now, in the non-fantasy world, which human agents occupy. But as the world you and I now inhabit is not like the fantasy world, an adequate social/moral theory must provide for a distributive value, either one of tolerating existing, or increasing inequalities, or one endorsing decrease (ultimate removal) of inequalities.

4. Which, then, of these two competing distributive values is the more defensible? Although the thesis, outlined above on its own, cannot lend support to the view, that equality is the correct distributive value in a non-fantasy world, where human agents are distinct and discrete individuals, however, it, together with the thesis of diminishing marginal utility (argued for explicitly in Chapter Six and implicitly in Chapter Ten *via* the notion of sufficiency which underpins the notion of need itself), can be used to establish that, of the two competing distributive values, that of equality is the more defensible.

As each of these distinct and discrete individuals operate under the principle of diminishing marginal utility, it would be more rational to make available to such agents the resources to meet their needs (at the three levels, as set out in Chapter Ten), than to deny the majority of such agents the resources to meet them. To give most of the resources to a few agents would only make sense if by so doing, the needs of the majority, deprived of the resources, could, somehow, be met. In the non-fantasy world we occupy this could not and would not happen. And as the privileged few derive less and less satisfaction from the larger and larger bundle of goods given to them (when these goods are real things like food, houses, clothes, shoes, cars, etc. and not money which is the ontological substitution for real things), it would not be rational to give such agents yet more, while the majority are suffering deprivation, through their needs not being met.

(Traditionally, the principle of diminishing marginal utility has been used by the utilitarians, such as Bentham, who, however, later found it not to his taste, even though he never formally ditched it altogether. As I use it here, the utility/disutility I am talking about does not refer to merely felt pleasure/pain, but also to the suffering of deprivation, whether this be experienced as felt pain or not.)

I have so far given one argument in favour of equality as the correct distributive value. The next set of arguments, I wish to advance, is, perhaps, best approached, initially, *via* certain criticisms, usually made against the notion of equality. Those who endorse inequality as the correct distributive value argue that their criterion is superior because its rival, equality, is both empirically false and conceptually insecure, if not logically misconceived. Its basic falsehood lies in the observation that, as a matter of fact, human agents are not equal, but unequal with respect to any characteristic one may care to cite. It is obvious that human agents differ with respect to physical features, like pigmentation of the skin, height, weight, as well as mental features, like intelligence and temperamental features, like being phlegmatic or volatile, lackadaisical or diligent, anxious or relaxed, and so on.

Of course egalitarians may not really be holding a clearly false empirical assumption. They are not so much saying that human agents are equal with respect to these traits, and, therefore, ought to be treated equally, but that they should be treated equally, in spite of the obvious differences between them. The former thesis may be called crude empirical egalitarianism, and the latter crude value egalitarianism.

In standard social/moral philosophy, either version runs into difficulties, which lead in turn to the charge of conceptual insecurity or even logical fallacy. Version 1 rests its argument (a) on a false empirical assumption, namely, that all human agents are equal, when they are not (in height, weight, intelligence, and so on); (b) but even if the empirical premise is correct, to argue from an empirical fact of equality ('is') to the prescription, that they ought to be treated equally ('ought'), is to commit the Naturalistic Fallacy. This version is hence doubly flawed — it combines empirical falsehood with fallacious reasoning.

Version 2 does not rest either on a false empirical premise or infer fallaciously from 'is' to 'ought'. But values or oughts are expressions of arbitrary, irrational, albeit sincere, commitments or choices. On this kind of meta-ethics, the rival distributive values of equality or inequality are essentially contestible, and both are equally 'valid'. Take your pick so long as you are sincere.

If the two meta-ethical possibilities exhaust the matter, then one should simply stop writing philosophy books on the subject (when the objective in social/moral philosophy is construed as the enterprise of constructing a substantive social/moral theory, in order to convince people, that it is a correct, adequate and relevant theory to adopt), or stop argumentation in the value domain in general. For on the former account, one is doing something logically illegitimate; on the latter, arguments are really neither here nor there.

But this book adopts a different methodology, as has been made clear in the first chapter. It wishes to argue that the distributive value of equality is viable, both factually and conceptually — (i) it rests on correct empirical assumptions about human agents; (ii) that correct factual/scientific assumptions can lend rational support (*via* epistemic implication) to value propositions of the kind 'human agents ought to be treated equally'; (iii) it rejects nominalism as a theory of meaning.

Nominalism holds that the only thing in common between two or more objects, called by the same name, is the name. If entity X (let us say that entity who used to smoke cigars, be photographed making a

V sign towards the end of the Second World War, etc.) and entity Y (let us say that entity who lived at the White House, was photographed with X at Yalta, etc.) are both called human agents or beings, then the name or label 'human being' is all that they have in common. It follows, then, that it is a perfectly arbitrary matter, what general label or name, we care to bestow on things. One could, on this epistemology, if one so wishes, bestow the label 'human being' on people with white skin only, and refuse to extend it to those whose pigmentation is darker. Indeed, one could include pet corgis in the category of human beings, while including one's black servants in the category of the canine.

Some anti-egalitarians could well belong to this school of epistemology, for they maintain that we have nothing in common, we differ in every characteristic one cares to cite, but nevertheless the term 'human' can still be bestowed on us all — all that we have in common is the name 'human'.

A non-nominalist theory of meaning holds that it makes sense to bestow a label or name on certain entities (especially when those entities are not artifacts but organic entities), only if these entities have certain things in common, that they share certain essential characteristics. To withhold the label 'human' from Louis Armstrong or Paul Robeson is an arbitrary act, for both entities share similar essential characteristics with other entities, like Churchill and Roosevelt, who are called human beings.

In other words, if the general term or name 'human being' or 'human agent' is used, then it must refer to certain characteristics, the possession of which, by an entity, qualifies it to be a member of that taxon, referred to by the term. There (conceptually) must be certain empirical assumptions which hold true about the members in question.

So which set of empirical assumptions, then, does one have in mind? To answer this question, turn back to the real definition of human agency given in Chapter Four. Note that the empirical characteristics mentioned are not those pertaining to obvious things, like actual differences in height, weight, intelligence and so on. They refer to capacities which human agents possess, like the capacity for frustration if intentions are not translated successfully into action (sub-thesis viii), like the capacity for feeling pain, acquiring skills, information (sub-thesis iv), or indeed the capacity for weight and height, etc. (It may sound stilted, but logically there is nothing wrong in saying that human agents have the capacity for weight and height. But it remains true that corpses, through decay, would gradually lose their weight and height. So in that deeper thermodynamic sense, only living agents, through being in a state of disequilibrium, could sustain the capacities for weight, height, as well as for thought, purposes, feelings, language, etc.) It is just that, for the purpose of arguing for the distributive value of equality, one needs only to invoke the possession of those capacities, which enter into the real definition of human agency, as set out in Chapter Four, and not the capacities for height and weight.

The actual empirical differences between human agents — such as, some are taller than others, some are darker in skin pigmentation than others, some weigh more than others, some score higher on I.Q. tests or Boy Scout tests than others, some speak English and others a babble of other tongues, some think of winning the football pools and others of winning the Nobel Prize in Physics — may be called surface characteristics. These are to be distinguished from deep characteristics, that is, the capacities for language, feeling pain and frustration, for day-dreaming, for height, weight, etc. While human agents differ in surface characteristics, they do not differ in deep characteristics. To count as a human agent, one must possess the latter — the dead have lost them and, therefore, do not qualify.

One needs then to look more carefully at the notion of capacity. Its logic is such that to maintain that X and Y, each, has the capacity for A or to do A, is compatible with maintaining that X and Y may not possess the capacity to the same extent or degree.

Capacities are capable of gradation. All human agents (except for those very damaged in the brain at birth) have the capacity to learn at least one language. (Common as well as scientific observation shows, however, that this capacity must be exercised by the age of two, or it is in danger of becoming so attenuated as to be virtually non-existent.) Yet we possess that vital capacity to different degrees as individuals. Some children may be competent language users by the age of two, others take a much longer period, up to six years or more in some cases. Some people acquire languages like the common cold. Yet others remain stubbornly mono-lingual in spite of effort and the best tuition. But this difference does not normally tempt people to maintain that the slower developers no longer possess the capacity in question. Why, then, should differences in other capacities lead them to assert the opposite?

To labour a point. All human agents, for instance, possess a heart, arteries, veins, blood, etc., that is, a circulatory system. But to admit this is not to admit that there must be no differences in the size of the heart, the type of blood carried, the rate with which the heart pumps the blood, the rate of oxidation, as clearly there are, and these vary from individual to individual. To admit these differences is not to admit that we are fundamentally different from one another. On the contrary, the science of physiology, for instance, is only possible because we possess the capacity for metabolism, of which the circulatory system is a part. The science is predicated upon our possession of the same deep characteristics, and our differential possession of surface ones. The latter refers to the different blood groups, to the different heart beats, etc. which enter into our personal constitutions and medical histories. So in the same way, one can say that we are fundamentally alike, in that we possess certain capacities (which enter into the real definition of human agency), but that we exercise them at a different rate, and we may even possess them to a greater or lesser extent (although in human beings, the range of differences is rather small as a matter of fact).

Essentially the same point is made by Rawls when he talks about 'range' properties. He says:

> the property of being in the interior of the unit circle is a range property of points in the plane. All points inside this circle have this property although their coordinates vary within a certain range. And they equally have this property, since no point interior to a circle is more or less interior to it than any other interior point. [11]

But these may also be called 'categorial' properties. Such properties possess a duality, of universality and specificity.

The eight sub-theses which enter into the definition of human agency, referring to certain capacities, possessed by entities, which are human, can then be construed as categorial features or properties, which agents to be human, must possess. Let us call these eight categorial features a. . .h. Corresponding to them are:

a^1 a^2 a^{10} $\quad$ b^1 b^2 b^{10} $\quad$ c^1 c^2 c^{10} $\quad$ d^1 d^2 d^{10}
a_1 a_2 a_n $\quad$ b_1 b_2 b_n $\quad$ c_1 c_2 c_n $\quad$ d_1 d_2 d_n

e^1 e^2 e^3 $\quad$ f^1 f^2 f^3 $\quad$ g^1 g^2 g^3 $\quad$ h^1 h^2 h^3
e_1 e_2 e_n $\quad$ f_1 f_2 f_n $\quad$ g_1 g_2 g_n $\quad$ h_1 h_2 h_n

The subscripts 1. . .n refer to individual agents and the superscripts 1. . .10 (just a convenient scale to use) refer to the range or degree of the capacities or features involved. Thus any two individual agents may differ as follows:

Individual I $\qquad$ a^3 b^5 c^2 d^8 e^9 f^4 g^7 h^4
$\qquad\qquad\qquad\quad$ a_1 b_1 c_1 d_1 e_1 f_1 g_1 h_1

Individual II $\qquad$ a^4 b^6 c^5 d^4 e^2 f^1 g^2 h^8
$\qquad\qquad\qquad\quad$ a_2 b_2 c_2 d_2 e_2 f_2 g_2 h_2

Those who hold that egalitarianism rests on an

empirical falsehood, have seized on the aspect of their specificity, and overlooked the aspect of their universality. But once reminded that categorial propertties are Janus-faced, one can then maintain (a) that, because human agents are equal (that is, in their possession of certain capacities — the universal aspect), they ought to be treated equally (but bearing in mind that the rational warrant for passing from 'is' to 'ought' is not that of strict implication or material implication but epistemic implication); (b) that, because human agents possess these capacities or categorial features to different degrees (that is, the aspect of specificity), the distributive value of equality, paradoxically, demands differential, not uniform, treatment of human agents.

Indeed, one of the arguments used by the critics of equality is precisely to say that it is objectionable, because it entails uniformity of treatment. But we shall see that this charge cannot be sustained, by coming to grips with the paradox, that has just been mentioned.

To do that, one must distinguish yet again between deep and surface concepts. The deep concept of equality corresponds to the deep categorial features of human agency in their universal aspect. It is this deep concept, which in turn generates differential treatment, when that concept is applied to the categorial features in their specific aspects.

The deep concept of equality holds that all human agents want their intentions translated into action, and would suffer frustration, if their execution is abortive. However, we also know that all human agents (though possessing the capacity or categorial feature of formulating intentions), as a matter of fact, do not formulate the same intentions. Agent X intends to become a novelist, while agent Y intends to be a cricketer. (Agent X intends to see a film while agent Y intends to do some shopping at a particular time.) In order that both X and Y do not suffer frustration, they must be able to translate their respective intentions into action. For agent X, minimally, this would require time, means to keep body and soul together, some space in the form of a table, if not a table in a room, paper and pen (or for the more technologically minded, a typewriter or word processor). For agent Y, it would also mean, minimally, time, means to keep body and soul together, space in the form of a cricket pitch, like-minded agents, bat and ball, etc.

The elements common to both agents in the realisation of their intentions are time (which is existentially scarce), and sustenance of the agents *via* food, shelter, etc. The other elements differ. So for agent X, it would be inappropriate to provide her/him with a cricket bat and ball, just as it would be inappropriate to give agent Y paper and pen. Nor would it be any more appropriate in the name of uniformity to issue both agents with a set of carpentry tools. As there is nothing in the notion of equality, resting on the categorial properties of human agency, which entails that all agents must have similar intentions and goals, therefore, it does not entail treating all agents as if they have similar intentions. On the contrary, the recognition that they do not (in conjunction with the deep concept of equality), entails that human agents have to be given differential treatment, depending entirely on what their intentions are. Uniformity of treatment would simply lead to universal frustration, or at least near universal frustration, because most agents would not be able to translate successfully their respective intentions into action.

Kant's moral philosophy is normally said to embody the notion of respect for persons. I suggest that content be given to this notion *via* the recognition that (a) human agents want intentions to be translated into action, and would feel frustration, if they were unsuccessful (sub-theses (vii) and (viii)), (b) that human agents, as a matter of fact, entertain different intentions, (c) that actions require access to the means appropriate to them, that is, the appropriate type of low entropic energy and matter, (d) therefore, avoidance of frustration entails differential treatment of agents. To respect someone as a person is then to respect her/his intentions by enabling them to be executed into action.

Differential treatment, entailed by the deep concept of equality, depends not only on the different intentions of agents, but also in certain contexts, on the (surface) differences between agents themselves. Take two agents both wanting to write a novel. Agent A is like the one outlined above, that is, an able-bodied agent who can use a pen or typewriter. Suppose, however, that agent B lives in an iron lung, paralysed from the neck down. Giving such an agent paper and pen would not enable her/him to execute the intention to write. The person, instead, would require a specially constructed device like the possum, which is an electronic instrument, that can be operated by the mouth or other parts of the body not paralysed. The two agents, though showing similar intentions, have very different requirements in realising their goal. Hence respect for person entails not only taking into account (i) the requirements appropriate to translating different intentions into action, but (ii) also the requirements which are peculiar to the individual agents themselves, and which may exist at any one time.

One may elaborate upon (ii) as follows: the extent of one's capacities is not a static but dynamic matter. Capacities may be enlarged or may be diminished. A normal agent's capacity for a certain activity could through illness (like a stroke) or accident be destroyed, or become much attenuated. To lose one's legs is to be deprived of one's capacity to walk. However, sometimes, exosomatic organs may be technologically available to replace endosomatic ones — the legless person could be given a pair of crutches, an invalid car, etc. which would enable the individual to be mobile. A person, who has lost her/his voice box, because of cancer of the larynx, could be fitted with an electronic device, thus enabling her/him to communicate to some extent.

But sometimes a damaged capacity is not so much compensated for by the provision of exosomatic organs, as by painstaking rehabilitation, and stimulation of the impaired organ. Even very severely handicapped agents could often overcome their handicaps to a significant extent, through a prolonged and difficult, but rewarding, process of rehabilitation. Impaired capacities, if not remedied, could become even more impaired.

Human agency is dynamic. Recall too that Chapter Seven argued for an epigenetic account of development. If so, social arrangements should ensure that capacities are enriched rather than diminished. Moreover, one must bear in mind that a very important element in the epigenetic events that constitute (post-natal) development is the psychological contribution based on the notion of the self image. Certain capacities, on the part of some agents, could remain undeveloped, if society through its institutions succeeds in labelling them as certified failures, or in marginalising such capacities. A society ought (as I have already argued, and will further elaborate upon in Chapter Ten) to celebrate all those capacities, which, when exercised (a) do not harm others, (b) can be fulfilled through activities, which are not zero-sum games, (c) and which do not make unsustainable ecological demands. In this way, all agents could be encouraged to develop themselves, without laying waste Nature, and beggaring their neighbours.

5. I have tried to defend the distributive value of equality in the version set out above. I will next briefly argue against the distributive value of inequality by looking at two possible charges against it.

The first consists of turning the table upon the inegalitarian by saying that it is the logic of inequality which entails uniformity, rather than its rival. But before doing that, let me enter a caveat. There are many forms of inegalitarianism, just as there are many forms of egalitarianism. The version of the former that I have been concerned with holds (a) that money wealth, the ever increasing possession and consumption of external goods that money can buy, constitute the central substantive value of the theory, (b) that the goods, obtained through securing this value, will be unequally distributed, with the end result that a few may be highly successful, a good many may be moderately successful, while even more will be quite unsuccessful.

Thesis (b) then involves a form of meritocracy. Meritocracy is a hierarchical system, like aristocracy. But unlike the latter, its fundamental rule decrees that success is not determined by birth or caste, but by personal effort in excelling in those activities, celebrated by the society in question. Meritocracy could conceivably celebrate skills in physical combat, ability to ride a horse or literacy. But today's meritocracy celebrates, by and large, (a) mentioned above. (In practice our meritocracy could be in danger of becoming a partial aristocracy as inheritance is permitted.)

As meritocracy necessarily singles out a limited set of activities for endorsement, while denigrating others, there is immense pressure to conform towards the norm. In contemporary civilisation (confining myself to the non-communist ones in order to simplify matters), parents, who naturally wish to see their offspring do well, expend an enormous amount of psychic and financial energy into producing successful children. In this country, certainly, parents know that exposing their children to a certain sort of environment would enhance their chances of success. Hence the urgency perceived by such parents to put them through the so-called public school system of education, Oxbridge and on to the City, Whitehall or the professions. This is often done without taking into account the inclinations and proclivities of the offspring.

If success is very narrowly defined, then the natural desire for success would ensure conformity, and hence uniformity of treatment. If little Johnny does not really want to be an accountant, but to be an organist, then pressure would be brought to bear on him, and he would be sent to a school together with others, who would be destined to become accountants, stockbrokers, etc.

Anxious parents have so far tried the 'environmental' path to success. (Yes, they do indeed engage in social engineering, contrary to what ideological rhetoric may permit them to say.) But lurking beneath is the hope that one day, through improved technology, there may be an easier, surer path to success. If only certain genes could be identified as the cause of intelligence (and hence success), then one can procreate through an assembly of such genes. Or perhaps one could populate the world through cloning of successful persons. This then is the logic of meritocracy carried to an extreme — the desire not merely to treat all agents uniformly, but also to reproduce exact copies of one or more type of human agents.

This in turn brings us to the second difficulty inherent in such a version of inegalitarianism. The desire to populate the world, through cloning of the successful type, brings out in the clearest possible way the incoherence of the theory itself. A hierarchical system is a zero-sum game. It necessarily has a few winners at the top of the pyramid, resting upon a broad base of losers. Not everyone logically speaking could be a winner. As we saw in Chapter Six, the goalpost in such a society is a shifting one — if everyone were a millionaire, then being a millionaire is not a sign of success. One must endeavour to be a multi-millionaire and so on.

The theory celebrates, as its central substantive value, things which by their very nature cannot be universally attainable. So its incoherence may be displayed as follows: (i) X is the substantive value which everyone is urged to attain — this implies that X is a good for everyone, that is, a universal good; (ii) yet given the nature of X, and the distributive value of inequality which follows from it, and endorsed by the theory, X could never be attained by all. Hence a good, which is meant to be a universaal good, is, by its very nature of being embedded in a zero-sum game, only a restricted good, that is, a good available only to some, but not all agents. The theory is logically constructed to the extent of recognising that its distributive value must be one of inequality, given the nature of its substantive value; but its incoherence lies in its attempt, nevertheless, to urge the substantive value to be a universal good, when by its very nature, it cannot be so.

This in turn raises the question: must a social/moral theory endorse a universal but not a restricted good? The answer to this is yes if you follow Kant. Kant holds (and no modern moral philosopher I know of has ever challenged him on this point) that 'ought' implies 'can'. One ought to do X if, and only if, it is possible to do or obtain X. But it is not possible for everyone to obtain X. Therefore, that one ought to do or obtain X cannot be a universal moral prescription.

The theory under criticism can get out of the difficulty only by reformulating itself as follows: one ought to try to do X, that is, to be successful, by being better off than others, in terms of money, status, power. (Note that 'one ought to try to obtain X' is not the same as 'one ought to obtain X'. To achieve X is to be successful. To have tried, but not to have attained X, is to fail to be successful. Honours will be heaped on the former, but dishonour on the latter.) However, this reformulation does not by-pass the Kantian dictum. When it says, for instance, that A ought to have tried to save the drowning person, this implies that A could have saved the drowning person (if A has so chosen to try). This in turn implies that A was at the site, where the person was drowning at the time, that A could swim and could have swum, or was able-bodied with a rope at hand, which he could have thrown as a lifeline to the drowning person, etc. But if A was not in a position to do any of these things, then it makes no sense to say either that A ought to have saved the drowning person, or that A ought to have tried to save such a person. Nor does it make sense to say that A ought to have saved the drowning person, when as it turned out, someone else had already carried out the rescue.

Analogously, lots of people in our society are not in a position to try to do the kind of things which would lead to success (as defined above). Just to take one example. It is hard to think of someone, who is a nurse, and remains a nurse, being in a position to try to be successful, in the accepted sense of success. Therefore, it makes no sense to say in such cases, that one ought to do or obtain X, or to try to obtain X. Moreover, as the nature of the good in question, that is, success as conventionally understood, is a logically, not merely a contingently scarce good (as the game involved is a zero-sum one), those who do not attempt, because they are not in a position to try, could not be held to be at fault on the grounds that they ought to have done so.

In an activity which is not governed by rigid rules, either legal or customary, laying down the limits of success (a nurse would have reached the height of the profession, when s/he becomes a matron, or what is now called a chief nursing officer), it may be possible, aided by extreme good luck and extreme hard work, in some cases to succeed in the accepted sense. One hears stories of barrow boys, penniless refugees, and so on, having succeeded spectacularly in businesses to become millionaires. But it is a mistake to believe that (a) all of us could, and should engage, in business activities (a society of only business people is a ridiculous one anyway), (b) that of those who do engage, that all would and could be successful — as business, by its very nature, is competitive, there are bound to be many failures, in order to support the few successes.

Increasingly, however, our society is finding a way for people to simulate success, or at least one aspect of it. While it is not logically possible for all to enjoy top income, power and prestige, it can be arranged for all to consume, without prior accumulation of wealth. Consume first, pay later. By turning everyone into a debtor, the virtue of ever increasing consumption can become a universal moral prescription. Nowadays, all that is required is to be eighteen or over in age, before one is given seemingly endless and unlimited credit, without further questions asked. Perhaps Kant was not far-sighted enough to have anticipated the creative refinements of mature capitalism to by-pass his dictum. Perhaps, advanced capitalism has revised part of the Lockean framework

309

within which (a) one is entitled to the fruits of one's labour, (b) the fruits of one's labour may be used to generate further wealth (money). It is no longer solely preoccupied with the accumulation of money, which does not rot, but also with its consumption. Money, as we saw, is not an entity which obeys the laws of thermodynamics, and is not ecologically scarce *per se*. It can indefinitely be increased. But, of course, the real trouble arises when it is used in exchange for real things, which are subject to the entropic laws, and are, therefore, ecologically scarce.

This then is the crucial challenge to our civilisation — how to square the operation of an entity, like money, with the operation of entities, like food, clean air, fertile top soil, water fit for drinking, etc.? It cannot be squared, not even by technology, no more than one can square the circle. The former is a physical impossibility; the latter a mathematical (logical) impossibility. But both forms of impossibility are equally impossible to overcome.

However, the partial revision of the Lockean framework mentioned just now should not be understood as transcendance of it. On the contrary, it is simply the restless nature of capital, whose essence is that of accumulation, expressing itself in this form, through the competition for the money, which is now put into the consumers' pockets *via* (almost) unlimited credit.

6. I have argued earlier that an adequate social/moral theory must have at least two values — a substantive value and a distributive value. It also transpires that some substantive values have a built-in distributive value of inequality — the example of the ever increasing possession and consumption of external goods illustrates this hidden link with inequality. Other substantive goods, like the one urged by this book, the acquisition of internal goods, based on the artistic mode of production, is capable of being equally acquired by all agents, although, as we shall see, in the history of that concept, some theorists have been

known to argue for an unequal, rather than an equal distribution of it. Two outstanding theorists, belonging to very different traditions, who take this line are Plato and J. S. Mill.

Plato's distributive stance, however, (i) is based on a very narrow conception of self-development as intellectual development itself — he was really only interested in an ability to do mathematics and philosophy (and thus to attain wisdom); (ii) consequently, on the plausible empirical assumption that not many people either would find mathematics and philosophy inherently fascinating, or are really good at them, necessarily the majority of the population would have to be ruled out. In this way, Plato arrived at his form of élitism, the rule of the philosopher-kings.

Mill was quite different. Although he was quite conscious of the limitations, both intellectual and otherwise, of the majority of his compatriots, he, nevertheless, believed that they were limitations, which were not inherent in any one class or group of persons, but could be overcome given proper education and more propitious opportunities for development. He thought that all people could develop in all sorts of ways (in spite of his own obvious preference for book learning), even though here and now, they might show no such signs of doing so.

However, after many years of agonising over the matter, he came to the conclusion that socialism/communism was to be rejected in favour of capitalism, in spite of his realisation that the former is more likely to ensure opportunities for self-development for all than the latter. Indeed, he endorsed capitalism with his eyes open, that it is a system, which only allows some people to develop, but not others (the majority). He discarded socialism or communism on the grounds, that it would stifle competition, and, hence, possibilities for further development. In other words, in the end, Mill opted for a form of social arrangement, which might give opportunities for experiment in self-development to a few, at best as a matter of fact, but at the expense of the majority. (This, however, is to overlook that under capitalism, self-development becomes distorted, and perverted to mean the very opposite, namely, to become the urge to possess, and consume endlessly external material goods.) This would still be morally superior to a type of social arrangement which would secure opportunities for self-development for all.

In Mill's opinion, some level of self-development, under socialism or communism, may exist, but it cannot improve, as it is a system which stifles competition. (Although Mill was concerned and prescient about the demand for conformity by democracy, he showed little awareness that the demands of capitalism in reality could lead to conformity, or to the stifling of competition itself — monopolies do not presumably advance the cause of competition, and the success of commodity production under capitalism (bourgeois) has led to the world wide domination of Coca/Pepsi Cola as a drink, driving out, in nearly all cases, local rivals, thus destroying, rather than encouraging diversity, as Mill thought. No single force has been as potent as bourgeois capitalism in creating a world-wide uniformity of expectation, of aspiration, of lifestyle — indeed, as some have maintained, the contemporary civilisation world-wide may most appropriately be called the 'Coca Cola Civilisation'.) With this revision, Mill should have consistently maintained that while he approved of self-development as a substantive good, it is, nevertheless, not a good that could be realised for all. It cannot therefore be a universal, but, at best, a restricted good for the few in his final analysis.

But there is another substantive value, namely freedom, which is commonly asserted by contemporary liberal thinkers to be the central substantive value of their theory, which I have yet to examine. It would be of interest to uncover what kind of distributive value it entails. Liberal theorists, on the whole, tend to imply that freedom must be unequally, not equally distributed, a thesis which is presented misleadingly in terms of a trade-off between freedom and equality — that is, more freedom for less equality or more equality for less freedom. Those of the rival persuasion also maintain that freedom is the substantive good, but that it requires, or at least is compatible with, equality as its distributive value. But as we shall soon see, the internal logic of the notion of freedom as a substantive good is much more complex than either view has bargained for.

In order to come to grips with the complexities of the issue, I propose to deal with freedom as freedom of action. Innocuous as that may sound, it is not uncontroversial from the standpoint of the standard literature about the concept. What is controversial is (a) whether freedom of action is the only kind of freedom worth having, and (b) what content is to be given to the notion of the freedom of action, even if one were to concede that it constitutes a significant type of freedom, although, admittedly, not the only sort worth having. This takes one into the controversy directly concerning the conceptions of negative and positive freedom, the two usually being regarded by philosophers to be essentially contested conceptions, that is to say, that even in principle and in the long run, no amount of argumentation could settle the controversy, so that one's choice between them becomes simply a question of (irrational or non-rational) commitment.

I do not wish here to go over the vast corpus of writing on this matter. I will only be commenting on certain strands of the controversy in order to show that it is not, as orthodox contemporary philosophy maintains, impossible to use argumentation to establish that one, or indeed, even both of the competing conceptions, may be unsound. The latter, is what I hope to establish, in spite of showing that each may contain some valuable points. I wish to argue for an analysis of freedom which can incorporate these partial insights, but also, to go beyond them.

Standard liberal theorists maintain that freedom is freedom of action, and that freedom of action is no more than the absence of legal interference and coercion — the view of so-called negative freedom. On this view, one is free to do X (an action) so long as there is no legal prohibition against it. The critics of negative freedom, however, argue that freedom may also be understood not only to mean freedom of action, but also freedom from certain (undesirable) states of affairs, and that in any case freedom of action itself means more than merely the lack of legal coercion and interference — there is not only freedom to do X (in the absence of legal prohibition to do X) but also freedom from Y (such as hunger, fear, etc.) This is the view of so-called positive freedom. [12]

I propose to resolve the controversy (in a critical and rational manner) in two ways — the first *via* teasing out a thesis about action from the real definition of human agency set out in Chapter Four, and the second, by adapting Bentham's analysis of the notion of legal right or freedom, and the corresponding notion of legal duty or obligation. It will be shown that the two approaches jointly lead to the following account of freedom:

(i) that freedom is freedom of action — score, 1 to so-called negative freedom and nil to so-called positive freedom;

(ii) that action (to be successfully completed or executed) requires the availability of the material means (that is, low entropic energy and matter) to execute the action — 1 to positive freedom, nil to negative freedom;

(iii) that action to be successfully completed, apart from (ii) above, also requires the non-interference on the part of other agents, the non-interference being ultimately guaranteed by law — 1 to Bentham and 1 potentially to negative freedom;

(iv) that, however, an agent A only possesses the legal right or freedom to do X, if there is a corresponding legal duty or obligation on the part of other agents, such as B or C, to refrain from interfering with A's execution of X — 1 to Bentham;

(v) a more refined analysis of (iv) above will show that the legal right or freedom to do X explicitly refers to the material means to do X, and guarantees legal freedom only to those agents with such means — 1 to positive freedom and possibly to Bentham;

(vii) but which agents in a particular jurisdiction have

access to the material means to execute X, and which
agents do not, is itself a matter underpinned by the
extant structure of legal rights and freedoms, and
their corresponding legal duties and obligations.

In detail then, what contribution can an exploration
of the notion of human agency make towards an understanding of the concept of freedom? But before I
do that, let me first clear up a matter of terminology.
I am arguing that freedom is to be understood as legal freedom (the term 'legal' may be used either to
mean a formal legal system, with which we are all
familiar today, or a more informal system of what is
sometimes called a 'pre-legal' system. But as we are
really concerned with contemporary society which is
embedded in a modern legal-rational state, I take it
that it is the formal system of municipal law (and at
times, international law when one is talking about
inter-state matters), that one is referring to). When I
refer to freedom in the mere context of analysing
human agency, I am not, therefore, referring to legal
freedom. For this reason (from now on), I will put
quotes around the word, whenever I use it, to indi-
cate that it is used not in a legal context, but merely,
heuristically, with an eye to casting light on the issue
of legal freedom itself.

In Chapter Four, we have already seen that human
agency implies action. To act, as distinct from to
think, involves (a) the use of certain parts of one's
body, like one's limbs or voice box (that is, endosomatic organs), or the use of such parts in conjunction with some other external physical objects (that is
exosomatic organs or instruments); (b) the occupation
by the items just mentioned of certain portions of
physical space and their sustenance in thermodynamic
terms. (a) and (b) constitute the material means (low
entropic energy and matter), by which actions are effected. That is to say, to be able to act effectively
and successfully, to translate one's purposes and intentions into action, the agent must either possess, or
have access to these means. In both cases, s/he may
be said to use and control them. And unless s/he can
do so, s/he would not be an effective agent. In some

actions, s/he must possess the components in order to control and use them, such as, when s/he walks or jumps, s/he literally must possess limbs, which are not defective. In others, s/he must consume certain external physical objects — to eat, s/he must have food. Yet in other instances, it is enough that s/he has access to, or be allowed to use them, when required — s/he does not need actually to possess the land s/he is allowed to walk across, or to possess the kidney machine, which purifies the polluted blood. To cover these instances of consumption, use and control, I will borrow the phrase 'the availability of the physical means or components of action'.

As we have seen, frustration follows if action is impotent (subtheses (vii) and (viii) of the real definition of human agency), that is, when the physical means or components are not available to the agent. Impotence occurs under two very different sets of conditions — (a) when these means fail to materialise without human intervention, or in spite of human intervention — for example, the agent might have been born a cripple, or that the crutches were destroyed in a gale, or research notwithstanding, we do not know how to prevent paralysis, following an attack of polio; (b) when they fail to materialise because of intervention on the part of other agents, direct or indirect.

(a) is of no relevance to one's ultimate concern with freedom as legal freedom, although it is a significant source of impotence of action, and its resulting frustration. Like morals, the law cannot and does not have anything to say on matters which are beyond human control; it would be futile if not irrational for it to do so. So I will concentrate on (b).

The most primitive direct type of prevention on the part of other agents is physical intervention, that is, when other agents maim limbs, eyes or other parts of the body, or seize the actual physical objects, such as spade or plough, which is required in the act of tilling. Another is incarceration of the agent — A locks up B, to prevent B from doing all sorts of things B might wish to do. An indirect, more sophisticated

method is simply that of ensuring that the physical
means are not available to B — for instance, A and
other like-minded agents might not sell certain things
to B. The non-white agents, who have the money and
want to buy a house in a particular suburb, may not
be able to do so, because the white residents may
simply not sell to them, even if they offer the asking
or a higher price.

The above account indicates that, in so far as agent
A can and does appropriate any given physical item
in the world, that item is no longer available to
another agent B, for the purpose of B's executing a
certain intention into action. B is only 'free' to do X,
if the physical means for doing X have not been pre-
empted, or are not being 'sat upon' by A.

It follows that if B were the only agent in the
universe, B would be maximally 'free', as *ex hypothesi*, there would be no other agent(s) to pre-empt
any of the physical components of B's would-be actions, including those, which s/he might not wish ever
to execute. But as this possibility belongs to the pro-
vince of what I have called fantastic theorising, I will
not pursue the matter further. In the real world, there
are always other agents, who by virtue of the fact of
their existence and their actions are there poised to
pre-empt the physical means of potential actions on
the part of any one agent. No one could be maximally 'free' in the real world.

Of greater relevance is the implication that 'freedom' involves three variables, agent A, the physical
items (for potential action) and B (other agent or
agents). The 'freedom' of A to do X, by appropriat-
ing the physical means or components for executing
X, is predicated upon the 'unfreedom' of B in respect
of doing X, or any action requiring the same physical
components for execution. This in turn means, more
'freedom' to A entails less to B. One cannot maximise
'freedom' *tout court*, for everybody. It is always a
question of 'freedom' to some agents (and how many)
and 'unfreedom' to other agents (and how many).

So, it emerges from an analysis of the notion of
action (together with the realistic assumption, that the

world we occupy is a multi-agent universe), that the notion of 'freedom' involves a triadic relationship and, hence, a ratio. Let us see next if the same relationship will obtain when we introduce another realistic assumption into the analysis, the existence of a legal system in human society.

As theorists of negative freedom have explicitly argued for the relevance of the law to the existence of freedom, it would be wise to start with their view. It would, however, also be wise to concentrate on the clearest writer on this subject, in my opinion, Bentham, a theorist commonly said to be working within the tradition of negative liberty and yet, as I shall show, his conception of it is very different from the standard one proffered. [13] Moreover, I also hope to show, as already indicated earlier, that by adapting his analysis of law, I can develop a framework, which would exhibit what are the points of validity and invalidity in each of these so-called conflicting conceptions of freedom, so that a more adequate unifying account of freedom, and its relationship to the notions of equality/inequality, may be explored.

His analysis of law shows that freedom, as the absence of legal interference, is not to be understood simplistically, to mean no more than that agent A enjoys freedom to do X, if there is no law prohibiting her/him from doing X, should s/he want to do X — the standard analysis given by negative libertarians. It is to be analysed out as follows: (i) if agent A is legally free (or has the legal right) to do X, this implies that there is a legal obligation on the part of B (let us call B or any other such agent the second party), not to prevent A from doing X, should A choose to do so; (ii) if agent B does prevent A from doing X, a duly competent law officer would prevent B (in the last resort by apprehending B and locking B up in person), from preventing A to do X (let us call the law officers, the third party).

In other words, A's legal freedom or right to do X is crucially dependent on B's, the second party's legal unfreedom to prevent A from doing X, and on the third party's legal obligation/duty to prevent B, from preventing A, to do X. Take A to be the owner-occupier of a house. The law sees fit to permit A, owners of houses (let us call this the first party), to paint the outside of the house any colour A pleases (because there is no legal prohibition against doing so). A is therefore said to be free to paint it how s/he wishes. This means that B (the neighbour, the second party) is not (legally) free to prevent A from painting it in a bilious yellow.

For every freedom (granted by the law) to one party (A) to do something, that same law (as a complete law and not only as a fragment of a law) is necessarily committed to denying a second party (B), the (legal) freedom to do what that party wants, rather than what A wants. And if B does interfere, A could appeal to law officers, the third party, to restrain B. In other words, the second party is under a legal obligation/duty not to interfere with A's legal freedom to do X, and the third party is also under a legal obligation/duty to ensure that the second party carries out its own legal obligation/duty. If only one, or neither, of these conditions obtains, A cannot be said to have the legal freedom/right to do X. (In practice, of course, it can happen that the law officers, on certain occasions, may be unwilling to enforce the law, that is, to make sure that B adheres to the legal obligation of not interfering with A's freedom to do X. But this does not show that B is not under such an obligation, or that the law officers themselves have not committed dereliction of their own legal duty.)

If this analysis is correct, then, whether the law could be said to promote a greater distribution of freedom, or a lesser distribution of freedom, (i) could only mean whether the freedom to do X is enjoyed by a smaller (or larger) number of people in the society affected by the legislation, compared with the number of second parties, who are prevented by the law from interfering with those, who are permitted to do X; (ii) would, therefore, depend on the specific legislation itself, and on the numerical strength of the first party, as opposed to the numerical strength of the second party.

For instance, historically the legal system under capitalism has been used to promote a lesser distribution of freedom in the economic domain, for the capitalist is allowed to do many more things with capital than the working classes, and the capitalists are smaller in number than the proletariat. Capitalists could offer wages as they see fit, could determine the conditions of work as they see fit, could fold up the factory as they see fit, etc. Workers on the other hand have simply to accept these conditions in favour of the capitalists, by entering into a contract to work for the owners of capital. The law, by guaranteeing so many legal freedoms to the employers of labour, necessarily denied legal freedoms to the employees to interfere with the employers' exercise of these freedoms. The capitalists were only legally unfree not to pay the wages to the workers, as laid down by the terms of the contract. Should the employees (the more numerous class) try to prevent the employers from closing down the factory and taking their investment elsewhere, by occupying the factory, preventing the removal of its contents, like the machines, and so on, the law (in the form of the police, magistrates, judges, etc.) would see to it that they are prevented from doing so. (Legislation was introduced permitting trade unions to be formed and to function in certain ways, such as through strike action, picketing, etc. so that they might secure certain concessions from the employers, by way of improved wages, better health and safety conditions at the workplace, and so on. This was an attempt to shift the grossly unequal structure of legal freedoms from the employers to the employees. But of late, legislation in this country has once again shifted back the balance of legal freedoms in favour of the owners of capital.)

To take another example. The law, as it stands, denies (legal) freedom to consumers to prevent the manufacturers in the food industry, from putting certain substances into their products, which could be harmful to them. If consumers were to take direct action, the police would ensure that they be prevented from denying the manufacturers the (legal) freedom to do what they like, with what goes into the making of their products. Of course, consumers could campaign for a law to be passed, which would prevent toxins from being used in food manufacture. But if such legislation were passed, then this new freedom — that is, freedom from poisonous foods — would be procured at the expense of the unfreedom, on the part of food manufacturers, to do what they like with the contents of their products. This would mean more people would enjoy this freedom — the consumers are more numerous — at the expense of a smaller group — the manufacturing class — suffering the corresponding unfreedom. This would replace the existing situation where a small group, that is, the manufacturing group, is enjoying the freedom to pollute food, at the expense of a very large group, that is, the consumers, suffering the corresponding unfreedom. The new legislation would shift the distribution of freedom from a small group to a very large group; and, in this sense, could be said to be maximising the distribution of freedom.

If the above analysis is correct, it would follow that it is confusing conceptually to hold that one is prepared to have less equality for greater freedom, or less freedom for greater equality. If the legal system upholds that only men could own, say, the house they live in, then this freedom for men (roughly a half of the human population) entails the unfreedom for women (the other half of the population) to own the house they live in. A legal system which says that people over the age of 18 or 21, male or female, may own the house they live in, would increase the distribution of the freedom to own a house from 50 percent to 100 percent of the adult population, by removing the corresponding unfreedom, on the part of women, to own houses. This, in turn, entails that men would be no longer free to prevent women from owning houses, a freedom they have formerly enjoyed. This former freedom has been removed from the group of men by law in order to bestow a corresponding freedom on the group of women. This example shows that the specific freedom in question (to own one's house) is now maximally distributed in the population of adult persons.

More formally, the points above may be spelt out as follows: ($\downarrow$ stands for 'entails')

Only men (over 18 years) may own houses — they have the legal freedom/right to do so — LI
$\downarrow$

The class of non-men over 18 years, that is, women, the second party, as well as any third party, has the legal obligation or duty not to interfere with LI — LII
$\downarrow$

Women are legally unfree, or have no legal right, to own houses — LIII
$\downarrow$

Men can legally prevent women from interfering with LI (by calling in the police; courts will uphold LI) — LIV
$\downarrow$

The specific legal freedom of house ownership is enjoyed by only roughly 50 percent of the adult population (strictly speaking, to derive LV from LI-LIV requires the additional premise that the adult population is roughly half male, half female) — LV

A change in the law says that:

Every adult has the legal right or freedom to own a house — LI_i which entails LI
$\downarrow$
$\downarrow$ LII_i which entails LII
$\downarrow$ LIII_i which entails LIII
$\downarrow$ LIV_i which entails LIV
$\downarrow$ LV_i which entails LV

The Benthamite analysis of a legal freedom/right may also be adapted to show that, in one sense, the controversy between negative and positive conceptions of freedom is trivial. The former, as stated earlier, is usually formulated as the freedom to do X, and the latter as freedom from Y, while X is an act the agent may want to bring about, Y is said to be a state of affairs, which the agent would rather not have to

322

endure. So one is said to be free or unfree to dine at the Ritz (dining at the Ritz is an action agents would like to do), but one is said to be free or unfree from hunger (being hungry is a state of affairs agents do not want to be in).

But this is a superficial linguistic difference — 'free to' (followed by a verb) as opposed to 'free from' (followed by a noun) — which in any case can be overcome by recasting the latter into the canonical mode. For instance, 'free from hunger', 'free from unemployment', 'free from polluted air', and so on, could be recast quite simply as 'free to work (when one wants to)', 'free to relieve hunger or to eat (when one wants to in one's hunger)', 'free to breathe unpolluted air', etc.

Nothing hangs on the linguistic formulation as such. The real points of substantive and significant differences lie elsewhere. These may be brought out by using the Benthamite analytical framework. Take freedom from unemployment, which translated into the canonical mode becomes, say, free to work at the Caterpillars factory in Scotland (analogous to being free to dine at the Ritz). In our legal system, the capitalist as owner and employer has the legal right or freedom to do what he likes with his investments and his assets, as we have seen. This entails that the owners of the Caterpillars factory in Scotland are legally free to close down the factory, and transfer assets and investments elsewhere should they see fit. This in turn entails that the employees of that factory are legally unfree to secure their employment with the firm in question, that is, they have a legal duty or obligation not to prevent, or interfere with, their employer's removal of assets and investments elsewhere. In other words, they are not legally free (that is, they do not have the legal right) to work at the Caterpillars factory when they want to, much as they want to. Conversely, should the company change its corporate plans, and decide to carry on business in that particular place, then the employees would be legally free to work there, in the same unmysterious way one is said to be free to dine at the Ritz.

Similarly, where the legal system permits the capitalists as manufacturers the legal freedom to spew forth toxins and other nuisances from their chimney stacks or whatever, the citizens affected are, correspondingly, unfree to breathe clean air. If citizens, who could be affected by such 'externalities', were to be guaranteed the legal freedom to breathe clean air, then this, in turn, would imply a corresponding legal unfreedom on the part of the producers of nuisances to emit them.

The real issues at stake are (i) whose legal freedom, whose legal unfreedom should society approve of and uphold through its legal system?, (ii) what criteria could be used (other than whim, arbitrary commitment, custom or the maximisation of profits) to determine between them in a rational manner?

To drive home the points above, let me take another example — freedom from hunger. (In canonical form, it reads — free to eat, when one wants to, in one's hunger.) In today's world, hunger and famine are quite often brought about by war, land-tenure policy, lack of money to buy food, rather than by the sheer non-existence of food itself in the world. (This, however, should not be used to mask another crucial issue, namely, whether the food produced, like the surplus of the American grain economy, based on EST, is a sustainable mode of food production.) For example, Oxfam [14] has shown that in Bangladesh after the 1974 flood, 4 million tons of rice were available, but the people could not afford to buy it. In Mexico, 80 percent of children in rural areas are undernourished, yet Mexico produces grain, to be fed to livestock (which consumes more grain than the entire population), and exported to the USA, to be made into beefburgers.

In Bangladesh, the legal system secures, to the owners of the rice, the legal freedom to dispose of it as they wish (including destroying the lot if no one could afford to buy it); it means that the hungry, correspondingly, do not enjoy the legal freedom to eat the rice, for any attempt to help themselves to it, without proper payment, would mean that policemen would put them in handcuffs, release CS gas at them, or even fire machine guns at them. In Mexico, the legal system, by sustaining the existing structure of landownership and guaranteeing to the landowners the (legal) freedom to do what they please, including using part of it to rear cattle and the other part to grow grain to feed the cattle for export, at the same time upholds the corresponding (legal) unfreedom on the part of the famished and the undernourished, to prevent the landowners from doing what they want to do, from diverting the grain to feed cattle, instead of humans. The existing Mexican legal system chooses to guarantee the freedom of a small group of landowners and ranchers, at the expense of the unfreedom to eat, on the part of the numerous famished and under-nourished.

If freedom is freedom of action (as opposed to merely thought), and if actions require the use or consumption of actual physical things, the successful execution of intentions into actions would require access to those physical things. This is one of the issues of substance between those, who hold the neg-ative conception and those, who hold the positive conception of freedom. The former maintains that the absence of legal prohibition (and hence coercion) alone constitutes freedom of action, providing both a nec-essary and sufficient condition. The latter asserts that the physical components of action must also be avail-able.

One way of reconciling the two is again by ex-tending the Benthamite analysis of a legal freedom/right and legal obligation/duty. As is obvious, the law can be used to uphold an existing structure of rights and corresponding obligations, or it can be used as a radical reforming tool to alter that *status quo*, so that those who under existing rights have no access to land to till, may now have them — the bestowal of this new legal freedom/right to till the soil, to grow food, to overcome hunger and malnutrition, is accom-plished by the removal of the existing legal freedom/right of the large landowners to do what they please with their possessions. Under the new dispensation, the former landowners would have no legal freedom or right to prevent the poor from parcelling out their estates and tilling their plots, just as under the extant dispensation, the poor have no legal freedom/right to prevent the landowners from doing what they please with their land.

Freedom from hunger, when food is available, can be solved by using the law in at least three ways: (a) more directly by altering the existing legal right of ownership to the rice or wheat, through expropriating the grain, and distributing it to the hungry masses — this is the method favoured by revolutionary governments, as an immediate solution to the urgent problem of hunger and famine; (b) more indirectly, by introducing legislation, to secure a minimum wage, child benefits, old age pensions, etc. through taxation of one kind or other, in order to make it possible for those without money to buy and pay for the food; (c) by altering existing rights about land ownership and tenure; (d) a combination of (a), (b) and (c).

But ultimately, whether it is money or physical things and services like rice, houses, education, medical treatment, that one is talking about, their distribution in any one society is governed by its legal system. Those who subscribe to the positive conception of freedom, may be interpreted to be arguing for the use of the law, to alter an existing pattern of rights and obligations, which might be highly inegalitarian (few landlords owning most of the arable land, whilst the masses have none or little to till), to an alternative structure of rights and obligations, which may be less unequal.

The crucial role of the law has, however, become masked and distorted under the conception of negative freedom, which simplistically holds, that one is free to do X, provided that no law prohibits one from doing X. On this misleading view, one would have to say that the penniless, as well as the millionaire, are, equally, free to act in a certain way, to execute their similar intentions into action, namely, say, to dine at the Ritz. Of course, as a matter of fact, the legal system does not behave in the way postulated by the theorist of negative freedom. For, if it is known in advance to the management of the Ritz that I do not have the money to pay for my meal, the management (the second party), in the form of the commissionaire, would bar my entry. Should I persist, insisting on my legal freedom to do so, the police would be called in (and later, magistrates and the courts, the third party), who would have no doubt, that I do not enjoy the legal freedom to dine at the Ritz. Negative libertarians, who wish to test this, may do so at their own cost. That is why the penniless, who understand freedom intuitively better than this kind of simple-minded theorist, very rarely, if at all, exercise the 'freedom' granted to them by negative libertarians. Indeed, such an exercise, carried out in the sincere belief that one enjoys the same legal freedoms as those who are able to pay, would land one in the loony bin. So much for taking some inadequate theory seriously.

To labour this point — that the penniless do not enjoy the legal freedom to dine at the Ritz — is demonstrated by the fact that there is no corresponding legal obligation/duty on the part of the management, the police, the courts, not to prevent the penniless from doing X, namely, dining at the Ritz. On the contrary, as I have shown, the second party appears to have the legal freedom/right to prevent such a person from doing X, which freedom is upheld by the third party. This proves, then, that such a person does not have the legal freedom/right to do X (at least on the adapted Benthamite analysis of what it is for an agent to have the legal freedom/right to do X).

The orthodox libertarian analysis of freedom, in terms, simply, of the absence of a law, which prohibits one from doing X, is, therefore, inadequate and seriously misleading. Logically speaking, it is true that the prohibition (should it exist in the legal system) — do not dine at the Ritz, or you may not dine at the Ritz — is the contradictory of the permission — you may dine at the Ritz. The absence of a prohibition entails a permission, as a prohibition can be shown to be the contradictory of a permission. [15] However, the analysis, as it stands, is incomplete. First, the permission itself (on the adapted Benthamite analysis of legal freedom/right) must entail a corresponding legal obligation/duty on the part of second and third parties, not to interfere with the exercise of the permission. But as second and third parties under the existing law have not such a legal obligation/duty, not to prevent A from dining at the Ritz, this shows that A does not have the legal freedom/right to dine at the Ritz, notwithstanding that the permission (you may dine at the Ritz) is an entailment of the absence of a prohibition (you may not dine at the Ritz).

The crucial point to grasp is that the permission constitutes a legal freedom/right, if and only if it entails, and there exist, corresponding legal obligations/duties on the part of second and third parties, not to prevent one, from exercising the legal freedom/right in question. Under this analysis, the permission, which actually exists in our legal system, is not that one may dine at the Ritz, but that one who has the money to pay for the meal may dine at the Ritz. This latter modified permission constitutes a genuine legal freedom/right, as it entails, and there exist corresponding legal obligations/duties on the part of second and third parties, not to prevent a person, who can pay, from dining at the Ritz. So if I can pay, am willing to pay and the management refuses to serve me, then I can take the hotel to court, on the grounds that it has acted against the law, and demand compensation from the management, for its having breached the law, and, hence, for my having suffered a legitimate legal grievance.

This also shows, that, although the modifying phrase, 'who can pay', in the revised permission, nowhere appears in explicit formulation, it does not mean that the revised permission is not the correct one. As Bentham would say, if the law in question were written out as a complete law, and not merely presented in a fragmentary fashion, as tends to be done, the crucial phrase, 'who can pay', having been inferred from the complete law, could be attached explicitly to the permission. (The complete law would have, amongst other things, to refer to another part of the legal code, which determines entitlement to goods and services — this part of the law, for the purpose of illustrating the point under discussion, could perhaps be formulated as 'In a purchase of goods and services, a person, without due payment, is not entitled to such goods and services'.) Its correctness is borne out by the fact that second and third parties have their respective legal obligations/duties, not to prevent one, who can pay, from dining at the Ritz. So the poor person's intuition is correct — the original permission is not a genuine legal freedom/right, although the revised permission is.

In its revised form, one can see more clearly why the so-called positive libertarians maintain that, in their view, formal freedoms are not real or genuine freedoms. The formal freedoms, such as, one has the right to dine at the Ritz, one has the right to live wherever one wants, one has the right to work in any job one chooses, etc. are precisely permissions of the kind, you may dine at the Ritz, you may live anywhere in the country you please, etc. Such formal freedoms, like such permissions, are not genuine freedoms. At best, they amount to no more than 'you may try to live anywhere in the country you please' or 'you may try to get any job anywhere you please'. However, the legal freedom/right to try to do something is not the same as the legal freedom/right to do something.

Take the so-called right to work in any job one chooses, which is an entailment of the absence of a prohibition against job choice. (In Tudor England, there were indeed legal prohibitions and restrictions about job choice, but with the development of capitalism, these laws were repealed to facilitate labour mobility.) This could not be taken, however, as a genuine legal freedom, because, for instance, if I fancy being a top ranking diplomat, but I do not have the right background, that is, I have not been to a university, never mind the right university and the right school prior to that, I speak impenetrable Scouse and so on, although I may possess other qualities which, I believe, would make me a good diplomat, I would never be taken seriously. The most one can say about my freedom is that I could write off for the forms, and fill them in. The Foreign Office could not get the police to arrest me for making an application, which establishes that I do have the legal freedom/ right to try to apply for the job of my choice, although it would think me a case suitable for treatment.

So once spelt out in this manner — you may dine at the Ritz provided you can pay for it, you may buy a house in any part of the country provided you can pay for it, you may obtain justice, if injustices have been done to you, if you can pay for it (or under limited legal aid, if you are fortunate enough to qualify under its stringent rules for assistance) — it becomes obvious that those who cannot pay cannot be said to enjoy such freedoms. Similarly, the right to work in a job of one's choice is incomplete and incorrect as it stands and is, hence, misleading, as such rights also are subject to other material requirements, analogous to the requirement of payment in the examples just cited — the right, properly characterised, is no more, then, than the right to try to get a job of one's choice. As it stands, it is incomplete, because it must be taken in conjunction with another law(s), which empowers the employer to be the arbiter of what it considers to be suitable qualities for the job, and of which candidate possesses them to the most desired extent. (Of late, this power of determination has been somewhat curtailed by the Race Relations and Equal Opportunities legislations.)

It also becomes obvious that the distinction between formal freedoms (as championed by the negative libertarians) and non-formal freedoms (as championed by the positive libertarians), breaks down. A proper analysis of freedom shows (i) that freedoms are legally defined and guaranteed; (ii) that they also refer to 'non-formal', material matters like the ability to pay.

Technological innovations do not affect the main thrust of the line of argument developed above, for such innovations also come under the legal structure of freedoms/rights and obligations/duties. The law has to decide who is to be entitled to the rewards of these innovations — the inventor, the agent, who finances the inventor, the entrepreneur who manufactures and markets the invention, the workers who work in the factories producing the goods, the general public who are also consumers of the product support the infrastructure of the society, through taxes, without which, there could be no inventors, entrepreneurs, factory owners, workers or consumers, etc. Usually under (bourgeois) capitalism, the entrepreneur and/or manufacturer take the giant share. But the question arises — is this fair? The legal system reflects the dominant conception of fairness and justice in the society in question, or at least, the conception of justice of the dominant group in society. (To say this, however, is not necessarily to deny that the law can also be used as a tool to bring about changes and reform in society in the direction of greater equality.)

The discussion in this section shows, then, that the adapted Benthamite analysis of legal freedom is a replicate of the analysis of 'freedom', which follows from the notions of agency and action. The latter's triadic relationship between Agent A, the physical means to execute action X, and Agent B (who has not pre-empted the means or physically prevented A from carrying out X) is analogous to the (neo) Benthamite analysis, which says that A is legally free to do X, if B (the second party) has a legal obligation not to prevent A from doing X, and if C (the third party) also has a legal obligation to prevent B from preventing A to do X. But a complete law about A's legal freedom to do X includes a clause about A's ability to pay for X, or for the physical means for executing X. This means that the two analyses are isomorphic — both involve triadic relationships (the second and third parties in the neo-Benthamite analysis standing in for B).

7. In the light of the discussion above, the relation between freedom and equality may now be summarised as follows:

(1) freedom, as freedom of action, is a substantive value or good; equality, however, is a distributive value, which governs the distribution of substantive goods, as well as procedural goods (such as a fair trial);

(2) but freedoms of action, when properly analysed, involve a distributive pattern of such actions;

(3) that distributive pattern is underpinned by law in modern states;

(4) whether the distributive pattern is one of equality or inequality depends on (a) the action which is said to be permitted by law, (b) the number of people, who are thus permitted to act in the society in question, in that particular way, (c) the number of people (the second party), who are correspondingly prevented by law to interfere with (b);

(5) the (standard) negative libertarians are right only in so far as they emphasise the relevance of the legal system to freedom of action, but are wrong, in having failed to realise that (2) and (4) above obtain;

(6) the positive libertarians are wrong in having failed explicitly to point out (3) above, but are right in emphasising, that freedom of action involves more than simply so-called formal freedoms, and that legal permissions, which are genuine legal freedoms/rights, have written in them (as a complete law), the material means by which an action is executed, a crucial means, being the ability to pay in a money economy;

(7) both negative and positive libertarians are, therefore, wrong in maintaining a strict dichotomy between formal and non-formal freedoms. The former holds that only formal freedoms count as genuine freedoms, and the latter, maintaining that only non-formal freedoms are such. The truth of the matter lies in holding that, on a proper understanding of a law, through a complete account, rather than a merely partial account of it, it is obvious that genuine freedoms refer to both sides of the dichotomy. The negative libertarians are, therefore, wrong in saying

that formal freedoms constitute genuine legal freedoms. The positive libertarians are misleading in holding that formal freedoms are not genuine legal freedoms, because the exercise of such freedoms can be affected by material requirements, such as the ability to pay. This way of putting things invites the unhelpful retort from the negative libertarians, that there is a distinction to be made between a freedom and the worth of a freedom, or the exercise of it. The criticism of the positive libertarians, on this retort, only shows that the worth of a freedom may have been affected by an inability to meet the material requirements, in order to exercise the formal freedom, and not that the formal freedom, even if it is not capable of being exercised on a particular occasion, does not exist or is not a genuine freedom. In order to pre-empt such a retort, they should have, instead, said that formal freedoms are not genuine legal freedoms, because the very concept of legal freedom includes such material requirements, that it entails the corresponding notion of legal obligation or duty, under which, second and third parties must not prevent one from exercising such freedoms. With formal freedoms (such as, you may dine at the Ritz, or enjoy the right or freedom to dine at the Ritz, even if you cannot pay for the meal), there are no such corresponding legal duties, which proves, that they are not genuine legal rights and freedoms;

(8) both conceptions are remiss in ignoring (2) and (4) above;

(9) it is perhaps important to bring out more clearly an implication of the analysis offered above, especially of (3), (6), (7) — namely, it follows that so-called economic rights are really a form of legal rights.

For example, to say that people enjoy the economic right to a pension, which increases with the rate of inflation, or average wage increase, is really to say that they have a legal right to such a pension. This entails a legal obligation on the part of second parties (pension funds), not to interfere with the enjoyment of such a right, and for the courts to enforce the legal obligation on the part of pension funds to comply in their behaviour.

The law, according as it sees fit, can either support an existing structure of economic rights, or alter it in the direction of greater equality or greater inequality. The law creates rights and freedoms — civil, political or economic. It is, therefore, not correct to maintain, that civil and political rights alone are the creations of the law. Economic rights, equally, are the creations of the law.

In this respect, the Marxist analysis is vindicated — liberal theorists are wrong in drawing a sharp dichotomy between civil/political rights and freedoms, on the one hand, and economic rights, on the other. And they are equally mistaken, when they further argue, that while the legal system (the state) is the guarantor of the former, it is no business of the state to bother with the latter. The state is equally concerned with both domains. Every state, through its structure of legal rights and obligations, upholds a certain distributive pattern of economic rights (and corresponding obligations to refrain from interfering with it), which it approves of. The liberal/democratic states of the first world approve, by and large, of a bourgeois capitalist structure of economic rights (and corresponding obligations to refrain from interfering with it, on the part of second and third parties.)

During the post war period of consensus under 'Buskellism', such states, like Britain, modified the structure somewhat to create the so-called welfare state, that is, by shifting the pattern of distribution of economic rights slightly more in favour of those without capital, and those not in a position to be gainfully employed. But since the late 1970s, these states once again, on the whole, have swung the pendulum back more firmly and definitively in favour of the owners of capital, and those who are fortunate enough to be gainfully employed.

If the above analysis is correct, it follows that in the last decade, far from it being the case that such states have increased their citizens' freedoms and rights (as their rhetoric says), the contrary in some of them is the truth — freedoms and rights have been diminished. In the increasing attempts in this country to privatise welfare provisions, for instance, the freedom to medical treatment when one is ill (in a legal system operating a National Health Service), will soon be replaced by freedom to medical treatment, when one is ill and when one is able to pay for it. In this move, freedom is being diminished, rather than enlarged, as those who cannot pay cannot be said to enjoy the new freedom.

CHAPTER TEN

HUMAN CAPACITIES AND NEEDS

1. There are two dominant views about the concept of needs in contemporary social/moral philosophy. The first says that all needs are wants, or disguised wants, for they are those wants which the individual would rather not pay for out of her/his own pockets, but would urge others to pay for them. The second says that all our wants are needs; as such, they are in need of urgent satisfaction.

They are, however, both based on a rejection of the claim that there is a valid logic of needs. That logic may be presented as follows: (1) human agents have wants as well as needs; (2) while some agents both want and need something, not all agents all the time have wants which are also needs, or needs which are also wants; (3) wants are subjectively determined — whatever an individual says s/he wants, or chooses, constitutes her/his wants; (4) needs are not simply subjectively determined; they are capable of objective determination. In other words, irrespective of what the individual wants, an outsider could be the arbiter of what s/he needs; (5) because of the purely subjective nature of wants, some wants can be said to be whimsical or unnecessary — hence there is no urgency or necessity to their satisfaction; (6) needs, on the other hand, imply urgency and necessity of fulfilment, for if left unmet, the individual, said to be in need, would come to harm, or be adversely affected in some identifiable and publicly recognisable way.

This logic has been challenged primarily in two

ways — by (a) the thesis of cultural relativism, an empirical claim about the actual diversities in cultural practices across space and time and (b) the thesis of philosophical relativism arising from (a).

If needs are a matter capable of objective determination, why is it the case that empirical (anthropological) evidence does not appear to support it? On the contrary, such evidence shows that there are endlessly different needs in different societies, in different places, and at different times. If needs are not merely culture-relative, then over time, one should see a trend towards similarities of needs between societies. Whether the earth is flat or round like an orange is a matter capable of objective rational determination. Al though the latter hypothesis met with resistance when first proposed, nevertheless, evidence accumulated by now makes it difficult (if not logically impossible) to deny that it is true. No such analogous rational consensus has arisen, it seems, with regard to needs.

A devout Hindu holds steadfastly to the view that s/he neither wants nor needs beef; the orthodox Jew that s/he neither wants nor needs pork; the committed Jehovah's Witness neither wants nor needs blood transfusion even were death imminent upon refusal. There appear to be as many needs, each often conflicting with one another, as there are forms of life. The form of life in question, if not the individual, determines what counts as a need and what does not. Wants are specific to individuals; needs are at best specific to cultures.

That there is cultural diversity in the determination of needs appears then to be an indisputable fact. However, from this fact alone it does not logically follow that there is and can be no rational procedure by which one can comprehend how the diversity has arisen, and why it exists. As we shall see, such rational comprehension is possible and available.

But normally this thesis of cultural diversity with its implied corollary that there is no way of giving a rational account of the matter is reinforced by, as well as itself justifying, the thesis of philosophical relativism. This is the view that needs embody values, and that values are logically incapable of objective and rational determination. Values are like wants. Their validity is created entirely by being (sincerely) adopted, chosen or committed to, and judged by canons of correctness or incorrectness internal and peculiar to each form of life. It is correct for a pious Hindu widow to throw herself on her husband's funeral pyre, for that is the canon of valid conduct as laid down by Hindu religious practices. It is correct for Eskimos to leave their aged parents to die on the ice. There is no non culture-bound criterion of validity in terms of which one can judge whether these practices are correct or incorrect.

But the thesis of philosophical relativism is not as unproblematic as it is often assumed to be. For a start, it appears to violate a very fundamental logical principle which in other contexts is universally accepted, that is, the principle of non-contradiction which says that both the thesis and its contradictory cannot logically speaking be true; p and not-p cannot both be true — either p is true or its contradictory not-p is true or both may be false. Yet the philosophical relativist endorses both p (patricide or abortion is morally correct) and not-p (patricide or abortion is morally incorrect) as true. It is not obvious that moral propositions are exempt from the operation of the law of non-contradiction. If they are indeed exempt, the relativist has not provided us with any account of why they are.

The relativist may, however, escape the charge of violating the principle of non-contradiction by saying that p is true, relative to the procedure for recognising truth in one form of life, and that not-p is true, relative to the procedure for recognising truth in another form of life. But this move simply transfers the charge to the meta-theoretical stage, namely, that it maintains that any procedure for recognising first-order truth is acceptable, including procedures which may directly contradict one another. [1]

But let us go back to the first dominant view about needs mentioned at the beginning of the chapter. In a system like ours, wants are predominantly met by one's ability to pay through success in operating the rules of the market; so then must needs, as all 'needs' are conceptually speaking only wants. It follows then, if some of these wants (which in need-logic are needs) cannot be met, because the individual, A, has no money to pay for them, then they will remain unmet, as there is no necessity for the community at large to meet them. For the same reason, all the wants of an individual, B (in need-logic, some of these wants are not needs and may be wholly frivolous and unnecessary), should be met, provided the individual is able and willing to pay for them. It is not necessary nor is it legitimate to redistribute money in B's pocket to give to A, even though it is the tenth holiday home B is proposing to buy with the money in the pocket, and A is living under bits of cardboard on the pavement, or under the bridge. If A says s/he is in need, that is simply to be translated into saying that A wants a roof over the head, but would like others to pay for it.

While this view downgrades needs to wants and dismisses their urgency, the second view upgrades all wants to be needs, and cashes in on their urgency. This means that the 'need' (in need-logic, a mere want) for B to buy the tenth holiday home is as urgent as the need (in need-logic, a need) for A to have immediate shelter over the head. For if the urgency is equal in both cases, as both are 'needs', then there is no justification to redistribute *à la* Robin Hood from B to A. A, of course, has B's best wishes to find the means to buy shelter, by trying to be successful in operating the rules of the market, but there is no moral obligation to part with some of her/his money to provide such shelter even though A, being elderly and mentally handicapped, is not likely ever to be successful operating the rules of the market.

2. How can one set about defending the logic of needs in the face of such a formidable challenge? Let us start by reminding ourselves of something which is

so obvious that even the (moderate) cultural-cum-philosophical relativists are quite prepared to concede. Even they would not wish to deny that we need oxygen to survive. What they maintain is that, anything other than the very obvious like oxygen, is culturally determined. But before pursuing what on the surface looks like an unpromising lead, let me clear away a red herring. We are not concerned here with the question whether the agent wants to live or to die. So the issue is not really that one needs oxygen only if one wants to survive. On this interpretation, needs are merely instruments for satisfying ends. But as ends are irrationally chosen, albeit sincerely chosen, by the individual (or community), needs are simply then cast into the means/end relationship of efficiency. Thus it is said that needs are simply efficient means to satisfy ends. You need to drink water, only because you have (sincerely but irrationally or non-rationally) chosen to live. You need glasses, only because you have decided you want to see the world clearly and not in hazy outline.

If needs are understood in this way, then needs are rational, for means are rationally determinable. But on such an interpretation, it is conceivable that an agent could choose not to see, not to talk, not to eat, not to drink, etc., in which case such a person could not be said to be in need of anything. However, this amounts to a *reductio ad absurdum*, for someone who systematically chooses (sincerely but irrationally or non-rationally) not to want all these things, is really choosing death, that is, to cease to be an agent. I am not here concerned with the morality or pathology of suicide. What one is discussing is a quite separate issue altogether, namely, that agency can only be sustained under certain conditions which are objectively and rationally determinable, irrespective of whether an individual agent wants to sustain it or not.

Given the metabolic constitution of the human agent and our scientific understanding of it, and of the properties of the gas called oxygen, it is an objectively and rationally determinable matter, that if such an agent were to be deprived of oxygen for a certain length of time, such an agent would die. (This account says nothing, to labour a point, about whether the agent wants or does not want to die.) The agent would at the very least be badly harmed, such as being brain-damaged, if not dead. Nor is this truth affected by the ignorance of the agent concerned with regard to human physiology, and the workings of the body's biochemical system.

This example of a need then can be shown to satisfy all the six theses which enter into the logic of needs as set out in section 1. Another example which does not concern human agents would illustrate theses (4) and (6). Fish, for instance, need water. Given their constitution, etc., fish taken out of water would become badly impaired or die after a certain period of time. This is an objectively and rationally determinable state of affairs, irrespective of whether the fish knows it to be so, and whether it wants to live or not.

Let us still stick to the mundane and the obvious. We need food, security, protection from the weather at the very least. As a society, we need to reproduce; we also need to bring up our young, etc.; and oddly enough, we also need to die (the other side of the coin of the need to reproduce).

The moderate cultural-cum-philosophical relativists may again claim they are not impressed by this list of needs even if they do not wish to dissent from it, on the grounds that the striking thing about them is how differently they are met from culture to culture. Nevertheless, I will persist, and try to show that the arguments are not all on their side, appearance notwithstanding.

Go back to food as a need of sustenance. We have already seen that the relativists gleefully remind us that food itself is a culture-bound concept. Not everything counts as food — pork is not food to Muslims and Jews. Lice are certainly not food to us, but are to certain peoples, like Eskimos.

The proposition 'not everything counts as food' has two sides to it: (a) it could mean not everything edible and is nourishing counts as food; (b) it could mean literally not everything counts as food because some things are not edible or nourishing for us humans; as such it does not entail the corollary, that anything may count as food, which the extreme relativist appears to imply. (On extreme relativism, see section 4.)

Examine (b) carefully first. It follows that no culture, no matter how exotic or fanciful to our modern ears and eyes, could conceivably regard, through a whim of its collective (or individual) will, deadly nightshade or avenging angel (a fungus) as food. In an objective sense, these plants cannot constitute food for human agents. A tribe silly enough to embrace cultural-cum-philosophical relativism, and to ingest the avenging angel as food, on the strength of such a thesis, would soon become extinct. What is edible for cows may not be edible for us human agents. The digestive system of cattle is differently constructed from ours. It produces an enzyme which could break down cellulose in plants, but which we do not possess, or possess weakly. As a result, grass is food for cows but not for us. Even cows, however, cannot digest the chemical ingredients present in fresh buttercups — in a meadow, these flowers are left well alone by them. Fresh buttercups are not food for cows, no more than they are for us.

So, what is food depends on (i) the type of organism one is, (ii) the digestive system one possesses, (iii) the biochemical contents of the thing that is ingested. If these fundamental biological truths did not obtain, then perhaps there would be no food shortage problem for the human population, as such a population could always ingest old bits of bark, and yet do nicely like goats. If these were not truths, it would not be a sick joke to present a hungry person with a plate of twigs and dead leaves. This means that for individual human agents to survive and human society to endure, a great deal of care and time must be devoted to meeting the need to eat, that is, for food.

The human constitution and the constitution of other organisms around it, as a matter of fact, rule out many many things as food. This may be a negative fact, but it is one of tremendous significance, if we wish to tackle the problem of endurance and flourishing.

Next, take the need for protection from the elements. The human organism, being warm blooded, has certain mechanisms for maintaining a constant body temperature. However, these would not function if the outside temperature becomes either too hot or too cold. We can die of too much heat or too much cold, unless we take steps to protect ourselves. To prevent hypothermia, one requires warm clothing, fire, shelter to keep out the wind, etc. To prevent death through excessive heat, one needs shade, fans, air-conditioning, etc. This need for protection from the weather is a real and genuine need, given our physiology.

Also consider the need to bring up our young. If the human offspring were like calves and foals, and could stand up and walk alongside its mother the moment it is born, then human societies would be organised very differently from the way they are. Human infants, as a matter of fact, take a much longer period to maturate (the rate of maturation is an epigenetic matter), quite apart from the fact that human societies have more to transmit to their young than non-human ones. So the need for the young to be with adults, to be nursed by them, to be taught by them is a real and genuine need.

These needs then exist because of the capacities we possess, in virtue of the kind of being we are, that is, beings with a certain physiological constitution, with a brain which can acquire language (the capacity for symbolling), skills, information, knowledge, with capacities for fear, love, laughter and so on. Our needs are rooted in our capacities. All human beings possess these capacities. (For earlier development of this argument, see Chapters Four and Seven.)

The possession of a capacity is, at least, a necessary condition if not a necessary and sufficient condition for saying a need arises. (See section 3 below for elaboration.) Failure to satisfy the need means that the capacity is not exercised, and might deteriorate, or even disappear altogether. To be minus a capacity, or to be in possession of an emaciated capacity, renders the agent less than whole. An agent without legs cannot execute an intention to move from one location to another, and would therefore suffer frustration (subtheses (vii) and (viii) in the real definition of human agency). That is why such an agent is said to require or be in need of crutches, a wheelchair or a specially adapted car to enable her/him to translate intention into action.

Similarly, a person who is very shortsighted is in need of glasses or contact lenses for, without either, s/he would not be able to execute the intention of looking at objects at a distance. To provide the agent with glasses or contact lenses would restore a diminished capacity to its full strength. The need for either type of technological products is based on the universal genuine need to see adequately for the purpose of daily living (of course, the degree of sharpness of vision depends on the activities the agent intends to engage in — vision good enough for negotiating around the house, and outside on the road, may not be adequate for doing fine work, like miniature painting), which in turn rests on a capacity of the human organism normally to have vision of a certain range.

Not only does the possession of capacities provide the basis for the concept of needs, but it also gives content to the notion of cruelty. To be cruel to another agent does not simply involve causing the agent pain (pain in the sense of felt pain, when something sharp is inserted into one's flesh) which it often does, but it may also involve depriving an agent of a capacity or preventing her/him from exercising it. Someone who removes the eyes of another is cruel, even if the operation were done under anaesthetics, so that the person felt no pain. It is cruel because it renders the agent emaciated and less than whole. Similarly, to put an agent under conditions of sensory deprivation is also cruel. It prevents the agent from executing intentions which are being entertained, from exercising the capacities to see, to touch, to smell, which s/he clearly possesses.

Cruelty of this kind has been and is perpetrated not only on human agents but also on non-human agents. Animals, like chickens in a battery 'farm', which are not allowed to move or flap their wings are being cruelly treated. Their capacity for movement is deliberately restrained. As a result, it is no wonder such animals develop forms of pathological behaviour. They are frustrated creatures.

3. But the crucial question arises about how these capacities are actually exercised and manifested in the concrete by different societies in very different habitats. It is here then that we find the diversities which so dazzle the cultural-cum-philosophical relativists. So they raise once again the question 'Where are the universal constants?'

One constant lies in the realisation (as argued in Chapter Seven) that every civilisation or society necessarily represses certain capacities and celebrates others. The repression of any one capacity may not be total, nor the celebration of any one capacity singleminded. For instance, some societies repress the capacity for aggression much more than others. Apart from repression, societies also use other strategems to divert it to other channels. Through the mechanism of sublimation, aggression need not be directed to bashing up people, but to winning games instead. As we saw, Fourier advocates sublimating the capacity for sadism, to turn would-be torturers to become useful citizens like butchers and surgeons.

Every society has evolved rules to contain aggression, whether it be in the form 'you may not kill your own kind', 'you may not kill civilians because not armed combatants in war', 'you may kill only in self defence', etc. In other words, those capacities, which if exercised could lead to destruction and mayhem, have to be carefully controlled, if not totally repressed; otherwise, the endurance of the society is at stake.

So it looks as though that not all capacities which human agents possess could be allowed expression. A civilisation must repress or at least rechannel those which could harm others, lead to its instability or destruction. That is why in the section above, I maintain that the existence of a capacity is only a necessary, but not a necessary and sufficient condition for the ascription of needs. Needs then are rooted in those capacities, which when exercised, pass the test of not harming others, or contributing to the instability or destruction of society. That is why it is odd to say that human beings have a need to be cruel, although clearly they have the capacity to be cruel. But to exercise such a capacity would do untold damage to others. At best, it can only be allowed to surface in an attenuated form. Society has to balance the frustration, caused to those prevented from exercising their capacity, against the harm caused to others. The rapist, no doubt, suffers frustration when he is prevented from raping his victims. But civilisations wisely channel such capacities in directions which are less anti-social.

Of those capacities which are allowed expression and exercise, and of the needs arising from their exercise, a very important point to bear in mind is that the way in which any one society meets these needs, rooted in our human capacities, depends ultimately on the best way available to it to ensure its endurance and continuity.

Take the need for food again. The habitat of the Eskimos, to say the least, was extremely harsh. Food was not easy to come by. Any chance of additional protein which is both crunchy and nourishing should not be spurned. Lice then was food. [2] In extreme circumstances, human flesh is food. People in cities under seige had to eat the dead. Recently, a plane carrying football supporters crashed in the South American jungle. The survivors, after a while, had to live off their dead friends, while waiting to be rescued. Even profound inhibitions and prohibitions can be overcome, if it becomes obvious that the only way to meet the need for food, is to eat what up to them has not been considered to be food. When the normal routine of life is rudely shattered, those who cling

346

tenaciously to cultural standards no longer appropriate to their changed circumstances, would literally end up dead and, moreover, extinguish their society in the process.

Potentially anything that is nutritious for the human being (what is nutritious is scientifically determinable) is food. Yet cultural-cum-philosophical relativists are right in saying that cultural norms intervene to select only certain items and to reject others as food. The selection itself, however, may not simply be the result of an arbitrary act of will. For a start, not all potentially nutritious items which are available taste as good. Not all, given the technology at any one given time in any one society, could domesticate the item in such a way as to make it give forth a productive yield. Societies too are constrained by factors like climate, geology and so on. What grows plentifully and readily in warm wet climes would not be available in colder more inhospitable areas, etc. In other words, far from the selection being arbitrary, it is the result of a variety of factors, such as the ecological possibilities of the habitat occupied by the society, and the type of technology it possesses. As neither of these two important factors (amongst others) remain constant and unchanging for all times, this in turn could affect the food preferences of a society over time.

As an extreme example of such a change take the Hindu Brahmanic caste and its roles in the history of Hinduism. Today, we regard this caste as the highest keeper of the Hindu taboo against beef eating and meat eating in general. Yet in Vedic times, this was not so. The Brahmins then were great meat eaters, and were the caste in charge of sacrificing animals for feasts and entertainment (entertainment is not to be understood in the contemporary sense of asking a few friends for dinner; it involved feeding whole communities). But following ecological changes, with deforestration setting in, the land could no longer support animals for food. By AD 700, the Brahmins had transformed themselves into a caste, which had renounced meat, and become the guardian of cows.

The cow, though no longer affordable as meat for the table, must be affordable, however, for other purposes, like giving milk, yielding dung both as fertiliser and fuel, pulling the plough and carts, if society were to be sustained. Hence the cow became sacred. [3]

This explanation would be true, even if, as a matter of fact, Hindus today do not themselves see the issue in such terms. Practising Hindus might just simply say that the reason why they do not eat beef is because because their religion forbids it. [4]

Once a food preference has acquired a normative significance, it can also serve the purpose of preserving and reinforcing the identity of the group. Jews, in the diaspora over the centuries, adhered to the prohibition against pork as part of their dietary laws, long after they had left the habitat from which the preference first evolved. Its preservation may have been seen (at least by some members of the community if not all) as the best way available to ensure the endurance and continuity of the community under changed circumstances.

The important point to bear in mind is that these rational explanations for the adoption and/or enforcement of a rule, in the total system of rules and values of the community, need not be the conscious reasons advanced and avowed for the behaviour in question, by each and every member of the group. For most members it is enough that the rule (against the prohibition against pork) itself serves as a reason for the behaviour of not eating that meat. Psychologically and conceptually, this makes sense. The latter, namely the conceptual possibility of a rule acting as a reason for behaviour, explains how it is possible that (i) individual agents need not have any idea why that rule is adopted in the first place, and why it is being currently enforced, (ii) for the community at large not to worry about the appropriateness or otherwise of the rule, so long as life remains relatively stable and routine. But when deep crises arise which threaten the endurance and flourishing of the community itself, as I have already mentioned, then some rethinking and reassessment will have to be made of the basic rules, if the community is to survive and flourish.

A dramatic example of this may be found in the history of the early Christian Church. Christianity teaches that those who die in a state of grace, go straight to heaven without an unpleasant temporary sojourn in purgatory. It follows from this proposition, that those just baptised (baptism having removed both original sin as well as other sins, mortal and venial, from the soul), should they die immediately afterwards, would enter heaven without hindrance. Fervent converts committed instant suicide at an alarming rate, to ensure they would enjoy the Beatific Vision. But the Church Fathers realised that this piece of theological inference and behaviour, though impeccable within its own logic, would undermine the endurance of Christianity. Hence the prohibition against suicide. Suicide was made a mortal sin. The souls of those who commit suicide would go to hell, and their bodies would not be allowed to be buried in consecrated grounds. The theological justification for the prohibition is then given by saying that as God has created life, God alone has the right to take it away. Today's Catholics, as individual believers, may be totally ignorant of the origin of the rule against suicide. Nor is the orginal reason relevant to modern Christianity. For a start, the Church has long evolved the institution of infant baptism. Today, converts are not likely, anyway, to kill themselves upon conversion in order to meet the Almighty, and to bask in His presence. However, over the centuries, the rule itself has acquired other roles within the system of rules, values and beliefs of the Roman Church. Today, were the Church to remove the prohibition, it would do so for such reasons as (a) ecumenism, (b) humanitarianism to the distressd relatives, not to mention charity to the dead themselves.

The human psyche is capable of both conservatism and innovation, both of which capacities are essential for endurance and continuity. In the absence of deep crises, the former takes a firm grip. On the whole, in such normal circumstances, the human psyche tends at first to suspect the unfamiliar and to reject it. Again, take food as an example. Before the arrival of people from the sub continent of India in this country, the British public at large rejected curry as food, referring to it as that disgusting, revolting, evil smelling substance which they would most certainly not give to their dogs. Now even in some of the smallest towns you are likely to find an Indian restaurant or a Chinese take-away.

In other words, what the cultural-cum-philosophical relativists see as evidence to support the view, that everything is arbitrarily endorsed, may not really be so. The evolution of cultural norms, their maintenance and change over time may be capable of rational explanation. And more importantly, the evidence does not support their conclusion that there are no genuine universal human needs.

Let us next examine the need for protection from the weather. How people meet this need, again, depends on the ecological constraints, and possibilities of its habitat, together with the technology available to it at any one time. In a cold climate, we need a fire to keep warm especially in the winter. The fuel in this country used to be wood. But by the seventeenth century, the country was suffering from an acute shortage of wood brought about by deforestation and increase of population. The need to keep warm was then met by burning coal. But to get the coal, a new technology had to develop. At first the people did not like coal, and thought it an inferior substitute, which it is. The rich preferred to pay more for the ecologically scarcer, but better product. The poor, however, had to put up with the inferior alternative. [5] An open fire in this country (very inefficient as a form of space heating but more comforting psychologically than more efficient alternatives) was traditionally the way to keep warm. Now, that has been supplanted by the technology of gas/electric heaters or of central heating. So the need to keep warm becomes expressed as the need to have central heating, or a gas fire, or solar panels fitted on the roof top (should that become the dominant technology), and not, on the whole, as the need for an open fire.

To the relativists, it then looks as if, while Americans have a need for air conditioning in the summer, other societies which also have hot sticky climates only have a need for a hand held fan, or at best an electric fan. From this, the relativists draw the conclusion that these needs are diverse, unrelated and simplicistically culture specific. But they are wrong, for these are only different ways to meet the same universal need, namely, the need to be protected from the weather, be it too hot or too cold. The different ways arise because they are the result of a complex interplay between ecological, technological, economic and other factors.

To illustrate the same point, I will next examine a need rooted in a psychological capacity, the need for entertainment. All human agents have a need for entertainment and rest. Some fulfil it gossiping with their neighbours under a tree, some playing boule, others by knitting (usually while gossiping), yet others by singing, dancing, telling stories, etc. Of late, much of these traditional forms of entertainment have been supplanted by a new means, namely, television, made possible by certain technological developments since the 1930s. So instead of saying one needs to sing, or read or play games, etc., we say, one needs a TV set. To concentrate exclusively on the different possible ways, or on the one dominant way at anyone time, is to overlook the significant fact they are all means of satisfying a single basic universal need.

What I have said is similar to the distinction made by Manfred Max-Neef between a need and its satisfiers. He writes:

First: *fundamental human needs are finite, few and classifiable.* Second: *fundamental human needs are the same in all cultures and all historical periods. What changes, both over time and through cultures, is the form or the means by which these needs are satisfied.* Each economic, social and political system adopts different styles for the satisfaction of the

351

same fundamental human needs. In every system they are satisfied, or not, through the generation, of different types of satisfiers. We may go as far as to say that one of the aspects that defines a culture is its choice of satisfiers. Whether a person belongs to a consumerist or to an ascetic society, her fundamental human needs are the same. What changes is her choice of quantity nad quality of satisfiers. Cultural change is — among other things — the consequence of dropping traditional satisfiers and adopting new or different ones. [6]

Whilst the needs are constant and universal, the satisfiers, or the ways in which different cultures meet these needs, are different. The whole burden of this book (and similar writing) is to argue that the way modern industrial civilisation has chosen to meet most of these needs, makes excessive demands on low entropic energy and matter, which is absolutely scarce, and then produces excessive waste, with which the biosphere and ecosystems cannot cope. For instance, to meet the need for protection from the weather, to heat a house in the winter to such a degree that one must strip to the shirtsleeves to be comfortable, and to cool it to such an extent in the summer that one requires a fire to keep warm, is just lunacy. To meet the need for mobility, a private car is not the most sensible form of transportation. To satisfy the need for food, eating highly processed junk food is again not a sensible thing to do, from the point of view both of health and of entropic demands. To eat fresh (or lightly cooked) carrots is infinitely better for one, and requires less low entropic energy and matter in its preparation than to eat tinned carrots or frozen carrots. Much as the advertisers love to tell us, a freezer in (nearly all) suburban households is not a need, that is, not an appropriate satisfier of the genuine need for food and its proper storage. Shops are readily available. Moreover, shoppers only buy frozen packets from the shops in order to put them into their own freezers. The real and genuine need for food (and its proper storage) is not served well by such a method. It is often said that buying tinned, frozen and generally processed food is a great convenience for the busy person. I admit that time is existentially scarce. But I dispute whether opening a tin of carrots involves less time compared to washing three sticks of carrots. In any case, in this civilisation, where the need for entertainment has been hijacked by television, whatever time is saved by cooking a TV dinner, is spent gawping at the box itself. The time could have been more creatively spent in cooking a decent meal, which satisfies at once the need for food, the need for entertainment and relaxation and the need for self-development.

So a rational choice of ways to satisfy real and genuine human needs should include the following criteria: (1) less demand on low entropic energy and matter, with correspondingly less production of pollution and waste; (2) reliance on the attainment of internal goods rather than possession and consumption of external goods to meet the psychological need for entertainment, to excel and do well; (3) to eliminate those satisfiers which, far from enabling agents to meet a need, harm the agents in question — this is borne out vividly by the 'food-chemical' industry in the 'food' it manufactures. Such 'foods', far from nourishing us, actually contain poisons and toxins. Many notorious E additives (though not all), hormones, antibiotics fed to animals, which are then further 'neutralised' by yet more poisonous chemicals, [7] and now irradiated food, things which may look good, but with the goodness destroyed, and often noxious substances put in their place, all pass off as 'food'.

Up to now, no culture has ever knowingly permitted toxins and poisons to pass off as 'food'. [8] Ours appears to have swallowed wholeheartedly its own myth of cultural-cum-philosophical relativism, thus appearing to conspire with profit-making to do precisely that. In doing so, the doctrine of relativism has become even more extreme, for the more moderate version merely says that not everything edible and nourishing counts as food. But it seems now prepared to say that anything (even poisons and toxins) counts as food, so long as one's culture decrees it to be so. This then again is in keeping with nominalism as a theory of meaning, which can be seen as part and parcel of the Faustian myth that man's will should dominate the world. Science and its EST enable man to conquer Nature. The conquest is further sealed by man's will, through the arbitrary imposition of names on the products of science and its EST. It enables the chemical 'food' industries and the advertising agencies to say 'this is ice-cream', even though this marvel of 'food' technology contains no cream, no fruit, but probably fish bones, petroleum by-products, chemical dyes and flavourings. Alas, the Humpty-Dumpty world has replaced reality — children offered proper ice-cream reject and denounce it, in favour of the 'real ice-cream' purveyed by the 'food'-chemical industry.

I will end this section by clarifying a point raised in section 2. There, I argued that it is a mistake to reduce needs to efficient means (which are considered to be rational) to achieve ends (which are considered to be subjectively, arbitrarily, irrationally or non-rationally chosen), for needs, which are universal and constant, are rooted in the capacities of human agency. However, a place can be found for the notion of instrumental rationality, if we are careful to distinguish between the needs themselves, which are universal and constant [9] and what Max-Neef has called the satisfiers of such needs, which may vary from culture to culture. Now satisfiers may be construed as rational and appropriate means, or irrational and inappropriate means to satisfy needs, which are themselves clearly not means. I have tried earlier to outline certain criteria of rationality and appropriateness, which will allow us to endorse certain means (satisfiers), and to reject others.

In contemporary literature on the subject, there is some confusion in the use of the notion of need even amongst those who take it seriously. The above distinction between needs and satisfiers (of needs) may help to clear up some of the confusions. Some need theorists, for instance, say that people today need a

TV set (A). Those who cannot afford the license fee ought to be exempted from payment. As argued by Max-Neef and myself, the 'need' in (A) is simply a satisfier (amongst others) of the need based on the capacity for rest and entertainment. As such, it is an instrument or device for satisfying the need, and not itself strictly speaking a need. However, it remains true that in a society where the more traditional and rival means for satisfying the need have been destroyed or eroded away, television has become the dominant (if not the sole) means of satisfying the need, there is a powerful pull towards transferring the normative implications and overtones of the logic of need to the dominant satisfier itself.

In other words, where television has usurped and displaced conversation, dancing, singing, etc., people who cannot afford the licence fee (even if they could afford the set itself) are indeed being deprived of entertainment, just as people, who are shut up in rooms painted white with nothing in them except strong fluorescent lighting, are said to suffer from sensory deprivation. It is no help to tell the individuals, who cannot afford the licence fee, to do without television, and to resort to singing and dancing instead. To tell them to do so is to ignore the fact that the dominance of a particular mode of satisfying a need has structurally rendered rivals and competitors, on the whole, impotent. What is required is a systemic change; guerilla action on the part of some individuals, though necessary, is not sufficient to bring about a change in the way in which needs are met or satisfied.

In the light of the above, it should be clearer that the force of 'need' in (A) is twofold: (i) it is a satisfier, not itself a need; (ii) the normative implications and overtones of the logic of needs are being transferred to the satisfier in the kind of context I have just discussed.

The above discussion can also throw light on why it is, that there appears to be a consensus about our need for oxygen. The consensus exists, with no one, not even the relativist, wishing to challenge it, because so far technology has not found a substitute for oxygen. If and when that day comes, the relativist would then argue that the need for oxygen is culturally determined, some societies claiming that they need oxygen, others that they need the substitute. What this shows is that oxygen is the satisfier, the only one available so far, of the need which the human organism has for combustion, based on the physiological, metabolic capacities, it possesses. What the thesis of relativism does not show, is that the claim that we need oxygen is so obvious, trivial, and, therefore, irrelevant to the thesis that needs are objectively and rationally determinable.

4. The concept of need implies the notion of sufficiency. The human capacities in which needs are rooted are bounded and limited (a) by the fact that we are mortal beings and (b) by a daily rhythm, by and large, determined by the rising and setting of the sun. Mortality implies that time is existentially scarce. However, we do not live the time allotted to us as an undifferentiated continuum, in which we can organise our activities entirely to suit our predilections or whims. To put things crudely — suppose one spends one third of one's lifetime in sleep. I cannot so order my life that I sleep continuously for say twenty five years (assuming that I live to seventy five), and then wake up to live the next fifty years non-stop. Our existentially scarce time is lived within a daily rhythm — the one-third we spend in sleep is normally during the hours of darkness. So although we need sleep, the amount of sleep is not unlimited during a day of life. There is a natural limit or sufficiency, even though it is true that individuals fluctuate within a small range — some need less than eight hours, and others a bit more than eight.

Within a day of life, one needs to eat during the moments outside sleep. But our metabolism is such that we need to eat a certain quantity at regular intervals, usually three times, unlike lions and tigers, whose metabolism enables them to absorb a huge quantity at one go, and then do without for a long period afterwards, unlike cows and horses which have to eat a little bit nearly all the time. It is no use, as far as we humans are concerned, eating all the meals a week in advance, for instance.

Within a day of life, one needs to do things (whether these activities are in aid of earning a living is immaterial). To force someone to sit still for hours doing literally nothing is a form of cruelty. But yet no one can indefinitely carry on an activity, be it sawing wood or writing a book, without feeling tired and needing rest. But, of course, rest is not needed in unlimited quantities.

At any moment in life, we are at one location only. It is impossible for us to arrange to be in two places at one and the same time. It follows that to satisfy the genuine need for shelter at any one time, we require access to one roof and one roof only. I cannot occupy two houses simultaneously. So while I am in residence at one, the others I may possess are strictly speaking redundant. Therefore, I do not need them and cannot meaningfully be said to need them.

If real things like food, houses, etc. are used to meet genuine human needs, then there is a limit to the amount of such things that a human agent could use in satisfying them. Yet neo-classical economists and other theorists tell us this is not so, that there is no sufficiency beyond which another shirt, or house, or car, or boat may be said to be redundant and irrelevant. They have long ditched the principle of diminishing marginal utility.

But what they say only makes sense because (a) they have also given up the notion of needs, claiming that it is conceptually incoherent; (b) they have reduced needs to wants — it is more plausible to think of an agent wanting more and yet more, than it is to conceive one needing more and yet more; (c) by channelling the specific need to do well and to excel towards the goal of the mere but ever increasing possession and consumption of external goods. (The difficulties and contradictions of this, I have already examined in the earlier chapters.)

As a result of (c), the additional houses, cars, boats that I possess serve as status symbols, and not as means to meet the need for shelter or mobility. The food I eat is not meant really to nourish the body, but to impress the world around me, and so on. As status symbols, it makes sense to possess and consume more and yet more of these things. It is this which lends substance to their axiom that 'needs' know no sufficiency. But there is no need to believe that the wholly genuine psychological need to excel can only be satisfied in this way — we can each excel through the acquisition of internal goods, and gain a sense of our own worth.

If the above analysis is correct, the underlying Marxist assumption that needs know no sufficiency is also equally unacceptable. Yet without this assumption, there is no need to embrace cornucopic socialism, which relies on science and its EST to exploit Nature, on the standard (to bourgeois as well as state capitalism) notions of productivity and efficiency, and the notion of exponential economic growth, to underpin the economy. Such relentless exploitation of Nature, even if it is on behalf of all human agents, not only of some, is redundant and irrelevant, if sufficiency obtains.

5. If one's concern is with all human agents (minimally all existing in the world today, maximally, future generations as well), and not merely human agents who live in affluent economies, then it is very important to make clear that there is a hierarchy of needs. I propose three levels to be lexically ordered as follows:
1. needs of survival or subsistence
2. needs of efficient agency
3. needs of enriched agency

By lexical ordering is meant that given scarce resources, before (3) be met (2) must be and, before (2) be met (1) must be. Within our affluent society, it is obvious that there are sufficient resources to satisfy all three levels of needs. (This is, however, not to say that in such societies there is not a minority, even a substantial minority, of people whose subsistence needs are in danger of not being met, given the inequalities inherent in most of them.) But particularly in the fourth world, this is not the case.

Level 1 must refer to the minimum number of calories sufficient to keep a person alive, to a minimum quantity of clean sweet water to drink and to wash to keep dehydration and certain diseases at bay. But agents who survive through meeting needs at level 1 are not really flourishing, efficient and effective agents. Minimally, level 2 must refer to a sufficient amount of nourishing food to ward off debilitating conditions like anemia, to accommodation with sanitation, to some degree of literacy, information and skills, which would enable the agents to do a job of work, and to cope with the world, both physical and social, at large. Minimally, level 3 must include some degree of leisure, as that is a necessary condition for rest as well as self-development.

It is obvious that many agents living in the fourth world and many parts of the third do not even meet the minimum requirement of level 1. Many more, in parts of the third world, hover precariously between levels 1 and 2. If lexical ordering is adhered to, then there is no doubt that there should be a massive transfer of wealth from the first to the fourth and parts of the third worlds. In the first world, as we have just seen, the needs of enriched agency have become distorted to mean the ever increasing possession and consumption of external goods, which have nothing to do with the satisfaction of genuine human needs. From the point of view of needs, this surplus is redundant and not required, and therefore should be diverted to meet genuine human needs at levels 1, 2 and 3 in the poorer countries of the world. But as we saw in the last chapter, redistribution *à la* Robin Hood is not what the dominant social philosophy in the first world endorses; instead, it favours economic growth which is really redistribution *à la* Matthew, either in the benign or, more often, in the malign sense.

The emphasis, on meeting needs at all three levels, entails reducing growth in the first world, and permitting growth in the third and fourth worlds, the level of growth being determined by how far such countries have reached in meeting the three levels of need. The slogan 'no growth', to cope with ecological scarcity, as it stands, is too crude. It is only partially correct as far as the first world is concerned. In such countries, where growth for growth's sake has rendered the debit column to be just as long, if not longer than the credit column, there is room not merely for zero-growth, but also for reduced growth (and all the other associated changes that must be made to make their society become a more ecologically sensitive and frugal one). The resources, thus saved, could be channelled into growth, which is needed in the poorer parts of the world, in order to meet their needs at all three levels. As low entropic matter and energy is ecologically scarce, the more of it consumed by the already affluent, the less there is for those who fall below the three levels of needs. For these reasons, there must be redistribution away from the rich to the poor.

Why should there be a lexical ordering amongst the three levels? This is because level 1 is a necessary condition of 2 and 3; 2 and 3 presuppose 1. This seems obvious enough. But does 3 necessarily presuppose 2? It is true that, in history, there have been a few agents who, in spite of being emaciated, managed to achieve great things — artists in the attic wrecked by TB, cold and often hunger, symbolise this possibility. But these cases are exceptions which prove the rule, and should not mislead one into believing that, far from being a drawback, to be emaciated is a requirement of self-development.

To be a whole and wholesome human agent, the needs at all three levels must be met. Hence the necessity for redistribution from those who have, to those who have not. But it is important to emphasise that the needs at level 3 must not be understood as the need for possession and consumption. That is not an appropriate way of satisfying the genuine need for self-development and enriched agency. If the need for enriched agency were to be satisfied in a non zero-sum manner, through the acquisition of internal goods, then the chances of all living agents today (as well as those who live after us, provided their numbers do not continue to grow exponentially) being able to flourish as whole human agents, would be much better secured.

6. The theory of needs is but one theory of justice or social justice. Other competing theories of social justice are those based on deserts and on rights. [10] Of the two possible alternatives, the former appears to be less invoked, while the latter, at the moment, is held by many writers in the field of social and political theory, to be the correct account of justice. Moreover, such theorists would also maintain that the theory of needs is essentially flawed, because the notion of needs itself is incoherent, or if not incoherent, it is at best a purely prescriptive notion with no agreed descriptive content.

I have challenged both of these criticisms and attempted a defence of needs, arguing that needs are rationally and objectively defensible. If that defence is plausible, I hope to go on further to argue that not only is the theory of needs, itself grounded on the capacities possessed by human agency, [11] rendered an intelligible theory of justice, it could also be used to show (a) that the theory of rights, as it stands, is not autonomous, but has to be backed up by some other justification, if it is not itself to be construed purely as a prescriptive thesis without descriptive content and, (b) that the theory of needs can provide that vital foundation for it. However, if such a foundation is indeed available, this in turn would entail that the theory of rights, far from being fundamental and prior to the theory of needs, is itself derivative from it. In other words, if the theory of needs is defensible in rational and objective terms, the theory of rights becomes redundant.

But before I develop these arguments, let me first

say something briefly about the standard ways of looking at rights. They may include the following:

(1) rights as natural rights;

(2) propositions about rights, as a species of moral propositions, are simply normative or prescriptive in character; such a character draws attention to matters, which in the opinion of the utterer, are of fundamental significance, so fundamental and crucial, that s/he says a 'no trespass' sign should be thrown around them.

(3) (i) natural rights are 'nonsense on stilts';

(ii) there are, therefore, no natural rights, only moral or legal rights;

(iii) moral rights are to be justified in terms of utility;

(iv) legal rights are simply those recognised by any one legal system;

(4) rights are based on deserts;

(5) the contractual model of (human) rights based on a conceptual analysis of the notion of 'right'; this account is much influenced by Hohfeld's analysis of legal rights.

Natural rights were traditionally understood to be universal rights possessed by all human beings, in virtue of a common essence in human nature. They are, therefore, distinct from actual legal rights as enshrined in legal systems. In their name, it makes sense to criticise legal systems which do not recognise them, and to claim that human beings ought to enjoy them, even though it is obvious that, as a matter of fact, they do not. Such a view has faced a variety of criticisms, ever since its clear enunciation in the seventeenth century. But I will deal with the modern criticisms first. In post war philosophical literature, the difficulties said to be inherent in the notion of natural rights have been formulated in Margaret Mac-Donald's classic article, entitled 'Natural Rights'. [12] There, she argues that propositions about natural rights are an unholy fusion of three logically different kinds of propositions — (a) a normative proposition to the effect that people ought to have such rights, even though as a matter of fact they do not have them; (b) a statement of fact — that every person is human 'by nature' in virtue of there being an essential human nature (such as, that s/he possesses reason or some other related feature); (c) but (b) is not really a factual proposition, but a disguised analytic one, as what constitutes human essence is merely given by a (verbal) definition of 'human being'. In other words, it is a nest of conceptual confusions.

This demolition of the notion of natural rights leads to ditching (b) and (c), retaining only (a). This then is view (2) listed above. As a consequence of the MacDonald-type critique, philosophers today fight shy of the term 'natural rights'. Instead, they talk about human rights, and avoid the kind of justification or foundation relied upon by the more traditional notion of natural rights. They also attempt to provide some sort of theoretical basis to the theory of human rights *via* a conceptual analysis of the notion of 'right' itself. This is then view (5) given above. As I will be devoting a lot of attention to it in a moment, I shall not comment any further upon it now.

There is, however, an older type of demolition of the notion of natural rights as given in (3) above. This may be said to be the legal positivist critique, especially that of Bentham. For him, the notion is a metaphysical one, as it fails to satisfy both the epistemological and ontological requirements of his positivist-cum-empiricist philosophy. For him, there are then only two types of rights, which can be said to be coherent and intelligible — legal and moral ones. The former refers, as we have seen, to those rights recognised by and enshrined in any one municipal legal system. The latter is to be understood in terms of utility — the notion of rights, then, is derivative from the principle of utility, which is the supreme axiom of his system. As such, it can be overridden by utility. On this view, then, as on mine (although the reasons are obviously different), rights are not autonomous.

Neither is the notion autonomous under view (4) listed above. This account of rights collapses into the notion of deserts. It is the Lockean or neo-Lockean,

Nozickian view in terms of the labour theory of value. One is said to deserve the fruits of one's labour and, hence, one has the right to the fruits of one's labour. But if so, it is desert which provides the basis for the right invoked. This then entails that the theory of rights is also rendered superfluous. (For more detailed criticisms of the Lockean thesis, see Chapter Six, and for the Nozickian thesis, see Chapter Two.)

After that brief diversion, I return to the task of showing that needs may generate rights and, thereby, provide a foundation for them. First let me take as an example of the latter something quite uncontentious, like the right to free speech. Rights theorists naturally take for granted that such a right is very important. Moreover, they also take for granted that it is unproblematic and obvious why it is so very important. As a result, they generally fail to ask themselves the fundamental question why it should be so. But suppose one were to take this question seriously, how would one answer it? I submit that one clear way, if not the only way of answering it, would lead to the theory of needs and the notion of human capacities.

J. S. Mill, a classical liberal, unlike contemporary modern liberals, took the question seriously and attempted to answer it. Let us then examine his justification for freedom of speech, or as rights theorists today put it, for the right to free speech. Mill gave at least two arguments in the essay, *On Liberty* — the epistemological justification and the ontological justification.

The former says, given that we are finite rational creatures, the only way such agents can discover truths is through a competition of ideas *via* criticism of them. Diversity and pluralism of opinions are therefore not celebrated for their own sakes but as a means, indeed the only means available to finite rational creatures to eliminate errors, and thus attempt to get at truths.

The latter consists of saying that being rational agents, it matters precisely how we get at truths —

364

they must be apprehended through criticism, that is, *via* the exercise of the rational faculty. Truths handed down by a god on tablets of stones or by swallowing truth pills are both fantastical and irrelevant to our concern as rational human agents. We need to affirm our being as rational beings through our attempts to get at truths in a critical manner.

The two justifications are inextricably linked with each other — if there were no truths whatever to be discovered in a critical fashion, then we cannot be said to be rational agents; as finite rational agents, the only way available to us to discover truths is to exercise our rational faculty and thus to reaffirm ourselves as such beings.

These two closely related justifications may then be said to rest ultimately on our possession of a capacity for critical, rational thought, even while admitting that it is finite in nature. A failure to exercise it amounts to a diminution or retardation of human agency. We have therefore a need to express ourselves (of course this need for free speech has to be qualified in practice by certain constraints like libel, incitement to violence, to hatred of others, etc.).

In other words, it is because we have a need to express ourselves based on the capacities for thought, for language, for speech, for criticism of what we speak (and write) that we possess, that it makes sense to assert that we have a (moral) right to free speech. Otherwise it is difficult to see why that right is considered to be so important. The need we have for expression provides a proper foundation for the right. Without such a foundation, one would be forced to say that expression of our thoughts happens to be something we bestow our approval upon, thereby implying that it would be no more or no less arbitrary to withdraw approval from such an activity. Yet rights theorists themselves emphasise the urgency of such a right, and in their condemnation of societies which do not appear to respect such ·a right, they imply that it is not simply a matter of arbitrary subjective whim and fancy to do so. But at the same time, they often themselves fail explicitly to provide arguments which could establish that the upholding of such rights is more than an issue of mere subjective choice or commitment, sincere though it be. (Of course, those who subscribe to view (2) above maintain that sincere commitment to the list of human rights is all that one can have by way of so-called justification.) [13]

Let us next take another example, this time a more contentious one from the point of view of rights theorists, the right to a social minimum. (As we shall see, some of them maintain that this right, like the right to work, the right to health, etc. are not genuine moral (or human or natural) rights. But I will for the moment ignore this aspect of their thought.) If one were to raise the question seriously why we should have such a right, an obvious answer lies in saying that we, as human agents, have needs for food, shelter, for clean water and air, etc. which constitute the general need for a social minimum. (On my interpretation, the force of the word 'social' is to draw attention to those problems I have already dealt with, in the earlier sections of this chapter about the various ways which societies have adopted to meet such a minimum. But to say that these means are culturally or socially determined is not to imply that they are arbitrarily and whimsically adopted.) The latter in turn is clearly based on the capacities we possess for a certain type of physiological and metabolic activities. The failure to satisfy these capacities can be shown to harm the agent in question. Hence the urgency to meet the needs generated by them, and in turn the moral urgency of the right to a social minimum.

I will next examine a standard analysis of rights given by rights theorists and then show why it is inadequate, if not downright misleading, so that such an analysis cannot be said to provide proper insight into the nature of rights, and the basis for attributing them to human (and other) agents. This account appears to be distinguished by the following features: (a) it is much influenced by Hohfeld's classical analysis of legal rights, especially his account of claim-right; [14] (b) as a result, the analysis of the notion of rights as moral or human rights has become distorted, in my view, by the analysis of legal rights; (c) in so far as that analysis pays any attention to the analysis of rights as moral rights, it appears to be modelled on the moral practice of promise-making, or forming agreements, or abiding by rules explicitly agreed upon or tacitly adhered to. In other words, it is a rule-based account, the rules here being moral rules or quasi-institutional ones which are the analogues of legal rules in the Hohfeldian account; (d) it would be fair, however, to point out that (a), (b) and (c) above may be said to be true of the account of rights as usually given by liberal rights theorists, whose primary contention is that only certain sorts of rights are genuine, namely, civil and political rights, but not others, which are sometimes called economic and social rights. To such thinkers, the latter category, though much endorsed by post Second World War ideological rhetoric world-wide, is, conceptually speaking, an unjustifiable extension of the term 'rights'.

Under the influence of (a), (b) and (c) above, rights come to be portrayed as 'things which can be possessed, exercised, demanded, waived, relinquished, transferred. . . . '. [15] I will argue later that while it is meaningful to say that rights can be possessed, exercised, demanded, it is not obvious that fundamental moral or human rights (as opposed to relatively trivial ones) can be generated *via* the above; moreover, it is also not obvious that it is morally permissible to waive, relinquish or transfer fundamental rights, although it may be allowable to do so in the case of relatively trivial ones.

But let me say something very briefly about (a), (b) and (c) now. (I will leave (d) for examination later.) As Hohfeld's analysis is a complex one, and the variations of it prolific on the part of writers influenced by it, I will single out what is considered generally to be the most central of the theses which make up his analysis, namely, his account of a claim-right.

A person has a claim-right to do or have something when another person has a duty to let him do or have that thing. An example of a claim-right is A's right to a piece of land which he owns corresponding to the duty of B and others to stay off the land. [16]

This then leads to the thesis of:

'strict correlativity' of rights and duties: A's right against B implies, and is implied by, B's duty to A. This position supplements the view contained in Hohfeld — that a claim-right implies a corresponding duty — by adding the reverse implication — a duty implies a corresponding claim-right. [17]

We shall see later how the thesis of strict correlativity gives rise to difficulties.

The thesis of strict correlativity generated by a Hohfeldian analysis of a legal claim-right is reinforced by an analysis of a moral right based on (c). The moral practice of promise-making or of entering into a voluntary agreement involves the following:
(i) there are two parties, A and B, the promisor and the promisee, such that A promises B to do X;
(ii) by thus promising, A has created a right invested in B;
(iii) and at the same time, a corresponding obligation in A to make good the promise;
(iv) it follows that whenever one says that one party (B) has a right, it entails that another party (A) has a duty to the other party (B);
(v) because it is a voluntary agreement or undertaking on the part of A and B, it implies that B is able voluntarily to release A from the obligation to carry out the promise, that is, B can and may waive the right invested in her by B's promise.

It is then a contractual model. It presupposes (1) that A and B are individuals who can meet and confront each other, (2) that A and B can understand what it is that they are doing, namely, that A must be able to realise that he is making a commitment to B, as a result of which he puts himself under an obligation to B, and creates in B a legitimate expectation that the commitment would be carried out.

The contractual model of moral rights which itself involves the thesis of reciprocity of rights and duties, thereby, merges with the Hohfeldian thesis of strict correlativity based on an analysis of legal rights. A legal claim-right is replicated by a moral claim-right.

> Moral claim-rights, like legal claim-rights, are the kind we most often have in mind when speaking of 'rights' without qualification. If A promises B that he will lend B a book, then B has a claim-right to be lent that book, corresponding to A's duty to lend it to him. [18]

(I will from now on use the term 'the contractual model' to refer to both (a) and (c) since the latter crucially covers the thesis of strict correlativity or reciprocity. However, if it is necessary for me to distinguish between (a) and (c), I shall do so.)

The symmetry established between a legal claim-right and a moral claim-right provides a unified framework for the analysis of rights, both legal and moral. Attractive though this project might be from a methodological point of view, I wish to contend that it is crucially flawed. A legal right is not the same as a moral right in spite of the surface similarities that might exist between them. I will argue that while the thesis of strict correlativity of rights and duties is part (not the whole, as Hohfeld and others appear to maintain) of a proper analysis of a legal right, it cannot be borrowed unthinkingly to apply to an analysis of moral rights *tout court*. It may obtain straightforwardly only in the case of that sub-class of moral rights generated *via* the practice of promise-making or of entering into voluntary agreements. If it turns out that not all cases of moral rights can be assimilated to this moral paradigm, then an analysis based on it can be and is highly misleading.

Promise-making is *par excellence* a rule-based activity, where the rules are explicitly understood and adhered to. (Its bindingness does not depend on the content of the promise made, but on the mode of promise-making itself.) It is therefore akin to legal rules which are, on the whole, also explicitly understood and adhered to. But an explication of the notion of moral rights in terms of rules, whether legal or moral, would only work if morality can be said to arise entirely out of rules which are explicitly adopted. This then leads to a more fundamental issue in meta-ethics whether the notion of morality can itself be reduced to rules which are consciously, explicitly and voluntarily chosen by human agents as individuals. This conception of morality is, of course, in keeping with the dominant account given of it by contemporary moral philosophers in the Western world. But this very large topic can only be mentioned without the possibility of it being pursued any further here. [19]

Let us see more precisely in what ways the contractual model may be said to give rise to certain difficulties upon reflection. For instance, intuitively, we think that it makes sense to say that parents have duties to their children, that present generations have duties to future generations, that we, human agents, have certain duties to animals. But on the contractual analysis of rights, it is not obvious that the three categories of human agents involved can be said to have duties, and, therefore, the three corresponding categories of agents can be said to have rights.

In the first example, it seems absurd to think that parents and children are parties to a voluntary agreement or undertaking. At a pinch, one could say that parents have undertaken to look after their offspring by their conscious decision to conceive them, or not to abort the foetus, once the mother realises that conception has taken place. (But this would not, however, take care of those cases where conception is quite unintentional and where abortion is, for one reason or another, not available.) But this kind of undertaking does not approximate to the contractual model outlined above, because in this case, the parents have promised themselves (or vowed to themselves), not their offspring, to discharge certain duties towards them. This may be said to be 'self-promising', quite different from the standard case relied upon by the contractual model which may be called, for want of a better term, 'other-promising'. If duties can be said to be created in the promisor even in the case of 'self-promising', and rights can be invested in a party who is not and cannot be a party to the act of 'self-promising', then this is a very different way of generating duties and corresponding rights from that envisaged by the standard account.

In the case of the unborn, it is even more absurd to think that future generations could be said to be parties to a voluntary agreement. A child already born is at least an individual which the parent can and does confront. But the yet unborn, *ex hypothesi*, are not individuals we can confront and meet face to face. They are just not there. As such they fail to meet presupposition (1) of the contractual model. Like the newly-born, the very young, they also fail to meet presupposition (2), for *ex hypothesi* it makes no sense to say that they could understand, here and now, the kind of contract they might be undertaking.

The baby, the infant and the unborn would one day come to understand the concept of a contract or a promise (in the case of the latter, one would have to say that any human baby born in the future, like today's newly-born, would one day come to have such an understanding). But animals are entirely different. They would and could never (empirically, conceptually and logically) come to understand such a matter as they lack the capacity for symbolling, which takes the form of verbal (or written) expression. They fail then to satisfy, even more radically than the unborn and the newly-born, presupposition (2) above.

The contractual model says that rights can be waived. Yet in these three controversial cases, it is not obvious that it makes sense to say that they can be waived. First, a clarification — the difficulties are two. The first is a moral difficulty, the second, a conceptual one. I will deal with the latter first, which has something to do with presupposition (2). That says that the two parties understand what it is to promise someone to do something, and to be promised by someone to do something. Those who cannot understand this, cannot also understand that there are certain rights invested in them. As such, they are not in a position to waive such rights either. Yet the contractual model holds that if someone has a right, it also makes sense for them to waive it. It follows then that it makes no sense to say that the newly-born, the very young, the unborn and animals can waive their rights. The only exception is that of a mature teenager. Suppose we take eighteen to be the age of adulthood, then one might concede that seventeen or sixteen year-olds could be in a position to waive such rights, and release their parents from their obligations towards them. (In the case of any child younger than that, it is not so much that we doubt their ability to understand the concepts of promise-making and promise-releasing, but that we doubt his/her proper understanding and grasp, not merely intellectually but also emotionally, of all the complexities of human existence at such a young age. This introduces an additional dimension to the matter.)

The second difficulty is a moral one. Even if the newly-born, the very young, etc. could meaningfully be said to be in a position to waive their rights, morally speaking, should such rights be waived? Take the case of a promise made betweeen two individuals where what is promised, although very important to the parties concerned, is not of fundamental significance to life as it is led. A might have promised B to help repair B's damaged fence. One could imagine B releasing A from his obligation to make good the promise, when he realised that A did not appear too keen to help, or had become too busy after the promise was made. But in a case where the promise touches on something of fundamental significance, it is not morally obvious that B could waive the right. Suppose A had promised B to help him dig a well, without which B would die of thirst. Suppose A was the only person for miles around with the appropriate tools for well-digging, then A's behaviour would not be excused by the fact of B waiving his right, even if for some reason or other he chose to do so. Should B die of thirst, A could hardly get away with it by the simple excuse that B had waived his right.

Consider the converse case. Suppose A were to promise B to kill himself because he, A, had let B down in some way. According to the contractual model, A had invested a right in B and created a corresponding obligation in himself to discharge the promise. But morally speaking, would one say that B was entitled to expect A to carry out the obligation, or that A had a moral duty to kill himself just because he had promised B to do so?

Moreover, the whole idea of waiving a right under the contractual model is subversive of the very tenet that human rights are a fundamentally important moral category, which can override other moral demands. For instance, some rights theorists, while not going to the extent of denying that the notion of needs is intelligible, nevertheless hold that the claim from needs is of lesser moral significance than that from rights, so that, in a case of conflict, the latter may override the former. But this putative claim to its overriding character is not easy to reconcile with the implication of the contractual model that rights can be waived. Anything which can be waived, *ipso facto*, from the moral point of view, cannot be of fundamental significance.

In the light of the above critique, rights theorists, who implicitly or explicitly adhere to the contractual model, are faced then with the following options:
(i) they can simply be consistent, and conclude that the categories mentioned above cannot be said to have rights, in which case, their conclusion would be morally counter-intuitive;
(ii) they can adopt a more moderate position by severing the link between rights and corresponding duties. On this modified view, it makes sense to say that B has duties to A without implying that A has rights and expectations to be treated in a certain way by B. Parents then may be said to have duties to their offspring, even though it is not correct to hold that children have rights against their parents. But this

version really amounts to jettisoning the contractual analysis of rights and duties — under it, it is not meaningful to say that B has rights unless A has duties towards it, and *vice versa*. On the revised interpretation, it appears meaningful to say that A has duties even in the absence of B having any rights against A;

(iii) they can say that the contractual model in such cases must not be understood and applied literally. The contract is meant to be a fiction — it is as if there were two parties involved which satisfy all the assumptions and presuppositions of the model. In this way, they might be able to make sense of the assertion that the categories of agents involved do have rights. However, the concession, that it is but a fiction, amounts to a tacit acceptance of the criticism, that the model is not really relevant and appropriate to the analysis of the notion of rights. In other words, they have as good as given it up. Moreover, the technique of construing something as a fiction is double-edged. It can be invoked to make sense of, and to justify almost anything in moral, social and political theory. For instance, should I so wish, I could invoke the technique, and argue that it is as if human beings are like animals without language, and that, therefore, the right of free speech is not an appropriate right for such agents. This does not appear to be an attractive way out.

So it looks as if rights theorists are trapped, at least if they adhere to the contractual model in their analysis of the notion of rights. If such theorists were to turn to the alternative that I advocate, they could meaningfully attribute rights to those categories, without having to rely on the unsatisfactory technique of fiction-postulating. But the price they would have to pay for this move, is that rights can no longer be held to be prior, more fundamental, more urgent than needs. They are derivative from needs, and have no autonomous existence of their own.

It is not difficult to show, that the rights which these categories of agents are said to enjoy, rest on the needs they have, and in turn, the capacities they possess. The newly-born, the young, animals, future peoples (when they become born) all have needs for food, for warmth, for shelter, for some one to be with them while they grow to be more independent, to become mature, etc. (Of course, the case of animals are somewhat different, but for the purpose of making the point here, there is no need to set out the differences.)

We have seen, in the earlier sections of the chapter, that the logic of needs does not presuppose (a) that the agents, said to be in need, necessarily know what their needs are, or indeed are able to understand what they are; or (b) that the agents, said to be in need, are individuals one can personally confront and meet, to talk to and come to an agreement with. Needs arise not through personal private negotiation between individuals, but through the capacities such individuals possess. To assess someone's needs, all that one needs to know are the characteristics of the agent in terms of the general capacities possessed, as well as the minor variations displayed between agents of the same species.

Needs, if not met, would lead to a diminution of such capacities and to diminished or impaired agency. That is why needs have a moral urgency to them that should not be ignored. It also accounts for why, when talk about needs is translated into talk about rights, it is morally odd to say that such rights could be waived.

The above characteristics would then explain why the so-called rights, invested in the three categories, are really disguised needs. As they fail radically to satisfy the presuppositions of the contractual model, it is not a wonder that they present difficulties to it. This in turn raises the question about the general relevance of the contractual model to an analysis and understanding of the notion of rights.

It appears that at best it can account for trivial rights, but not fundamental ones, which are usually dignified today with the label 'human' attached to them. Promises and agreement mutually made between (competent language-using) individuals do, of course, create rights and corresponding duties. These in turn could be annulled or suspended through mutual agreement. Moreover, the party in whom the right is invested may also unilaterally release the other party from his/her obligation. But the suspension or release is morally permissible only in the case of relatively trivial matters, as we have seen. In matters touching the vital areas of life, it is not obvious that the model is suitable. For instance, surely rights theorists themselves would not wish to say that the right to free speech could be waived by (human) agents, who are said to possess this fundamental human right. Nor, as we have also seen, is it relevant to a discussion of rights, where the agents involved are without speech, or are incompetent, immature language users.

So while not wishing to deny that the practice of promise-making or entering into agreements on a voluntary basis plays a pretty large part in human existence, it remains correct to say that, nevertheless it cannot be leaned upon to cast light on those issues in life which are of fundamental moral significance.

So far I have only discussed three categories of human and animal agents which are problematic as far as this model is concerned. But rights theorists could retort that the failure to accommodate them is not all that damaging, as they themselves do not consider them to be key issues in their account of human rights. They are primarily concerned with what Minogue calls 'separating rights', not what he calls 'uniting rights'. [20] Rights of children, of future peoples, of animals, right to a social minimum, to welfare, etc. belong to the latter, which Minogue appears to deny as genuine rights anyway. (Strictly speaking the rights of future peoples do not all fall into the category of uniting rights, for the right to free speech may be one of the rights they are said to possess. It is, however, open to Minogue to argue that young children and animals do not enjoy the right to free speech, and, therefore, all their rights may be construed as uniting rights.) But the right to free speech is, in the opinion of rights theorists, a genuine human right and an extremely important one at that.

Sometimes, separating rights are said to constitute civil and political rights, whose *raison d'être* is the protection of individual freedom; uniting ones are said to constitute economic and social rights, whose aim has nothing to do with promoting the ideal of freedom, but the ideal of social justice. In the literature on the subject of rights, liberal supporters of the theory usually perceive a profound discontinuity between civil and political rights on the one hand, and economic social rights on the other, and, moreover, maintain or imply that only the former type can count as genuine rights. [21]

So let me next examine the right to free speech, and see if the contractual model applies to it. If it turns out that it does not approximate to it, then I would have shown that even in a matter considered as essential to the concern of (liberal) rights theorists, it does not work. One may then conclude that it is truly irrelevant and should be abandoned — it is time to adopt an alternative foundation even for separating rights, based on human needs, and the capacities we possess.

A possible reason for holding that economic and social rights are pseudo rights is precisely that such rights fail to conform to the contractual model. Take again the right to a social minimum. It is clear who is said to have the right — it is the poor, the unemployed. (Of course, who counts as poor may vary from society to society.) But is it obvious who has the duty or obligation to ensure that the right will be satisfied? No party has apparently voluntarily contracted with those said to have the right, to ensure that they be given the social minimum. Unlike the case of children, the unborn and animals, where one knows how to locate the party with the duties, but has difficulty construing that children, etc. are the party with the rights, this example has no difficulty in locating the party with the right, but has difficulty identifying the party, which can be said to have the corresponding duty. Since the analysis of rights, based on the contractual model, requires a reciprocity between rights and duties, this line of reasoning concludes that as economic and social rights fail to satisfy the demand, they then must be construed as pseudo rights.

However, if this is a crucial reason for denying economic and social rights the status of being genuine rights, then by the same argument, perhaps, one too must conclude that even separating or civil and political rights are not genuine.

If A is said to enjoy the right to free speech, it follows that B is said to have the obligation not to interfere with A's right, and *vice versa*. But it seems implausible, if not outright absurd, to think that A and B have voluntarily and mutually undertaken, and promised not to interfere with each other's exercise of free speech. A and B might never have met, and even if they had, they might never have discussed the subject whatsoever. But without prior explicit agreement, how could rights and duties have been generated?

Again, if pressed, one could fall back on the contract as a fiction. It is as if A and B had mutually agreed not to interfere. But as I have already pointed out a crucial drawback to this technique, I will leave the point without pursuing it further.

Moreover, as I have also already indicated, it is equally absurd to conceive of A and B mutually waiving their respective rights to free speech, thereby relieving themselves of their respective obligations to their respective rights.

So-called liberal rights theorists could retort that I have misrepresented the role of such separating rights in the history of political thought and rhetoric. They are meant to make claims and demands against government, not individuals. To this, the following response may be apt: to construe the state (or government) as the party in whom the corresponding obligation lies is, of course, done *via* the social contract as a fiction. Locke seems to have favoured this device. We, as individuals, have entered into a contract with the state, whereby we have the duty to obey its edicts, provided it protects our natural rights to life, liberty and property. However, the drawbacks of fiction-making apart, such a device cannot in this context, at least, be used to generate rights on the part of citizens, which the state is then said to have the obligation not to interfere with. On Locke's account, we already have such rights, which he termed 'natural', prior to the fictional contract. The fictional contract, therefore, does not, and cannot serve to generate rights in the one party and corresponding obligation or duty in the other. It can at best be used to argue that the state has the right to expect obedience from us because we have promised to obey its edicts, provided our so-called rights are protected and not violated. But this is a very different thesis from the contractual model which is meant to yield an analysis of the notion of rights, and to account for how rights and corresponding duties are generated.

In short, one could say that the contractual model is applicable, neither to separating (that is, civil and political) rights, which the theory endorses as genuine, nor to uniting (that is, economic and social) rights, which are condemned as pseudo. On the other hand, my analysis of rights, in terms of needs and capacities, has the virtue of being able to make sense of both separating and uniting rights, as well as the rights of children, future peoples and of animals. It follows that liberal rights theorists are not correct in maintaining that there is a radical and profound discontinuity between civil, political rights on the one hand and economic, social rights on the other. Even if one were to concede that while the former serves to promote the ideal of freedom, that is, political justice, the latter a very different goal, such as social justice, it remains true that we, human agents, given the capacities we possess, have as much a need for political justice as we have for social justice. The demand for both sorts of rights is a demand in the name of needs. So one is not unreasonable in concluding that there is no deep chasm between the two, and that it might be more appropriate simply to call both fundamental moral or human rights, the common aim of which is to promote justice. (See Chapter Nine for detailed argumentation on this point.) This alternative unifying analysis is, therefore, superior, and to be preferred, both on conceptual and methodological grounds.

So far I have discussed the notion of rights as moral (or natural or human) rights. I would next like to explore another dimension to the matter, namely, the transformation of moral rights to become legal rights, and in this way, I hope to link up my discussion of legal rights in Chapter Nine with my account of moral rights, as disguised needs, in this chapter. I have earlier criticised rights theorists in general for having analysed the notion of moral rights as if an analysis of legal rights was appropriate to the purpose. In this, they have been influenced by Hohfeld's analysis of legal rights, as we have seen. I will now try to show that his account of legal rights is partially but not wholly correct. For a more adequate analysis, one has to turn to Bentham.

As Bentham points out, moral rights are not identical with legal rights. In any particular legal system, the latter may not entirely coincide with the former. The former may, however, be used to criticise inadequacies in the latter, and advocate reform in its name. The notion of moral rights belongs to that domain which, today, is commonly called in jurisprudence influenced by legal positivist thought, 'law as it ought to be' (Bentham calls it 'censorial jurisprudence'), while the notion of legal rights belongs to the domain of 'law as it is' (Bentham calls it 'expository jurisprudence').

Some fundamental moral rights (in my analysis, they are needs) are considered to be so important that they have become incorporated into the legal system as legal rights, or are urged to be thus incorporated. My arguments in the last chapter show that the legal system underpins any structure and distribution of legal rights, thereby including those moral rights which have become legal rights. I have also there given a neo-Benthamite analysis of the notion of legal rights.

It follows from that analysis that to say, for

instance, A (the first party) has the legal right to free speech, entails that B (the second party) has a legal duty or obligation not to prevent A from exercising A's right, and that C (the third party which consists of law-enforcing officials) has a legal duty or obligation to prevent B, from preventing A, from exercising A's right. On this analysis of what might be called a legal separating right, it is clear which party has the right and which parties have the corresponding duties and obligations.

A similar analysis may also be given of what might be called a legal uniting right. To say that A has the legal right to a social minimum entails that B (the second party, in this case, the DHSS officials) has the legal duty not to prevent A from claiming it, and that C (the third party, in this case, the DHSS ombudsman, or whatever other legal body is designated as arbiter in such matters) has the legal duty to prevent B, from denying A, his/her legal right to a social minimum.

In other words, on my analysis of what it is to have the legal right to a social minimum, it is obvious which party has the right, and which parties the corresponding legal duties and obligations. The parties involved can be clearly identified. Those, who are said to have such a right, are those deemed in that particular society to earn less than a certain amount per month or per annum. The duties lie with B, the DHSS officials in the first instance, then with C, the Welfare Ombudsman. Beyond C, there may be still further legal provisions to allow grievances to be pursued, indeed all the way to the House of Lords in this country, and even to the European Court of Human Rights. The chain of agents bearing the corresponding duties is clear, and must exist, if A is said to enjoy the legal right to a social minimum. Of course, as we have also seen in the last chapter, in a complete account of the law on this issue, one would also have to refer to various tax laws and other similar measures, which ensure the transfer of wealth from the rich to the poor, if the legal right to a social minimum is a genuine legal right.

In the case of children, future peoples and animals, again it is clear that they can be said to enjoy certain legal rights, only if B (parents in the case of children already born, society in general in the case of posterity and animals) does not act to deny A the rights, and if C (law officials) prevents B (existing adults or present people) from denying A such rights. So if we are really serious, for instance, about the legal rights of future generations, then we have to legislate to control, either directly or indirectly, activities which lead to pollution, deforestation, exhaustion of non-renewable low entropic energy and matter, ecological degradation and bankruptcy, which would make it very difficult, if not impossible, for future peoples to meet their needs. If B were caught violating these laws, then C (law officials) have the legal duty to apply sanctions against B.

The same goes for animals. If animals have certain legal rights, then this implies that B (human agents) have a legal duty or obligation not to act in such a way as to deny them these rights, and that C (law officials) have a legal duty to prevent B from denying animals their rights.

In conclusion, let me summarise the thrust of the arguments in this section as follows: I hope to have provided a way of analysing those moral rights considered to be so crucially significant and important as to be dignified by the label 'human' before it, in terms of needs, which can take account of all those contexts we intuitively feel to be covered by the notion of fundamental moral rights. (Admittedly, I have not attempted to give an account of those moral rights, which arise out of promise-making and other voluntary undertakings between individuals, in terms of needs. It could be that I am unable to give a convincing account even should I try, although I regard that as an open issue for now. My omission to do so here is explained by my more limited aim of arguing that the category of 'human rights' can be successfully grounded in terms of needs, and not the more general thesis, that all rights can be so grounded.) By so doing, I have also provided a critical and rational foundation or justification for it, thus relieving it of the possible charge that it has no descriptive content, and is a 'pro-word' with only normative force. But if my arguments succeed, they imply, however, that the theory of rights, as a theory of justice, is redundant. I have also given an account of the transformation of certain fundamental moral rights to become legal rights and, in turn, an analysis of the latter along quasi-Benthamite rather than Hohfeldian lines.

CONCLUSION

A social philosophy, to be adequate and relevant, must be in accordance with the science of thermodynamics, the principles of ecology (amongst other sciences) and the non-linear model of causation embedded in the latter. The former tells us (i) that energy and matter can neither be destroyed nor created, but only transformed, (ii) that transformations of energy entail loss of usable or available energy in the form of heat as waste. The latter two tell us that addition to, or removal of an element(s) from an ecosystem(s), could generate far-reaching consequences through the interactions of parts which are interdependent upon one another.

Together these epistemically imply the following general principles for determining social arrangements:
1. in the exchange between human agents and Nature, the former ought not to employ EST, as such a technology would (a) deplete the non-renewable supplies of low entropic energy and matter at a rate which renders a civilisation based on it non-sustainable, (b) overload the ecosystems and the biosphere with its waste to such an extent as to cause severe disruption, so that the way of life resting on it, is rendered also non-viable in the long run;
2. that the exchange between human agents and Nature be mediated by EST, a technology which (i) uses renewable supplies of low entropic energy and matter at a rate compatible with ecological renewability, producing 'waste', which is also compatible with their

ecological recyclibility;

3. an EST mediation in turn calls for (i) a conception of human needs based on the notion of sufficiency, not infinite, ever-expanding insatiety; (ii) hence the rejection of the value, which focuses human satisfaction upon the ever-increasing possession and consumption of external material goods; (iii) an alternative source of abiding satisfaction, which lies in self-development, as a means of meeting the genuine human need to excel, in the achievement of internal goods, which themselves, on the whole, do not make impossible demands upon the ecologically, that is, absolutely, scarce supplies of low entropic energy and matter;

4. the above solution to the question 'What sort of person ought one to be?' entails the rejection of a zero-sum game, of egoism, competitiveness and envy in the relationship between human agents; instead, it allows for a non zero-sum game to be played in which all could be winners, and makes co-operation possible;

5. the above theses enable one also to overcome, or at least, to erode to a greater extent (i) the dichotomy between egoism and altruism, (ii) the dichotomy between work and leisure, (iii) the dichotomy between human and non-human life, which so centrally dictates the way the former has treated the latter, for the last four hundred years;

6. they lead to the rejection of the doctrine of (exponential) economic growth, which involves redistribution according to the Matthew Principle; instead they entail redistribution in the direction of equality according to the Robin Hood Principle; the notion of equality, properly analysed, does not entail either envy or uniformity of treatment;

7. they also involve the rejection of both bourgeois capitalism and that version of socialism which is also currently a form of state capitalism, that is to to say, the expansive or cornucopic version of socialism; instead they imply a form of socialism, which may be said to be ascetic as far as material goods for consumption and use are concerned, but rich in

opportunities offered to all, to achieve abiding satisfaction, through the attainment of internal goods.

A social/moral theory or philosophy constructed without reference to, and in ignorance of how the world of Nature really works, cannot be said to be a relevant solution to the basic problems raised by such a philosophy, namely, of endurance and flourishing, of how we ought to live with regard to Nature at large, to one another and with regard to our integrity and identity. Such a theory or theories must be dismissed as fantastic. Most social philosophies, at least the dominant orthodox ones since the seventeenth century, are such fantastic theories. Those which are not, like Fourier's, have been ignored or ridiculed. It is time to realise that their basic insights might not, after all, be as insane and inane as they usually have been made out to be. The boot may now be on the other foot — the charge of irrelevance could be made to stick in the case of the orthodox theories.

CHAPTER 1   A RATIONAL BASIS

1. See K. Lee, *A New Basis for Moral Philosophy*, (Routledge and Kegan Paul, London, 1985).

2. For details, see Lee, *A New Basis*, Chapter IV, section 9.

3. See, for instance, R. Elliot and A. Gare, *Environmental Philosophy*, (Open University Press, Milton Keynes, 1983).

4. When people talk about the mechanistic paradigm of explanation and prediction in science, they could have one, or more, of the following in mind:

(a) that Newton, Galileo and others established the (modern) science of mechanical motion;

(b) that they used mathematics to formulate the laws of motion;

(c) that the physical world is actually a machine (to be studied and understood by sciences like the science of mechanical motion using mathematics for the formulation of their laws);

(d) that the fundamental stuff of the universe is matter in motion (for instance, Hobbes' materialism) to which everything else in the universe may be reduced;

(e) that the universe is a deterministic one — given the laws of nature (discovered under (a), (b) and (c) above), the positions and velocities of the particles of matter at time t, one could predict precisely their positions and velocities at time t_1 (Laplacean determinism).

It is held that quantum mechanics in this century has upset most if not all the theses above, but in particular (e).

Heisenberg's uncertainty principle, it is said, has overthrown the view that the universe is a deterministic one, replacing it with the view that it is indeterministic — that is, one cannot simultaneously predict both the velocity and the position of a subatomic particle. One might do the one or the other. Sometimes, it is said that the principle of causality has been superseded. At other times, it is also said that the distinction between the observer and the observed has broken down. From these claims, some scientists turned philosophers, like Capra, have concluded that there is room for mysticism.

My challenge of classical physics and its mechanistic paradigm is neutral as to (e). It is more specifically addressed against (c) and (d). I think the relation between classical Newtonian physics about macro objects, and quantum physics about subatomic particles, is much more complicated than what is implied by a mere acceptance of Heisenberg's principle of uncertainty. But this is not the place to pursue these issues. Nor do I believe that one has to lapse into mysticism given the relevance of Heisenberg's principle to quantum mechanics. I am here concerned only to reject reductionism, which ignores the occurrence of emergent properties, and which fails to recognise that the laws to be found in biology, ecology, psychology or sociology are about phenomena at a much higher level of organisational complexity than those studied by physics. In other words, it is to say that while the laws of biology have to take into account the laws of physics, the latter alone cannot explain biological phenomena. It may provide necessary conditions, but not necessary and sufficient conditions, for the occurrence and, hence, understanding of biological phenomena.

I am also concerned to challenge the mechanistic linear model of causation embedded in classical physics, when it is applied to other domains of phenomena like ecological ones. That the ecological world behaves like a machine is unacceptable. But for discussion on this point, see Chapter Two, section 1.

5. Marx, one may say, was less prescient than Charles Fourier, a social philosopher whose insights have been dismissed by Marx as utopian and frivolous, and ignored by others. In Chapter Eight, I will try to show that Fourier could be said to have anticipated some of the arguments now put forward by those who take thermodynamics and ecology

seriously in their social vision.

For a harsher judgment on Marx on the issue, whether he could have known about the matters dealt with by what is now called the science of thermodynamics, and its potential significance for social philosophy, see J. Martinez-Alier, *Ecological Scarcity*, (Blackwell, Oxford, 1987), especially Chapter 3 and Chapter 14, section on 'Marxism and Ecology'. He maintains that Podolinsky, a Ukrainian socialist, had explicitly drawn Marx's attention to the problem, through his correspondence with him (and also Engels had kept Marx informed about Podolinsky's view as requested), but that Marx had chosen to ignore it.

6. Quoted by J. Rifkin and T. Howard, *Entropy, A New World Vision*, (Paladin Books, London, 1985) p. 55; also, A. Schlipp, *Albert Einstein: Philosopher Scientist*, (Harper and Row, New York, 1959).

7. A. Eddington, *The Nature of the Physical World*, (University of Michigan Press, Michigan, 1958), p. 74.

8. For a critique of the view that it would still not be right to blow up the world even if one were the last human agent(s) alive, see Paul W. Taylor, *Respect for Nature*, (Princeton University Press, New Jersey, 1986). Here the argument consists of maintaining that Nature has a value independent and irrespective of the existence of human agents, who have intentions and goals, which require the use and the consumption of materials provided by Nature, in order to be successful in executing them in action. But one can get to Taylor's conclusion by another route — by arguing that human agents are only morally entitled to Nature's resources if these are used to meet genuine human needs. To blow up the world, even though one might be the last human agent(s) alive, could hardly be said to constitute a genuine human need. This line is pursued by this book — see Chapters Seven and Ten for a discussion on what constitutes genuine human needs.

CHAPTER 2   ECOLOGY AND THERMODYNAMICS

1. Quoted by E. J. Kormondy, *Concepts of Ecology*, (Prentice-Hall, Inc., Englewood Cliffs, New Jersey, 1976), p. x. For an accessible account of ecology in general, see P. R.

Ehrlich, *The Machinery of Nature*, (Simon and Schuster, New York, 1986).

2. Also cited by Kormondy, *Concepts*, p. xi (quotation is from A. Macfadyen, *Animal Ecology: Aims and Methods*, (Pitman, London, 1957)).

3. F. Capra, *The Turning Point*, (Simon and Schuster, New York, 1982), p. 272. (This view about self-organising systems is part of what is called the Systems View or Systems Philosophy; for an account of the latter, see E. Laszlo, *Introduction to Systems Philosophy*, (Gordon and Breach, New York, 1972).

4. Kormondy, *Concepts*, p. 7. E. P. Odum also points out, in *Ecology, The Link Between the Natural and Social Sciences*, (Holt, Rinehart and Winston, Inc., New York and London, 2nd edn, 1975), p. 4 that homeostatic processes through negative feedbacks are, of course, best known to most people as:

> homeostasis in the individual, as, for example, the regulatory mechanisms that keep body temperature in man fairly constant depite fluctuations in the environment. Regulatory mechanisms also operate at the population, community, and ecosystem level. For example, we take for granted that the carbon dioxide content of the air remains constant, without realizing, perhaps, that it is the integration of organisms and environment that maintains the steady conditions despite the large volumes of gases that continually enter and leave the air. Homeostasis at the population level is not always evident; nevertheless, the size and rate of function of most populations tend to remain within certain limits, not only in mature nature, such as a mature forest where the biological structure buffers the external environment, but even in young nature that is exposed to fluctuating physical conditions.

However, as far as the development of ecosystems is concerned, it would be wise to qualify the general account above by saying, as E. P. Odum does, in *Fundamentals of Ecology*, (W. B. Saunders & Co., Philadelphia and London, 3rd edn, 1971), pp. 257-58 that:

> While the basic assumption that species (in an ecosystem) replace one another in a successional gradient 'because

populations tend to modify the physical environment making conditions favorable for other populations until an equilibrium between biotic and abiotic is achieved'. . . is certainly valid, it may be an oversimplification. . .

On this point, see also J. Emlen, *Ecology: An Evolutionary Approach*, (Addison-Wesley Publishing Co., Massachusetts and London, 1973), especially pp. 351-62. Refer to point 5 in the text.

5. Capra, *The Turning Point*, p. 273.

6. Capra, *The Turning Point*, p. 269; see also E. Jantsch, *The Self-Organizing Universe*, (Pergamon Press, Oxford and New York, 1980).

7. 'Resilience and Stability Of Ecosystems' in E. Jantsch and C. H. Waddington (eds), *Evolution and Consciousness*, (Addison-Wesley Publishing Company, Reading, Massachusetts and London, 1976), p. 79. He continues on the same page to write:

Since 1940, there has been a series of similar catastrophic changes in the Great Lakes that has led to major changes in the fish stocks. The explanations for these changes have been explored in part, and involve various combinations of intense fishing pressure, changes in the physical and chemical environment, and the appearance of a foreign predator (the sea lamprey) and foreign competitor (the alewife and carp). Whatever the specific causes, it is clear that the precondition for the collapse was set by the harvesting of fish, even though during a long period there were no obvious signs of problems. The fishing activity, however, progressively reduced the resilience of the system, so that when the inevitable unexpected event occurred, the populations collapsed. If it had not been the lamprey, it would have been something else: a change in climate as part of the normal pattern of fluctuation, a change in the chemical or physical environment, or a change in competitors or predators. These examples. . . suggest distinct domains of attraction in which the populations forced close to the boundary of the domain can then flip over it. The important point is not so much how stable populations are within a domain, but how likely it is for the system to move from one domain into another and so persist in a changed configuration.

8. M. Maruyama, 'The Second Cybernetics: Deviation-Amplifying Mutual Causal Processes', *American Scientist*, Vol. 54, No. 2, (1963), p. 166. Maruyama characterises negative feedbacks as 'deviation-counteracting' loops and positive feedbacks as 'deviation-amplifying' loops. But both are aspects of mutual causal systems (that is, the non-linear model of causation to be discussed in greater detail later in the text). See also Maruyama, 'Paradimatology and its Application' in *Cybernetica*, Vol. XVII, No. 2, (1974), pp. 136-57.

9. W. Ophuls, *Ecology and the Politics of Scarcity*, (W. H. Freeman & Co., San Francisco, 1977), p. 21.

10. I wish to draw the reader's attention to two points:
(a) classical physics is meant to apply to the macroscopic world but not to the sub-atomic world. The latter is dealt with by quantum physics. The causal paradigms of these two physics are said to be different. Classical physics seems to employ what may be called the unidirectional (linear) causal paradigm; quantum physics, the random process paradigm. The former aims ideally at the production of causal laws which are universal and deterministic in character; the latter at statistical laws which are probabilistic in character. But the non-linear model, also called the mutual causal paradigm, is different from either. On the differences between the three, see H. Henderson's adaptation of Maruyama's account (see note 8 above) in *The Politics of the Solar Age*, (Anchor Books, New York, 1981), p. 336. (However, I do not necessarily agree with them on every one of the points they have raised, or with the way they have precisely formulated them);
(b) what I have to say on the subject of non-linear causation (as well as my critique of mechanistic linear causation) are at best rudimentary and exploratory. Philosophers have concentrated, by and large, either on linear or random process causation, and have neglected the third variety. Work, done so far on the latter, has been mainly carried out by non-philosophers, or by philosophers who are not regarded as mainstream. It is time that so-called mainstream ones be alerted to this matter.

11. For the sake of making clear the point under discussion, the thesis of methodological individualism is given this interpretation, leaving aside other possible interpretations as well as other associated complexities, such as the respective ontological status of entities, like individuals and society. For

one view of these issues, see D. H. Ruben, *The Metaphysics of the Social World*, (Routledge and Kegan Paul, London, 1985). For a general view, see S. Lukes, *Individualism*, (Blackwell, Oxford, 1979).

12. See L. B. Lombard, *Events, A Metaphysical Study*, (Routledge and Kegan Paul, London and Boston, 1986), for a thorough exploration of the concept of events.

13. H. L. A. Hart and A. M. Honoré, *Causation in the Law*, (Clarendon Press, Oxford, 1959).

14. What they overtly hold as the criteria for singling out an event as the cause are two: (a) that of abnormality and (b) that of the voluntary intervention of another (human) agent. For them, the abnormal factor must be an event and not a standing condition — in the egg-shell skull example, the fragility of the skull may certainly be said to be an abnormal matter, but for them, it does not count, as it is a standing condition which exists prior to the event, the tapping on the head. See Hart and Honoré, *Causation*, pp. 307-8.

15. My emphasis on the systemic boundaries can be used to deflect the criticism that a reference to the whole set of necessary conditions sufficient for the occurrence of the effect could lead to the 'for want of a nail, a shoe was lost' type of situation, which is in danger logically of including everything which has ever existed in the universe, to be a necessary condition. I am concerned with the systemic boundaries that obtain at the time the effect is said to occur. Although X's birth is undoubtedly a necessary condition for his possessing an egg-shell skull, his birth did not form part of the systemic boundaries that obtained at the time the book fell on his head.

16. Both the so-called realist and the positivist philosophies of science agree that one of the goals of science is to generate non-accidental generalisations (whether of a universal or statistical kind). They differ in the ways they account for their non-accidental character.

17. This in turn raises the question — what constitutes a system? I do not profess, here and now, to be able to deal with it, only to draw attention to it. Some systems are relatively easy to identify because they have fixed physical boundaries. Others are not so readily identifiable — for instance, an ecosystem does, of course, have physical boundaries, but these are less determinate than those of, say, an organism

itself.

18. Paul R. Ehrlich *et al.*, *Human Ecology*, (W. H. Freeman and Company, San Francisco, 1973), pp. 217-18. (A graph illustrating the difference between linear and non-linear dose response is shown on p. 218.)

19. Ehrlich, *Human Ecology*, p. 217.

20. Ehrlich, *Human Ecology*, p. 218.

21. Paul R. Ehrlich *et al.*, *Ecoscience*, (W. H. Freeman and Company, San Francisco, 1977), p. 548.

22. See details at note 7 above.

23. For a technical account but, nevertheless, accessible to lay persons, see F. W. Atkins, *The Second Law*, (Scientific American Books Inc., New York, 1984); for less technical versions, see, for instance, J. Rifkin and T. Howard, *Entropy, A New World Vision*, (Paladin, London, 1985).

24. Atkins, *The Second Law*, p. 7.

25. See, for instance, A. Goudie, *The Human Impact on the Natural Environment*, (Blackwell, Oxford, second edition, 1987) for an account of the consequences of human transformations of low entropic energy and matter for the world's ecosystems.

26. S. Angrist and L. Hepler, 'Demons, Poetry and Life: A Thermodynamic View', *Texas Quarterly*, (10, September 1967), pp. 27-8; quoted by Rifkin and Howard, *Entropy*, p. 51.

27. Rifkin and Howard, *Entropy*, p. 52.

28. H. F. Blum, *Time's Arrow and Evolution*, (Princeton University Press, Princeton, NJ, 1968), p. 94.

29. Example used by G. Tyler Miller Jr. in *Energetics, Kinetics and Life*, (Wadsworth, Belmont, California, 1971); cited by Rifkin and Howard, *Entropy*, p. 65.

30. Miller, *Energetics*, p. 291.

31. N. Georgescu-Roegen, 'Energy, Matter and Economic Valuation' in H. Daly and A. F. Umaña (eds), *Energy, Economics and the Environment*, (AAAS Selected Symposium 64, Westview Press Inc., Colorado, 1981), pp. 54-5.

32. Daly and Umaña, *Energy*, p. 55-6.

33. Comment of Harrison Brown *et al.*, in *The Next Hundred Years*, (Viking Press, New York, 1957); cited by Georgescu-Roegen in Daly and Umaña, *Energy*, p. 55.

34. Rifkin and Howard, *Entropy*, p. 49.

35. Georgescu-Roegen in Daly and Umaña, *Energy*, p. 63.

36. W. Murdoch and J. Connell, 'All About Ecology' in I.

G. Barbour (ed.), *Western Man and Environmental Ethics*, (Addison-Wesley Publishing Co., Reading, Massachusetts and London, 1973).

CHAPTER 3   ECOLOGICAL SCARCITY

1. William Ophuls defines it in *Ecology and the Politics of Scarcity*, (W. H. Freeman & Co., San Francisco, 1977), p. 127 as follows:

> Ecological scarcity is an all-embracing concept that encompasses all the various limits to growth or costs attached to continued growth that have been mentioned . . . . As we have seen, it includes not only Malthusian scarcity of food, but also impending shortages of mineral and energy resources, biospheric or ecosystemic limitations on human activity, and limits to the human capacity to use technology to expand resource supplies ahead of exponentially increasing demands (or to bear the costs of doing so).

2. E. J. Kormandy, *Concepts of Ecology*, (Prentice-Hall Inc., Englewood Cliffs, NJ, 1976) p. 42; see also J. Harte and R. Socolow, *Patient Earth*, (Holt, Rinehart and Winston Inc., New York, 1971), Chapter 16.

3. This is the 'small is beautiful' school of thought, the more 'pessimistic' member of which may be said to be N. Georgescu-Roegen.

4. See L. B. McGowan and J. O'M. Bokris, *How to Obtain Abundant Clean Energy*, (Plenum Press, New York and London, 1980), pp. 132-34.

5. See Bokris, *Energy: the Solar-hydrogen Alternative*, (Architectural Press, London, 1976); also McGowan and Bokris, *How to Obtain*.

6. See, for instance, J. Rifkin and T. Howard, *Entropy, A New World Vision*, (Paladin, London, 1985), pp. 117-18.

7. See Preston Cloud, 'Mineral Resources in Fact and Fancy' in H. Daly (ed.), *Toward a Steady State Economy*, (W. H. Freeman and Company, San Francisco, 1973).

8. See E. Goldsmith, 'Settlements and Social Stability' in D. Meadows (ed.), *Alternatives to Growth*, (Ballinger,

Cambridge, Massachusetts, 1977), p. 331.

9. See W. D. Metz and A. L. Hammond, 'Helium in Conservation Program: Casting it to the Winds', *Science*, (183, 1974), pp. 59-63; see also J. Harte and R. Socolow, *Patient Earth*, (Holt, Rinehart and Winston Inc., New York, 1971), Chapter 6.

10. Ophuls, *Ecology*, p. 62; see also Harte and Socolow, *Patient Earth*, Appendix 1.

11. Rifkin and Howard, *Entropy*, p. 128.

12. Ophuls, *Ecology*, p. 65.

13. On a detailed discussion of this distinction as understood by orthodox economists, see Harold J. Barnett and Chandler Morse, *Scarcity and Growth*, (Johns Hopkins University Press, Baltimore, 1963), especially Chapters 1 and 3.

14. Economists and others refer to the Western advanced industrialised world (but including Japan) as the First World; the Soviet Union and Eastern Europe as the Second World, the Asian and Latin American economies as the Third World; and some of the African economies as the Fourth World, those which do not even qualify to be so-called 'developing' economies like the Third World ones.

15. See A. C. Fisher and F. M. Peterson, 'The Environment in Economics: a Survey' in *Journal of Economic Literature*, (March 1976), pp. 1-33; cited by Daly, *Steady-State Economics*, (W. H. Freeman & Co., San Francisco, 1977), p. 40.

16. Barnett and Morse, *Scarcity*, p. 11.

17. Donald E. Carr, *Energy and the Earth Machine*, (Abacus edition, Sphere Books Ltd, London, 1978), p. 279.

18. Daly, *Steady-State Economics*, pp. 125-26.

19. *A Blueprint for Survival*, (published by *The Ecologist*, Vol. 2, No. 1, 1972), p. 42.

20. *A Blueprint for Survival*, p. 42.

21. Ophuls, *Ecology*, pp. 110-11.

22. William Vogt, *Road to Survival*, (Victor Gollancz, London, 1949), p. 16.

23. Some philosophers of science seem to maintain that a scientific theory is suspect, if not actually pseudo-scientific, if it cannot make precise and accurate predictions — its scientificity is a measure of this predictive power so that it is more scientific, the more precise the prediction it makes. On this

criterion, one must admit that thermodynamics when applied to the ecosphere itself (rather than to more specific contexts like the efficiency of steam engines, Carnot's preoccupation which set the science going) is not capable of making very precise predictions. But this is the fate not only of thermodynamics (and also ecology) but a whole lot of other theories as well, including the theory of evolution. This test of scientificity is so stringent that, if accepted, one would have to withdraw the label 'scientific' from a variety of theories, which are firmly accepted and acknowledged to be, otherwise, scientific. Its ideal seems to be based on classical astronomy as the paradigm of scientific theorising. But the subject matter of many sciences, unlike that of astronomy, is not amenable to such a severe test, there being too many variables for which one simply has no precise data, which have to be taken into account, for a high degree of accuracy in making predictions.

CHAPTER 4   HUMAN AGENCY

1. However, my use of this term does not entirely coincide with Steiner's. (On the analysis of the notion of action and its relationship with freedom — the latter theme to be pursued in Chapter Nine, section 6 — my view and Steiner's have things in common, and his has helped to clarify my own.)

2. See J. Harte and R. Socolow, *Patient Earth*, (Holt, Rinehart and Winston Inc., New York, 1971) chapter on DDT.

3. A critic could, of course, argue as follows: my argument only works if one were to understand the preservation of the species as a form of selfishness. But those who usually oppose selfish to non-selfish behaviour are talking about something else, namely, what is in the interest of the individual, not the species.

Two things may be said in reply:
(a) pursuing an action not in accordance with ecological requirements can, sometimes, as I have mentioned in the text, re-bound on that very individual — the fishing industry, in over fishing, destroys itself. Now a truly determined selfish individual would, at a point, just before the industry collapses and becomes no longer viable, pull out and go elsewhere to pursue similar actions of ecological devastation, until that

sphere too grinds to a halt. But this course of action is necessarily not open to everyone affected by the ecological collapse. Moreover, such persons would, sooner or later, run out of situations to exploit in this way. Such a mode of behaviour would only avoid ecological disaster if it is confined to a minority of agents. This, then, is linked to the free rider issue dealt with in secton 3. The free rider is a moral parasite, a prey upon others;

(b) a selfish individual may, however, include in his/her conception of self interest, the well-being of others — s/he might care about her/his children and grandchildren, if not the fate of the panda and other endangered species. But to care for the well-being of one's children and grandchildren is already to have a conception of the preservation of the human species. If every generation were to adopt the ecological imperative of leaving the earth, in nearly as good a state as it found it, as far as entropy for the next generation and the generation after is concerned, then the endurance and stability of human society, together with the endurance and stability of the ecosystems, would have been secured.

As I have already devoted a section in Chapter One to examining the thesis of egoism and its bearing on ecological scarcity, there is no need, here, for me to say anything further about point (b).

4. His article 'The Tragedy of the Commons' first published in 1968 has been much anthologised. See, for instance, G. Hardin and J. Baden (eds.), *Manning the Commons*, (W. H. Freeman and Company, San Francisco, 1977).

5. Hardin and Baden, *Manning the Commons*, p. 20.

6. See Mancur Olson, *The Logic of Collective Action*, (Harvard University Press, Cambridge, Massachusetts, 1982).

7. However, some individualist theorists deny that there are such things as collective goods. They contend that appropriate devices or technologies could always be designed, which would render all such goods individual goods, so that they will then fail to pass criterion 2 listed in the text. (And if criterion 2 is irrelevant, so is criterion 3.) Take clean air. On this view, should air become so polluted that it is positively dangerous to breathe it, we can each buy a container of clean air, strap it to our backs with a nozzle clamped on our noses. At least, this course of action is open to those with the money to buy the device in question.

Similarly, law and order, too, could be individualised and privatised because one can (with the proviso of money being available) buy guns, hire body guards, wear bullet-proof vests, ride in bullet-proof cars, live behind electronically controlled fortresses, etc.

To some extent, clean air has already been privatised — those who can afford to, tend to move from areas where the air is more polluted to live in more salubrious (usually more expensive) suburbs. But this example shows that privatisation may, at best, be only partially successful even for those who can buy the wherewithal to escape the collective bad. Those who live in green belts with relatively cleaner air may still have to travel through, or work in, areas which are not so wholesome. Maybe this problem will finally be solved when advanced industrialised nations have exported all dirty industries to developing nations. But this *cordon sanitaire* is only an illusion as Nature does not respect national political boundaries. The examples of Chernobyl and acid raid (the Scandinavians claim that most of the pollutant(s) comes from Britain) clearly show that there is no room for complacence or *shadenfreude* should an ecological disaster happen. The crisis over the ozone 'hole' illustrates the same point.

8. K. Lee, *The Positivist Science of Law*, (Avebury, Gower Publishing Co., Aldershot, England, 1989), Chapter Four, section 3.

9. By individualism I am referring, in this context, to that thesis, sometimes called abstract individualism, namely, that human beings possess the characteristics they do, independent of the society of which they are a part, and the corollary that an essential characteristic is their selfishness. This thesis is, in turn, maintained as either that of psychological egoism or of rational ethical egoism — see Chapter One, section 3 for further discussion.

Kant's task in moral philosophy is to try to make the link between self interest and duty, to convince such egoists that, nevertheless, they have duties which do not coincide with their self interest. In other words, Kant has already accepted the polarisation between self interest and altruism (duty), but nevertheless tries to reintegrate the two in his moral philosophy.

10. See E. Cassirer, *Kant's Life and Thought*, trans. J. Haden, (Yale University Press, New Haven and London, 1981),

especially pp. 89-90 and pp. 235-36.

11. Ophuls does make this point, see *Ecology*, pp. 150-52.

CHAPTER 5   REPRODUCTION AND CONSUMPTION

1. Those, who follow Marx's denunciation of Malthus (including those who do not regard themselves to be Marxist or neo-Marxist like Murray Bookchin), simply see Malthusian scarcity as an ideological counter to mask the horrendous issues of social injustice and inequalities, which exist between countries and between groups in individual countries. I do not dispute that it has been and can be so used. However, to leave matters at that level of analysis is to overlook that Malthusian scarcity would still exist, even should we succeed in righting all the social injustices and inequalities that, undoubtedly, plague and stunt the development of vast portions of the world.

2. See E. Goldsmith (ed.), *A Blueprint for Survival*, (*The Ecologist*, Vol. 2, No. 1), p. 2.

3. H. Daly, *Steady-State Economics*, (W. H. Freeman & Co., San Francisco, 1977), p. 164.

4. Daly, *Steady-State Economics*, pp. 162-63.

5. J. S. Mill, *Utilitarianism, Liberty and Representative Government*, (Everyman's Library, J. M. Dent and Sons Ltd., London, 1954), p. 163.

6. See K. Lee, *Three Legal Theorists — Hobbes, Bentham and Kelsen*, forthcoming, Chapter on Bentham.

7. See John Ardagh, *The New France*, (Penguin Books, Harmondsworth, third edition, 1977), p. 453; on a discussion between the use of the stick or the carrot, or between negative and positive incentive policies, see M. Bayles, *Morality and Population Policy*, (The University of Alabama Press, Alabama, 1980), especially pp. 63-6.

8. From the perspective advocated in this study, the problem cannot be simplistically presented as one of the interests of the individual pitted against the interests of others. The whole point is to argue that the interests of the self and those of others need not be quite so polarised, once the ecological model of interdependence has been fully grasped.

9. On China's population policy, see H. Y. Tien, *China's Population Struggle: Demographic Decisions of the People's*

Republic, 1949-1969, (Ohio State University Press, Ohio, 1973) and H. Y. Tien (ed.), *Population Theory in China*, (M. E. Sharpe Inc., White Plains, New York and Croom Helm, London, 1980).

10. See H. Henderson, *Creating Alternative Futures*, (Berkeley Publishing Corporation, New York, 1978), p. 173.

11. E. J. Piel and J. G. Truxal, *Man and Technology*, (McGraw Hill Book Co., New York, 1973), p. 191.

12. J. Rifkin and T. Howard, *Entropy, A New World Vision*, (Paladin, London, 1985), p. 126.

CHAPTER 6   ECONOMICS

1. See the pioneering work of F. Soddy, *Matter and Energy*, (Home University Library of Modern Knowledge, London, 1912); *Wealth, Virtual Wealth and Debt*, (Allen and Unwin, London, 1926).

2. See E. Fox-Genovese, *The Origins of Physiocracy*, (Cornell University Press, Ithaca and London, 1976).

3. See Hunter Davies, *George Stephenson*, (Hamlyn Paperback edition, UK, 1980), Chapter 2.

4. I do not wish to give the impression, however, that there have been no other conceptions in the history of the subject. But this is not the place to deal with the complexities of the historical development of the subject.

5. The non-orthodox ones, from this point of view, include N. Georgescu-Roegen and H. Daly amongst others.

6. See A. Turk, J. Turk & J. T. Wittes, *Ecology, Pollution and Environment*, (W. B. Saunders Co., Philadelphia, London and Toronto, 1972), pp. 124-26; for case studies documenting the environmental and social problems caused by the use of EST in developing countries, see M. T. Farvar & J. P. Milton (eds), *The Careless Technology, Ecology and International Development*, (Natural History Press, Garden City, New York, 1972).

7. See, for instance, H. Daly, *Steady-State Economics*, (W. H. Freeman & Co., San Franciso, 1977), pp. 102-23; P. Ekins (ed.), *The Living Economy*, (Routledge and Kegan Paul, London, 1986).

8. On points (1), (2), (3), see V. Packard, *The Waste Makers*, (Longman, London, 1961); *The Hidden Persuaders*,

(Penguin, Harmondsworth, 1974). On point (4), see F. Hirsch, *The Social Limits of Growth*, (Harvard University Press, Cambridge, Massachusetts, 1976). For an account very different from that advocated by this book, of the rise of modern consumerism, see Colin Campbell, *The Romantic Ethic and the Spirit of Modern Consumerism*, (Blackwell, Oxford, 1987).

9. A. M. Okun, *Equality and Efficiency: the Big Trade Off*, (Brookings Institution, Washington, 1975), pp. 2-3; cited by Daly, *Steady-State Economics*, p. 121.

10. See Daly, *Steady-State Economics*, p. 121.

11. See K. Lee, *Three Legal Theorists — Hobbes, Bentham and Kelsen*, forthcoming, Chapter on Bentham.

12. See ibid.

13. See ibid.

14. Daly, *Steady-State Economics*, p. 121.

15. See K. Lee, *The Positivist Science of Law*, (Avebury, Gower Publishing Co., Aldershot, England, 1989), Chapters 1 and 6.

16. 'Man can work only as nature does, that is by changing the form of matter, and in this, he is constantly helped by natural forces. . . .We see then that labour is not the only source of material wealth, of use-value produced by labour. As William Petty puts it, labor is its father and the earth its mother.' (quoted by H. Henderson, *The Politics of the Solar Age*, (Anchor Books, New York, 1981), p. 216.)

17. K. Marx, *Capital*, (International Publishers, New York, 1967), Vol. 1, p. 505

18. R. Wilkinson, *Poverty and Progress: An Ecological Perspective on Economic Development*, (Praeger, New York, 1973), p. 4.

19. Daly, *Steady-State Economics*, p. 92.

20. It is presumably this sense of capital that Immanuel Wallerstein has in mind when he writes in *Historical Capitalism*, (Verso, London, 1983), pp. 71-2:

> One of the strengths of the anti-systemic movements is that they have come to power in a large number of states. This has changed the ongoing politics of the world-system. But this strength has also been a weakness, since the so-called post-revolutionary regimes continue to function as part of the social division of labour of historical

capitalism. They have thereby operated, willy nilly, under the relentless pressures of the drive for the endless accumulation of capital . . . within the framework of the capitalist world-economy, the imperatives of accumulation have operated *throughout* the system. Changes in state structures have altered the politics of accumulation; they have not yet been able to end them.

21. See, for instance, Daly, *Steady-State Economics*.
22. See Boulding in H. Daly (ed.), *Towards a Steady-State Economy*, (W. H. Freeman & Co., 1973).
23. Cited by Daly, *Steady-State Economics*, p. 14.
24. Daly, *Steady-State Economics*, pp. 17-18.
25. Daly, *Steady-State Economics*, pp. 35-6.

CHAPTER 7   CIVILISATION

1. See K. Lee, *A New Basis for Moral Philosophy*, (Routledge and Kegan Paul, London, 1985), especially Chapters Two and Three.
2. See J. Elster, 'Self-Realization in Work and Politics: the Marxist Conception of the Good Life' in E. Paul *et. al.* (eds), *Marxism and Liberalism*, (Blackwell, Oxford, 1986).
3. See S. Lovtrup, *Epigenetics, A Treatise in Theoretical Biology*, (John Wiley and Sons, London and New York, 1974), p. 13. On the subject of epigenetics, I try to follow Lovtrup; but as it is not an easy matter to follow, I could have got him wrong. I urge readers to check for themselves. See also D. J. Pritchard, *Foundations of Developmental Genetics*, (Taylor and Francis, London, 1986).
4. See T. G. R. Bower, *Human Development*, (W. H. Freeman and Co., San Francisco, 1979). Bower regards human development to be epigenetic, but maintains that the term 'development' can only be meaningfully confined to that period of one's life between birth and 20 years. However, he holds that death is epigenetic — see pp. 432-33. His reason for saying that from 20 years onward to death strictly cannot count as development, is that major high-level types of development, such as associated with a child's grasping of the principle 'I am a boy/girl', no longer takes place. He thinks that adults do not show basic developmental changes barring a

few like St. Paul who are exceptions to the rule. He says: 'I know of no evidence indicating genuine developmental change in the adult's basic world view, whether of the self, of the social world, or of the physical world.' p. 432.

One's view (or, at least, the ordinary human being who is not an expert in the scientific fields) of the physcial world would depend very much on the dominant scientific theories of the day. My argument is that, up to now, that dominant corpus of knowledge has not placed sufficient emphasis on the science of thermodynamics and the principles of ecology nor drawn the attention of the ordinary person to them. If the ordinary person could grasp their significance and relevance, then there might be changes (assuming that people are rational and act on rational beliefs which they may not, of course, as history often shows) to the person's conception of the physical world, the social world and the self.

Moreover, adults do not show, on the whole, basic changes only so long as the social world for them remains static and unchanged, more or less. When their social world alters through conquest, revolution, death in the family, the Wall Street crash, they do change pretty drastically — notable examples in recent years are the Japanese Emperor Hirohito, who was overnight undeified by General MacArthur, and the last Manchu Emperor, who became mere citizen and comrade Puyi. Both apparently survived these radical changes with equanimity, claimed relief from no longer having to bear the old labels and adjusted their personalities to cope with their reduced circumstances — in the Manchu Emperor's case more drastically than in the Japanese Emperor's. Less exalted examples can be found in anthropological literature when both the physical and social worlds of tribal peoples are ruthlessly destroyed leaving once proud, dignified and competent people to become alcoholic, dependent and degenerate. My example of women in war time also bears this out. War upsets the social world. Women, as a result, are forced to find new roles and, therefore, new conceptions of the self. Similarly, widows. Their social world, too, will have been shattered by their husbands' sudden and unexpected deaths.

5. On the relevance of the study of monozygotic twins to this controversy, see Bower, *Human Development*, especially pp. 401-05.

6. See E. Kamenka, *The Ethical Foundation of Marxism*,

(Routledge and Kegan Paul, London, 1962).

7. I am in agreement with Marx here. But for Marx a society of artists is predicated upon a civilisation, which seems to rely on using science and its EST to dominate Nature, to make her serve human ends. However, the argument of this book is that a society of artists, as a truly human society, is predicated upon precisely the rejection of a civilisation that subordinates Nature to serve human ends, regardless of whatever effects these may have on Nature, by means of its science and EST.

8. See V. Packard, *The Waste Makers*, (Longman, London, 1961).

CHAPTER 8   WORK AND THE TWO SOCIALISMS

1. Socialism itself is not an easy concept to delineate. But, for this discussion, I am using it to include the following features — it is a type of social arrangement (i) which is committed to equality as the correct distributive value (see Chapter Nine); (ii) which recognises that there are genuine human needs that have to be met (with the recognition that these would not be met for all human agents through the operations of the market (see Chapter Ten)).

2. Fourier laid emphasis on (ii) referred to, under 1, above. He talked about a social minimum, but permitted a small degree of inequality between people. But he rejected a system of production which produces for exchange rather than use. His Harmonians had to bring capital with them, and income above the minimum was to be determined by a formula which gives 5/12 to labour, 4/12 to capital and 3/12 to talent. (But he also gave alternative formulae.) He also restricted the amount in the accumulation of unearned income, by varying the rate of interest paid on invested capital according to the size of the individual's holdings. In his system, while capital had some room to play, it was not expected to play the role of ever-increasing accumulation (regardless of the absolute level already reached), which is its central role under capitalism, both bourgeois and state. Hence, one could say he did not subscribe to the logic of capital thus understood.

For commentaries in English on Fourier's writings, see the Introduction by J. Beecher and R. Bienvenu to their edition of

Fourier's writings, *The Utopian Vision of Charles Fourier*, (Jonathan Cape, London, 1972); N. V. Riasanovsky, *The Teaching of Charles Fourier*, (University of California Press, Berkeley and Los Angeles, 1969).

For another example of the ascetic model of socialism see William Morris and his works which will be discussed in section 8.

3. See K. Polanyi, *The Great Transformation*, (Beacon Press, Boston, 1957), pp. 176-77. L. von Mises holds this view but according to Polanyi, it is not original. Bishop Whateley had said it 150 years before Mises.

On the subject of the progressive alienation of work under the demands of the capitalist mode of production, see H. Braverman, *Labor and Monopoly Capital, The Degradation of Work in the Twentieth Century*, (Monthly Review Press, New York and London, 1974).

4. L. von Mises, *Human Action: A Treatise on Economics*, (Hodge & Co., London, 1949), p. 13.

5. In the twentieth century, it has been realised that the alienating conditions under which work is organised, in terms of breaking down the processes of production into simple-minded, boring, repetitive operations and machine-minding, may itself be counter productive in terms of increasing output. What informs this view, however, is a business philosophy (in the spirit of Taylorism) which advocates making places of work more attractive, aesthetic, giving workers some say over the work process, etc., rather than an attempt to decrease alienation for its own sake. Some car manufacturers have put this philosophy into practice. One reads of such factories being clean, airy, tastefully laid out, even decorated with potted plants, and so on. But apparently, this instrumental move to attenuate alienation can ironically be too successful. Workers began to take more pride in the work they did; inspired to such an extent to produce a high quality product of which they did not have to be ashamed, they spent a much longer time to produce the object. As such the company would have to sell at a much higher price in order to maintain the same level of profits. But this might work out not to be worth its while — it is more profitable producing shoddy goods, which sell more cheaply with a large volume sale and rapid turnover than high quality ones, which do not sell as fast and as many. So workers had to be told not to take too

seriously the notion of pride in careful workmanship.

6. Some critics say unkindly that Fourier's concern for the sexually deprived was born out of the fact that he himself never seemed to have success with women.

7. The psychological compulsion to work is the other side of the coin of the work ethic. We see it very clearly in the case of Japanese workers and businessmen who refuse to take any holidays whatsoever. They appear to have no resources within themselves to lead a meaningful and satisfying existence outside work itself. In other words, so successfully have they been indoctrinated in the work ethic that for them it is no longer possible to conceive of leisure, the supposed contrast to work, under the instrumental conception of work.

8. Beecher and Bienvenu, *The Utopian Vision*, p. 288.

9. W. Ophuls, *Ecology and the Politics of Scarcity*, (W. H. Freeman & Co., San Francisco, 1977), pp. 60-1, Box 2-1.

10. Beecher and Bienvenu, *The Utopian Vision*, p. 199.

11. See C. Pateman, *Participation and Democratic Theory*, (Cambridge University Press, Cambridge, 1970).

12. See J. Schumpeter, *Capitalism, Socialism and Democracy*, (Allen and Unwin, London, 1974).

13. F. E. Manuel, *The New World of Henri Saint-Simon*, (Harvard University Press, Boston, 1956), p. 302. See also S. Wolin, *Politics and Vision*, (Allen and Unwin, London, 1961).

14. Manuel, *The New World*, p. 87; see Wolin, *Politics and Vision*, p. 376.

15. *Selected Writings of Henri Comte de Saint-Simon*, trans. Markham, (Macmillan, New York, 1952), p. 69.

16. Perhaps we see this most vividly borne out by post-war Japan.

17. *Capital*, I, Moscow, 1962, p. 384.

18. Marx and Engels, *The German Ideology*, (Lawrence and Wishart, London, 1977), pp. 44-5.

19. Marx, *Grundisse*, trans. M. Nicolaus, (Allen Lane, London, 1973), p. 612.

20. *Capital*, III, Moscow, 1962, pp. 799-800.

21. See R. Wilkinson, *Poverty and Progress: An Ecological Perspective on Economic Development*, (Praeger, New York, 1973).

22. See. I. Mészáros, *Marx's Theory of Alienation*, (Merlin Press, London, 1970), p. 247.

23. ibid.

24. Marx and Engels, *Collected Works*, (Lawrence and Wishart and Progress Publishers, Moscow, London, 1976), Vol. 5, p. 472.

25. Marx and Engels, *Collected Works*, Vol. 5, p. 472.

26. Marx and Engels, *Collected Works*, Vol. 5, p. 471.

27. Marx and Engels, *Collected Works*, Vol. 5, p. 474.

28. Marx and Engels, *Collected Works*, Vol. 5, p. 471.

29. Marx and Engels, *Collected Works*, Vol. 5, p. 474.

30. For a detailed and insightful account, see W. Leiss, *The Domination of Nature*, (Beacon Press, Boston, 1974).

31. Leiss, *The Domination of Nature*, p. 85.

32. Leiss, *The Domination of Nature*, pp. 122-23.

33. Leiss, *The Domination of Nature*, pp. 138-39.

34. Leiss, *The Domination of Nature*, p. 146.

35. Leiss, *The Domination of Nature*, p. 147.

36. Leiss, *The Domination of Nature*, p. 59.

37. Leiss, *The Domination of Nature*, p. 59.

38. Leiss, *The Domination of Nature*, p. 164.

39. To appreciate the difficulties faced by a Marxist who wishes to take this critique seriously, see Braverman, *Labor and Monopoly Capital*. The difficulties are never made explicit by Braverman but lie just below the surface, itself a sign, perhaps, that they cannot be resolved without abandoning the cornucopic conception of socialism, erected upon an industrial civilisation using science and its EST to dominate Nature, in order to increase productivity and efficiency for the purpose of meeting ever expanding human needs. (When I had just finished writing this book, I came across Frank Webster and Kevin Robins' *Information Technology: A Luddite Analysis*, (Ablex Publishing Corporation, Norwood, New Jersey, 1986). Their analysis and mine appear to be similar in many respects — see pp. 42-73. However, the similarity they emphasise between Marxist and non-Marxist attitudes to technology lies in both parties accepting technological determinism in some form. I stress, on the other hand, their acceptance of EST and their common ideology, that is, scientism, of exploiting Nature through EST to serve human desires or needs which are ever expanding and, therefore, infinite.)

40. The quotations in this section all come from A. L. Morton (ed.), *Political Writings of William Morris*, (Lawrence and Wishart, London, 1973). See also E. P. Thompson, *Romantic to Revolutionary*, (Lawrence and Wishart, London, 1955) and *The*

Communism of William Morris, (William Morris Society, printed in Dublin, 1965); J. Benham and J. Harris (eds), *William Morris and the Middle Ages*, (Manchester University Press, Manchester, 1984).

CHAPTER 9 REDISTRIBUTION

1. For a critique of this notion of wealth, see, for instance, P. Ekins (ed.), *The Living Economy*, (Routledge and Kegan Paul, London, 1986).

2. See Walter Rodney, *How Europe Underdeveloped Africa*, (Bogle-L'Ouverture, London, 1978).

3. Such an argument seems to underlie the administration of Mrs. Thatcher since 1979: on the one hand, tax cutting in personal income tax of those particularly at the higher levels, increase in the level of exemption from capital gains tax, and so on, and on the other, recouping such lost revenue by increasing VAT, and prices on essential goods and services like gas and electricity, which have the effect of enriching the rich whilst impoverishing the poor. The aim of these fiscal policies is avowedly that of re-invigorating the British economy, that is, to increase economic growth.

4. J. Rawls, *A Theory of Justice*, (Clarendon Press, Oxford, 1972).

5. A. Schnaiberg, *The Environment: from Surplus to Scarcity*, (Oxford University Press, Oxford and New York, 1980), p. 425.

6. See D. Pepper, *The Roots of Modern Environmentalism*, (Croom Helm, London, 1984), pp. 204-11; see also M. Bookchin, *Toward An Ecological Society*, (Black Rose Books, Montreal, 1980).

7. However, there may be exceptions to this rule (i) where the greatest impact may be made by abstention on the part of the largest group within society, and (ii) where abstention, required on the part of minority groups, could be interpreted as a form of genocide. The People's Republic of China recognises this problem. Its one-child family policy only applies to the majority Han ethnic group and not to the other minority ethnic groups.

8. I have tried elsewhere to show why sexual and racial discrimination is arbitrary and unjustified — see K. Lee, *A*

New Basis for Moral Philosophy, (Routledge and Kegan Paul, London, 1985), Chapter Four.

9. To say this does not necessarily commit one in advance to any particular philosophy of mind. All that it commits one to maintaining is that possessing a body is a necessary condition for human agency. Whether it is also a sufficient condition remains an open question.

10. D. H. Munro, *Empiricism and Ethics*, (Cambridge University Press, Cambridge, 1970), p. 200.

11. Rawls, *A Theory of Justice*, p. 508.

12. See I. Berlin, *Four Essays on Liberty*, (Oxford University Press, London, Oxford, New York, 1969), Essay III.

13. See K. Lee, *Three Legal Theorists — Hobbes, Bentham and Kelsen*, forthcoming, Chapter on Bentham.

14. See for instance, their leaflet, *Eight Commonly Held Myths about World Hunger*, (Oxfam Publications, Oxford, 1987).

15. See H. L. A. Hart, *Essays on Bentham*, (Oxford University Press, Oxford, 1982), p. 114 where he borrows the Aristotelian square of opposition to illuminate the point that prohibitions are the contradictory of permissions.

CHAPTER 10 HUMAN CAPACITIES AND NEEDS

1. For a stringent and comprehensive attempt to refute relativism, see H. Siegel, *Relativism Refuted*, (D. Reidel Publishing Company, Dordrecht, Boston, 1987).

2. See Marvin Harris, *Good to Eat*, (Allen and Unwin, London, 1986), for numerous such examples.

3. Harris, *Good to Eat*; see also his *Cannibals and Kings*, (William Collins and Sons, London, 1977), Chapter 12.

4. This is the distinction between etic and emic explanations. See Harris, *Cultural Materialism*, (Random House, New York, 1983). It raises the controversy in the philosophy of the social sciences, whether a social practice can be fully and exhaustively explained in terms of the participant's account of it, or whether the participant's account is not the last word and, sometimes, not even the first word in explaining social life.

Let me raise here a point which might already have struck some readers — namely, a similarity between Harris' thesis of cultural materialism and mine about the justification of certain rules of conduct and values (ESVs), in terms of thermodynamic and ecological considerations. Harris maintains that rules of conduct, thrown up by anthropological evidence, no matter how initially bizarre and puzzling, can, nevertheless, be explained by reference (in many instances, if not in all) to ecological requirements which obtain in any one society. His thesis is, therefore, an explanatory one. As such, it may face the difficulty of providing a sense (which is non-tautological) for saying that ecological requirements are more fundamental and basic than other determinants in explaining anthropological data. In contrast, my preoccupation is not an explanatory but a justificatory one. As such, I do not need to face and meet his problem. All that I am arguing for is this: when faced with a choice of rules and values (at a time of crisis when society is at an energy watershed), it would be rational to adopt certain rules and values and reject others by reference to thermodynamic and ecological requirements.

5. See R. Wilkinson, *Poverty and Progress: An Ecological Perspective on Economic Development,* (Praeger, London, 1973), pp. 113-18.

6. P. Ekins (ed.), *The Living Economy*, (Routledge and Kegan Paul, London, 1986), p. 49. Note, however, that my analysis of needs does not entirely coincide with that given by Max-Neef or those of the other authors in this anthology of articles.

7. See, for instance, *Guardian*, 7 April 1987, p. 29 — an article by James Erlichman entitled, 'Cover-up that may help Superbugs', about a milk additive called penicillinase to 'obliterate' the antibiotics contaminating the milk, yielded by cows treated by penicillin for mastitis. See also G. Cannon, *The Politics of Food*, (Century Press, London, 1987).

8. Towards the end of the nineteenth century, to its credit, the legislators in Britain (to take one example) passed laws, such as the various Food and Drugs Acts, based on the doctrine of strict liability on grounds of public interest to stamp out adulteration of food and other substances. It is true that food, which has deliberately been made impure, has always existed. But up to now, such impurities have been recognised to be a bad thing, which progressive legislation has tried to prohibit. But today, unfortunately, this appears no longer to be so. Instead, legislators appear to conspire with

adulterators to permit the introduction of dangerous sub-stances (far more lethal than the water which traditionally adulterated milk, or the chalk which diluted flour) into what we eat and imbibe.

9. On an evolutionary view of organisms, it is strictly speaking true that nothing is static and, therefore, constant. But here the time involved, over which species changes take place, covers millions of years. For the purpose of constructing a social philosophy, here and now and in the imaginable future, such possible changes to the human species may be ignored. The human species, as we know it today, has been in existence for a million years at least, but is itself, however, a short span in the whole evolutionary scale of things. It is to this species and its capacities that I am addressing the problems of social philosophy.

10. See D. Miller, *Social Justice*, (Clarendon Press, Oxford, 1976) where he discusses three theories of social justice, rights, deserts and needs. But if my arguments, that will follow, were to succeed, the theory of rights would become superfluous. This leaves, then, two rival theories, deserts and needs. I follow Miller here in maintaining that it is not easy to identify what constitutes desert, and that the concept-ual problem surrounding its identification thereby renders it impractical, if not impossible, to apply. See Miller, *Social Justice*, Chapter III.

11. However, I did qualify this by saying that the exist-ence of any one capacity is only a necessary condition for what counts as a need. If the capacity itself, when realised, could lead to harming others, then it ought not be expressed, or it could be manifested only with qualification, such as *via* sublimation, or at least partial, if not total, repression. That is why it would be odd to say that we have a need to harm others, although we clearly have the capacity to do so. How-ever, there is a corrresponding need not to be harmed by others. This need arises from the various other capacities (a-part from the capacity of harming others) that we possess as human agents, which could be severely impaired, should they be damaged by the actions of fellow human agents.

12. This has been much anthologised. For a handy refer-ence, see J. Waldron (ed.), *Theories of Rights*, (Oxford University Press, Oxford, 1984).

13. Two points for comment here:

(a) those who subscribe to view (4) would have difficulty accounting for the right to free speech (or to free assembly, to free association, etc.). The labour theory of value may have ready application in the case of the right to private property. However, in what way can one be said to deserve the right to free speech? It seems to have nothing to do with the fruits of one's labour. It could, perhaps, be instrumentally justified as a means to protecting the institution of private property. But even if such a case could be made on this basis, it would not show that the right is a fundamental one, like the right to property, which is founded on the view that one deserves the fruits of one's labour;

(b) of late, there have been more systematic attempts to provide a rational foundation for rights which does not rely on view (2) — see, for instance, L. W. Sumner, *The Moral Foundation of Rights*, (Clarendon Press, Oxford, 1987).

14. Sumner writes: 'Where the analysis of rights is concerned, the beginning of wisdom, though not the end, lies in Wesley Hohfeld's celebrated classification of "fundamental legal conceptions".', *The Moral Foundation*, p. 18; Waldron, in his Introduction to *Theories*, says: '. . . it must be acknowledged that most of the pioneering work in the analysis of the concept of a right has been done in relation to legal rights . . . . The account . . . given by Wesley N. Hohfeld in 1919 is justly famous.' pp. 5-6.

15. Sumner, *The Moral Foundation*, p. 13.

16. Miller, *Social Justice*, pp. 58-9.

17. Miller, *Social Justice*, p. 60.

18. Miller, *Social Justice*, p. 59. (Of the major writers on natural rights in the post-war period, H. L. A. Hart does not make the mistake of thinking that the model of promise-making plays a part in generating natural rights — see 'Are there any natural rights?' in Waldron, *Theories*, and *The Concept of Law*, (Clarendon Press, Oxford, 1961). There are several points raised by Hart in his writings on the subject which, if developed, could, in my opinion, lead to the view that needs provide the foundation for rights — but I hold no brief for Hart, naturally.)

19. See, for instance, L. E. Lomasky, *Persons, Rights and the Moral Community*, (Oxford University Press, New York, 1987), where it is argued that rights are to be understood and justified in terms of the commitment, on the part of indivi-

duals, to 'projects'. (Projects must include in large part explicitly adopted rules by the individuals, if not an exclusive part.)

20. See K. Minogue, 'Natural Rights, Ideology and the Game of Life' in Kamenka and Tay (eds), *Human Rights*, (Edward Arnold, London, 1978), p. 19.

21. See Miller, *Social Justice*, pp. 78-9; Minogue in Kamenka and Tay, *Human Rights*, p. 33.

BIBLIOGRAPHY

Ardagh, J. (1977) *The New France*, Penguin Books, London

Atkins, F. W. (1984) *The Second Law*, Scientific American Books Inc., New York

Attfield, R. (1987) *A Theory of Value and Obligation*, Croom Helm, London, New York and Sydney

Barnett, J. and Morse, C. (1963) *Scarcity and Growth*, Johns Hopkins University Press, Baltimore

Bayles, M. D. (1980) *Morality and Population Policy*, The University of Alabama Press, Alabama

Beecher, J. (1986) *Charles Fourier: The Visionary and His World*, California University Press, Berkeley

Benham, J. and Harris, J. (eds) (1984) *William Morris and the Middle Ages*, Manchester University Press, Manchester

Berlin, I. (1969) *Four Essays on Liberty*, Oxford University Press, Oxford and New York

Blum, H. F. (1968) *Time's Arrow and Evolution*, Princeton University Press, Princeton, NY

Bokris, J. O'M. (1976) *Energy: The Solar-Hydrogen Alternative*, Architectural Press, London

Bookchin, M. (1980) *Toward an Ecological Society*, Black Rose Books, Montreal

Boulding, K. (1966) 'The Economics of the Coming Spaceship Earth' in H. Jarret (ed.), *Environmental Quality in a Growing Economy*, Johns Hopkins University Press, Baltimore

Bower, T. G. R. (1979) *Human Development*, W. H. Freeman & Co., San Francisco

Braverman, H. (1974) *Labor and Monopoly Capital, the Degradation of Work in the Twentieth Century*, Monthly

Review Press, New York and London

Campbell, C. (1987) *The Romantic Ethic and the Spirit of Modern Consumerism*, Blackwell, Oxford

Cannon, G. (1987) *The Politics of Food*, Century Press, London

Capra, F. (1982) *The Turning Point*, Simon and Schuster, New York

Carr, D. E. (1978) *Energy and the Earth Machine*, Sphere Books Ltd., London

Daly, H. (1977) *Steady-State Economics*, W. H. Freeman & Co., San Francisco

—— (ed.) (1973) *Towards a Steady State Economy*, W. H. Freeman & Co., San Francisco

Daly, H. & Umaña, A. F. (eds) (1981) *Energy, Economics and the Environment*, Westview Press Inc., Colorado

Davies, H. (1980) *George Stephenson*, Hamlyn Paperback Edition, London

Doyle, L. & Gough, I. (1984-85) 'A Theory of Human Needs', *Critical Social Policy*, 4, pp. 6-38

Eddington, A. (1958) *The Nature of the Physical World*, University of Michigan Press, Michigan

Ehrlich, P. R. (1971) *The Population Bomb*, Pan Books, Ballantine, London

—— (1986) *The Machinery of Nature*, Simon and Schuster, New York

Ehrlich, P. R., Ehrlich, A. & Holdren, J. P. (1973) *Human Ecology*, W. H.Freeman & Co., San Francisco

—— (1977) *Ecoscience: Population, Resources and Environment*, W. H. Freeman & Co., San Francisco

Ekins, P. (ed.) (1986) *The Living Economy*, Routledge and Kegan Paul, London

Elliot, R. & Gare, A. (1983) *Environmental Philosophy*, Open University Press, Milton Keynes

Elster, J. (1986) 'Self-Realization in Work and Politics: The Marxist Conception of the Good Life' in E. Paul *et. al.* (eds) *Marxism and Liberalism*, Blackwell, Oxford

Emlen, J. M. (1973) *Ecology: An Evolutionary Approach*, Addison-Wesley Publishing Co., Massachusetts, London

Farvar, M. T. & Milton, J. P. (eds) (1972) *The Careless Technology, Ecology and International Development*, Natural History Press, Garden City, New York

Fourier, C. (1972) in J. Beecher and R. Bienvenu (eds), *The*

Utopian Vision of Charles Fourier, Jonathan Cape, London

Fox-Genovese, E. (1976) *The Origins of Physiocracy*, Cornell University Press, Ithaca and London

Gauthier, D. P. (ed.) (1970) *Morality and Rational Self-Interest*, Prentice-Hall, Inc., Englewood Cliffs, New Jersey

Georgescu-Roegen, N. (1971) *The Entropy Law and the Economic Process*, Harvard University Press, Cambridge, Massachusetts

—— (1976) *Energy and Economic Myths*, Pergamon, Oxford

Goldsmith, E. (ed.) (1972) *A Blueprint for Survival*, published by *The Ecologist*, Vol. 2, No. 1

Goudie, A. (1987) *The Human Impact on the Natural Environment*, 2nd edn, Basil Blackwell, Oxford

Hardin, G. & Baden, J. (eds) (1977) *Manning the Commons*, W. H. Freeman & Co., San Francisco

Harris, M. (1986) *Good to Eat: Riddles about Food and Culture*, Allen and Unwin, London

—— (1983) *Cultural Materialism, the Struggle for a Science of Culture*, Random House, New York

—— (1977) *Cannibals and Kings*, William Collins & Sons, London

Hart, H. L. A. 'Are There Any Natural Rights?' in J. Waldron, (ed.) (1984) *Theories of Rights*, Oxford University Press, Oxford

—— (1982) *Essays on Bentham*, Oxford University Press, Oxford

—— (1961) *The Concept of Law*, Clarendon Press, Oxford

Hart, H. L. A. & Honoré, A. M. (1959) *Causation in the Law*, Clarendon Press, Oxford

Harte, J. & Socolow, R. (1971) *Patient Earth*, Holt, Reinhart and Winston Inc., New York

Henderson, H. (1981) *The Politics of the Solar Age*, Anchor Books, New York

—— (1978) *Creating Alternative Futures*, Berkeley Publishing Corporation, New York

Hirsch, F. (1976) *The Social Limits to Growth*, Harvard University Press, Cambridge, Massachusetts

Holling, C. S. (1976) 'Resilience and Stability of Ecosystems' in Jantsch & Waddington (eds), *Evolution and Consciousness*, Addison-Wesley Publishing Co., Reading, Massachusetts

Hospers, J. (1961) *Human Conduct*, Harcourt, Brace & World, Inc., New York

Jantsch, E. (1980) *The Self-Organizing Universe*, Pergamon Press, Oxford, New York

Jantsch, E. & Waddington, C. H. (eds) (1976) *Evolution and Consciousness*, Addison-Wesley Publishing Company, Reading, Massachusetts

Kamenka, K. (1962) *The Ethical Foundation of Marxism*, Routledge and Kegan Paul, London

Kormondy, E. J. (1976) *Concepts of Ecology*, Prentice-Hall Inc., Englewood Cliffs, New Jersey

Laszlo, E. (1972) *Introduction to Systems Philosophy*, Gordon and Breach, New York

Lee, K. (1985) *A New Basis for Moral Philosophy*, Routledge and Kegan Paul, London

—— (1989) *The Positivist Science of Law*, Avebury, Gower Publishing Co., Aldershot, England

—— (forthcoming) *Three Legal Theorists — Hobbes, Bentham and Kelsen*

Leiss, W. (1974) *The Domination of Nature*, Beacon Press, Boston

Lomasky, L. E. (1987) *Persons, Rights and the Moral Community*, Oxford University Press, New York

Lombard, L. B. (1986) *Events, A Metaphysical Study*, Routledge and Kegan Paul, London

Lovtrup, S. (1974) *Epigenetics, a Treatise in Theoretical Biology*, John Wiley & Sons, London and New York

Lukes, S. (1979) *Individualism*, Blackwell, Oxford

MacDonald, M. 'Natural Rights' in J. Waldron (ed.) (1984) *Theories of Rights*, Oxford University Press, Oxford

McGowan, L. B. & Bokris, J. O'M. (1980) *How to Obtain Abundant Clean Energy*, Plenum Press, New York and London

Mannison, D., McRobbie, M. and Routley, R. (eds) (1980) *Environmental Philosophy*, Australian National University, Canberra

Manuel, P. E. (1956) *The New World of Henri Saint-Simon*, Harvard University Press, Cambridge, Massachusetts

Martinez-Alier, J. (1987) *Ecological Economics*, Blackwell, Oxford

Maruyama, M. (1963) 'The Second Cybernetics: Deviation-Amplifying Mutual Causal Processes', *American Scientist*,

Vol. 54, No. 2

—— (1974) 'Paradimatology and its Application to Cross-disciplinary, Cross-professional and Cross-cultural Communication' in *Cybernetica*, No. 2

Marx, K. (1967) *Capital*, Vols. 1 and 3, International Publishers, New York

—— (1973) *Grundrisse*, trans. M. Nicolaus, Allen Lane, London

Marx, K. & Engels, E. (1977) *The German Ideology*, Lawrence and Wishart, London

—— (1976) *Collected Works*, Lawrence and Wishart, London & Progress Publishers, Moscow, Vol. 5

Meadows, D. (ed.) (1977) *Alternatives to Growth*, Ballinger, Cambridge, Massachusetts

Mészáros, I. (1970) *Marx's Theory of Alienation*, Merlin Press, London

Mill, J. S. (1954) *Utilitarianism, On Liberty and Representative Government*, Everyman's Library, J. M. Dent & Sons Ltd., London

Miller, D. (1976) *Social Justice*, Clarendon Press, Oxford

Minogue, K. R. (1978) 'Natural Rights, Ideology and the Game of Life' in E. Kamenka and A. Tay (eds), *Human Rights*, Edward Arnold, London

Mises, L. von (1949) *Human Action: A Treatise on Economics*, Hodge & Co., London

Morris, W. (1973) in A. L. Norton (ed.) *Political Writings of William Morris*, Lawrence and Wishart, London

Munro, D. H. (1970) *Empiricaism and Ethics*, Cambridge University Press, Cambridge

Murdoch, W. & Connell, J. (1973) 'All About Ecology' in I. G. Barbour (ed.) *Western Man and Environmental Ethics*, Addison-Wesley Publishing Co., Reading, Massachusetts

Nozick, R. (1974) *Anarchy, State and Utopia*, Blackwell, Oxford

Odum, E. P. (1971) *Fundamentals of Ecology*, W. B. Saunders Co., Philadelphia, London

—— (1975) *Ecology, the Link between the Natural and Social Sciences*, 2nd edn, Holt, Rinehart and Winston, Inc., New York

Okun, A. M. (1975) *Equality and Efficiency: the Big Trade-Off*, Brookings Institution, Washington

Olson, M. (1982) *The Logic of Collective Action*, Harvard

University Press, Cambridge, Massachusetts

Ophuls, W. (1977) *Ecology and the Politics of Scarcity*, W. H. Freeman & Co., San Francisco

Oxfam (1987) *Eight Commonly Held Myths about World Hunger*, Oxfam, Oxford

Packard, V. (1961) *The Waste Makers*, Longman, London

—— (1974) *The Hidden Persuaders*, Penguin, London

Parfit, D. (1984) *Persons and Reasons*, Clarendon Press, Oxford

—— (1981-82) 'Future Generations, Further Problems' in *Philosophy and Public Affairs*

Pateman, C. (1970) *Participation and Democratic Theory*, Cambridge University Press, Cambridge

Paul, E. *et. al.* (eds) (1986) *Marxism and Liberalism*, Blackwell, Oxford

Pepper, D. (1984) *The Roots of Modern Environmentalism*, Croom Helm, London

Piel, E. J. & Truxal, J. S. (1973) *Man and Technology*, McGraw Hill Book Co., New York

Polanyi, K. (1957) *The Great Transformation*, Beacon Press, Boston

Pritchard, D. J. (1986) *Foundations of Developmental Genetics*, Taylor and Francis, London

Riasanovsky, N. V. (1969) *The Teaching of Charles Fourier*, University of California Press, Berkeley and Los Angeles

Rawls, J. (1972) *A Theory of Justice*, Clarendon Press, Oxford

Rifkin, J. & Howard, T. (1985) *Entropy, A New World Vision*, Paladin Books, London

Rodney, W. (1978) *How Europe Underdeveloped Africa*, Bogle-L'Ouverture, London

Ruben, D. H. (1985) *The Metaphysics of the Social World*, Routledge and Kegan Paul, London

Saint-Simon, H. (1952) *Selected Writings of Henri Comte de Saint-Simon*, trans. Markham, Macmillan, New York

Schlipp, A. (1959) *Albert Einstein: Philosopher Scientist*, Harper & Row, New York

Schnaiberg, A. (1980) *The Environment: from Surplus to Scarcity*, Oxford University Press, Oxford and New York

Schumpeter, J. (1974) *Capitalism, Socialism and Democracy*, Allen and Unwin, London

Siegel, H. (1987) *Relativism Refuted*, D. Reidel Publishing Company, Dordrecht, Boston

Singh, N. (1976) *Economics and the Crisis of Ecology*, Oxford University Press, Delhi

Soddy, F. (1912) *Matter and Energy*, Home University Library of Modern Knowledge, London

—— (1926) *Wealth, Virtual Wealth and Debt*, Allen and Unwin, London

Steiner, H. I. (1974-75) 'Individual Liberty' in *Proceedings of the Aristotelian Society*, No. LXXV

—— (1975) *Political Obligation and the Concept of Sarcity: An Argument Concerning the Rule of Law, Based Upon an Analysis of the Concepts of Liberty and Justice*, Manchester University, Phd. thesis

Sumner, L. W. (1987) *The Moral Foundation of Rights*, Clarendon Press, Oxford

Taylor, P. W. (1986) *Respect for Nature*, Princeton University Press, Princeton, NJ

Thompson, E. P. (1955) *Romantic to Revolutionary*, Lawrence and Wishart, London

—— (1965) *The Communism of William Morris*, William Morris Society, London and Dublin

Thomson, G. (1987) *Needs*, Routledge and Kegan Paul, London & New York

Tien, H. Y. (1973) *China's Population Struggle: Demographic Decisions of the People's Republic, 1949-69*, Ohio State University Press, Ohio

—— (ed.) (1980) *Population Theory in China*, M. E. Sharpe Inc., White Plains, New York, Croom Helm, London

Turk, A., Turk, J. & Wittes, J. T. (1972) *Ecology, Pollution, Environment*, W. B. Saunders Co., Philadelphia and London

Vogt, W. (1949) *Road to Survival*, Victor Gollancz, London

Waldron, J. (ed.) (1984) *Theories of Rights*, Oxford University Press, Oxford

Wallerstein, E. (1983) *Historical Capitalism*, Verso, London

Webster, F. & Robins, K. (1986) *Information Technology, a Luddite Analysis*, Ablex Publishing Corporation, Norwood, New Jersey

Wilkinson, R. (1973) *Poverty and Progress: An Ecological Perspective on Economic Development*, Praeger, New York

Wolin, S. (1961) *Politics and Vision*, Allen and Unwin, London

INDEX